PSEUDOCAPITALISM AND THE OVERPOLITICIZED STATE

Pseudocapitalism and the Overpoliticized State

Reconciling politics and anthropology in Zaire

S. N. SANGMPAM

Avebury

Aldershot · Brookfield USA · Hong Kong · Singapore · Sydney

Published by
Avebury
Ashgate Publishing Ltd
Gower House
Croft Road
Aldershot
Hants. GU11 3HR
England

Ashgate Publishing Company
Old Post Road
Brookfield
Vermont 05036
USA

British Library Cataloguing in Publication Data
Sangmpam, S. N.
  Pseudocapitalism and the Overpoliticized
  State: Reconciling Politics and Anthropology
  in Zaire. - (Making of Modern Africa Series)
  I. Title   II. Series
  330.967751
ISBN 1 85628 660 6

Library of Congress Cataloging-in-Publication Data
Sangmpam, S. N.
  Pseudocapitalism and the overpoliticized state : reconciling
politics and anthropology in Zaire / S. N. Sangmpam
    p. cm. -- (The making of modern Africa)
Includes bibliographical references.   ISBN 1-85628-660-6
  1. Zaire--Social conditions. 2. Social change--Zaire. 3. Zaire-
-Politics and government. 4. Political anthropology--Zaire.
I. Title II. Series
HN811.A8S26   1994   94-27723
306'.096751--dc20   CIP

Printed in Great Britain by Ipswich Book Co. Ltd., Ipswich, Suffolk

Contents

List of tables and figures

Preface

Commenting about Zaire, Benoît Verhaegen once said, 'The real challenge to our time and our country is not growth – the colonizer, in that respect, was unbeatable – but development or growth control.' To paraphrase him, the academic challenge for Zaire and Africa is not the growth of empirical data and information, which is immense, but the development of the information. This book is not about 'new facts' on Zaire or its political history. I am not a historian. Zaire/Congo is one of the best-documented African/Third World countries, and, on purely empirical and descriptive grounds, there is nothing new to be discovered. Except for precolonial societies, on which much work needs to be done and easily dismissed by most social scientists other than anthropologists, most details about the Leopoldian/colonial rule, the Congo Crisis, and the Mobutu era are well documented. For this reason, I do not provide detailed accounts of these historical episodes.

I attempt a theoretical explanation of known facts about Zaire. Because theory explains observable phenomena, I believe that, for scholars interested in change in Zaire and Africa, it, and not 'thick descriptions,' offers the best chances for social prescriptions. Not long ago, authoritarianism was hailed as the solution to underdevelopment; today 'democratization' has replaced authoritarianism as the answer. The democratization process that began in 1990 in Zaire has been stalemated since August 1992, resembling in many ways the 1960–65 crisis-ridden 'democratic' rule. Although the stalemate is partly explained by local factors, it is not unique to Zaire. Zaire not only shares violent resistance by authoritarian rulers to democratic change with other African countries, but, more importantly, the stalemate of democratic change

African countries, but, more importantly, the stalemate of democratic change as manifested by the inability of the countries that have already made the transition to democracy to provide the needed consensus for socioeconomic change. Zambia, Congo, Mali, Benin, Mauritania, and even Senegal attest to this situation. The strong and false belief in authoritarianism and 'democratic institutions' and 'good governance' as the answer to socioeconomic problems stems from evolutionary assumptions in the dominant paradigms of the state and society in the Third World.

In this study, I offer an alternative explanation of the society and state in Zaire and draw implications for social change. I argue that despite formal 'democratic' trappings, competitive ('democratic') rule does not fundamentally differ from authoritarian rule; they are genetic twins, sharing the same manifestations of an overpoliticized state that subverts social change. To understand this type of state requires one to rethink the theory of the society in which it exists, which is possible only by repudiating evolutionism and bringing precolonial societies back to the center of the debate. Political science must meet anthropology.

Because I favor theory over description, the argument of the book has to contend with two competing epistemological positions: one that defends the 'canons of the same' and another that advocates 'deconstruction' and 'otherness.' In an attempt to deconstruct the dominant Western discourse about the 'others' (non-Western societies), one of the objectives of deconstructionism is to challenge the so-called Western concepts and methods. This concern seems to miss the point; there are no 'Western' concepts or methods but concepts and methods articulated in a Western language by scholars born in the West. If this were not true, then even noneducated Westerners would be familiar with dialectical materialism or structuro–functionalism. The truth is that these two concepts/methods are familiar to both Western and non-Western scholars only because they study them. And if given the opportunity to learn about these concepts, both noneducated Westerners and non-Westerners are likely to understand the concepts. They can understand the concepts because, however abstract, concepts and methods reflect and represent the empirical world or social behavior. The concept of God is universally understood because it echoes the anxiety of human existence. The concept of hegemony and its derivative domination, its refinement by Gramsci and his disciples notwithstanding, reflect human and social activities and behaviors that are found in all societies, Western or non-Western, capitalist or noncapitalist. Without their contact with Western scholars, non-Western scholars would have been able to develop the concept of hegemony without calling it 'hegemony' in their own language. The same holds true for the concept of mode of production. Concepts used by non-Western scholars are not 'Western' because they reflect the scholar's empirical world; they are universal.

Yet the non-Western scholar confronts a harsh reality. Because of variations in social and historical realities, Westerners express or understand universal concepts in their own language and signs different from those in the non-Western world. Given the imperial dominance of the Euro-American world over the rest of the world, this situation has serious implications for theory building. Although the imperial order does not negate the universal character of the concepts and methods, it imposes its set of assumptions on the reality under study and, hence, on the explanation. Consider again the notion of hegemony. Because of variations in social and historical realities, hegemonic behavior does not manifest itself in the same way in all societies; in some, it is manifested through class relations, in others through other nonclass relations, including lineage relations. Likewise, as world history confirms, mode of production or economic system need not revolve around capitalism. Yet because of its dominance, the Euro-American world, in which hegemony manifests through class configurations and the mode of production is and revolves around capitalism, imposes the 'imperial' reality on the social reality everywhere. It *assumes* class hegemony everywhere and the ubiquity and inevitability of capitalism. Historical particularities are assumed to be universal phenomena, and subconcepts, such as capitalism and class, are turned into universal concepts.

A critique of the 'canons of the same' should not, therefore, be directed to 'Western concepts and methods' but to the underlying assumptions of the imperial reality espoused by both Western *and* non-Western scholars. Because they are situated at the very beginning of the theory-building process, assumptions determine the choice of methods and concepts and, thus, vitiate the explanation. The explanation, in turn, affects social prescriptions. Questioning underlying assumptions is, therefore, crucial to critical theory. For this reason, it is senseless to suggest, as some do, that those who criticize Western scholarship do not necessarily succeed because they still use Western concepts and methods; concepts are not the issue, assumptions are. One can successfully critique a theory – whatever its origin – by attacking its assumptions while using the same concepts and methods as the theory being criticized. V. Y Mudimbe's *The Invention of Africa* is a case in point.

The focus on the wrong target ('Western concepts and methods') explains the subjective idealism of deconstructionism and discourse theory. Avoiding the 'white man's' and 'Western' methods and concepts, deconstructionism or postmodernism has reimposed its own ideology of the 'subject' and the 'individual.' Although it is crucial that subjects tell their own story, it is still a story of their involvement in social relations and structures. These require that the story be told by capturing first the particularity of the social reality, hence subconcepts, and using appropriate universal methods and concepts.

To attempt an alternative explanation of the society and state in Zaire, I have used universal concepts but seriously questioned the basic assumptions and subconcepts underlying the paradigms of society and state in the non-Western world (to which I refer incorrectly as 'third world'). For this reason, I have given primacy to the analysis of the much-silenced precolonial societies and focused critically on subconcepts, such as lineage, class, and capitalism. Being essentially a critical study, the book takes issue with the social prescriptions that have been proposed for Zaire and Africa by showing that their failure and unfounded optimism result from the pitfalls inherent in the theories on which they are based. As I argue in the last chapter of the book, attempts at proposing new explanations remain the only sure way for better prescriptions for Zaire and Africa. For the younger generation of African scholars, it is better to fail in theory building than to succeed in storytelling.

References to the sources used are given at the end of each chapter. However, because, in some cases, the references are incomplete, and I do not mention many of the sources that I consulted, I provide a supplementary list of the sources in lieu of a general bibliography at the end of the book.

As is always the case for scholarly writing, I have benefitted from the comments of others. Professors Crawford Young and Michael Schatzberg of the University of Wisconsin-Madison, Goran Hyden of the University of Florida, and Richard Dillon of Hobart and William Smith Colleges read earlier versions of some chapters and offered helpful comments. Professor Georges Nzongola-Ntalaja of Howard University provided advice and guidance. As the writing progressed, I received comments on the manuscript from two anonymous reviewers. Although I did not agree with some of his comments, Professor John Higginson of the University of Massachusetts-Amherst helped me improve the manuscript. For their advice and support, my deepest appreciation goes to Professors Abebe Zegeye and Robin Cohen of the Centre for Modern African Studies at the University of Warwick, both of whom have been instrumental in the publication of this book. Finally, I thank the editors of *Comparative Politics* for allowing me to reproduce here, in a somewhat modified version, my article 'The Overpoliticized State and Democratization: A Theoretical Model' that first appeared in *Comparative Politics*, 24 (July 1992).

Needless to say, the views and weaknesses in this work are strictly mine and do not engage the aforementioned individuals or institutions.

S. N. S.
Syracuse, N.Y

1 The problem, the theory and the concepts

This book is about the theory of the state in the Third World as exemplified by Zaire. Since the 1950s, the theme of underdevelopment has dominated political debate, especially in Africa, Asia, and Latin America. In addition to its structural features, underdevelopment is characterized by generalized socioeconomic deprivation as measured by low GNP, high infantile death rate, short life expectancy, high illiteracy rate, malnutrition, and political authoritarianism and strife. Various solutions have been proposed to combat underdevelopment. Central to these solutions is the role assigned to the state as the 'engine of development.' Until recently, it was thought that an authoritarian state could better perform 'developmentalist' tasks. In recent years, the state has been invested with the capacity to move toward democracy, which presumably will lead to socioeconomic development. The belief in the state is reinforced by the call to 'bring-the-state-back-in,' according to which the state and its policies reflect almost autonomous institutions and the actions of those occupying these institutions.[1] It comes as no surprise that this type of state can perform developmentalist tasks.

The intensity of the debate about the importance of the state in social change has led to a succession of paradigms of the state–society relationship. The state–society relationship is made problematic, however, by the way society is perceived or analyzed. Modernization theory assumes an imaginary society because the real society in the Third World is perceived as 'transient.' In imperialism-inspired theories, overemphasis on the role of capitalism and imperialism distorts the understanding of Third World Society. Other views of society are based on its temporary manifestations. Two noteworthy examples are the 'deepening of capitalism' that supported the authoritarian–bureaucratic state model and 'societal disengagement,' which is at the center of the soft state paradigm. The implications for the theory of the state are predictable. Theoretical paradigms derived from these models of society scarcely provide a convincing explanation of the state. Tailored in many cases to reflect and fit temporary manifestations of society, they easily border on faddism, which, in turn, affects solutions. For insofar as the role assigned to the state in social change is predicated upon an understanding of the state and its relation with society, failure to explain the latter makes solutions that are proposed ineffective. As Gavin Kitching points out: 'This is why good theory is important. For good theory helps one to identify causes and constraints accurately, while bad theory leads to simplistic conceptions of both causes and constraints. These in turn lead to simplistic prescriptions for policy and action in which some constraints are overlooked or wished away.'[2]

The goal of this book is to show that claims about the role of the state in social change, including democratization, can be made only after the theoretical status of the Third World state has been clarified. Implicit in this goal is the need to question the dominant paradigms of the state and society. To do this, I use Zaire as an empirical case. I argue that, even in its 'democratic' version, the state in Zaire (and in the Third World in general, even though not considered in this study)[3] is structurally different from the capitalist democratic state of the West. As such, it defies analyses based on the dominant paradigms and assumptions about its role in social change. Whereas many recent publications about Zaire describe and analyze Mobutu's authoritarian rule, my goal is to explain the state in both its 'democratic' and authoritarian versions to better understand its actions. Zaire's experience with both competitive ('democratic') rule from 1960 to 1965 and authoritarian rule in the post-1965 period, as well as the post-1990 'democratization' process, makes it a particularly fitting example.

Zaire is used as a springboard to contribute to the search for a theory in comparative analysis. I intend to generate propositions–hypotheses that will be tested in other African/Third World countries. Therefore, I must avoid the conceptual parochialism that characterizes the dominant paradigms of the state in the Third World, especially in African studies. To generate theoretical hypotheses that can be tested in other countries, my definition of the core problem ('explicandum') will take into account what Zaire has in common with other Third World countries. The approach offers an advantage: by concentrating on similarities in what needs to be explained, I can (1) do an informed critique of the theoretical paradigms that, even though not necessarily concerned with Zaire, address issues that Zaire shares with other Third World countries and (2) generate informed hypotheses and, thus, avoid explanations tailored to fit only Zaire. This, it must be repeated, does not mean that I am proposing an explanation of all African, let alone Third World, countries. Defining what Zaire shares with other countries so as to derive informed hypotheses from it is not the same as explaining all Third World countries.

1. The Problem

The state is a set of relationships and interactions among social classes and groups that is organized, sustained, and regulated by political power. As the nodal point of the transformations of these relationships, political power implies the monopoly of the (legitimate)[4] means of coercion and a set of institutions over a given territory. The manifestations of the state in Third World countries differ from those in Western countries. The state's pervasive role in managing a variety of activities in society, despite the recent emphasis on 'privatization,' makes its relative autonomy even more problematic in the Third World. The institutional setting of the state is often authoritarian,[5] based on a one-party state or military rule. In general, free democratic expression is absent. (Authoritarianism does not preclude the fact that society is differentiated and pluralistic in Third World countries).

Even states with nonauthoritarian rule share fundamental characteristics with Third World authoritarian states, which are manifested differently from those in Western countries. In Ecuador, for example, a supposedly democratic state, the president was taken hostage in protest by his own military in 1986. In Tunisia, another 'democratic' state, a senile president clung to power until he was overthrown by his own minister in 1987. In Senegal, the 'African model' of the democratic state, the opposition leader, unable to reach a compromise with the ruling party, vowed to call in the military to take over. In a totally unrelated incident, he was accused of 'insulting the president' and threatened with a jail term after he questioned the president's financial dealings in 1985.[6] The behavior of the opposition in Senegal is not mere 'peregrinations' of the opposition leader as some have claimed. That rumors of a coup d'état led to the dismissal of top military officers in 1988 and the opposition raised the specter of civil war during the 1993 elections belies the claim. Since independence in 1960, only one political party has been in power and 'won' all major elections, including the most recent 'rigged' presidential elections of February 1993. In India, the 'largest democracy,' every election is marred by deaths, which cannot be simply dismissed as 'some fatalities.' In Malaysia, democratic rule is, in effect, oligarchical rule, in which representation counts but contestation does not. In Guatemala, democracy coexists with state-sponsored murders of the opposition and native South Americans and is threatened by coups and coup attempts (e. g., President's Serrano's coup in May 1993). In 1992, Peru's and Venezuela's 'democracies' were respectively overthrown by President Alberto Fujimori and almost overthrown twice by the military supported by the Venezuelan masses. In short, what is called a 'democratic' state in the Third World is almost indistinguishable in crucial aspects from its authoritarian counterpart. Douglas Chalmers describes these common manifestations in Latin America:

> In an institutional regime [in Western countries] there is a constant tendency to establish a fixed and recognized set of legitimate participants, set arenas for action, and rules for decision. In the politicized state [in Latin America] a premium is placed on redefining the groups, classes, and interests involved,

3

the way in which they should encounter each other, and the way in which the outcome is determined. ... Politicization contributes to, and is reinforced by, the central role of the state. ... The control and manipulation of the state apparatus are ... a major element in political struggle.[7]

In this sense, Third World regimes based on elections or fairly open elections are not liberal democracies. Because they form, with authoritarian rule, two sides of the same coin, I refer to them – for lack of a better term – as 'competitive rules,' although I am aware that liberal democracies are competitive.[8]

The particularity of the state in the Third World resides also in its crisis. In structural-functionalist analyses, the concept of crisis is identified as a dysfunction within a system presumably in equilibrium; its resolution is contingent upon the establishment of new institutional means.[9] For my purposes, a political crisis may be defined as an eruption of conflicts, a set of contradictions resulting from the prevailing relations among classes or groups as they strive to modify political relationships that govern them. A corollary to this is often, but not always, institutional change. Both Western countries and Third World Countries can and do experience political crises. Political crises in Third World countries, however, exhibit higher intensity, are more persistent, and have a lower rate of resolution than those prevailing in Western countries. Third World countries are characterized by a specific form of political competition marked by violent eruption of conflicts. From 1958 to 1965, about 70 percent of Third World countries experienced violent conflicts ranging from secession to open warfare, and 68 military coups were successful. From 1966 to 1985, about 130 coups occurred in Third World countries; of about 10 million violent, conflict-related deaths in the world, 99.94 percent were in Third World countries and only 0.06 percent were in Western countries.[10]

This number has since increased. Samuel Huntington provided a vivid description of this enduring situation in 1965:

> 'Instead of a trend towards competitiveness and democracy, there has been an erosion of democracy, a tendency to autocratic military regime and one-party regimes. Instead of stability, there have been repeated coups and revolts. Instead of unifying nationalism and nation-building, there have been repeated ethnic conflicts and civil wars.'[11]

Zaire shares these manifestations of the state with other Third World states, having been under both competitive rule and authoritarian rule. The state has assumed a pervasive role in societal activities and in economic processes. Under competitive rule, Zaire experienced two secessions, two major popular uprisings, two succesful coups d'état, and various struggles and centrifugal movements. Under authoritarian rule, the country had attempted military coups, two invasions, and a variety of minor conflicts. Institutional arrangements were shaped by the sharply authoritarian leadership of a single party–state. Unable to express itself through legal means until the 1990 democratization process, political opposition was expressed outside the constitutional framework. The post-1990 democratization process has been marred by violence, death, and social despair.

These manifestations of the state in Zaire and other Third World countries show that the state is 'overpoliticized.' By overpoliticization I mean (1) the use of overt compulsion by those holding power to organize political representation, participation, and competition for the social product (i.e., goods and services); (2) the fluidity of state power and constant insecurity characterizing holders of state power in their relations to other social actors; (3) political participation and competition outside established institutions; (4) the lack of compromise over the outcome of political competition; and (5) the general use of open violence and confrontation in such participation and competition. Overpoliticization clearly distinguishes the Third World State from the capitalist democratic state of the West. It is an invariant, that is, a constant phenomenon in both authoritarian and competitive rules in Zaire and the Third World. Given this fundamental difference, I refer to the state in Zaire as an 'overpoliticized state.' I hope to show that the term is not a mere semantic substitution for such terms as 'overdeveloped' or 'peripheral.' To avoid confusion, I will prefer it to 'politicized' state, as used by Chalmers and others. No society or state is without politics; by definition, every state is politicized because political competition is involved. 'Overpoliticized' distinguishes the state in Zaire and the Third World from the capitalist democratic state and stresses its specific manifestations more accurately.

My specific objective, then, is to answer the following central question: How does one explain the overpoliticized state in Zaire, that is, the invariant reliance by political actors on overpoliticization in both competitive rule (1960–65 and post-1990 democratization process) and authoritarian rule (1965–1990)? Only then can one delineate the structural limits of the state, clarify its theoretical status and address the role of the state in social change.

2. The Theory and Summary of the Argument

The concept of the state, as already noted, is indissociable from that of society. Most analyses of the state recognize this relationship. Of crucial importance, however, is not so much the recognition of the link as the extent to which society determines the state and what is determinant. This old debate remains important today as challenges are mounted by proponents of rational choice, deconstruction, and neostatism, who advocate the return of the 'subject' or 'rational actor' to the center of inquiry. To be sure, the role of the individual in social life cannot be denied. But reliance on the rational actor cannot explain why the state in Zaire shares, as the above description of the problem clearly shows, the features of overpoliticization only with other Third World states and not with the state in Western countries.

As the nodal point of societal relationships, the state necessarily embodies the particularity of these relationships. Consequently, it cannot be discussed without specifying a form of material production and its appended set of relations and practices. This approach is neither deterministic nor exclusively Marxist as is often claimed. That Marx insisted on this link is undeniable. But he is not the only thinker to have done so. This view was also strongly held by Aristotle and such liberal thinkers as Adam Smith, John Locke, James Madison, and Alexander Hamilton. Adam Smith, of all people, wrote: 'The necessity of civil government grows up with the acquisition of of valuable property. ... And till there be property there can be no government, the very end of which is to secure wealth, and to defend the rich from the poor.'[12] Well before Adam Smith and Karl Marx, the people of the Kongo kingdom took the link between the state and social relations of production as a given. Indeed, 'for Kongo villagers in particular, government [was] not something established to govern a limited territory; a government [was] the representative of a particular power [emanating from a senior lineage's relations of production].'[13] Marx differed from these thinkers – in this specific instance – only by his staunch opposition to the oppression of the propertyless classes that resulted from this link. Therefore, to explain the overpoliticized state in Zaire, the focus ought to be the unbreakable link between the state and society, especially its relations of production; the latter will be referred to as 'core relations' to suggest that they determine society's forms of political and ideological organizations as well as its overall direction and modalities of socioeconomic change.

However, proposing to explain the state by society's core relations does not take one far enough. Society in Zaire (and in the Third World) is not similar to the capitalist society of the West. One does not need to repudiate the idea of the 'global village' to be convinced of this. The specificity of the Third World society is revealed by its structural traits. (I take for granted that society comprises ethnic, religious, racial, and other noneconomic dimensions; my focus is its core relations.) Among the traits Zaire shares with other third world countries are: (1) the noncentral position of the capitalist core relations in society, which is expressed by the detachment of most social behaviors from these core relations; (2) lack of integration and of interdependence in the economy from geographical, sectoral, and input–output perspectives; for example, agricultural products from a given geographical region are not used by the manufacturing sector in other regions; (3) sectoral inequality in terms of productivity and specialization of material production; the best illustration of this situation is the reliance of Third World countries on one or two export products; (4) partial commodification of (socio)economic production, that is, most economic activities are disconnected from and not commodified by the capitalist sector; (5) scanty internal markets; (6) external economic domination and strong dependence on the world market; (7) oscillation of social classes and groups between capitalist relations of production and precapitalist relations; (8) marginal position of indigenous social classes in the structure of capitalist ownership of the means of production and in the process of capitalist reproduction; (9) distortion, lack of distinctiveness, and lack of the organized cohesion of class structure present in capitalist countries; and (10) existence of competing forms of ideology. The most visible effect of these features, as noted earlier, is socioeconomic deprivation. I refer to this particularity of society as 'pseudocapitalism.'

It follows that the explanation of the overpoliticized state is possible only after explaining why society is specific, that is, different from the capitalist society of the West. In other words, the explanation of the overpoliticized state is subordinated to that of pseudocapitalism. Failure to explain pseudocapitalism adequately has severe implications for the theory of the state in the Third World. As I show in chapter 2, such failure explains the pervasive evolutionism in and weaknesses of the dominant paradigms. The assumptions that these societies are at an 'earlier stage' of capitalist development, that they will become capitalist, that they are capitalist, or that they would have become capitalist had it not been for Western capitalism and imperialism have two results. First, they lead to bad theory, to use Kitching's words. Second, they, coupled with bad theory, do a disservice to the search for solutions; by diverting attention from the real target of inquiry and possibly 'good theory,' they freeze alternatives. Explaining pseudocapitalism (why society is specific), on the other hand, offers one crucial advantage: It helps to identify the structural forces that make societal core relations specific; this, in turn, allows a better explanation of the overpoliticized state and a better appreciation of the possibilities and constraints for action. As David Easton has forcefully argued in a recent important theoretical work, a theory of the structure (never mind the disagreement on what is the structure) helps explain 'visible' political institutions; it also helps identify constraints.[14] In this book, the explanation of pseudocapitalism (hence, its difference from capitalism) is the sine qua non for an understanding of the overpoliticized state.

The specificity of pseudocapitalism lies in its complex combination of core relations. This complexity imposes a common requirement on all researchers who take advice from the people of the Congo, Adam Smith, and Karl Marx to undertake the perilous task of explaining society and the state in the Third World. In addition to paying close attention to capitalist core relations, one has to investigate local, precolonial core relations. Obviously, this requirement can be met without using the term 'mode of production.' Nevertheless, as a heuristic device, the concept of mode of production helps to organize data about core relations of societies that followed different historical roads. Only through it can pseudocapitalism and its complex core relations be sorted out and, ultimately, the state explained. To investigate the combination of the core relations under pseudocapitalism in Zaire, I rely on the concepts of the capitalist mode of production and lineage mode of production (capitalist mode and lineage mode, in short).

The thesis of this book, then, that is, the answer to the central question raised earlier, can be summarized as follows: The overpoliticized state in Zaire is an outcome of pseudocapitalism. The latter results from the neutralization of capitalism by the dynamism (and not stagnation) of the lineage mode of production of precolonial societies. As such, pseudocapitalism, because of its distorted core relations, repudiates the fundamental rules of the capitalist democratic game, especially the equalization of opportunities, which is the necessary ideological requirement for liberal democracy. The result is reliance on overpoliticization in the competition for the social product in both competitive and authoritarian rules. These two types of rule become almost identical twins from the same

7

parent, the overpoliticized state. As a structural outcome, the overpoliticized state generates feedback effects on pseudocapitalism that subvert efforts for social change.

My purpose for using the concept of mode of production is not to apply the theory of the 'articulation and transition of modes of production,' which I reject in chapter 2. Nor is it to show, as Goran Hyden does, that because of the lineage mode the 'economy of affection' (i.e., 'traditional ways') affect and shape the postcolonial state and development in Africa.[15] Although Hyden is correct on methodological grounds, his dualistic explanation of African state/development is questionable (see chaps.2). Recourse to mode of production in this study differs from other studies that have used the same concept; I propose here an explanation of contemporary society and state without falling back on dualism or on evolutionary assumptions as imperialism-inspired theories do. In congruence with this explanation, the concept of mode of production allows for a structural–historical interpretation of precolonial civilizations and cultures because it brings together coherently those aspects of history, anthropology, and economics that political scientists have ignored in their analyses of the state.

The concept of mode of production has lost the luster it generated in the 1970s. Calling it an exhausted concept, scholars who had previously embraced it have recently retreated from it and often cite its irrelevance.[16] The repudiation of the lineage mode of production concept is even more pronounced. Various reasons have been given: the presence of centralized state and tribute, the 'extensive' use of slaves in some precolonial societies, the different functioning modes of lineage in different societies, the 'fabrication of ethnicity' by colonial officers, and the absence of the lineage organization in its pre-colonial form, especially in the urban areas today. The retreat from the concept denotes not its fallacy but its uselessness in the hands of its earlier proponents. Mode of production became a grandiose model about 'primitive societies,' which had no bearing on today's society. Those who attempted to apply it to today's society fell into the trap of evolutionism and dualism. As such, the concept was open to fierce criticisms, which forced its proponents to retreat from it. Its rejection evokes an urge to deny even what is factually undeniable – that lineage was central in precolonial social configurations. Historical and anthropological studies and, more importantly, native knowledge of the societies involved confirm this not only in Africa but in Asia and precolonial America as well.

This is not to ignore recent attempts by historians to question fundamental anthropological assumptions about lineage societies. Nor do I suggest that all the reasons they give to question these assumptions are wrong. Jan Vansina and Robert Harms in their recent works on the forest peoples[17] take issue with anthropological models that show how lineage structures dominated power and exchange relationships in Africa. According to Vansina, 'There was far more inequality, irregularity of norm and practice – with regard to membership, succession, inheritance, marriage – than the lineage model allows for.'[18] In a similar vein, Harms has written that Nunu society cannot be conceptualized only in terms of lineage and community; competition, individual initiative, achievements, conflicts, and strategies must also be considered. Although these authors

8

are right, these are not reasons to deny the primacy of lineage. Perhaps as a political scientist I take for granted the points they make and treat the debate among historians and anthropologists as *fausse querelle*. Lineage is inconceivable without inequality, individual initiative, competition, or conflicts. The coexistence of individual initiative or conflict and lineage is no more mysterious than the coexistence of social class and individual competition or initiative.

In any case, in this book, lineage is *not* the explanation; recognizing its primacy is not the same as viewing lineage as the explanation of everything, which is a major pitfall in kinship studies. At issue is the concept of mode of production through which lineage acquires its explanatory power. Consider, for instance, Kitching's comments on the applicability of the concept to Africa: 'The problem with this justification of the modes of production literature is not so much that it was not able to achieve these purposes, as that most of them could have been achieved equally as well or better without it.' According to him, one does not need the concept of mode of production to show (1) 'how pre-capitalist modes of production and social formations had been permeated by or 'articulated with' the capitalist modes of production by which they were dominated'; and (2) 'that beneath the apparently 'mutualist' and cooperative facade of kinship lay relations of exploitation and dominance of which kinship categories and norms were, in part at least, an ideological justification/mystification.'[19]

Kitching's position is consistent with what I suggested earlier but only up to a point. One does not need the concept of mode of production to show that forces and relations of production in African peasant agriculture were altered by its incorporation into territorial and international markets in the colonial period. Nor does one need the concept of mode of production to show that there were conflicts within the lineage structure. However, it is doubtful that one can prove that capitalism dominated (or not) African precolonial relations or that there was class exploitation (or not) within the lineage structure without recourse to the concept of mode of production. I do not believe it is that simple to demonstrate, as Kitching claims, why the manner of control and circulation of bridewealth cattle favored the power of elder over junior men in many African societies. How does one prove these claims? Marshalling empirical and historical data will not explain why in Western Europe there is no circulation/control of bridewealth resulting in the power of elder over junior men as there is in Africa. Nor will historical evidence in itself explain why capitalism has not been able to become exclusive at the expense of precapitalist relations in the Third World.

Comparing empirical descriptions cannot provide answers to the kinds of questions being raised here. Empirical descriptions can only support an explanation, not provide it; the explanation is, perforce, theoretical. Social reality is a complex whole made up of a variety of interconnecting practices. It is difficult to attempt a comparison or an explanation of these different social realities and practices without simplifying and reconstructing them through abstraction in a theoretical model. Although a model is not a taxonomy, it does discriminate between these practices; it distinguishes those that are determinant from those that are not. A model helps to account for fundamental causes because under its discriminating eye not every observed reality, however important on the surface, is determinant. A theoretical model is an abstract representation of reality; it is not synonymous with social relations themselves. Its aim is to render observed facts intelligible at a different level of knowledge than obtained by immediate observation. To do so requires the development of concepts, which is indissociable from the method one develops to shed light on social reality.

These observations apply to the concept of mode of production, whose aim is to model complex social reality. It is especially useful because of the crucial need to compare and explain societies that have followed different historical trajectories and that display intriguing, observable facts. Comparing and explaining, to be sure, have been done by scholars with different theoretical orientations. It is not valid to claim the usefulness of the concept of mode of production by itself vis-à-vis other concepts and models. Its usefulness can be ascertained only by raising the issue of its underlying method and its potential contribution to explanation. Proponents of the concept exaggerated the importance of 'their discovery' and made an elaborate typology of it in the 1970s. They failed to recognize that mode of production was not, after all, a first-time discovery because it was only a model within the structural–historical method. Taken out of context, the concept of mode of production fell into the usual trap of models: it became an end in itself, rather than a contribution to an explanation of today's observable realities.

The concept of mode of production is indissociable from the structural–historical method that explains societies by focusing on the means of existence, relations of production, and their appended political and ideological ties. Mode of production helps to model these practices and relationships through subconcepts such as relations and forces of production and surplus product. The debate about the broad and restrictive definitions of a mode of production is well-known and will not be repeated here.[20] In this work, a mode of production is defined as a theoretical representation of the forces and social relations of production and of the means by which the relations of production allow the extraction of surplus product from a class, a group, or an individual. As already indicated, the relations of production and the means by which surplus product is extracted are referred to as 'core relations.' They shed light on the forms of ownership, distribution of social resources, accumulation, and the overall sociopolitical organization of society. Core relations are 'ideological core relations' when they refer to the precolonial (lineage) mode; in this case, the relations of production and the extraction of the surplus product are organized by ideological coercion (e.g., a curse, threat of impending disaster from gods or the ancestors, or threat of mishap, illness, and misfortune). (Ideological coecion differs from physical coercion which consists of use or threat of use of force, internment in jail, police or army action, or death.) Core relations are 'capitalist core relations' when economic coercion (wage) intervene to extract surplus product; under capitalism economic coercion is generally supported by pysical coercion. By surplus product I mean the extracted product that constitutes the difference between the total product and the subsistence of those who directly produce it. Taxes, duties, and tributes are forms of surplus product, but they are state-drained resources and are not specific to any society. For this reason, I do not consider them as part of a mode

of production. This distinction helps clear the confusion about precolonial centralized and noncentralized societies. I will argue that, contrary to the prevailing
view, tribute-paying in centralized societies does not differentiate their mode of
production from that of noncentralized societies.

Outline of the Book

I develop the above argument in the next seven chapters. In chapter 2, I critique
the dominant theoretical paradigms of the state and society in the Third World to
demarcate them from the thesis of this book. I argue that the misinterpretation of
Third World society, evolutionism, and the geographical parochialism that
characterize most studies vitiate the dominant paradigms of the state in the Third
World.

In chapters 3 through 5, I explain pseudocapitalism/society by using the available anthropological and historical record. In chapter 3, I describe precolonial
societies and show that despite some differences, these societies relied on lineage, which regulated their social, political, and economic activities. In chapter 4,
I use a theoretical and critical interpretation of the empirical data provided in
chapter 3 to develop the concepts of the lineage mode and ideological routinization and to explain the dynamism of precolonial societies. I argue that lineage
societies were characterized by an absence of class relations. As a result, the
state, politics, and the extraction of surplus product relied not on physical coercion, as in a class society, but on ideological coercion instead. As in other modes
of production, ideology was also needed to reproduce social conditions of existence in the lineage mode. Consequently, the lineage mode displayed, unlike any
other mode of production, a double dependence on ideology. This stronger
dependence explains the higher level of ideological routinization in lineage
societies, the very source of their dynamism. In chapter 5, I show how this
dynamism, which dictated a noncapitalist path of development in precolonial
times, neutralizes capitalism. By linking precolonial societies (see chap. 3 and 4)
to colonial and postcolonial society, I demonstrate that contrary to claims by
transition and dualist theorists, precolonial societies were not supposed to make
a transition to capitalism. The higher level of ideological routinization and its
attendant structural effects were the dynamism (and not stagnation) that
explained the noncapitalist path of development of these societies before the
advent of Western capitalism. As internal dynamism, the higher level of ideological routinization and the attendant noncapitalist path of development
contradict claims by imperialism-inspired theories about colonial and postcolonial society. Rather than what 'almighty capitalism' did or did not do,
precolonial societies played the bigger role in structuring today's society. By
neutralizing its implantation, the higher level of ideological routinization caused
capitalism to adopt contradictory and highly exploitative and disintegrating
policies. The result was pseudocapitalism.

In chapters 6 through 8, I explain the overpoliticized state, the central issue of
this book. I claim that, because of pseudocapitalism, the overpoliticized state is
characterized by its reliance on overpoliticization in both competitive rule and

authoritarian rule. Therefore, I show first empirically the reliance on and manifestations of overpoliticization in both forms of rule (chap. 6 and 7) before providing a theoretical answer to why pseudocapitalism led to overpoliticization (chap. 8). In chapter 6, I analyze how the 1960–65 competitive rule relied on overpoliticization in the competition for the social product. In chapter 7, I show how authoritarianism under Mobutu during the 1965–90 period was also an expression of the reliance on overpoliticization in the competition for the social product. And finally, in chapter 8, I provide a theoretical answer to the central question of the book by explaining why in both rules political competition is based on overpoliticization. The overpoliticized state is to pseudocapitalism what liberal democratic state is to capitalism. By taking into account the neutralizing power of the lineage, I show that, unlike capitalism, pseudocapitalism freezes the means of compromise by creating structural conditions that lead to overpoliticization. I conclude the chapter with a discussion of the implications of the overpoliticized state for social change by analyzing, among other things, the post-1990 stalemated democratization process in Zaire. The main points of the argument are summarized in figure 1. 1.

3. Leading Concepts

Although most concepts used in this work are defined in one way or another throughout the text, I need to provide at the outset a more complete definition of the leading concepts of the study to guide the discussion. In addition to the concepts of state, overpoliticization and mode of production already defined, there are four other leading concepts: lineage, capitalism, pseudocapitalism, and social product.

Lineage

Lineage is used here as a generic term. It implies descent reckoning and differs from kinship reckoning. Descent is deeper and involves, generally, a corporate group reckoned by steps of filiation to a common ancestor. Kinship is shallow and emphasizes the distinction of proximate generations and the unity of the sibling group, which includes half-siblings. Kinship includes what is generally referred to as relatives and does not presuppose a common ancestor. The rights and obligations of its members differ from those of descent reckoning, which are deeper and more constraining. Rather than being largely nominal as it has become in contemporary Europe, descent relations create a network of relations in which the actors have very well-defined roles. Moreover, in descent reckoning a fictitious aspect coexists with reality, whereas kinship relations necessarily involve a real network of relations. Although kinship does exist in the West, descent reckoning does not. In non-Western societies, on the other hand, both kinship reckoning and descent reckoning exist, with descent reckoning dominating social relations.[21]

Figure 1.1. A diagrammatic Summary of the Argument

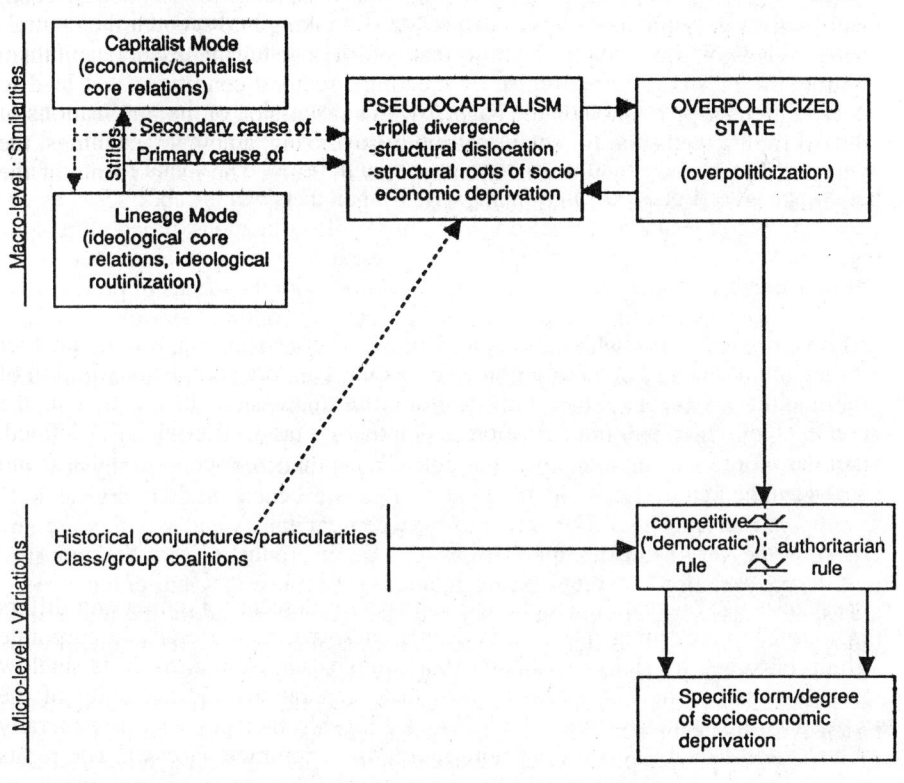

KEY
→ direct or determinant influence
--► indirect or secondary influence
⌒ almost the same

13

A discussion of the characteristic features of capitalism frequently raises the issue of periodization: the timing of the advent of capitalism and its phases.[22] While attempting to propose a research strategy about capitalism, Rodney Hilton has suggested studies of the predominating methods and relations of production and the interrelationships of the economic, social, and political aspects of society.[23] Both Marxist and non-Marxist writers defining capitalism have focused on one or more of these elements. For my purposes, these predominating methods and relations are more important than periodization itself (which does not deny the significance of the periodization). The features I discuss characterize capitalism and intrinsically distinguish it from other modes.[24]

Capitalism exhibits eight major features. The first and most important is best understood in reference to the transition from feudalism to capitalism. The decline of the feudal social order was accompanied by a new social relationship between landlord and peasant/tenant–serf. Rather than owing labor services or dues in kind to the landlord, the serf, freed of servile obligations, relied more and more on wage labor to pay rent. Of all the characteristics of capitalism, this type of relationship is at its core. Workers are separated from the means of production at two levels: ownership and process of production; both are controlled by the capitalist/entrepreneurs who extract surplus labor. The relationship between the owners of the means of production and the workers is reduced to a contract requiring the workers to perform only those tasks contained in the contract while allowing them the freedom to choose the employer. Owners extract surplus labor from the workers economically – through wage – and not through physical or ideological coercion. (Legal, ideological, and physical coercion do intervene, but as support mechanisms.) The relations between capitalists and workers are so crucial at the very heart of capitalism as a mode of production that they constitute its core relations (capitalist core relations). Because they are crucial, they also shape class structure in capitalism, which revolves around the capitalist and the working classes. This does not mean that class relations are reducible to two classes; there is a connected chain of secondary strata and groups.[25]

As a corollary, private property constitutes the second major trait of capitalism. Extensive private property existed in the ancient world of Greece and Rome. Family-owned private property also existed in imperial China. Yet none of these three countries was capitalist. Not every type of private property implies capitalism; it can coexist, in different forms, with different modes of production. Because the fundamental societal division under capitalism opposes the capitalist class and the workers, the notion of private property acquires a special meaning. At the center of private property rights in a capitalist society are those rights the capitalist/entrepreneur enjoys vis-à-vis the worker. Because of the pivotal position of the capitalist–worker relationship (capitalist core relations), capitalist society in its entirety depends on these core relations. This dependence explains the extensiveness and pervasiveness of private property rights under capitalism, for these core relations deeply and complexly affect other private actors who come to 'venerate' private property. State regulations are not precluded because state intervention in private property can occur in any type of society. However, in a capitalist society, unlike lineage mode societies such as imperial China, the state does not intervene to create or allocate private property – even though it protects property rights. An exception here is the intervention of the state in allocationg land to private actors in 'frontier zones' (e.g., in the United States).

The third characteristic of capitalism is its extensive commodification. The transition from feudalism to capitalism involved the use and circulation of money. In fact, the accumulation of monetary capital was seen by Marx as a necessary (but not sufficient) condition for the emergence of capitalism.[26] The importance of this monetary capital grew with the role played by merchants and usurers during the transition. Capitalism came to be characterized by the production of commodities for exchange on the market, but it is not reducible to the development of commodities and the market; the accumulation of monetary wealth is not its exclusive attribute. The particularity of commodification lies in the whole of social production taking the form of a commodity. That is, the production of commodities for exchange by capitalists/entrepreneurs is possible only to the extent that they first purchase two other types of commodities: labor power and the means of production. On the one hand, the separation of workers from the means of production leaves workers with only their labor power to sell; on the other hand, the means of production, not being possessed by the workers, are purchased as products elsewhere. The extraction of surplus labor by capitalists is possible only under these conditions. Capitalist core relations dictate commodification.

Extensive commodification leads to the fourth trait of capitalism, which is complementarity. Given (1) that revenues that workers receive as payment for their labor power are used to purchase commodities for their personal subsistence and (2) that capitalists have to purchase means of production (and their own means of consumption) from other enterprises, capitalism is characterized by a complementarity of activities in its system of commodity circulation. In this system, referred to by Marx as 'department 1' and 'department 2,' some enterprises ('department 1') produce means of production for sale to capitalists; others ('department 2') produce means of subsistence for workers and capitalists alike. These exchanges denote the complementarity of economic activities from sectoral, geographical, and input–output perspectives under capitalism; this is well reflected by terms such as capital goods and intermediary goods. However, complementarity is not an exclusive attribute of capitalism; a socialist economy can also display this trait. Structural complementarity under capitalism differs from socialism or other modes of production because *capitalist relations* pervade sectoral, geographical, and input/output exchanges, giving them their specific form.

The combination of the previous four traits generates capitalism's fifth feature, namely, its geographical and social entrenchment. It becomes a 'culture' directly affecting social actors and their behaviors. Owing to the centrality of capitalist

15

core relations and the dependence of the entire society on them, the mode of social organization rests on such notions as liberty, rights, property, and equality. This situation is not negated by Daniel Bell's notion of 'cultural contradictions of capitalism' as a 'radical disjunction of culture and capitalism' in the 1960s and 1970s;[27] Bell is right only in the sense that the usual congruence between capitalism and culture was temporarily replaced by the 'accidental' disjunction of the 1960s and 1970s.

The sixth feature of capitalism concerns the pervasion of capitalist relations through agriculture and industry. There are no longer 'landowners' in the precapitalist sense of the term, but only agrarian capitalists. Even small farmers depend on and operate in congruence with capitalist relations. Industrial capital is the basis of production; it has primacy over merchants' or usurers' monetary wealth.

Steady technical progress, the tendency to expand, and its attendant accumulation worldwide constitute the seventh characteristic of capitalism, and not its main defining feature as is often claimed.

Finally, the eighth characteristic, although debatable, is that the major portion of capital is directly or indirectly of national/local origin rather than foreign. That is, the portion of productive capital invested by local entrepreneurs far outweight that contributed by foreign investors.

One can refer to the above eight features as capitalist convergence. The combination of these features and the central sustaining role of capitalist core relations fundamentally distinguish capitalism from other modes. Indeed, capitalism demarcates itself from other systems by subordinating to its core relations all social relationships and all conditions under which the social product is generated. Capitalism does not differ only from other modes of production but also from pseudocapitalism, to which I will now turn.

Pseudocapitalism

Earlier in this chapter (sect. 2), I identified pseudocapitalism by its features. In chapter 5, I discuss empirically and theoretically these features in the precise case of Zaire. As used in this study, pseudocapitalism is not 'one of the many variations of capitalism.' Nor is it the result of the 'stagnation' of precolonial societies, which is the standard explanation of modernization/dualist theory. Although it denotes the 'articulation of two modes of production,' as argued by imperialism-inspired theories, pseudocapitalism is *caused*, as I show in chapter 5, by the neutralization of the capitalist mode by the dynamism of the lineage mode and not by the subjugation of precolonial societies/lineage mode by imperialism/capitalist mode as maintained by these theories. For this reason, pseudocapitalism is not the same as 'peripheral capitalism.' Although some of the descriptions of peripheral capitalism are similar to those of pseudocapitalism, the latter concept implies a different type of causality.

Bearing in mind this crucial distinction, the features of pseudocapitalism differ from the eight characteristics of capitalism or only partially resemble them: (1) The crucial role played by the capitalist core relations in shaping class structure

16

in capitalism stands in contrast to the noncentral position of the capitalist core relations in pseudocapitalism, which is reflected, among other things, by the distortion and lack of organized cohesion of class structure. (2) Although the pervasiveness of private property under capitalism results from the dependence of the entire society on the capitalist core relations, in pseudocapitalism, by comparison, private property is neither determined by the capitalist core relations nor is as extensive as under capitalism because it competes with a high level of state-controlled or lineage-owned, or feudal-like property. Moreover, the extensiveness of private ownership by local social actors in capitalism contrasts with the marginal position of indigenous social actors in the structure of capitalist ownership under pseudocapitalism. (3) Whereas capitalism is characterized by extensive commodification, in pseudocapitalism most socioeconomic activities are disconnected from and not commodified by the capitalist sector. (4) The complementarity of activities in capitalism's system of commodity circulation is contradicted by pseudocapitalism's lack of integration and of interdependence in the economy from geographical, sectoral, and input–output perspectives, scanty internal markets, and external economic domination and strong dependence on the world market. (5) Capitalism's social and 'cultural' entrenchment differs from the detachment of most social behaviors from capitalist core relations and the existing competing forms of dominant ideologies in pseudocapitalism. (6) Unlike in capitalism, where capitalist relations pervade industry and agriculture, pseudocapitalism is characterized by the prevalence of merchants' or usurers' monetary wealth; agriculture, which generally dominates industry, is only partially penetrated by capitalist relations. (7) Instead of capitalism's steady tendency to expand, pseudocapitalism is generally characterized by its stagnant socioeconomic reproduction and specialization of material production.

Social Product

By social product I mean that the claimable goods and services – the object of political competition – are a by-product of direct or indirect social involvement. That is, they have been contributed to by different social actors in different capacities, regardless of whether these goods are private or public property.[28]

I use these concepts to support, in chapters 3 through 8, the argument summarized here. Before doing so, however, I need to clear the path by discussing in chapter 2 some of the dominant theoretical paradigms of the state and society.

Notes

1. See P. Evans, D. Rueschemeyer, and T. Skocpol, eds., *Bringing the State Back In* (Cambridge: Cambridge University Press, 1985).
2. G. Kitching, *Development and Underdevelopment in Historical Perspective* (London: Methuen, 1982), p. 183.
3. I attempt to generalize in S. N. Sangmpam, 'The Overpoliticized State and Democratization: A Theoretical Model,' *Comparative Politics*, 24, 4 (July 1992): 401–17.

4. The term 'legitimate' is in parentheses because control over political power does not necessarily need legitimacy.
5. By authoritarianism I mean a political mode of organization characterized by strong and autonomous governmental structures that seek to impose on the society a system of interest representation based on enforced limited (political) pluralism. In this mode of organization spontaneous interest articulations are eliminated and a limited number of authoritatively recognized groups that interact with the government apparatus is established. See J. Malloy, ed., *Authoritarianism and Corporatism in Latin America* (Pittsburgh: Pittsburgh University Press, 1977), p. 4.
6. See *Jeune Afrique*, No. 1365, pp. 28–29.
7. Douglas Chalmers, 'The Politicized State in Latin America,' in Malloy, *op. cit.*, p. 25, 30, 31.
8. I have deliberately avoided the use of the term 'semi-competitive,' which is usually found in the mainstream literature on democratization, to escape the evolutionary assumption attached to it.
9. See Sidney Verba, 'Sequences and Development,' in Leonard Binder et al., *Crises and Sequences in Political Development* (Princeton: Princeton University Press), p. 302.
10. I have calculated these figures and made estimates from S. Huntington, *Political Order in Changing Societies* (New Haven: Yale University Press, 1966), pp. 4, 40; Scott Thompson, ed., *The Third Wolrd: Premises of U.S. Policy* (San Francisco: ICS Press, 1983), p. 80; Ruth Leger Sivard, *World Military and Social Expenditures 1982* (Leesburgh, VA: World Priorities, 1982), p. 15. Note that the 0.06 percent of deaths in the West occurred in its marginalized zones (northern Ireland and Turkey).
11. S. Huntington, 'Political Development and Political Decay,' *World Politics*, 17, 3 (1965): 386–430.
12. Adam Smith, *An Inquiry into the Nature and Causes of the Wealth of Nations* (Chicago, 1952), pp. 309 and 311.
13. Wyatt MacGaffey, *Custom and Government in the Lower Congo* (Berkeley: University of California Press, 1970), p.263.
14. See David Easton, *The Analysis of Political Structure* (New York: Routledge, 1990). For a review, see S. N. Sangmpam, 'Political Theory to the Rescue of Comparative Analysis: David Easton's The Analysis of Political Structure,' in *The Review of Politics*, 54, 4 (Fall 1992).
15. Goran Hyden, *No Shortcuts to Progress: African Management in Perspective* (Berkeley: University of Californial Press, 1983), especially pp. 11–22.
16. See B. Jewsiewicki, ed., *Mode of Production: The Challenge of Africa* (ste-Foy, Canada: Safi Press, 1985).
17. See Jan Vansina, 'Lignage, IdŌologie et Histoire en Afrique Equatoriale,' in *Enquetes et Documents d'Histoire Africaine*, 4 (1980): 133–45; 'The Peoples of the Forest,' in David Birmingham and Phyllis Martin, eds., *History of Central Africa*, Vol. 1 (New York: Longman, 1983), pp. 75–117; 'Towards a History of Lost Corners in the World,' *The Economic History Review*, 35 (1982): 165–78; and Robert Harms, *Games Against Nature* (Cambridge: Cambridge University Press, 1987).
18. Vansina, 'Towards a History of Lost Corners in the World,' p. 175.
19. G. Kitching, 'Suggestions for a Fresh Start on an Exhausted Debate,' in Jewsiewicki, ed., *Mode of Production: The Challenge of Africa*, pp. 117–118.

20. For a broader view, see N. Poulantzas, *Political Power and Social Classes* (London: NLB, 1975), pp. 13–14; and Perry Anderson, *Lineages of the Absolutist State* (London: Verso, 1979), p. 405; for a more restrictive view, see B. Hindess and P. Q. Hirst, *Pre-capitalist Modes of Production* (London: Routledge, 1977), p. 9; J. Taylor, *From Modernization to Modes of Production* (London: McMillan, 1979), p. 109; D. Crummery and C. C. Steward, eds., *Modes of Production in Africa* (Beverly Hills: Sage, 1981), chap. 1; Ernesto Laclau, *Politics and Ideology in Marxist Theory* (London: NLB, 1979), pp. 34–35.

21. For a complete discussion on lineage and kinship, see Meyer Fortes, *Kinship and the Social Order* (Chicago: Aldine Publishing Co., 1963), pp. 276–310; Wyatt MacGaffey, *Custom and Government in the Lower Congo*, p. 86; Jacques Maquet, *Power and Society in Africa* (New York: McGraw-Hill Book Co, 1971), p. 42; and I must thank Professor Grace Harris of the department of anthropology at the University of Rochester for discussing these differences with me.

22. See Douglas C. North and Robert P. Thomas, *The Rise of the Western World* (Cambridge University Press, 1979), p. 102; Jerome Blum, Rondo Cameron and Thomas Barnes, *The Emergence of the European World* (Boston: Little, Brown and Co., 1970), p. 45; Rodney Hilton et al., *The Transition from Feudalism to Capitalism* (London: Verso, 1978); Etienne Balibar, 'The Basic Concepts of Historical Materialism,' in Louis Althusser and Etienne Balibar, *Reading Capital* (London: NLB, 1970), pp. 34–35.

23. Rodney Hilton in *Transition from Feudalism to Capitalism*, p. 153.

24. For this characterization I have referred to Hilton, ibid.; Taylor, op. cit.; Samir Amin, *Unequal Development* (New York: Monthly Review, 1976); Hindess and Hirst, *Pre-Capitalist Modes of Production*; Blum et al., op.cit.; John Vaizey, *Capitalism* (Praeger, 1971); Nicos Poulantzas, *Classes in Contemporary Capitalism* (London: NLB, 1978); Daniel Bell and Irving Kristol, eds., *Capitalism Today*; L. Afanasyev et al., *The Political Economy of Capitalism*; Anthony Giddens, *Capitalism and Modern Social Theory* (Cambridge: Cambridge University Press, 1971); and K. Marx, *Capital*, 3 Vols.

25. On classes in capitalism, see Poulantzas, *Classes in Contemporary Capitalism*; Eric Wright, *Class, Crisis and the State* (London: Verso, 1979); Anthony Giddens, *The Class Structure of the Advanced Societies* (New York: Harper and Row, 1973).

26. See Marx, *Capital*, Vol 2 (Moscow: Progress Publishers, 1965) and *Grundrisse* (London: Penguin Books, 1973), p. 506.

27. Bell and Kristol, eds., *Capitalism Today*, pp. 27–57.28. For a fuller elaboration of the concept, see S. N. Sangmpam, 'American Civilization, Name Change, and African American Politics' (mimeo).

28. For a fuller elaboration of the concept, see S. N. Sangmpam, 'American Civilization, Name Change, and African American Politics' (mimeo).

2 Paradigms of the state and society in the Third World: A critique

In this chapter, I critique the dominant theoretical paradigms of the state and society in the Third World to demarcate them from my central thesis. I support my claim that the misinterpretation of society has led to the failure to explain the state by assessing two types of studies: those that attempt to explain society and those that propose a theory of the state. Much has been said about the various conceptual frameworks that deal with these twin issues. The debate about modernization theory and imperialism-inspired theories is well known. So is the debate about the various models of the state, including my own critique of the authoritarian-bureaucratic-corporatist state, the inherited postcolonial state, and the soft state models.[1] The critical comments in this chapter are directed only to those theories that raise directly the salient issues defined in chapter 1. The discussion on society centers on dualism/modernization, some versions of imperialism-inspired theories, and, marginally, culture. As for the state, the focus is the 'democratizing state' paradigm because, as just mentioned, I have discussed other paradigms of the state in my previous writings.

1. Dualism, Imperialism, and Culture

Of the three paradigms that attempt to explain society in the Third World, dualism is, perhaps, the most enduring. The dualist thesis divides society in the Third World into two sectors. Each sector is given a name that denotes a dichotomy: a capitalist and a noncapitalist sector, a modern and a traditional sector, or an advanced and a backward sector. The radical opposition between

20

the two sectors is both sociological and economic. According to the Dutch economist J. H. Boeke, social dualism is the clash of an imported social system with an indigenous social system of another style; such a dual system is a lasting formation. In Third World societies, the penetration of capitalism into their precapitalist agrarian societies results in a form of social disintegration. Neither of the two societies dominates or includes the other. Consequently, one policy for the whole country is not possible, and what is more beneficial for one section of society may be harmful for the other.[2] Economic dualism, to which Boeke also subscribes, argues that there is a dichotomous use of production functions in the traditional and modern sectors. The traditional sector is characterized by its limited needs, lack of risk taking, lack of business qualities, fatalism, resignation, and stagnation. The modern or capitalist sector is receptive to change, is market oriented, and follows maximizing behavior.

Many criticisms have been leveled against the theory.[3] One criticism argues, on the basis of the empirical evidence, against the ideas of widespread unemployment in the traditional sector and of the lack of risk taking in the traditional sector. Another criticism addresses the more fundamental issue of the interrelationship between the two sectors. The dualist idea argues that the two sectors are not connected to each other, but it has been demonstrated that even the most remote areas of the Third World have been linked to the modern sector via the imperatives of the world market.

All these are good criticisms, but there is more to be said against dualism. What prevents the dualist argument from explaining pseudocapitalism/Third World society is its underlying assumption. Dualism is the non-Marxist (and sometimes Marxist) version of evolutionism and expresses the idea of almighty and indispensable capitalism. It is predicated upon the passage from the precapitalist sector to the capitalist one. The dichotomic distinction between the stagnant and modern sectors leads, as Tamas Szentes points out, to the need for a policy of the diffusion of capitalism.[4] To be sure, capital is not synonymous with capitalism; some theorists of dualism do advocate a model of economic development based on capital formation without necessarily prescribing capitalism as a development option. This difference notwithstanding, much of the dualist argument is predicated upon the passage from the precapitalist sector to the capitalist one. Even capital formation is, according to Arthur Lewis, possible only through capitalists because only they can save.[5]

Dualism has found its best expression in foreign policies of assistance and development and has not lost its academic roots. Among today's proponents of dualism is Peter Bauer, who has been in the forefront of dualist theory since the 1950s. Although some of his policy recommendations may have been modified, his dualist assumptions remain solid:

> The small size and low productivity of farms in much of the third world reflect the want, not of land, but of ambition, energy and skill, which also explains the low level of productive capital. .... Over most of the third world, economic achievement declines as we move further from the impact of the

Western economic contact. ... Throughout the third world, the most prosperous regions are those with the most extensive commercial contacts with the West.'[6]

As mentioned earlier, Hyden's work on 'the economy of affection' is also reminiscent of the dualist approach. This 'economy of affection' is founded on an intricate network of support, communication, and interactions among structurally defined groups connected by blood, kinship, community, or other affinities. It constitutes an obstacle to (capitalist) development because it maintains peasants' autonomy and prevents the occurrence of such variables as agricultural surplus. According to Hyden, the traditional ways of this 'uncaptured' peasantry shape modern politics. Taking these factors into account precludes any strategy of development through state action because the state is weak in the face of peasant autonomy. Hyden's strategy of development includes, among other things, the strengthening of Africa's emergent bourgeoisie of merchants and manufacturers. They alone can create the economic and political structures capable of eliminating the uncertainties of the economy of affection and stimulate a city-based strategy of development.[7]

Neither Bauer nor Hyden can be faulted on the basis of their policy recommendations. Proposing that Western governments help Third World countries with capital investments is by no means aberrant. What is questionable is the theoretical foundations of these policy recommendations: they assume a dualist framework, in which a stagnant sector can be activated only by a dynamic, capitalist sector. In other words, proponents of dualism explain pseudocapitalism by the stagnation of precolonial Third World societies; the latter can be activated only by capitalism. In an evolutionary fashion, capitalism is thus construed as the natural final stage of development. As in earlier evolutionary studies, such as W. W. Rostow's *The Stages of Economic Growth*,[8] proponents of dualism still view precolonial societies in the Third World as lifeless entities waiting for their metamorphosis into a 'superior' state or stage of being.

Marxist critics of dualism have generally been within the limits of the 'almighty capitalism' thesis. For those who categorically reject the idea of dualism, the backward sector is but the other side of the same coin, the capitalist world system.[9] For those who accept the idea of dualism, dualism is not the outcome of unexplained backwardness but of capitalist infiltration.[10] And those who reject the idea of dualism but admit, nevertheless, that capitalism operates along with precapitalist relations of production argue that these relations have been maintained by capitalism.[11] Imputing dualism or the lack thereof to capitalism is to credit capitalism with omnipotence and to fall, from a different angle, into the trap of evolutionism. Precapitalist societies are thus deprived of any vitality.

In a similarly evolutionary fashion, imperialism-inspired theories also attempt to explain society in the Third World.[12] Briefly, four major points lie at the core of the Marxian theory of transition. First, the transition from one mode of production to another necessarily involves an articulation of at least two modes of production; this juncture is likely to result in their temporary coexistence but not necessarily in their equality. For example, the transition from feudalism to capitalism did not lead immediately to the disappearance of the feudal social order; aspects of feudalism coexisted with those of emerging capitalism. The form of the articulation, its attendant coexistence, and the length of time for the persistence of the old mode of production depend on the types of modes of production present. Second, any mode of production comprises three spheres or 'instances': economic, political and ideological. Depending on the prevailing mode of production, one of the three spheres emerges as the dominant sphere. Under feudalism, the political sphere dominated whereas the economc sphere dominates under capitalism. The transition from one mode of production to another requires a shift in the leading role among the spheres of the articulated modes. For instance, when capitalism, as a new mode of production articulated with the already existing feudal mode, it sought to reproduce itself and to maintain its dominance by replacing the political (dominant) sphere of the feudal mode with its own economic sphere. Third, the success of the displacement of the old dominant sphere by the new mode and its sphere is a function of the internal dynamics of the preexisting mode of production. Rather than being mechanical, the transition from one mode of production to another depends on how real social forces are set in motion by the relations of production: 'The origins of the capitalist mode of production must initially be related to the dynamics of the previously dominant mode, to the extent to which its articulations within the social formation (evidenced in the use of the legal, military and political power necessarily involved in the reproduction of the feudal mode) can establish preconditions for the emergence of the elements that capitalist production necessarily has to combine to reproduce itself.'[13] In the transition from feudalism to capitalism, competing explanations have been advanced to account for the transition: demographic change,[14] class struggle,[15] the specific conditions of class struggle,[16] long-distance trade,[17] internal crisis and external/trade factors,[18] and internal crisis and the specificity of feudalism as an European phenomenon.[19] Fourth, the transition from one mode of production to another in a given concrete society involves social change. For example, the transition from feudalism to capitalism involved rising competition, polarization of forces, and the emergence of a capitalist class producing for the market and owning the means of production and of a mass of the population deprived of access to these same means of production and forced to sell their labor power.[20]

These theoretical guidelines are unassailable as a reflection of the well-known case of the transition from feudalism to capitalism. Otherwise, they are shaky in their basic assumptions, especially in regard to nonfeudal societies. Most questionable is the central assumption that there must be a transition to a 'superior' mode – that in the particular case of non-European societies, such a transition must lead to capitalism. Pervasive is the idea that modes of production operate in successive stages; that the 'communal' mode is anterior to all other modes; and that the state appears only when social class appears, hence,

23

when there is a transition to another mode (e.g., to the tributary or capitalist mode). There are also attempts to show how precolonial non-European societies were characterized by feudalism, with the implication that they would also lead to capitalism or that they were capitalist. Even observers who would like to dissociate themselves from evolutionism irresistibly fall back on it.[21]

The evolutionary view has serious consequences. Precapitalist societies in Africa, Asia, and South America are stripped of any ability to self-perpetuate; they are reduced to lifeless entities waiting for their metamorphosis into capitalism, the 'superior' stage, despite the evidence to the contrary. Indeed, studies devoted to the Middle East, South Asia, and pre-Columbian South America, including those by some proponents of the 'transition to capitalism' thesis, show that, in many ways, these societies were more advanced than feudal Europe.[22] Thus, for instance, in comparison with China and Egypt, 'the beginning of the feudal order in Europe (...) meant a surplus of modest size but also an absence of political, administrative, and economic centralization.'[23] And before the sixteenth century, European (hence capitalist) hegemony did not exist; on the contrary, in terms of trade, merchant wealth, money and credit, 'in the thirteenth century, Europe lagged behind the Orient.'[24] There is no indication, however, that these non-European societies were supposed to become capitalist. Because they ignore this crucial fact and view the transition to capitalism as a natural law, proponents of the transition thesis and imperialism-inspired theories struggle to explain why these societies, advanced as they were, did not become capitalist; they blame the excessive centralization of non-European empires or European imperialism for not allowing the transition to capitalism. Although it may be true that 'there was no inherent historical necessity that shifted the system to favor the West rather than the East,'[25] there was a reason for it: The West and the East were two different types of society that followed two different historical roads with different fortunes.

The mistakes of the proponents of the theory of transition are even more pronounced in the case of tropical Africa, where, echoing dualism, they blame the 'stagnation' of precolonial societies for not making the transition to capitalism. Some authors argue that, unlike their counterparts in Asia (e.g. China), sub-Saharan African precolonial societies were stagnant because of their dualistic structure, which relied on poor internal subsistence agriculture and the monopoly of a dominant group over long-distance trade. They maintain that closely linked to this dualistic structure were the passivity of the aristocracy, the despotic ruler's exploitation of neighboring states rather than of subjects within the state, and the absence of outside impetus. All these factors, the argument goes, failed to galvanize the forces of production. Furthermore, once long-distance trade declined, the forces of stagnation strengthened themselves. As a result, these societies were too poor and stagnant to make a transition to capitalism.[26]

The societies discussed here offer evidence that seriously questions the validity of the stagnation thesis. Accumulation via trade will be discussed in greater detail in chapter 3. It suffices here to indicate that trade activities, including the slave trade, contributed a great deal to economic accumulation in such societies as the Kongo and Luba. The tributary character of their states more than encouraged trade activities. The connection of these activities to monopolized long-distance trade is undeniable, but it did not contribute to stagnation. In these societies, long-distance trade meant exchanges of goods that were produced in different regions. The production of subsistence or luxury goods, in turn, involved changes in the forces of production, including the organization of labor. Data from the Central Zaire Basin, along with those presented in chapter 3, support this contention. In this region, the accumulation of resources by the traders allowed them to invest in new forms of agrarian activities, especially fishing. Major forms of investments included capital (tools), insurance (redistribution), social (marriage), and prestige. At the same time, these activities created the opportunity for new alliances among social groups, which led to the rise of ethnicity in the region.[27] Other important signs of change were the appropriation of certain high-yielding natural resources, such as copper mines and fields of saline grasses, by the holders of political power. In addition, the concentration of servile labor and the possibilities to dispose of the produce generated the appropriation of intensive fisheries, the artificial construction of territorial holdings, and the creation of plantations. 'Toward the end of the nineteenth century some residential groups, which were engaged in commerce and fishing, seemed to evolve toward associations, and individualism began to prevail whenever a generalized market in goods had been solidly planted.'[28] Vansina discusses other changes in the production forces:

> Kuba history clearly is characterized by economic development. Agricultural potential increased dramatically, the social and technological division of labor became more and more pronounced, trade at all levels intensified, and at least one city, the capital, developed. A demographic increase, whether it resulted only from migration or also from natural increase in the population, accompanied this growth. These are the factors that Michal Tymowski lists as criteria of genuine economic development. The Kuba economy was booming in the 1880's, and its development was not recent. Its dynamics extend well back into the seventeenth century.[29]

He continues, 'Nowhere in the whole history of Central Africa is the evidence so clear, even though it is skeletal, in showing that our traditional ideas about the immobility of African society are wrong.'[30]

How does one then explain the persistence of the stagnation thesis in light of this evidence? Its proponents recognize that there was some change in the forces of production, but they do not seem to be convinced by the evidence. Why? Because change is premised on the transition to capitalism, or at least to a class society; and when capitalism did not occur, proponents of the transition theory call it stagnation. Catherine Coquery-Vidrovitch makes the point: 'Whatever its origin, this egalitarian system seems to have hindered economic progress, precisely because it forbade the concentration of wealth and power and hence, a differentiation into social classes based on the social division of

25

labor.' After deploring the absence of an aristocracy that would have created exploitation and progress, she concludes, 'Thus a whole series of technological innovations would have been encouraged, accelerating in turn the division of labor and, consequently, aiding the maturation of a civilization in the Western sense of the term, comparable to that of India, China, Egypt, or the Near East.'[31] The assumption of transition to capitalism is even clearer in Samir Amin's work: 'It seems, however, that the large-scale trade of premercantilist Africa, remarkable though it was in some regions, being linked with relatively poor formations of the communal or tribute-paying types, would not have been able to generate by itself the capitalist mode of production.'[32]

India, China, Egypt, and the Near East were presumably not 'poor formations' and, thus, led to 'civilization.' Why then did they not make the transition to capitalism? The answer may be that the process was stifled by their integration into the European capitalist world. The integration of China and Egypt into the capitalist world did not really take place until the nineteenth century. Why did they not, by contrast to sub-Saharan African societies, develop along capitalist lines? Given a whole series of technological innovations in China (e.g., the rotary mill, invented almost at the same time as it was in Europe, and the wheelbarrow, developed earlier than it was in Europe), one would have expected China to make a transition to capitalism, if not at an earlier period than in Europe, at least at the same time or before Europe penetrated China. Yet this did not happen. What does this say about the theories of transition and stagnation? The view that China, Egypt and other tribute-paying societies did not become capitalist because they were centralized is not convincing.[33]

This is not to suggest that African societies were as 'developed' as or 'more developed' than other societies. The purpose here is to clarify that analyses that subscribe to the stagnation thesis are based on the wrong assumptions. African and other precolonial non-European societies were not based on the capitalist mode of production nor were they bound or expected to make a transition to it. The type of economic or social change they experienced was not and did not have to be capitalist. Failure to recognize this crucial point has severe interpretive implications. After advocating the existence of an aristocracy as the necessary class impetus to progress in Africa, Coquery-Vidrovitch is puzzled by the absence of such impetus even though other conditions were present. 'In truth,' she writes, 'once the process of state-building had begun, it is difficult to understand why this transcendence [to class-based progress] did not take place.'[34] The reason is simple: the transcendence could not take place where it was not supposed to take place. State-building is not synonymous with a class society, let alone a capitalist one. The lineage mode, as I show in the next three chapters, operated with a logic of its own. Because it was inconsistent with capitalist change, the change in African precolonial societies could not lead to the transcendence. Moreover, there is no evidence that a class-based society necessarily leads to 'progress' or capitalist accumulation. Ancient Rome, feudal Europe, and today's Third World societies are all class societies. None of them – except feudal society's transition to capitalism –

shows impressive 'progress.' Class relations are not a prerequisite for 'civilization' or 'development' nor is their absence proof of the lack thereof.

To assume a transition to capitalism leads to excessive emphasis on imperialism in explaining today's Third World societies. The role played by capitalism and imperialism in distorting society in the Third World is well known. Capitalism's intrinsic tendency for expansion, resulting in the struggle for overseas markets, is recognized by most imperialism-inspired theories. So is its ability to integrate the Third World into the world market and to affect it negatively. This general tendency is demonstrated differently among theorists of imperialism and theorists of dependency and world-system. Overall, both Marxist and non-Marxist versions of imperialism recognize the loss of sovereignty/autonomy of the dominated zones, which is accompanied by economic, political, military, and cultural domination of the Third World.[35] The expansionist tendency, which is explained by underconsumption at home, results in the collective exploitation of the (Third) world and the division of the colonies into spheres of influence.

Imperialism-inspired theories illustrate the influence of capitalism on the Third World with other indicators: the use of trade and cheap manufactured goods as a means to destroy 'traditional' crafts and artisanship; the expansion of plantation agriculture at the expense of a portion of peasant agriculture; the division of labor, leading to the reliance of the Third World on the production of raw materials for export; and the transfer of value from Third World countries to the capitalist countries of the center. Furthermore, capitalist investments are concentrated in sectors that reduce competition with Third World countries and in those with a higher rate of return. Capitalism thereby disproportionately influences some industries of the Third World and creates enclave economies or 'development islands.' Finally, capitalism associates local groups/classes as 'junior partners' in its pattern of development, which reduces their ability to conceive autonomous development.

These facts cannot be denied, as I will demonstrate in chapter 5. Nevertheless, as an explanation of pseudocapitalism, they fall short because of the evolutionism in imperialism-inspired theories. By categorizing precolonial societies as transient, the assumption of a 'transition' to another mode of production leads to excessive emphasis on the role of imperialism. The role of precolonial societies is removed from analysis, while almighty capitalism, given unlimited and exclusive power to make and break Third World societies, is at the forefront. John Taylor and Samir Amin, whose works reflect the better attempts on this issue, are cases in point. They base their analyses on modes of production and show that the patterns of capitalist infiltration led to the distortion of Third World societies. Yet neither answers convincingly the question of *why* the distortion occurred. Despite Amin's discussion devoted to precolonial and precapitalist modes of production, he fails to provide an explanatory link between these and contemporary 'peripheral social formations.' The burden of the explanation of contemporary peripheral social formations is shifted almost entirely to imperialism and capitalism of the center.[36] Why devote a lengthy discussion to precolonial modes if they have no bearing at all on the explanation of today's societies? Amin does say, in passing, 'The form assumed by peripheral formations will ultimately depend on the nature of the precapitalist formation subjected to attack,' and that traditional social structures hinder the spread of commodity exchange. He also speaks of 'resistance from precapitalist formations.'[37] But he says no more about why. Amin's evolutionary claim that the stagnation of the forces of production in African precolonial societies could not lead them to capitalism, coupled with his reliance on the faulty notion of the tributary mode, prevents him from seizing the essence and dynamics of precolonial modes. This, in turn, prevents his otherwise pioneering work to address properly the issue of pseudocapitalism.

Taylor relies on the faulty notion of Asiatic mode of production. He specifies and explains how the ideological 'instance' was determinant in the modes of production of precolonial non-European societies. He uses this theoretical matrix to shed light on contemporary Third World societies. At this level, however, serious cracks appear in his argument. To explain the 'uneven and restricted development' in the Third World, Taylor rightly maintains that 'apart from the limitations placed on its penetration of agriculture by its *coexistence* with noncapitalist modes of division of labour, it [capitalism] is also confined to particular sectors by the reproductive requirements of the industrial capitalist mode of production.'[38] Yet, he speaks of the 'forceful penetration' of imperialism and its separation of the producers from their means of production. How does one explain the coexistence in the face of such a 'forceful penetration?' Although Taylor underscores the determinant role of ideology in precolonial modes, he does not bring this into the explanation of the coexistence. On the contrary, Taylor argues that imperialism blocked even the ideology ('determinant instance') itself: 'The displacement forcibly induced by imperialist penetration *blocking the reproduction of the determinant instance of the non-capitalist mode* produces a series of effects that give the transition to capitalism its particular restricted and uneven form in Third World formations.'[39] Given that the burden of explanation falls totally on imperialism, one wonders why Taylor analyzed precolonial modes; they do not significantly contribute to the explanation.

Another powerful case for almighty capitalism is made by world-system and dependency analyses.[40] The strength of the world-system theory lies in its bold way of defining capitalism, but this boldness is precisely the source of its weakness. Capitalism is defined as a historical system that spread and swallowed other parts through its division of labor, making Latin America, Africa, and Asia 'peripheral zones' on which a different type of labor control (e.g. coerced cash crop labor) was imposed. 'By the late nineteenth century, for the first time ever, there existed only one historical system on the globe. We are still in that situation today.'[41] Given this seemingly irresistible, all-powerful push by capitalism to reduce various entities to a single system, one understands why Immanuel Wallerstein abandons the notions of society and the state. This repudiation unavoidably leads to the neglect of precapitalist, non-European societies and their active role in the making of 'peripheral' zones. These zones appear, thus, to be the exclusive by-product of capitalism. This point is made even more explicit by some dependency theorists. Although recognizing the impact of precapitalist modes of production, they dismiss them as viable obstacles to capitalism. Dale Johnson, for instance, writes:

> It is obvious that Asian, African and Middle Eastern civilizations had advanced on the basis of non-capitalist modes of production prior to European colonization and that elements (or at least the effects) of these non-capitalist modes have persisted to some degree to this day. But it is a serious theoretical error to weave what remains of pre-capitalism and pre-colonialism with legacies of prior historical forms of capital accumulation and a now-growing incidence of wage labor, into a new synthetic fabric labeled 'articulation of modes of production,' wherein a dominant capitalist mode is hemmed in and constrained by pre-capitalist modes.[42]

The point is not so much that he is opposed to the notion of articulation as that he upholds precapitalism to be subordinated totally to the capital accumulation process.

Evolutionism also characterizes the works of those who repudiate the dependency point of view and claim to espouse a more Marxist perspective. They believe that the major barrier to capitalist development in the Third World today is created by the backwardness of the forces and relations of production. (One notes here the dualist argument among Marxists as well.) For such development to occur, they argue, a complete transformation of these forces and relations is essential. Given that the transition to capitalism is the rule and that Third World societies cannot on their own effect the transition, these writers contend that only foreign capitalism can be the 'transforming engine.' Indeed, for them 'direct foreign investment, from the developed to the Third World countries, will tend to break down pre-capitalist relations and lead to the development of capitalism in LDCs[43] (less developed countries). They fail to explain how foreign capitalism would accomplish this task and why it has not been accomplished in spite of a flow of investments to the Third World for the last two centuries, not to mention other forms of infiltration before then. What caused the backwardness in the first place?

All in all, in imperialism-inspired theories, the transition from precolonial, non-European modes of production to the capitalist mode is not only possible but inevitable. As a result, the role of precolonial societies in the making of postcolonial societies is not examined. The internal dynamics of precolonial societies that may have blocked the implantation of capitalism are removed from the explanatory process. The focus is on the intrusion of almighty capitalism to either block the 'free' transition to capitalism of these precolonial societies or to 'dictate' the capitalist transition to them. Most, if not all, of capitalism's interactions with precolonial societies are viewed as deliberate and unrestrained attempts to 'get what it wants the way it wants it.' Pseudo-capitalism is explained as the outcome of the subjugation of passive, lifeless precapitalist societies by almighty capitalism. Amiya Kumar Bagchi sums up:

29

This recognition of the overriding nature of the initial conditions created by Western Europe as the cradle of capitalism also shows why it is not very sensible to ask whether, independently of European contact, transition to capitalism could have taken place in other parts of the world. For, once the contact had taken place with a society which was further along on the capitalistic path, the lagging societies could not possibly develop in an autonomous fashion. In that respect, capitalism is probably far more of a contaminating system than all the systems that preceded it. We shall argue ... that contact with Western European capitalism retarded the development of anything resembling capitalism in third world countries.[44]

This view may help strengthen political struggle against imperialism, but it raises more questions than it answers. Consider the now popular notion of the 'Third World's own responsibility.' More and more the idea that colonialism and imperialism caused underdevelopment is seen as a myth. The lapse of time since colonialism ended is used as 'evidence' that the West bears no responsibility in Third World underdevelopment. The argument is not valid, but it exposes the weaknesses of the thesis according to which capitalism would have occurred or was occurring in precolonial societies. The proponents of the thesis need to answer some questions. Why was this 'capitalism' slow to occur? By 1885, when Africa was officially carved up, there was no sign of capitalism in these societies nor was there any sign of it in Asia before colonial rule was effectively established. The claim that slave trade was Africa's first contact with capitalism and recent attempts by some Africanist scholars to show that capitalism existed in Africa[45] are not only theoretically indefensible – slavery, simple contact, and market are not capitalism – but consistent with the evolutionary logic according to which African societies had to follow the 'natural' European/American capitalist path. At any rate, why did European capitalism occur earlier? And if capitalism existed or was in the making, why would European capitalism be more successful and powerful than the other? As untenable as the position of those rejecting the exploitative responsibility of colonialism and imperialism may be, one has still to contend with these questions. Answers to them cannot help but suggest some serious defect in precolonial societies or even in their people's minds.[46] They, paradoxically, seriously weaken the position of the very societies that some proponents of the transition to capitalism theory seek to defend. The transition and almighty capitalism arguments, which are one and the same, vitiate the debate about the development path in precolonial societies and, hence, that about today's societies.

Dissatisfaction with both modernization/dualist theory and imperialism-inspired theories has revived an interest in culturalist theories. Some of the culturalist theorists have maintained the theme of modernization theory: the culture of the Third World is blamed for underdevelopment.[47] Other writers choose simply to underscore the cultural factors that make the Third World different, insisting on the 'ethnocentric' Western model of development.[48] This is not the place for an in-depth critique of the cultural approach.[49] Suffice to say that culture, in its rather vague and porous acceptation, cannot be dismissed as an explanation. However, its very porousness can scarcely help establish clear causal links between it and pseudocapitalism; the definition limits its explanatory power. When its definition is made more explicit, culture becomes, as an explanation, a tautology. Every society has a culture, which, one is told, is 'that which lies outside the sphere of political economy';[50] that is, what is made of beliefs, values, cognitions, and emotional commitments.[51] Because by definition these beliefs are specific to each society, it follows that the particularity of (Third World) society is explained a priori. In other words, they are particular because they are culturally specific. It becomes difficult, if not impossible, to explain similarities among Third World countries when each of them is culturally specific and explains itself. Furthermore, barring dualism or eclecticism, it is impossible to bring together in a conceptual framework both internal and external factors that explain the state of Third World societies. The culturalist approach, by definition, militates against such an integrated framework by repudiating those factors that are not 'part of the culture' or that do not lie outside political economy. Even if one accepts that culture is linked to sociopolitical and economic factors and can, as such, shed some light on pseudocapitalism, the mechanisms by which it does so should be specified. In the absence of such specification the relationship established between culture and the characteristic features of the Third World remains unpersuasive. In this study, I do not repudiate in toto culture as an explanation. Because I view it as part of the overall political economy and civilization, the role it plays in shaping society will be understood only through the analysis of the precolonial mode of production and societies, pseudocapitalism, and over-politicization that I provide in the next chapters.

I have argued that the dominant paradigms fail to properly explain society in the Third World (pseudocapitalism). This, however, is not meant to deny any contribution of imperialism-inspired theories. Imperialism-inspired theories have uncovered the expansion of capitalism and, indeed, its exploitative and growth-generating ability in the Third World. Yet, this does not make capitalism 'almighty' in the presence of 'passive' precolonial societies. By raising the issues in terms of capitalist implantation and not capitalist expansion, one inescapably discovers the 'hidden power' of precolonial societies. Although imperialism-inspired theories are correct on the issue of capitalist expansion, they fail to make this discovery and thus cannot explain why capitalism did not implant itself. Failure to understand the differential development path of precolonial societies, coupled with the assumption of the transition to capitalism, leads to questionable explanations of today's Third World societies – pseudocapitalism. In the same vein, I take it for granted that culture can be a clue to understanding society in the Third World. This is possible only by specifying the linkage mechanisms between the two. By defining itself outside the political economy and modes of production, the conventional notion of culture limits its explanatory power.

As go the theories of society, so go the theories of the state. Failure to explain society adequately has repercussions on the theories of the state that

31

are proposed, including the 'order-creating' state, the authoritarian-bureaucratic state, the inherited postcolonial state, the neocolonial state, the patrimonial state, the soft state, and the democratizing state. As said earlier, because I have already discussed many of these paradigms in published articles, I focus here on the democratizing state argument whose claim that society in the Third World is conducive to liberal democracy contradicts my overpoliticized state thesis.

2. The Democratizing State

The ongoing process of democratization in the Third World has led to a huge body of political science literature devoted to the issue of democracy from both empirical and normative points of view. The pluralist argument is well known,[52] as are the criticisms against it.[53] The various theories dealing with the prerequisites or preconditions of democracy have been amply debated. I will comment on the level of economic wealth and development, social structure, external environment, cultural context, and autonomy of political actors as they pertain to my thesis.

Whereas the debate about democracy in Western countries has been about how to improve it, in the Third World the question has been whether it can be established. From a macrocomparative perspective, if the proposed preconditions are any indication, the answer is negative. For *socioeconomic development*, it has become evident that a high level of income is not a sure ticket to democratic rule. One needs only to refer to rich Third World countries to understand this. Many Western European countries became democratic when their per capita GDPs were between $300 and 500 (in 1960 U.S. dollars);[54] many rich Third World countries have passed that level (the average annual income in the Third World is U.S. $790), without being democratic.

Culture also has been discussed as a prerequisite. It has been argued, for instance, that Protestantism leads to democracy whereas Catholicism generally does not.[55] The argument reflects only what already exists; bad functionalism assumes that because most countries with a Protestant majority are democratic, there must be a causal relation between the two. According to this argument, because Latin America is Catholic and not democratic, Asia is Confucian and Buddhist and not democratic, and the Middle East is Moslem and not democratic, it follows that their forms of religion are not conducive to democracy. However, one needs to explain the cases of Italy, Belgium, and France, which are democratic despite the strong influence of Catholicism. How is it that Spain and Portugal, whose democratization is not to be confused with that in Brazil or Argentina, are democratic. Japan's democracy also must be accounted for ; Japan is not Protestant. In Africa, Catholicism, in spite of the formal trappings and appearances, does not have a strong hold as is the case in Latin America, nor does Islam (except in the northwest and the East), let alone Buddhism or Confucianism. Yet Africa is not democratic.

Discussions on *social structure* generally center on class structure and regional, occupational, ethnic, and religious groups. These groups, it is argued, provide the basis for the limitation of state power, hence for the control of the state by society through the adoption of democratic political institutions.[56] Undoubtedly, as means of controlling state power in an already existing democratic state, these different groups play an important role. They may be a necessary condition for the maintenance of democratic rule, but they are not a sufficient condition for such maintenance and do not explain the establishment of democratic rule. Although most Third World countries do not have political pluralism, most, if not all, of them are pluralistic in terms of occupational, ethnic or religious groups. Such a pluralism has not led to democratic rule.

The establishment of capitalist democracy has also been associated with *foreign intervention*. Myron Weiner, for example, has argued that the 'British colonial model of tutelary democracy has been more successful than other colonial models in creating democratic institutions and processes in newly independent countries.'[57] Yet, as the author himself recognizes, the majority of former British colonies are not democratic. Although competitive rule has been maintained in India, Sri Lanka, and the islands of the Caribbean, British tutelary democracy has not created democratic institutions in British Africa or the Middle East. Moreover, as part of the Commonwealth, most of the Caribbean competitive rules (Jamaica, Dominican Republic, the Bahamas, Antigua and Barbuda, and Grenada) still recognize the queen of England as head of state. Under these conditions, it is misleading to use the Caribbean countries as evidence of the contribution of British colonial rule to democracy in the Third World. One could hardly imagine an authoritarian Third World country under the authority of the queen of democratic England. However 'independent,' these islands do not much differ from France's overseas Caribbean territories of Martinique and Guadeloupe, which are perforce democratic. The real tests of the proposition are, therefore, India and Sri Lanka. In comparison to British Africa, it can be hypothesized that the longer duration of British colonial rule in these countries contributed to the persistence of competitive rule there. However, the hypothesis does not hold for two reasons. First, Pakistan (until November 1988) and Bangladesh (until 1991) were not competitive, let alone capitalist democratic rules, even though they were colonized at the same time as India. Second, the hypothesis, and indeed the whole argument, of crediting the type of colonial rule with the establishment of democracy is predicated upon the faulty inherited state thesis that would make us believe that democracy, like the postcolonial state, were 'inherited' from colonial rule.[58]

The fates of West Germany, Italy, and Japan in the postwar period are often cited as examples of how foreign imposition of democracy can work. Studies that have quite convincingly shown strong similarities in structural conditions between Japan and Western Europe[59] are generally dismissed as 'structuralist' or 'predeterminist.'[60] Yet, the resistance of South Korea (which, incidentally did not share the structural preconditions with Western Europe the way Japan did) to the imposition of democracy by the United States in the postwar period is not addressed. Nor is any explanation advanced about why (today's wave of

33

'democratization' notwithstanding) most U.S. attempts to impose democracy in the Third World have not generated working democratic rules like those prevailing in West Germany, Japan, and Italy.

These questions apply to the role assigned to *social actors* in the making of democracy as well. Both Marxists and non-Marxists emphasize the role played by the individual in the establishment of democracy. For non-Marxists, the emergence of democracy is a function of creating a political environment in which a responsible opposition is allowed. Within that environment the political elite must build institutions of participation, bargaining, and compromise. For Marxists, the rule of democracy is a function of class struggle.[61] Other writings on democratization stress the role played by national or local idiosyncratic events: unexpected events, insufficient information, audacious choices, plasticity and talents of individuals.[62] Any attempt to challenge these claims, aimed at pointing to the limits of the role of social actors, is denounced. Yet, it is not explained why the roles of both the elite and the popular masses have not led to democracy in the Third World. Scarcely a Third World country is without opposition, however minimal. To be sure, much of this opposition is illegal and functions under subnormal conditions. If anything, this only reveals the limits imposed on individuals involved in the opposition, which raises the question of why, under most circumstances, the opposition does not work. There is no doubt that, except in such cases as 1789 France where the populace played a big role, most democratic rules in the West were at their inception a product of the 'elite,' who, in many cases hijacked mass democratic movements.[63] There is, therefore, a priori no reason why, being rational actors, the elite in the Third World would not devise strategies for democratization. Yet, in many cases such attempts by the elite have been unsuccessful; in some cases the elite has simply not tried. Unless the elite in the third world is irrational – and there is need to explain why irrationality would characterize only them – then it must be concluded that the role of the elite is not a sufficient condition for the establishment of liberal democracy.

The role of the elite in the making of liberal democracy is the non-Marxist equivalent of the Marxist notion of hegemonic class. Central to the hegemony thesis is the idea that capitalist democracy is a mechanism of concession/compromise devised by the capitalist hegemonic class. This mechanism aims to satisfy, to some degree, the interests of other classes. The hegemonic class exploits workers with their consent, and at the ideological level a mystifying equilibrium/peace needs to be established between the hegemonic class and the exploited people.[64] That mystifying peace and equilibrium are created via democracy is undeniable. My objection is that one does not *need* to bring in hegemony to explain the role played by social actors (ruling class) in the making of democratic rule. To do so is to create a false impression that hegemony is an exclusive attribute of capitalism and that a hegemonic class can, at will, allow the establishment of democratic rule.

Admittedly, Gramsci used the term hegemony in the restrictive sense of 'hegemony under capitalism.' But even here, to reinterpret his idea and suggest that hegemony creates institutions that help to 'coordinate' the interests of exploiter and exploited strikes me as being an ex post facto formulation, perhaps more in tune with the situation in the late nineteenth and twentieth centuries than in the early days of liberal democratic rule. Indeed (and this brings one back to the role of class struggle in the making of democracy), democratic rule of these earlier days was 'restricted to men possessing property and/or educational qualifications. The justification for this took the line that the ability to deliberate on distinctively public and political concerns (directly or through representatives) in an enlightened and critical manner could only be imputed to individuals possessing a stake in the market system – entrepreneurs, professionals, rentiers, at most the more established self-employed workers.'[65] Under these conditions, the disfranchised masses had to fight their way into the system. How, then, would the hegemony thesis apply here? Democratic rule, albeit incomplete, *preceded* the later attempts by the ruling classes to open up the system under the pressure of the disfranchised classes. Liberal democracy does not emerge under any type of hegemony. One needs to specify structural limits within which the hegemonic class operates. Failure to do so entails serious consequences. For example, one would be led, in view of the elite accommodation in Colombia, or in other Third World countries, to call them liberal democracies but would be unable to explain why Colombia faces perpetual guerilla warfare and martial law.

Emphasis on the role of class struggle in the Marxist critique of structuralism is well known, and justified, given the superformalism associated with the Althusserian revolution. Yet, I do not think that, in assessing the conditions of democracy in the third world, an emphasis on the role of class struggle is warranted. Class struggle in the Third World has not been lacking. One of the best known social revolutions took place in a Third World country – Mexico. By any standard, the Mexican Revolution of 1910–17 was a momentous class struggle. The Constitution of 1917 was clearly aimed at democracy. Yet one does not need to be reminded by the famous Mexican writer Carlos Fuentes to be aware of the 'death' of the revolution and its democratic dream. In defining the overpoliticized state earlier, I indicated how protracted wars and strifes have characterized the Third World. Many of them have been class conflicts, and open ones at that. In fact, for the last five decades there have been far more instances of class confrontations in the Third World than in Western countries. Many of these conflicts have been about freedom and equality, and, hence, about democracy; yet, democracy is still elusive.

I do not deny the role played by the European bourgeoisie in dismantling the ancien régime. Nor do I wish to minimize the crucial impact of the struggles of the masses in capitalist societies for the rule of democracy. My purpose is to illustrate the fact that all these factors by themselves do not bring about liberal democracy. There are other conditions one must take into account. They are different in the Third World. If by the saying 'man proposes, God disposes,' one seeks to convey the idea of the limits imposed on social actors, then the same limits must be recognized with respect to capitalist democracy. One may say 'humans propose, structural conditions dispose.' This recognizes class struggle and other structural constraints in the making of capitalist democracy. For this, one does not need to subscribe to predetermination. After all, ancient Greece and Rome under the Republic were 'democratic.' Political struggles and class conflicts did shape both democracies. But is there any evidence that they were liberal democracies? I think not. As Giovanni Sartori points out: 'The difference between ancient and modern democracies is not simply one of geographic and demographic dimensions requiring completely different solutions, but also one of ends and values. ... How can we possibly think that when we advocate democracy today, we are pursuing the same aims and ideals as the Greeks?'[66]

Historical time does not explain why Greece and Rome were not liberal democracies. Had they existed only fifty years ago, their structural conditions still would not have made them liberal (capitalist) democracies in spite of the existence of class struggles. Latin America, Africa, and Asia have waged struggles for democracy while liberal democracy flourishes in Western Europe and North America. Yet, these struggles have not led to the development of liberal democracy. If liberal democracy is such a natural occurrence, why did centuries of precolonial history in Africa, Asia, and Latin America not lead to its emergence? Why did it not emerge in eighteenth-nineteenth-century Africa and Asia when they were not fully colonized and when the idea of liberal democracy was taking shape in the Western world? Arguing that Third World nations are 'young' and will democratize with time only creates confusion. There is no proof that the West was created before Africa, Asia, and South America. They are young in relation to what? The argument is irremediably an evolutionary one.

Huntington concluded in 1984 that the prospects for the spread of democracy in the Third World were not good, especially for the Middle East, East Asia, and Africa.[67] Eight years after his assessment, changes in many Third World countries replaced authoritarian with competitive rule – Haiti (which shifted back and forth between authoritarian and competitive rules), the Philippines, Pakistan, South Korea, and most Latin American countries. To this list one must add African countries, including Zaire, that are on the verge of establishing competitive rule or that have already done so. In each of these instances, local and idiosyncratic conditions did play a role. Huntington himself would view the advent of competitive rule in these countries as a sign of the spread of democracy. So too would others. In this sense one would argue that Huntington's assessment has been modified; democracy is spreading. Maybe so, except that this 'democracy' is the opposite of the definition of democracy proposed by proponents of democratization in the Third World. For all of them, political violence, that is, overpoliticization, is not (or should not be) part of democracy. According to Weiner, civilian democratic rule should avoid a 'renewal of societal violence and the failure of a civilian government to keep adversarial politics within an orderly framework'; and 'for those who seek democratization the lessons are these: mobilize large-scale non-violent opposition to the regime.'[68] For Larry Diamond, Juan Linz, and Seymour M. Lipset, democracy meets three essential conditions, two of which are '(1) meaningful and extensive competition among individuals and organized groups (especially political parties) for all effective positions of government power at regular intervals and *excluding the use of force*, and (2) a highly inclusive level of political participation in the selection of leaders and policies, at least through regular and fair elections such that no major (adult) social group is excluded.'[69]

Few Third World countries would meet these conditions. Most, if not all, competitive rules have no fair elections; many exclude some social groups from the competition; and in some, the competition has been limited to one or two political parties that dominate the political scene. In most recent cases of 'democratization,' elections have been rigged. In most, if not all, of these cases, there has been bloodshed and other violence. The use of political violence does not differentiate Third World 'democratic' rules from their authoritarian counterparts. There is overpoliticization in 'democratic' Sri Lanka, as it faces the Tamil movement, as there was in authoritarian Ethiopia, as it faced the Eritrean movement. Election-related deaths in 'democratic' Ecuador's 1988 presidential elections or in Jamaica's parliamentary elections are no less a sign of overpoliticization than a failed coup attempt in authoritarian Kenya (before the 1993 elections) or the coup-related murder of President Thomas Sankara of authoritarian Burkina Faso. The removal of Prime Minister Benazir Bhutto of 'democratic' Pakistan from office by the president under military pressure in 1990 is as good a testimony to overpoliticization as the overthrow of the Hissen Habre government in Chad by rebels in the same year.

The overpoliticization of the policy debate in competitive rule and its similarities with authoritarian rule are demonstrated in many ways. First, competitive rule is often a coerced option. Consider El Salvador after the May 1984 elections, Grenada after the December 1984 elections, and Panama after the 1989 overthrow of the Noriega government. In all these cases 'democracy' arrived as the result of U.S. overt or covert interventions. This is also partly true for Argentina in 1983 and Brazil in 1985.[70]

Second, whenever rules of the game resembling a capitalist democracy exist at time t − 1, prior to a policy debate/change at time t0 (i.e. at the present), the rules are not likely to endure the test of change. They are likely to be disrupted by overpoliticization; hence, the compromise they imply cannot be reproduced by the change that prevails at time t + 1 (i.e. in the future), as is the case in Western countries. Examples are the postindependence 'democratic regimes' of Africa and Asia, which turned authoritarian just a few years after independence. Consider also those countries that attempted a first, second, and third round of democratization only to fall back into authoritarianism: Argentina before October 1983, Brazil before January 1985, Uruguay before February 1985, Nigeria, Ghana and Haiti.

Third, in many cases the proclaimed democratic rule is replaced by de facto authoritarianism by a 'dominant' party. The cases of the *Partido Revolucionario Institutional* (PRI) in Mexico, *Union Progressiste Sénégalaise* (UPS, today's Socialist Party) in Senegal, and the *Parti Destourien* in Tunisia before 1987 illustrate this situation.

Fourth, the rules of the game, that is, 'democratic' institutions, are coercively devised by the holders of state power (as opposed to emanating directly from capitalist core relations) to deny equal opportunities to some would-be participants. The accommodation of the elite in the Latin American 'old democracies' of Costa Rica, Venezuela, and Colombia is a case in point. Here, democracy is reduced to accommodation among a limited group of political parties that narrowly define the political options open to selected participants in their quest for a share of the social product. In fact, political parties are the state; only a limited number of major parties participate in the accommodation and determine what democracy ought to be. Consequently, the role of interest groups is defined by the power holders:

> In a perfectly pluralist system, an interest group would want to be as independent of the government as possible (to maximize bargaining power); in a perfectly corporatist system, however, the goal of interest groups is to maximize its integration into the government (to maximize access to the pie that the government is cutting). Actual practice in our three countries [i.e., Costa Rica, Venezuela, and Colombia] is broadly corporatist, with varying overlays of pluralism.[71]

Fifth, overpoliticization in competitive rule is revealed by the 'crisis syndrome.' As in authoritarian rule, decisions about and outcomes of the distribution of the social product are often contested by the opposition outside the limits of established rules, procedures, and institutions. An example includes the boycott of parliamentary sessions by the 'legal opposition,' a practice that should not be confused with filibustering; in most cases, the boycott results from massive electoral fraud by the party in power. In nearly all cases of competitive rule, elections are contested by the opposition because they have been rigged or tampered with. The Philippines (1986), South Korea (1988), Haiti (1988), Mexico (1988 and 1991), and Pakistan (1990) are only the latest examples; even the supposedly 'strong democracy' of Costa Rica can be included. One needs only recall the 1948 armed insurrection in the form of civil war that resulted from flagrant electoral fraud by the Calderon regime. When massive fraud is not the problem, death and violence prevail. This is obvious to anyone with even a superficial knowledge of elections in countries like India and Sri Lanka. The opposition also uses the threat of military coup: Senegal in 1984 and 1988; Argentina in 1987, 1988, and 1990; the Philippines; and most Latin American competitive rules whose militaries are de facto rulers exemplify this situation. The opposition's response outside constitutional limits may also take the form of guerilla warfare. Again, the Philippines, Latin America, and the pre-1966 African 'democracies' are illustrative cases.

Sixth, overpoliticization in competitive rule is further revealed by the actions of the holders of state power. In India political power has been assumed by one family since 1947, apart from the 1964–66 Shastri government and the short eclipse of Indira Gandhi from 1977–80. (The 1989 victory of the opposition is inconsequential for the argument.) This longevity was made possible by building a network of undemocratic support within and outside the Congress party by manipulating both economic and political resources and by relying on sharply authoritarian actions, such as the emergency powers act of 1975 and the muzzling of the opposition parties. As a result, Indira Gandhi's temporary removal from office in 1977 took the form of personal revenge against her by the opposition parties. Her assassination in 1984 and that of her son, Rajiv Ghandhi, in 1991 are also clear indications of overpoliticization in India's 'democracy.' In the words of Eugene Kim and Laurence Ziring, 'The purpose of the Indian government seems to be expressed in the concept of managed anarchy rather than sophisticated political competition.'[72] India is not unique. In Latin America, martial law has coexisted with competitive rule.

Seventh, competitive rules are characterized by what may be referred to as the Brazilian syndrome. Although the procedural trappings of 'democracy' and liberties do exist, they are devoid of any democratic substance (more so than in liberal democracy). Practices consistent with authoritarianism linger on under competitive rule. As Fernando Henrique Cardoso puts it (in the case of Brazil), 'We have a regime of liberty, but we are not living under a regime of democracy.'[73]

Conclusion

In short, then, the evidence contradicts the claims of the democratizing state paradigm that the Third World state is liberal democratic or has the potential of being so. Why have the various prerequisites of democracy not led to liberal democracy? And, why do authoritarian rules share crucial similarities with competitive rules? A theory of democracy in the Third World must answer these two questions. Neither a normative stand on democratization nor an exhaustive description of the conditions of emergence, maintenance, or demise of competitive rule can answer them. The recent shift of emphasis in the literature to strategies of democratization is unlikely to serve its purpose unless these questions are answered first.

The two questions are not properly answered because of the misinterpretation of the Third World society. Reliance on the explanation of society provided by dualism/modernization theory and imperialism-inspired theories has severe consequences for the theory of the state. On the one hand, it leads to the normative posture adopted by the democratizing state paradigm, which borders on evolutionism and functionalism. Rather than explain why there are differences between the Third World and Western countries, it emphasizes what is lacking in the Third World in comparison to the West. This, in itself, is not aberrant; the difference between the terms of comparison can be shown by what one term does not possess. However, in a normative/evolutionary approach, a high premium is placed on the 'lacking factor'; it is both the explanation and the solution. It is also a stage to be reached. An example is the search for 'democratic institutions' and 'good governance' – the lacking factors – that proponents of the democratizing state and soft state paradigms, inspired by modernization theory, propose as the solution to African problems. On the other hand, overemphasis on imperialism has led to the questionable (although not completely false) conclusion that the lack of democracy results from the fact that the state was inherited from colonial rule and Western imperialism.[74]

Part of the problem is excessive parochialism in these paradigms, itself the result of the misinterpretation of the third world society. Distinctions (important but secondary) such as new authoritarianism, old authoritarianism, populism, and the period of democratization are made at the expense of perceiving fundamental patterns of overpoliticization in Third World countries; this obscures common features of competitive and authoritarian rules. The result is overemphasis on descriptions of authoritarian rules and the 'transition to democratic rule.' Truncated explanations of authoritarianism and the 'transition to democracy' are also proposed at the expense of an explanation of why both types of rule display crucial similarities. Moreover, the problem is defined with emphasis on such limitations as 'Latin America,' 'sub-Saharan Africa,' 'Middle East,' and 'South Asia,' rather than concentrating on fundamental similarities among these countries concerning the core problem. As a result, the truncated definitions of the core problem correspond to explanations tailored to fit each geographically defined empirical situation.

It is clear that Zaire shares crucial traits of the state with other Third World countries (this is not to deny differences in some aspects). On the other hand, Zaire and the Third World in general do not share these similarities with Western countries. The state in Zaire can be properly explained only by viewing it as a reflection of the Third World state in general. Therefore, informed by the common features that Zaire shares with other Third World countries, I will propose alternative explanations of society and the state that are not tailored to fit only Zaire, but can serve as hypotheses for other Third World countries. In the next three chapters, I attempt such an alternative explanation of society from which I will derive an alternative explanation of the state in the last three. Because precolonial societies are crucial in theorizing about today's society (i.e., pseudocapitalism), they need to be described first before interpreting them theoretically. The description is given in the next chapter.

Notes

1. On modernization theory, see Anthony D. Smith, *State and Nation in the Third World* (New York: St. Martin's Press, 1983); Daniel Offiong, *Imperialism and Dependency* (Washington, D.C.: Howard University Press, 1982); Tamas Szentes, *The Political Economy of Underdevelopment* (Budapest: Academia Kiado, 1976), esp., part 1; Dean Tipps, 'Modernization Theory and the Comparative Study of Societies,' in *Comparative Studies in Society and History*, 15 (1973), 199–240. On imperialism-inspired theories, see Suzanne Bodenheimer, 'Dependency and Imperialism: The Roots of Latin American Underdevelopment,' in *Readings in US Imperialism*, ed. Fann and Hodges (Boston: Porter Sargent, 1971); Bill Warren,

Imperialism: Pioneer of Capitalism (London: Verso Editions, 1980); Aristide Zolberg, 'Origins of the Modern World System: A Missing Link,' *World Politics*, 33 (1981), 253–81; Ronald Chilcote, ed., *Dependency and Marxism: Toward a Resolution of the Debate* (Westview Press, 1981). On the bureaucratic-authoritarian-corporalist state thesis, see Guillermo O'Donnel, *Modernization and Bureaucratic-Authoritarianism* (Berkeley: Institute of International Studies, 1973). For a critique of the bureaucratic-authoritarian state and the inherited postcolonial state models, see S. N. Sangmpam, 'The State–Society Relationship in Peripheral Countries: Critical Notes on the Dominant Paradigms,' *The Review of Politics*, Vol. 48, No. 4 (Fall 1986): 596–619; for a critique of the soft state model, see S. N. Sangmpam, 'Neither Soft Nor Dead: The African State is Alive and Well,' *African Studies Review*, Vol. 36, No. 2 (September 1993): 73–94.

2. J. H. Boeke, *Economics and Economic Policy of Dual Societies* (New York, 1953).
3. See Keith Griffin, *Underdevelopment in Spanish America* (London: George Allen and Unwin, 1969), pp. 19–31; Laclau, *op. cit.*, chap. 1; Tamas Szentes, *The Political Economy of Underdevelopment*, pp. 75–85.
4. Szentes, *The Political Development of Underdevelopment*, p. 83. See B. Higgins, 'The Dualistic Theory of Underdeveloped Areas: Economic Development and Cultural Change,' in G. M. Meier, ed. *Leading Issues in Development Economics* (New York, 1964).
5. Arthur Lewis, 'Economic Development with Unlimited Supplies of Labour,' *Manchester School*, May 1954.
6. Peter Bauer and Basil Yamey, 'The Third World and the West: An Economic Perspective,' in Scott Thompson, ed. *The Third World: Premises of US Policy* (San Francisco: Institute for Contemporary Studies, 1978), pp. 102, 104.
7. See Goran Hyden, *No Shortcuts to Progress; Beyond Ujamaa in Tanzania: Underdevelopment and an Uncaptured Peasantry* (Berkeley: University of California Press, 1980); and 'Fostering Progress in Africa.'
8. W. W. Rostow, *The Stages of Economic Growth* (Cambridge: Cambridge University Press, 1960).
9. A. G. Frank, *Latin America: Underdevelopment or Revolution*, pp. 221–230.
10. Szentes, *op. cit.*, pp. 84–85.
11. Laclau, *op. cit.*
12. Theories of imperialism, dependency, and world-system differ from each other, even though the demarcating line is often blurred. Dependency theory, in turn, is divided into many schools, including dependent development, internal colonialism, subimperialism and new dependency. The discussion here is not about the theories of imperialism per se, but focuses on these theories that derive from the concept of imperialism or share some of its concerns. More specificaly, those theories that address the issue of society in the third world. Thses are dependency and world-system theories, to which is added the theory of transition of modes of production.
13. John E. Taylor, *From Modernization to Modes of Production*, p. 146.
14. D. North and R. P. Thomas, *The Rise of the Western World*
15. Maurice Dobb and Paul Sweezy in Hilton et al., *The Transition from Feudalism to Capitalism*
16. Hindess and Hirst, *Pre-Capitalist Modes of Production*, pp. 265–285.
17. Dobb and Sweezy, in Hilton, ed., *The Transition from Feudalism to Capitalism*; Henri Pirenne, *Economic and Social History of Medieval Europe* (New York: Harcourt, Brace and World, Inc. 1937); Roger Godlieb, 'Feudalism and Historical

Materialism: A Critique and a Synthesis' *Science and Society*, Vol. XLVIII, no. 1 (Spring 1984): 1–37.

18. I. Wallerstein, The Modern World-System, Vol. 1; S. Amin, *Unequal Development*

19. Perry Anderson, *Lineages of the Absolutist States* and *Passages from Antiquity to feudalism.*

20. Bill Warren, *Imperialism: Pioneer of Capitalism* (London: Verso, 1980), p. 13.

21. See Norma Stoltz Chinchilla, 'Interpreting, Social Change in Guatemala: Modernization, Dependency, and Articulation of Modes of Production' in R. Chilcote and D. Johnson, eds. *Theories of Development* (Sage, 1983) pp. 159–169; see also, Norma Stoltz Chinchilla and James Lowell Dietz, 'Towards a New Understanding of development and Underdevelopment,' *Latin American Perspectives*, 8 (Summer–Fall): 138–147.

22. See Jacques Soustelle, *Daily Life of the Aztecs* (Stanford: Stanford University Press, 1970); Saiyid A. A. Rizvi, *Landmarks of South Asian Civilizations* (New Delhi: Munshiram Manoharlal Publishers, 1978); K. N. Chaudhuri, *Asia Before Europe: Economy and Civilization of the Indian Ocean from the Rise of Islam to 1750* (New York: Cambridge University Press, 1990); S. Amin, *Unequal Development*; S. Amin, *Eurocentrism*; Janet L. Abu-Lughod, *Before European Hegemony: The World System A.D. 1250–1350* (New York: Oxford University Press, 1989).

23. Amin, *Unequal Development*, p. 55.

24. Abu-Lughod, *Before European Hegemony*, p. 18.

25. Ibid., p. 12

26. See Amin, *Unequal Development*, pp. 50–57; and Catherine Coquery-Vidrovitch, 'The Political Economy of the African Peasantry and Modes of Production,' in P.C.W. Gutkind, eds., The Political Economy of Contemporary Africa, pp. 100–109.

27. Robert Harms, *River of Wealth, River of Sorrow*, Parts 2, 3, and 4.

28. B. Jewsiewicki, 'Lineage Mode of Production ...,' pp. 105–106.

29. Vansina, *The Children of Woot*, p. 196.

30. Vansina, *Kingdoms of the Savanna*, p. 123.

31. Coquery-Vidrovitch, *op. cit.*, p. 104.

32. Amin, *Unequal Development*, p. 51.

33. Samir Amin (in *Unequal Development* and *Eurocentrism*) and Immanuel Wallerstein (in *The Modern World-System* I) have argued that capitalism was prevented in China, Egypt, and other tribute-paying societies by the centralized nature of their empires.

34. Coquery-Vidrovitch, *op. cit.*, p. 108.

35. For a summary of theories of imperialism, see Ronald Chilcote, *Theories of Comparative Politics* (Boulder,CO: Westview Press, 1981), chapter 7.

36. See Amin's 9 theses in *Unequal Development*, pp. 198–203.

37. Ibid., pp. 204, 294, and 334.

38. Taylor, *op. cit.*, p. 213.

39. Ibid., p. 215. Emphasis added.

40. See Immanuel Wallerstein, *The Modern World-System*, 3 vols; Samir Amin, *Accumulation on a World Scale*; *Unequal Development*; *Eurocentrism*; and Andre Gunder Frank, *Crisis in the Third World*.

41. I. Wallerstein, 'World-System Analysis' in Anthony Giddens and Jonathan H. Turner, eds. *Social* Theory Today (Cambridge: Polity Press, 1987), p. 318.

42. Dale Johnson, 'Class Analysis and Dependency,' in Chilcote and Johnson, eds., *op. cit.*, p. 238.
43. James Weaver and Marguerite Berger, 'The Marxist Critique of Dependency Theory: An Introduction.' in Charles Wilber, ed. *The Political Economy of Development and Underdevelopment*, 3rd Edition (Random House, 1984), p. 59.
44. Amiya Kumar Bagchi, *The Political Economy of Underdevelopment*, p. 13.
45. See John Illife, *The Emergence of African Capitalism* (Mineapolis: University of Minnesota Press, 1983).
46. Laurence Harrison, *Underdevelopment Is a State of Mind*, comes close to this position.
47. See ibid.
48. See Lucian Pye, *Asian Power and Politics* (Cambridge, MA: Harvard University Press, 1985); Howard Wiarda, 'Toward a Nonethnocentric Theory of Development: Alternative Conceptions from the Third World,' in Wiarda, ed., *New Directions in Comparative Politics*, pp. 127–150; *Ibid.*, his 'Ethnocentrism and Third World Development,' *Society*, Vol. 24, No. 6, September/October 1987, pp. 55–64.
49. Some of the criticism can be found in Chilcote, *Theories of Comparative Politics*, pp. 234–240; see also, James A. Bill and Robert L. Hardgrave, Jr., *Comparative Politics* (University Press of America, 1981, pp. 113–116.
50. Peter Worsley, *The Three Worlds: Culture and World Development* (Chicago University Press, 1984), p. 60.
51. Sidney Verba, 'Conclusion,' in L. Pye and S. Verba, eds, *Political Culture and Political Development* (Princeton University Press, 1965), p. 515. Aaron Wildavsky, 'Teaching and Taking: A Seminar on Cultural Theory,' *Political Science Teacher*, Vol. I., No. 1 (Winter 1988): 3.
52. See Robert Dahl, *A Preface to Democratic Theory* (University of Chicago Press, 1956) and *Polyarchy* (Yale University Press, 1971).
53. See Graeme Duncan, ed. *Democratic Theory and Practice* (Cambridge University Press, 1983); Quentin Skinner, 'The Empirical Theorists of Democracy and Their Critics: A Plague on Both Their Houses,' *Political Theory*, I (1973), pp. 287–306.
54. Jonathan Sunshine, quoted by S. Huntington in 'Will More Countries Become Democratic?' *Comparative Politics 85/86* (The Dushkin Publishing Group), p. 151.
55. See Laurence E. Harrison, *Underdevelopment is a State of Mind*.
56. Huntington, 'Will More Countries Become Democratic?' p. 152.
57. Myron Weiner, 'Empirical Democratic Theory and the Transition from Authoritarianism to Democracy,' in P.S., Vol. XX, No. 4, Fall 1987, p. 862.
58. For a critique of this view, see S. N. Sangmpam, 'The State–Society Relationship in Peripheral Countries: Critical Notes on the Dominant Paradigms.'
59. See Perry Anderson, *Lineages of the Absolutist State*, especially Conclusions.
60. See Larry Diamond, Juan Linz, and S. M. Lipset, eds. *Democracy in Developing Countries: Africa* (Preface typescript).
61. See Goran Therbonn, 'The Rule of Capital and the Rise of Democracy,' in David Held et al., *States and Societies* (New York: University Press, 1983), pp. 261–271.
62. Guillermo O'Donnell and Philippe schmitter, eds., *Transition from Authoritarian Rule: Tentative Conclusions About Uncertain Democracies* (Washington, DC.: Johns Hopkins University Press, 1986), pp. 5, 20.
63. See Barrington Moore, *Social Origins of Dictatorship and Democracy* (Boston: Beacon, 1966).

64. See Adam Przeworski, 'Material Bases of Consent: Economics and Politics in a Hegemonic System,' *Political Power and Social Theory* (1980); Poulantzas, *Political Power and Social Classes*; For a review, see Robert Alford and Roger Friedland, *Powers of Theory* (Cambridge: Cambridge University Press, 1986), Part III. For an understanding of the concept of hegemony, see Antonio Gramsci's *Prison Notebooks* and *The Modern Prince*.
65. Poggi, *The Development of the Modern state* (Stanford: Stanford University Press, 1978) p. 123.
66. Giovanni Sartori, *The Theory of Democracy Revisited*, T2 (Chatham House, 1987), p. 879.
67. Huntington, 'Will More Countries Become Democratic?'
68. Weiner, *op. cit.*, pp. 864, 866.
69. Diamond et al., *op. cit.*, p. 14.
70. Andrew Young, U.S. ambassador to the United Nations under President Carter, indicated this in a television interview on March 23, 1985 in Washington, D.C., when pointing to the fact that 'democracy' in Argentina and Brazil was the result of Carter's human rights policy toward these countries.
71. J. Peeler, *Latin American Democracies*, p. 104.
72. E. Kim and L.Ziring, *An Introduction to Asian Politics* (Englewood Cliffs, NJ: Prentice Hall, 1977), p. 137.
73. Fernando Henrique Cardoso quoted in Frances Hagopian, 'Democracy by 'Undemocratic Means'? Elites, Political Pacts, and Regimes Transition in Brazil,' *Comparative Political Studies*, Vol. 23, no. 2 (July 1990), 147–170.
74. See Basil Davidson, *The Black Man's Burden* (New York: Times Book, 1992); H. Alavi, 'The State in Post-Colonial Societies: Pakistan and Bangladesh'; Samir Amin, 'la question démocratique dans le tiers monde contemporain,' *Africa Development*, Vol. XIV, no. 2 (1989): pp. 5–25 ; for a critique, see Sangmpam, 'Critical Notes on the Dominant Paradigms.'

3 Precolonial societies in central Africa

In this chapter, I describe precolonial societies to establish the empirical base for a theoretical interpretation of society in chapter 4 and 5. Since Meyer Fortes and E. E. Evans-Pritchard's *African Political Systems*, anthropologists have debated the merit of the bipolar division they established between stateless societies and state societies. Such a classification is flawed insofar as it postulates statelessness in some societies. For this conventional classification I substitute one that compares noncentralized societies to centralized ones.

1. Noncentralized Societies: Ambuun, Bading, Basongo, and Ngombe

The Ambuun, the Bading, and the Basongo, on the one hand, and the Ngombe, on the other, are geographically located far apart. The Ambuun (also referred to as Bambunda), the Bading (or Ding), and the Basongo live in the savannah of southwestern Zaire in the Bandundu–Kuilu region. The Ngombe live in swampy forests on both sides of the Congo (Zaire) River in the northwest between Lisala and Mbandaka. Lineage[1] constituted the backbone of social relations in these societies. It included roughly the same major units: the nuclear family, the extended family, the subclan, and the clan. In all of them the nuclear family, although independent in some aspects, remained subordinated to the requirements and needs of the whole lineage. The mode of descent reckoning was based on patrilineage among the Ngombe, and matrilineage characterized the descent reckoning among the Ambuun, the Bading, and the Basongo.

45

The Ngombe extended family comprised three to eight adult males with their children and their sisters. The members of an extended family recognized the leadership of the eldest male member, called *sangwasu* (our father). The Ngombe called the subclan *etuka*, which consisted of 'a kinship group numbering less than thirty men with their children of both sexes, as well as their sisters who reside elsewhere with their husbands but remain members of the *etuka* of their birth. The bonds of this group [were] closer and more secure than that of the village group, based as they [were] on common descent from an ancestor who is seldom more than four generations removed from the youngest members.'[2] The Ambuun extended family, *Nzo* (house), revolved around a deceased or living grandmother, but was led by an elder man (*Ngâ-nzo*). Above the *Nzo* stood the subclan (*eyot* or *eyor*), the largest localized and organized clan section. It was autonomous and generally occupied a specific territory in the village. Like the extended family, the subclan was generally led by an elder man, even though descent was traced back to a woman. Its membership included all women and their daughters' children of both sexes up to five generations, as well as their brothers, who might reside elsewhere with their wives.

After the subclan came the clan in all these societies. It had two quite contradictory roles. On the one hand, it differentiated its members from other members of the larger society (subtribe or tribe). On the other hand, it lacked the cohesion characteristic of the subclan and extended family. Among the Ambuun, the Bading, and the Basongo, a clan could be defined as 'a group of people who reckon[ed] their descent in the matrilineal line by steps of filiation to a common ancestor. It include[d] both deceased and living members of both sexes, that is, those living on the ground and those living underground.'[3] The clan was localized, totemic, and exogamous. Its members called each other brothers and sisters or uncles and aunts. This 'brotherhood' or 'sisterhood' allowed a stronger sense of sharing among the clan's members than was found among members of the larger society. This sense of sharing also obtained within the Ngombe clan, which included 'the descendants of the patrilineal ancestor whose name it bears, and its members call each other 'brothers' in distinguishing themselves from members of any other major lineage.'[4]

These lineage structures coincided with or shaped the political and administrative structure in these societies. The lineage, in addition to its own internal organization, politically and administratively structured the villages and chieftainships. Hence, a discussion of the political and administrative organization includes three levels – the lineage, the village, and the structure above the village – although in some cases the distinction between the lineage and the village is not easy to make. Among the Ambuun, the Bading, and the Ngombe, no formal politico-administrative authority governed all the clans' members because their major segments, the subclans, were autonomous. However, this did not prevent the clans' members from invoking the authority of the more prominent chiefs, who were generally heads of the senior subclans or villages. Nor did this autonomy preclude the existence of a formal authority over the clans at an earlier period. In fact, the patterns of segmentation of the lineage and the recounting of it by the elder Ambuun seem to point in that direction. At any rate, the politico-administrative organization of the lineage was much more visible at the level of the lower units, that is, at the subclan level. The Ambuun *eyot* and the Ngombe *etuka* expressed their autonomy by organizing themselves as political and administrative units under the leadership of the eldest male of the group. He was named *Ngâ-bol* among the Ambuun and *mosuko o nganda* among the Ngombe. Among the Basongo, the clan played a much more centralizing role, politically and administratively, for its members under the leadership of its chief. Although the normal succession was automatically determined by seniority, in all these cases the rule of succession allowed for an adult, younger man to head the group. This occurred whenever the dying head of the lineage handpicked his successor, or the current head, for some reason, relinquished his leadership to a younger adult male. Among the Ambuun the would-be head could also be elected by the elders of the lineage.

As a political and administrative figure, the head of the lineage organization fulfilled several functions. He played the role of referee for the whole organization, acting to maintain cohesion and order. He made sure that a member of the lineage did not take another fellow member to court; any dispute among members of the lineage was submitted to his arbitration. In any interlineage dispute, he accompanied and represented the involved members of his lineage. The head of the lineage was also consulted on all important matters, such as the education of the youngsters, their marriages, and migration. Moreover, he had prime responsibility for the health of his subjects, for whom he was the ambassador in all relationships with other lineages. Finally, he was the guarantor of the group's property. In fulfilling all these functions, the head of the lineage benefited from the support of the lineage council, which comprised the heads of the subunits within the lineage organization. Among the Ambuun, for instance, the council was made up of the heads of the extended families (*Ngâ-nzo*).

What was lacking administratively and politically at the lineage level was supplied by the village. The village was either an integral part of the lineage organization – as in the case of the Ngombe village – or its coordinating structure among the Ambuun, the Bading, and the Basongo. For the Ngombe, 'the village [was] a community of one hundred and fifty to three hundred members who inhabit[ed] contiguous plots along a road or forest path, with the continuity broken only between the several segments, *bituka*, of the whole. Like all other Ngombe social units, the village [was] composed of the agnatic descendants of the ancestor for whom the group is named, although, as at other levels, some few may trace descent from the founder through a female link.'[5] In the three other societies, the village (characterized by its generally large size among the Ambuun) was also made up of several subclans. Unlike the Ngombe village, however, the village subclans among the Ambuun, the Bading, and the Basongo usually belonged to different clans and did not trace their descent from a common ancestor. Only some exceptionally small villages were single-lineage villages. Lineages that made up the village were not equal; in most cases, a prominent or senior lineage dominated village politics.

Whatever its ethnogeographical specificity may have been, the village was subordinated to the lineage organization, which dictated its structuring. The Ngombe village was headed by a chief (*kumu*); he was elected by the unanimous choice of the villagers representing their respective lineage organizations. As a rule, the office of the *kumu* was held by one of the two specific units of the lineage organization: the subclan and the extended family. The chief of the village was assisted by a notable judge (*mowe*) in his function of arbitrating cases of adultery, theft, homicide, and so forth. Both the chief and the *mowe* formed the political link between other villages and their own. Among the Ambuun, the village chief (*mfum a bol*) was chosen from the senior subclan of the village, which, as a rule, held the office of the chief. This explained the frequent assimilation of the office of the village chief with that of the senior *Ngâ-bol*, the head of the senior subclan of the village. Upon his death, the village chief was replaced by his brother on the mother's side or his sister's son. It follows that the succession to the village headship heavily depended on how the head of the senior subclan was chosen. The village chief was assisted by a council of elders representing different lineages. Like the Ngombe chief, the Ambuun village chief had jurisdiction over matters related to theft, adultery, homicide, property, and so forth. He also oversaw the political relations with other villages. Among the Bading, the village chief was referred to as the *nkum* or *ngaal*. The procedures surrounding his election and succession were similar to the ones prevailing among the Ambuun. He was generally the head of the senior lineage, which often made him a landowner. However, landownership was not the strict *sine qua non* to become a chief because there are reported cases of chiefs who did not own land. Unlike the Ambuun village chief, the Bading chief had a small council made up of only one or two members who belonged, generally, to his own lineage or allied lineages.[6]

In all these cases, the village chief received deference from his subjects. He also received, from time to time, tribute from them, which marked recognition of the chief as a political leader. However, given the fusion between lineage and political organization, the tribute was often, at the same time, a recognition of the ownership rights of the chief's lineage over land.

The tribe was a prolongation of both the lineage structure and the political structure. As a lineage organization, the tribe did not possess a membership that could claim with some certainty descent from a common ancestor.[7] Probably as a result of this uncertainty about the descent reckoning, the tribe lacked a coordinating center and a unitary state apparatus to maintain a hierarchy. Unlike in centralized societies, no lineage structure was associated with a founding king by which to organize a hierarchical and centralized society politically. The politico-administrative structure that displayed direct connections with both the lineage and the village was the subtribe (or chieftainship). The latter was a group of clans and villages whose descendants claimed a common ancestor with a depth of some fifteen to twenty generations. The primacy of the lineage structure had political implications for the subtribes. Among the Ambuun, for instance, some senior clans whose more prominent subsections owned lands had the explicit or implicit respect of the less prominent ones; the heads of these senior clans emerged as political figures of the subtribes. This pattern culminated in the consolidation of some major chieftainships, each being controlled by a prominent clan.[8] The emergence of these chieftainships would probably explain why the Kuba – a centralized society since before the eighteenth century – claimed to have copied its political organization from the Ambuun, a society known for its decentralization.[9]

Among the Basongo and the Bading, chieftainships also emerged in response to the patterns of lineage landownership. Indeed, the landowner was generally the head of a senior clan around which other clans clustered. He was called *muwil* among the Basongo and *ngaal* among the Bading.[10] Such clustering usually culminated in a larger political entity, thus conferring some political authority on the senior clan's head. His functions were judiciary and administrative, resembling those of the village chief but surpassing them in magnitude. Among the Basongo, perhaps because of the smallness of the entire society and the minimal role played by the village chief, the chieftainship and its chief played a more important role. The amount of tribute paid to the chief in foodstuffs and labor service (e.g., clearing his fields) seems to have been more than that received by the chieftainship office among the Ambuun and the Bading. The rules of investiture and succession of the head of the chieftainship were similar to those applying to the lineage head and village chief, differing only in their more solemn character. Despite all this, chieftainships did not lead to the centralization of political power. As in the case of the village chief, tribute paid to the chieftain played a dual role: it was tribute to him as a political leader and also as the head of the senior clan, hence, as a landowner.

Lineage also dictated and determined the ideological discourse. The lineage defined itself as the sum of the living and dead, who traced their descent to a common ancestor. In so doing, it elevated dead ancestors to such a high status that all social relations were subordinated to their prescriptions. The reliance on the dead ancestors determined for the most part the requirement of seniority attached to most social relations. Seniority implied closeness to the ancestors; as such, it endowed one with supernatural and divine power. Among the Ngombe, for instance, the position of the eldest male member of the extended family, the *sangwasu*, was vital for the whole group, 'for it [was] he who petition[ed] the ancestors to give the group a successful hunt or success in other ventures, and it [was] likewise within his power to curse or bless any individual in the name of the ancestors.' Seniority was also a criterion for power at the subclan level. Here the head was the oldest living father, 'recognized as having considerable influence with the ancestral spirits who he will soon join and as having more wisdom than the others because he [had] lived more years and [had] seen the village before.' Likewise, the village chief, the *kumu*, who was an elder man in the lineage structure, was endowed with supernatural powers by the ancestors: 'If the villagers fail to heed his decision on such subjects as warfare or the moving of a village, or if they fail to show him due respect, he may cause the ancestors to withhold all good things from the village – game, offspring, or success in war.'[11]

With but slight modification, this seniority power applied to the Ambuun, the Bading, and the Basongo as well. As the quintessence of seniority, the lineage head played the intermediary role between living members and dead ones. Even in those instances where he was not the eldest member of the lineage, his appointment by the dying predecessor enhanced his status in the eyes of the ancestors and qualified him to be the link between them and the living members of the lineage. Far from being the source of his power, the investiture of the lineage head only consecrated and reaffirmed the powers that emanated from the ancestors and that allowed him to speak and act on their behalf. The power emanating from his position in the lineage (his designation by the dying predecessor) was attested to by burial rites: 'Oshium, you are now gone underground. Chief Okan who stands here has been designated by yourself to look after women and men. We are now staying with him. Chief Okan is now in charge of women and men. ... Here is your wine, here is your meat. May chief Okan [live] in peace without fear or worry.'[12] To ensure acceptance of the new lineage chief by the ancestors, the Basongo organized a ritual hunt. If the hunt produced game, it signaled acceptance; an unproductive hunt was interpreted as the ancestors' rejection of the new lineage head. In the latter case, the search was reopened.[13] By virtue of his ancestor-derived authority, the lineage head was feared by his subjects, even though his was anything but tyrannical power. Any member of the lineage who did not submit to his instructions was likely to be punished and cursed. For example, a young woman who did not marry the lineage head's choice could easily be threatened with barrenness. On the other hand, by presiding over ancestral rituals, the lineage head was equipped to bless members of the lineage for their various undertakings and to protect them against sorcerers and other evils.

The prime importance of dead ancestors among the Ambuun permeated most activities of life. Insofar as living members of the lineage were the branches of a tree whose roots were its dead members, the dead were credited with creating happiness for the living. To benefit from such happiness one had to obey one's ancestors' prescriptions, imitate their good deeds, and also make them happy. For this reason, living members assumed the responsibility for debts accumulated by the deceased members as well as their unfinished court hearings. Dead members were always evoked in terms similar to those applied to the living members to maintain the presence of the ancestors within the lineage. Their presence was further reinforced through the selective reincarnation of the ancestors in the newborn of the lineage. A kaolin (*mpio*), jealously conserved, symbolized such a presence among the living members.

Not obeying ancestors' prescriptions was tantamount to provoking their anger; the result was often a mishap, such as sterility, drought, or disease. These misfortunes also occurred as the result of revenge by an ancestor who had felt mistreated by other lineage members while alive. To calm them and to exorcise the evil spirit, ancestral cults and sacrifices were organized. The usual form of sacrifice consisted of offering a chicken or goat to the ancestors. The head of the animal was cut off and its blood sprinkled on the ancestor's grave and on the participating crowd before words were pronounced by the officiating elder. Among the Ambuun, a more specialized form of ancestral sacrifice was organized in the case of revenge by a mistreated ancestor. Misfortune expressed itself in the form of epilepsy suffered by one or several members of the lineage. To expel the curse (called *obel*), the body of the vengeful ancestor was exhumed and small portions of his bones were mixed with other healing ingredients, kaolin, and water or palm wine in a pot. The mixture was then presented to the living members of the lineage as a beverage. Yet not all ancestors were forgiving. A class of ancestors who died as sorcerers or wrongdoers remained irrevocably devilish. They did not live with the 'good' ancestors; they were relegated to caves and other desolate places and became perpetual wanderers, causing misfortune to living people. Sacrifices by members of the lineage did not calm them; only a diviner (witch doctor) could do so.

Lineage ideology spread through the larger society via sorcery. Although the sorcerers' killing power affected only the members of their own lineage group, other means existed through which members of other lineages could benefit from and be affected by it. Whenever an intralineage dispute between two members caused one member to wish the death of another lineage member, he or she benefited from the complicity of the sorcerer. A magical 'sale' of the cursed relative was made to the sorcerer, who could then eliminate him or her. Given the complex network of interlineage alliances, such magical sales were able to spread what was fundamentally a lineage-based practice to society at large. The pervasiveness of sorcery had its own side effects; it led to the proliferation of antisorcery practices and institutions.

Economic Organization

Like most African societies, the main economic activities in these societies consisted of hunting, agriculture, animal husbandry, fishing, gathering, and handicrafts. The forms of labor cooperation varied from one activity to another. In agriculture, slash-and-burn, along with shifting cultivation, constituted the main practice: 'Every year a new area is cleared, and the grasses and tree limbs are burned and the ashes used as fertilizers. After further preparation by hoeing, which takes different forms, the main crop is then sown or planted. Rotation of different crops on the same field is practiced until the soil is exhausted, which occurs usually from two to four years after the first planting. The field then lies fallow in order to regenerate for a number of years, which may be as many as twenty.'[14] A variety of crops, including yams, sweet potatoes, sugarcane, millet, bananas, sorghum, beans, groundnuts, and American crops, such as maize and cassava, were grown. The forms of labor cooperation in agriculture depended on the activities involved and crop cycles. Clearing and burning forest fields were men's activities, whereas clearing and burning undergrowth, planting, and harvesting were mainly women's activities. In forest areas crop cycles were alternating processes in which men did the slashing and burning while women did the planting, weeding, and harvesting. In the less dense regions where landscape was dominated by undergrowth, labor coperation tended to be less, and much of the burden throughout the crop cycle fell on women. Unlike some West African societies, such as the Gouro of Côte d'Ivoire,[15] the Ambuun and the Bading were rarely involved in activities where men and women worked together at every stage. Activities at certain stages were carried out by men, at some stages by women, and at others by both men and women together. Labor cooperation, however, was no substitute for individual activities that, on the whole, dominated the production process.

Animal husbandry was generally less developed. The Ambuun, the Bading, and the Basongo raised pigs, goats, chickens, and sheep. The labor process consisted of raising livestock and managing the space for it. Fishing and gathering were practiced in various ways. Men and women shared the activities, some of which involved some forms of cooperation, especially fishing. The main handicraft activities were weaving, basketwork, iron smithing, pottery, and woodworking. For environmental reasons, hunting was the most important economic activity among the Ngombe. Warfare was politically important and complementary to hunting. 'Agriculture [was] an activity in which lineage ancestors [had] very little interest and in which there [was] almost no cooperative activity on the part of lineage brothers.'[16] Whatever amount of work was devoted to agriculture was aimed at providing the bare minimum for a complete meal. Therefore, the major form of cooperation among Ngombe villagers concerned hunting (and warfare). This cooperation manifested itself frequently in the *bokai* hunt, in which all the men of the village set up a huge circle of nets in the forest and drove the animals from the center to the perimeter, where they were killed by the men stationed at the nets.

All four societies used similar instruments of labor. The Ambuun, the Bading, and the Basongo had the edge over the Ngombe because their economic activities were diversified. Land was the principal means of production, and instruments of labor included swords, axes, hoes, knives, machetes, and bows and arrows. As means of payment, these societies used shells (*nzim*), raffia squares (*mbal*), and sometimes salt.

As in the case of the political and administrative organization, social relations of production in these societies were dominated by lineage. As a result, there was hardly any relation of production beyond the clan. The tribe was not a corporate landholding body, and thus did not hold the positive right to actually allocate plots of land to its members. At the subtribe level, with the arguable exception of the Basongo, the same held true even though the senior lineage of the chieftainship owned lands that the villagers used for hunting and for which they paid tribute. Both the tribe and the subtribe did, however, exercise the negative right to exclude foreign communities (other tribes and subtribes) from using the land within their territorial limits. Among the Ngombe, the lack of positive right applied to the clan as well. With no actual right to allocate land to its members, the clan's responsibility was reduced to defining certain area limits within which all clan members shared hunting and fishing rights prohibited to outsiders. Among the Ambuun, the clan's negative rights were from time to time accompanied by the positive right of actually allocating land to its members when they moved from one village to another where the clan had a local section.

The relations of production appeared more clearly structured at the lower levels of lineage units – the subclan and the extended family levels. Here the lineage head stood at the center of a network of relationships involving the ownership of the means of production and the extraction and distribution of the surplus product. By virtue of his ancestor-derived powers, the lineage head was the chief protector and manager of the group's land, waters, and forests. Land was inalienable because it was ultimately the property of the ancestors, and living members were simply guardians.[17] To be sure, no explicit allocation of land to lineage members was necessary because all members made their own choices as to which part of the land to till. Nevertheless, the tacit approval of the lineage chief was necessary; he had the power, when dissatisfied, to disapprove explicitly of one member's choice of land. The primacy of hunting over agriculture among the Ngombe and the relative abundance of land among the Ambuun, the Bading, and the Basongo helped prevent recurrent conflicts over land.

No rigid rule governed the ownership of the instruments of production. In general, instruments such as axes or hoes were owned by individual members of the lineage. Lineage members also owned their houses, furniture, livestock, their fields, and the produce of their work on the fields. Individual ownership did not strictly mean private property; other members of the lineage still exercised some usufruct rights over such instruments and goods, and the lineage head held indirect rights of ownership. Within the limits of normal expectations, instruments of labor could easily be borrowed, lent, and shared among members of the lineage.

Owing to his vast ancestor-based authority, the lineage head also indirectly controlled the labor process. The bulk of labor cooperation in these societies took place under the aegis of the lineage. Work or production teams did not exclusively rely on members of the lineage; the inclusion of outsiders was a normal occurrence. However, except in the case of collective hunting, most participants were members of the same lineage or allied lineages. The lineage head could approve or disapprove of the inclusion of outsiders in the lineage-based team; he could sanction or disapprove of hunting, fishing, or gathering in some fields, waters, or forests owned by the lineage. Finally, he could, in the name of the ancestors, extend or withhold his blessing for such productive activities.

The extraction and redistribution of the surplus product constituted two important aspects of the relations of production. The extraction took two forms: (1) contributions to some kind of trust fund for the entire lineage, and (2) the surplus product taken by the eldest members of the lineage from its junior members. Both forms of extracted surplus took place under the aegis of the lineage head. The trust was made up of livestock, agricultural produce, tools, or money. Its sources were various. Among the Ambuun, the Bading, and the Basongo, in addition to mandatory or voluntary contributions by lineage members, goods inherited from any deceased member were part of it because the deceased member's children, spouse, or brothers did not have any special claim to such goods. Bridewealth received by the lineage was also part of the trust. These contributions – some of which were strictly mandatory, as among the Basongo – and inherited goods were held by the lineage head.

For extraction of the surplus intended for the lineage head, the justification in all these societies was the same. The intermediary role played by the lineage chief between the ancestors and the living members of the lineage entitled him to it. The surplus was intended for the ancestors he represented. By virtue of his supernatural power over juniors, the lineage head, and indeed other senior members of the lineage, obtained from them a variety of goods and labor services. These ranged from foodstuffs to clearing their fields for cultivation. The requirements for the extraction varied; they went from lax among the Ambuun to strict among the Basongo. Among the Ngombe, where the village was an integral part of the lineage structure, the village chief was a surrogate for the eldest lineage member. Hence his relationship with the villagers was not one linking a political authority to subjects. Rather, he extracted from the villagers as a lineage head. He received from them deference and certain rare animals (in whole or part) – the leopard, the python, certain species of birds, the tail of a crocodile, and the trunk of an elephant. In all societies, the lineage head and other elders at each level of the lineage structure received meat as a gift, were offered a chair when they approached, and had a pipe of tobacco prepared for them. When game was killed, it was not to be cut until the lineage head and elders had so ordered; and certain parts of the game were to be reserved for them.

Both goods put in trust and those extracted by the lineage head were redistributed in many ways among the members of the lineage. To be sure, the lineage head did use some of the extracted surplus for his own benefit. Meat, fish, and other goods were consumed by his family; he also used for himself or his family some luxury goods given to him. The bulk of extracted surplus, however, was given back to the lineage members. The prime beneficiaries were sick people, widows, orphans, old people, those in debt, and anyone in need of support. The surplus was also redistributed through the brideprice paid for acquiring wives for junior members and through collective meals in which lineage members participated.[18]

2. Centralized Societies: Kongo, Kuba, and Luba

The Kongo Kingdom

Society

The Kongo kingdom is one of the best-known African precolonial kingdoms. A clear picture of its social and political life has been drawn from written records of missionaries, officials, and traders. Emerging in the fifteenth century, and probably earlier, the kingdom extended, by the sixteenth century, into the territories of today's Zaire, Congo, and Angola.[19] Lineage stood at the center of the social relations of the kingdom. From the fifteenth to the nineteenth centuries, the lineage structure was modified by political vagaries and social transformations in the kingdom. This was particularly true with regard to power distribution; some units in the lineage networks came to play a greater role while others' roles declined.[20] Because of these changes, lineage came to revolve around some basic units: the clan (*mvila* or *mbila*), the subclan (*kanda*) and the extended family (*ngudi*, mother or house). The house was, in turn, divided into smaller segments. At the very bottom of the hierarchy was the nuclear family. Descent was reckoned in the matrilineal line – without excluding patrilineal relationships.

The clan was the highest lineage unit. Twelve major clans are said to have founded the kingdom and influenced its social and political life. The clan was a group of individuals tracing unilineal descent from a common ancestress and included both the living members and those living in the other world: 'The Kongo clan is a collectivity which lives or makes the individual live. ... By itself the clan is the equivalent of [what is for Europeans] the paternal house, the family, the religious and civil society. ... It includes two categories of people: the ancestors who live underground and their descendants who live under the sun. The grave in the ancestral land constitutes the entrance door for the latter to join the former.'[21] As in noncentralized societies, the Kongo clan lacked cohesiveness at the upper level. Although it displayed such cohesiveness in the earlier years of the kingdom, it lost it in later years, probably after 1700[22] owing to its fragmentation into autonomous *kanda*. Not only are genealogical links absent at the clan level today, but the Kongo clan also is questionably an exogamous corporate group. It was the subclan, or *kanda*, that embodied the characteristic bonds of the lineage organization. Unlike the clan, the subclan was a localized and exogenous corporate group. Each *kanda* resided in a village or in several villages in the same area and maintained the basic characteristics and elements of the original clan. The clan remained its point of reference because by referring to the larger clan the members of a *kanda* could avoid incestuous relations with other *kanda* of the same clan. They also could have access to the clan's land and could enjoy security and share a sense of solidarity with other members of their clan. Every *kanda* had an exclusive body of common affairs, defined names, traditions, and membership. It was totemic. Each *kanda* was made up of three *ngudi* (houses).

As a result of matrilineal descent within the lineage structure, the son belonged to his mother's and maternal uncle's lineage. One's lineage thus included one's mother and maternal aunts, one's maternal uncles, one's nephews, nieces, cousins, and brothers and sisters on the mother's side. In general, only the offspring from free (as opposed to slave) women, were members of the lineage. Lineage members called each other 'mother,' 'brother,' or 'sister,' which helped develop a strong sense of sharing. The *kanda* was the referent point to distinguish between free men and slaves; belonging to a lineage made one free, whereas the opposite meant slave status. It also provided access to land.[23]

Each level of the lineage structure displayed a leadership, which expressed itself through a nomenclature including senior (*nkuluntu*), elder (*mbuta*), chief (*mani* or *mfumu*), and leader and uncle (*nkazi*). Each title carried with it a portion of the authority that added up to the pyramidal whole. 'Every individual member of a *kanda* was a relative elder on a continuum of eldership which reached from the named elders in the other world to the most junior member of this; each contained within himself the jural and spiritual authority of the *kanda*.'[24] At the top of the lineage pyramid was the *mani*, who, as a female or male senior, headed the whole *kanda*. The other segments of the lineage structure were headed by the *mbuta* and *nkuluntu*, whose houses (lineage subdivisions) owned land locally or whose talents had earned them a strong voice in local affairs. As the Kongo kingdom crumbled and centrifugal forces accentuated its fragmentation after the eighteenth century, the *nkazi* came to assume the leadership of the lineage at the local level at the expense of its central authority.[25]

As a rule, seniority was require to succeed to one of the leadership positions in the lineage structure. To succeed a lineage head, one had to be the predecessor's brother or nephew on the mother's side. No rigid sex preference governed titleholding, especially that of the highest level of the lineage (the *mani*). The lineage head was chosen by a committee of elders of the lineage group. The electoral code was broken with the disintegration of the kingdom as some ambitious *nkazi* came to rely on economic resources to secure peripheral power. On the whole, however, the lineage structure did perpetuate itself and renew its leadership through a representation mechanism. As the chief representatives of the lineages, the lineage heads fulfilled administrative and judiciary functions of their *kanda*, whose names they took. In the name of the lineage, the lineage head married off the female members to other lineages and regulated relations among the component subgroups of the lineage organization. The lineage leadership also buried deceased dependents, sponsored and represented dependents and clients (e.g., by speaking for them and finding land for them to cultivate), and exercised authority over slaves, especially in questions of sale and redemption. Most of these functions were shared with the heads of lower lineage segments. Thus, for instance, at the lowest level, the *nkuluntu* judged civil and communal matters and represented their group in their internal and external relations.

Lineage structure shaped the village organization as well. The villages, *vata*, were usually very small. Generally built far away from major roads, they differed from towns, or *mbanza*.[26] A village was made up of several lineages evolving around a core lineage whose head was the village chief (*mfumu*). The core lineage owned the land on which the village stood. Village chiefs were assisted by councils of elders representing their respective lineages. Chiefs were in charge of justice, war, commerce, and public works. As lineage seniors, they organized ancestral cults and rituals and ordered such labor services as house building and wine making from their subjects for their own use. As representatives of the ancestors, village chiefs enjoyed vast authority and were granted high marks of deference, such as special greetings and the observance of silence when they passed.[27]

On the ideological front, the Kongo society was not very different from noncentralized societies. Kongo's lineage-based ideology also focused on two major factors that went hand-in-hand: the primacy of the ancestors and seniority. By defining the lineage as a continuum whose ends were its dead members in the other world and its living members in this world and by granting a superior position to the dead, the Kongo people allowed social relations to be dominated by the ancestors. And given that seniority was the means to ensure closeness and access to ancestors, it was also a requirement for attaining a position of leadership. The ancestors, *bakulu* (note that *nkulu* = old, senior), lived underground, next to streams, and in forests. They lived in villages similar to those of the living members. Their world was without pain, suffering, and hard work. The dead, without being seen, lived with the living members of the lineage, worked with them, and participated in all their undertakings. On them depended the success or failure of such undertakings. The passage from this world to that of the ancestors was ensured by both the spirit and one's corpse. Both allowed dead lineage members to become *nkulu*, that is, ancestors who kept their before-death personalities and ranks.

The perception of the dead members of the lineage had four major consequences: (1) the ancestors had to be invoked by the living when the living were searching for happiness; (2) securing happiness by invoking the ancestors was conditional upon making them happy first; (3) the task of invoking the *nkulu* was left to the elders of the lineage, which reinforced the code of seniority as the ultimate criterion of closeness to the ancestors; (4) the status of some deceased members as wanderers who caused misfortune and their complicity with sorcerers meant that living lineage members had to find means to counter their influence. To ensure the happiness of deceased members, the Kongo made sure that proper burial accompanied the deaths of their fellow lineage members; elaborate funerals accompanied the deaths of the elders. The burials themselves bore witness to the ancestors' lives after death. Deceased notables were sometimes accompanied in their graves by their slaves, generally slave wives, whereas other dead lineage members were buried with their personal belongings. The dead were also given palm wine by the living members of their lineages. 'At the graveside, a person respected in this function as a religious person amassed earth and water, carried it on his shoulder then, with face averted, covered the corpse.' Living members of the lineage addressed the following message to the dead: 'Where you are going, convey our message to the ancestors, and where we are staying, may we live prosperous.' Then they trod the clay.[28]

After performing these burial ceremonies and rituals, living members of the lineage were entitled to ask favors, from their ancestors, ranging from success in hunting and fishing to bearing children. As in the noncentralized societies, graves were the sites of the encounters and communication between the ancestors and the living members of the lineage. Such grave-based rituals of communication were generally performed by the children of the *kanda*. They visited the graves every new moon, lamented the dead, and deposited wine and food for them. The children were chosen because of the spiritual power the father exercised over them. Kongo ancestors were not responsive to the invocations of living members whenever rituals or sacrifices offered to them did not meet their approval. The consequence was a persistent mishap or failure in one's life or undertakings. The Kongo saw in these misfortunes the return of the ancestors. They exhumed the body of the ancestor, inquired into the mistake, and reburied it with the correct rites.

Personal communication with the ancestors was allowed to all lineage members. However, the lineage elders remained the prime intermediaries between lineage members and the ancestors because of their closeness to the latter. Indeed, 'the elders in the other world were believed to be at the apex of a continuum of relative eldership which extended from them to the most junior member of the *kanda* in this world. Each relative elder could bless or curse the junior. The junior was expected to respect the elder, consult him or her and offer gifts of tribute. The elders of the *kanda* performed such functions with respect to their elders in the other world.'[29] As in noncentralized societies, the lineage head's or elder's position as intermediary only revealed his lack of control over people and things; lineage land and whatever grew on it belonged to the ancestors. The right to bless and curse also belonged ultimately to them. But, by the same token, the position of intermediary gave the lineage head tremendous leverage over lineage members, for any power to act was derived from the ancestors. As the representative of the ancestors, the lineage head or elder was thus the visible hand through which the invisible hand of the ancestors ensured the fertility of women, the productivity of palm trees, the abundance of game in the lineage's forests and that of fish in its streams and ponds. It was also through the lineage head that the ancestors protected their descendants against evil spirits, sorcerers, and death.[30] Rituals that accompanied the investiture formalized the power of the newly installed elder/notable to domesticate ancestral powerful forces. The investiture that made one a *mfumu* (chief) was meaningless if one was not at the same time an elder.[31]

In addition to the ancestors, the Kongo ideological universe included numerous other 'spirits' of different origin. Among these spirits were those

58

dead who were rejected by the ancestors and who became devilish wanderers, *matebo*, and the *bi simbi*, who were associated with waters, earth, and forests. Unlike the *matebo*, the *bi simbi* were not seen. Like the *matebo*, however, they could also be captured and used by sorcerers to harm living people. The *nkita* were powerful spirits, heroes who died violently in war, murder, or suicide. They were invoked through the *kimpasi* (initiation rites) to rid a society of jealousy and tensions.[32] The *mbumba*, represented in the form of a giant snake, was invoked for fertility, but could also provoke infertility, disease, and death. Finally, the sky spirits (*nkadi mpemba*) 'could help man to acquire wealth, to defend himself against the evil deeds of others, to combat the many manifestations of sorcery and to manipulate the natural world to his material ends.'[33] These various spirits led to the proliferation of two antagonistic forces: the evil forces, or sorcery (*ndoki*), which caused harm to the living members of the lineage, and the forces of goodness set in motion to counter the actions of the sorcerers – the *nkisi* in the hands of the *nganga* (witch doctor/diviner).

Production forces in the Kongo kingdom did not differ much from those prevailing in noncentralized societies. The Kongo practiced hunting, fishing, gathering, agriculture, and handicrafts as main economic activities in various forms of labor cooperation. In agriculture, the major economic activity of the Kongo, the forms of labor cooperation and the overall process of production took place under the aegis of the lineage. The elaborate rituals at the opening of the farming season and those aimed at obtaining fertility and a good harvest from the ancestors were performed by the lineage head in the presence of lineage members.[34] Lineage cooperation, however, did not preclude individual activities or a restricted form of cooperation.

Trade and slavery explained the Kongo kingdom's advantage over noncentralized societies with regard to accumulation. The two factors were stimulated by the centralization of the Kongo state. In the Kongo, as in other African precolonial societies, the causes of slavery included war, crime, sale debt, famine, and rejection by one's lineage. As productive forces, slaves were used as means of transportation, labor power in agricultural and other work, means of payment for debt, and as wives. They were, above all, used to increase the ranks of the lineages that acquired them. Trade, on the other hand, focused on such luxury items as iron, salt, cloth, animal skins, and shell (*nzimbu*), in addition to perishable food products. The market played an important role in trade activities because of the uneven regional distribution of these products. Three factors facilitated the impetus of trade and slavery in the accumulation process. The first was the geographical position of the kingdom itself, which opened it to European trade. The Kongo kingdom entered early into trade relations with the Portuguese. Exchanges with European products stimulated internal demand, which increased the volume of domestic products geared toward exchange. Even when the kingdom disintegrated from the seventeenth century onward, trade channels still increased as the Portuguese and the Dutch competed for supremacy.[35] The second factor was the kingdom's early exposure to the Atlantic slave trade. The trade not only reinforced slavery but totally modified its raison d'être. A highly lucrative venture, it enabled the Portuguese and Kongo officials, elders, and would-be traders to accumulate wealth by trading people. The third factor, the tribute requirements and the myth of kingship, stimulated the circulation of goods and slaves. Concerning slavery particularly, the king's authority over people seems to have facilitated in many ways the flourishing of the slave trade with the Portuguese.[36] It is worth noting that the Kongo, like noncentralized societies, used shells (*nzimbu*) and raffia cloth as payment in most of their transactions.

The Kongo relations of production revolved around land ownership because land was the principal means of production. The larger clan, let alone the whole society, did not hold the positive right to allocate land to individuals; the subclan (*kanda*) did. The larger clan, however, did influence the patterns of landownership. Indeed, given that the Kongo kingdom emerged out of twelve original clans (which later fragmented into *kanda*), the original clans were viewed as the original landowners. This explained why the original clans' ancestors were the 'actual' owners of land. Consequently, even though the *kanda* came to assume the positive rights to allocate land, it exercised these rights on behalf of the original clan ancestor. Hence, one understands the fundamental requirement of the Kongo society: land was the property of the lineage, and as such, was inalienable. The ancestors owned it, and the lineage managed it; lineage members had only usufruct rights.

For practical reasons, the *kanda* and the extended family, *ngudi* (or house), held the rights over land. Through their leaders, they allocated portions of it to individual lineage members. The notion of the inalienability of land was not rigid within the subunits of the same lineage or allied lineages of 'father' or 'sons.'[37] They were given access to land whenever it was needed. As in noncentralized societies, individuals were allowed to own some types of property: clothes; money; furniture; utensils; houses; livestock; instruments of labor, hunting and fishing, and witchcraft; and their own cultivated land and its products. Such individual property did not exclude other lineage members from using it within the limits of normal expectations. Nor did individual property exclude the organization of lineage property or trust. The trust comprised goods inherited from deceased lineage members that did not go to the nuclear family. (In noncentralized societies, the nuclear family did not have special claim over the deceased's goods.) The individual goods left by deceased members without nuclear families also went to the lineage trust, as did slaves, proceeds from funerals, and bridewealth. Once again, as the representative of the ancestors, the lineage head controlled the trust.

The extraction of the surplus product was justified by the ancestor-derived preeminence of the lineage elder/head: 'The *kanda* could become powerful instruments in the extraction of surplus product. Their internal structure was flexible, authority at each level being legitimated by the holder's position on the continuum of eldership and by his or her power to bless or to curse his juniors. ... If power was concentrated, an extremely hierarchical structure could develop, with the lineage heads extracting a considerable proportion of the surplus product.'[38] A whole range of ideological postulates influenced the extraction of the surplus product. By virtue of their ancestor-endowed power, lineage heads had the authority to sell lineage members they 'owned'; they also had the power to kill or to enslave them. His political motives notwithstanding, De Cleene's observation is à propos: 'The lineage head, who is in the indigenous conception the closest to the ancestors, has for this reason a quasi religious authority over all clan members. No one can disobey him, since all are convinced that he speaks and acts in the name of the ancestors. Obedience and loyalty to him are for them natural sentiments.'[39] The high value attached to seniority established a network of relationships based on the subordination of the juniors to their elders. This subordination was expressed by labor, services, and deference owed the elders by the juniors:

A man remains a cadet (*nleeke*) until he is about forty, perhaps longer. As a cadet he is likely to be assigned to service tasks at funerals; only occasionally is he invited to practice being an elder by being given secondary speaking roles at weddings and the like. His advancement depends on his personal character, his ability, and the number of his older relatives. As they become infirm he will have increasing opportunities to serve as *nkazi* at some of the less important events. Otherwise he is at the beck and call of his elders, whose tone toward him is often peremptory.[40]

The *nkuluntu* (elders, seniors) were given a share of the harvest. They also imposed levies and tolls. By being the most closely associated with agricultural production, women were easily the target of the elders' extraction. 'At the harvest, women formed a pile of dried kidney beans, a pile of maize, and so forth, then handed to the *nkuluntu* his part for subsistence, separating it from what was to be conserved for the next cultivation. The rest was shared among houses.'[41] Closely linked to the *nkuluntu* were the *kitome*, who as village 'priests' were indissociable from the lineage structure and eldership. As 'the owners and masters, lords or chiefs of the land,' they also extracted a surplus in agricultural products said to exceed, in the mid-seventeenth century, that received by the state governor. Even when there was some shift in political succession from matrilineage to patrilineage, 'Among the ruling groups generally, goods were, by the late eighteenth century, normally owned by the minimal lineage, the nephews inheriting from their potential uncles and paying tribute to them.'[42]

In addition to agricultural produce, extraction took other forms. Here, as in noncentralized societies, lineage elders used the brideprice as a mechanism to extract a surplus. The brideprice constituted, among other things, an exchange for the labor power of the women lost to another lineage.[43] As in noncentralized societies, surplus product and collective property were redistributed among lineage members. The redistribution also took many forms: mainly, it assisted sick people, widows, orphans, old people, those in debt, and any lineage member who sought support. Brideprice paid to acquire wives for lineage members and common meals were other usual forms of surplus redistribution. Redistribution also took place at a lineage member's death or birth and at judiciary events.

The State

The Kongo was a centralized kingdom in which political and social organization at the local level was articulated into the larger state structure. Its geographical limits were the result of an expansion by a lineage-based political leadership. Although the reasons for political expansion are not clear, some historians have speculated that the need to control the copper trade was the driving force.[44] They agree, however, that lineage played a crucial role in the rise of the kingdom. How and when this role was played is an issue left to historians, as is the question of whether the arrival of the first king in Mbanza Kongo (Sao Salvador), the capital city, was through secession or invasion.[45] Here it is enough to point out that the invading or seceding forces sought to establish their rule in the capital city and the surrounding areas by creating alliances with local lineages through marriage. The first decisive alliance took place between *Ntinu* Wene (King Wene), the leader of the conquering forces, and the local clan head, the *Mani* Kabunga (the titleholder Kabunga). As the lineage head, the *Mani* Kabunga was the land owner and the earth priest (*kitome*) for the area. The king married a daughter of Kabunga's lineage, Nsaku Vunda, which sealed the alliance between the king and the Nsaku Vunda lineage. As a result, *Mani* Kabunga accepted *Ntinu* Wene as his overlord. The recognition of King Wene by *Mani* Kabunga was total, with the king adopting the title of *Mani* Kongo or *Ne* Kongo. From the capital city, *Mani* Kongo was able to expand his authority on a territorial basis. Four new provinces were conquered and added; two other provinces were incorporated into the kingdom following their recognition of the king's authority. The six made up the territorial administration of the kingdom. In each of the provinces, local lineages constituted the transmission belt between the central administration and localities. However, the lineages of the central province, Mpemba, formed the core of lineage-based politics. They were the ruling elite, the *mwissikongo*, from which the king came. As mentioned, it is generally admitted that there were twelve such core lineages. The domination of the core lineages was somewhat mitigated in the two provinces that had accepted the authority of the king voluntarily. Governorship of the province remained in the hands of the lineage that ruled at the time of incorporation.

The political and administrative structure of the kingdom was formed by the village, the district, the province, and the central administration, which was dominated by the royal court. The village politico-administrative organization has already been described. The king was not involved in the election of village chiefs, which was linked to that of the lineage head. However, some districts depended directly on the king, who appointed their functionaries; others depended on the province's governor, who appointed the administrators. The officials appointed by the king at the district level came directly from the royal lineage; otherwise, local lineages provided them.[46] Above the districts were the six provinces, each headed by a governor directly appointed by the king. At the center, in the capital city, the king was surrounded by officials who were in charge of his policies in many areas: the royal quarters in the capital city, justice, tax, treasury, police, and security. He was also assisted by a royal council made up of twelve members generally believed to represent the twelve core lineages of the kingdom. All the functionaries were called *mani* and formed the aristocracy.

The king stood at the center of the state apparatus. Given that the Kongo kingdom was more centralized than were most precolonial states in Africa,[47] the king's personality was preeminent indeed. No doubt, environmental constraints and other forces, such as localized armies and religious divisions, did not make the Kongo a fully unitary kingdom. Yet the king's supremacy was pervasively felt by his subjects, whom he controlled and owned. He made and unmade the unity of the kingdom. Even the defense of the local interests by some powerful lineage heads did not challenge this unity, at least in the fifteenth and sixteenth centuries. The king's power had mystical and quasi-religious overtones. He was the kingdom. As in Southeast Asia and in other African kingdoms,[48] the wealth and fecundity of the land depended on him. As his vigor went, so went the wealth of the kingdom. Each year he and his wife performed rain and fertility rituals to bring prosperity to the kingdom. The king wore much regalia, which attested to the sacral character of the kingship. Only at his inauguration and death and in the event of war were the subjects allowed to see the king's symbol of omnipotence (*ngoma*). Moreover, the king could not be seen eating. The 'king was at the center of a whole system of rules, taboos and obligations which isolated him, mystically protected him, and caused people to express respect and fear toward him. ... The homage rendered to the holder of supreme power thus appeared to be directed toward a semi-divine person.'[49]

The power of the king, however, was not unlimited. Three organs counterbalanced and kept it in check. The first was the Royal Council. For all his power, the king was still a *primus inter pares* in relation to the lineage representatives. They had to be consulted on certain crucial issues, such as wars or appointments of the twelve representatives at the council, including the principal judge, the principal secretary, and the official in charge of the king's household. The second counterbalancing organ comprised the office holders of the king's household made up of relatives, sons, and nephews of provincial governors and their *mwissikongo* supporters sent to be educated at the king's court; religious functionaries; and, especially in the late sixteenth century, slaves. The third organ consisted of those lineage heads who, not being part of the core lineage, had supplied the king with women from their lineage; in so doing, they gained access to the court through their nephews born of the marriages.[50] In light of this evidence, some authors have argued that the Kongo kingdom was a combination of despotism, absolutism, theocracy, aristocracy, and constitutional monarchy.[51] I shall return to this issue in chapter 4.

Both the extensive power of the king and the centralized form of the Kongo state had implications for the state's extractive policies. In the same way he owned his subjects, the king owned the whole land of the kingdom. Therefore, the use of land by the subjects was conditional upon the payment of tribute. Tribute was also paid to the king's treasury to maintain the state apparatus. Tribute consisted of slaves, salt, ivory, raffia cloth, animal skins, live animals such as pigs and chickens, agricultural products, shells, and labor service. These items were collected by state officials, each of them specializing in those products easily obtainable in their own regions. For instance, although many regions sent agricultural produce, the governors of the coastal regions sent salt and shells. Some tribute came from king-controlled areas; for example, shells (used as currency) were produced in royal fisheries. The burden of tribute collection fell on state officials at the provincial and district levels. Governors and district officials, in turn, relied on the villages for the task. Each district corresponded to a rental (tributary) unit and included the revenue of a dozen villages.[52] The execution of the policy was, at the village level, the responsibility of lineage heads, who extracted tribute from members of their lineage. In a hierarchical order, each lineage head returned the tribute to the village chief who, in turn, gave it to the district official and so on up to the king. The governor took the tribute to the king twice a year.[53]

The collection of tribute for the king also rewarded officials. The amount of compensation and the form it took varied according to the ranks of the officials. At the very top, the prime beneficiaries were members of the core lineage of the kingdom. High territorial officials also received from the king a share of the tribute in the form of offices or of gifts of rare goods not produced in their own regions. It was estimated that the gross income of the king was 175,000 *kofu* (3,500,000,000 *nzimbu*). After distribution to officials his net income was only 14,000 *kofu*.[54] Officials also received an income by withholding some of the taxes and dues on their pieces of land or by retaining a portion of the taxes collected. The need to retain a portion of the taxes and the dependence on the royal court had two consequences. First, state officials were likely to commit abuses; there were, from time to time, reports of arbitrary exactions by state tax collectors, which led to villagers' open revolts (e.g., expelling the tax collectors) or passive resistance. Second, insofar as state officials received an income from the royal court and lacked solid economic bases in their own regions, they were not likely to secede from the central government; the result was the political stability of the kingdom. Even those officials who held rights to land and had a local lineage base were so closely tied, via marriages, to the king's lineage that they seldom contemplated the possibility of seceding. It is worth noting that the king's movable goods, wives, and slaves belonged to the office; his successor inherited them.

The Luba Empire and Kuba Kingdom

Society
The Luba empire emerged around A.D. 1500 and ended in the nineteenth century. It extended to territories in today's Kasai and Shaba regions. The Kuba kingdom[55] also arose around the same period or a little later in the seventeenth

century. It was located entirely in today's Western Kasai region, bordered by the Kasai River in the west, the Sankuru River in the north, the Lulua River in the south, and by the 22° 30' meridian in the east.

The Luba reckoned their descent in the patrilineal line. The basic lineage structure was the nuclear family. The highest lineage unit was the clan, which does not seem to have been totemic. Between the two lay intermediary units. The *kisaka* and the *tshisamba* constituted, at each end, the pillars of the lineage organization. The *kisaka* was formed by a group of nuclear families, that is, a *pater familias* and the families of each of the sons. The *tshisamba* was the equivalent of a superclan, corresponding to a territorial chieftainship. As with the societies discussed earlier, the Luba lineage structure displayed its cohesiveness more at the bottom than at the top. Given their patrilineal reckoning, the Luba organized their succession at each of these lineage levels on the male side. The eldest brother was first in the line, then came the sons of the eldest brother, and so forth. Lineage affairs were debated by a group of elders who also were in charge of genealogy.

The Kuba reckoned their descent in the matrilineal line. Whereas the Luba shifted from matrilineage to patrilineage, the Kuba evolved from a patrilineal mode of reckoning to a matrilineal one. The clan was the largest lineage unit and was divided into sections or subclan units. The clan section was the cornerstone of the lineage relationship, tracing its descent to a grandmother or a great-grandmother. It was the residential unit within the village, and its composition varied over time. Through its elders, it was in charge of lineage affairs, such as marriage, inheritance, and succession to office.

The Luba lineage structure, like that of the Kongo, shaped the village organization. A village (*kibundji*) was made up of one or several extended families (*bisaka*). In general, however, multi-lineage villages were more common than single-lineage ones. The *kisaka* that founded the village was the core lineage of the village and dominated the others. As such, it owned land and was the leading candidate for village leadership. However, among the Luba of the Shaba region, this was not always the case. In some villages, the village chief was not necessarily the landowner. A *mulopwe wa nsi*, a second type of chief, controlled land. Both chiefs were united by a special rite, thus artificially creating a lineage bond between them.[56] Such a union resembled what anthropologists refer to as 'perpetual kinship.' The rules of succession and the investiture of the village chief were dictated by lineage structure. Patrilineage prevailed, as did its sacral aspect as provided by lineage ideology. The village chief was assisted by a council of elders made up of lineage heads. The council and the village chief fulfilled judiciary and administrative functions of interest for the village. The village chief received tribute in agricultural products and livestock from his subjects.

Among the Kuba, the village was also made up of one or more lineages, with the lineage dictating village organization. However, the shift from patrilineage to matrilineage and the ensuing compromise between the two modes of reckoning caused the village to mitigate somewhat the influences of the lineage structure on it. This probably explains why the village chief was appointed by the village council rather than by the core village lineage. Still, the village chief (*kubol*) was assisted by the village council (*malaang*), which was made up of lineage heads.[57]

Unlike the Kongo, the Luba developed a structure above that of the village that was the direct prolongation of the village's double characteristic of being both a lineage and a political organization: the chieftainship. As a lineage structure, the chieftainship was a superclan divided into lineage subunits. It was ruled by what may be called a grand chief. As a rule, the head of the chieftainship (the *mulopwe*) was the head of the core lineage subunit, that is, the core *kisaka* of the core village around which other villages clustered. This association of the grand chief with the oldest line allowed him to claim lineage bonds with deceased chiefs, thus endowing him with supernatural powers. The succession to the dying grand chief was designated either by the dying chief himself or by the chieftainship council. Under normal succession rules, the grand chief was replaced by his brother. In the absence of a brother, he was replaced by his son, and if there was no son to inherit power, the chief's nephew inherited it.[58]

As a political and administrative structure, a chieftainship was composed of several villages, of which the grand chief's was the core. In some chieftainships, some of the villages were recognized as aristocratic villages. The grand chief was assisted by an executive council at the central level and by a local administrative body. The executive council consisted of twenty-five to thirty councilmen (*bamfumu* or *bamena ba mikombo*), who represented the nobility, that is, the leadership of the ruling lineages. The grand chief's own lineage provided the most influential members of the council. In addition to deciding on the succession and the investiture of the grand chief, members of the council fulfilled many functions related to justice, war, foreign affairs, the treasury, constitutional respect, and the personal affairs of the grand chief. At the lower and local level the grand chief was represented by the village chiefs and other lineage heads. They collected tribute for the grand chief and performed many other tasks facilitating his rule. The grand chief himself appointed the councilmen, received tribute, distributed goods on main occasions, presided in court, offered rituals to the ancestors, and required labor service from his subjects. He also distributed land and decided about seasonal hunting and fishing.

The Kuba also developed chieftainships that later became constituent parts of the kingdom. Chieftainships may have emerged as the Kuba made the transition from patrilineage to matrilineage. With this shift, support for the grand chief came not only from heads of the subunits of his own lineage group but also from other unrelated lineage groups. In other words, the Kuba chieftainship was supported locally by matrilineages (*mbaangt*, or founding clans) via their elders, who were not necessarily members of the grand chief's lineage. At the center of power, the grand chief was assisted by a council made up of representatives of the supporting lineages. The court, on the other hand, was made up of commoners who were not members of the founding clans. All in all, the political and administrative structure of the chieftainship included the grand chief, *kum*, the ruling lineage (the grand chief's lineage), the founding clans, *mbaangt*, and the commoners. The Kuba chieftainship was composed of one to twenty villages. The succession to the throne of the grand chief was not by his sons but by the offspring of marriage between the women of the ruling lineage and the men of the founding clans.

The Luba ideological universe strongly resembled those of the Kongo and of the noncentralized societies. The ever-present cult of the ancestors was indissociable from the code of seniority. The Luba's attachment to the ancestors (*bakishi*) was also indissociable from their concept of the lineage group as a continuum whose ends were its deceased members in the other world and its living members. The ancestors not only owned the lineage property but were the source of happiness, success, and health for the living members of the lineage. They lived near streams, in trees, and not far from the villages. Many practices bore witness to this belief. Like the Kongo and the noncentralized societies, the Luba burial ground was surrounded by the deads' belongings as a reminder of their presence. The ancestors were reincarnated in newborn babies.

The living members of the lineage could obtain happiness, health, and success in their undertakings on the sole condition that they invoked the ancestors properly, placated them with offerings, feared their displeasure, and provided huts for their accommodation. The placement of goods and food on the grave and the libation of beer were but two of the offerings designed to placate the dead. If offended or mistreated, the dead became vindictive, causing harm and mishap to living members of the lineage. In this case, special rituals were required to appease them. More ominous, however, were the 'bad dead' (*bafu ba kizwa*), who included sorcerers, people who did not live on good terms with their fellow lineage members, and people who were buried in alien ground. They were rejected by the 'good' ancestors, doomed to solitude, and were thus prone to cause misfortune and illness to living members. Diviners were called upon to pinpoint the bad dead. Like the Kongo and the Ambuun, the Luba often exhumed the body of a dead person to destroy the evil spirit.[59]

As in the Kongo and in the noncentralized societies, the Luba attachment to their ancestors brought into prominence the elders of the lineage. The lineage elders were, by virtue of their age, juniors to the ancestors, yet were close to them within the lineage continuum. As juniors to the ancestors, lineage heads were required to serve them. Their closeness to the ancestors qualified lineage elders to represent them among the living members of the lineage. The overall result was a vast degree of deference shown to lineage elders by their juniors, who believed their elders possessed supernatural powers to curse or bless members of the lineage. They could make a young woman barren or create misery for a young family. If happy, they could make one fecund and successful. Communication between lineage members of the other world and those of this world could take place only through lineage elders.

The prominent role played by lineage elders was reflected in the lineage-based political structure, that is, in the village and the chieftainship. Indeed, both the village chief and the grand chief of the chieftainship were living proof of lineage eldership with their powers and functions derived from the ancestors. The village chief, like the grand chief, was covered by *bufumu*, that is, authority and power, and by *bulopwe* (sacred power) to a lesser extent. Acquisition of such power by the grand chief was accompanied by special rites, such as the seclusion of the grand chief-to-be in a hut without doors or windows and his sexual intercourse with his niece. He was also presented with human blood – which he sometimes drank. He kept some body parts of his predecessor (e.g., genitals and head) as signs of power.[60] The act of investiture sought to officially establish the chief's seniority and also revealed that the lineage senior had been endowed with mediating power between the ancestors and the living.[61] For this reason, a real or fictitious descent line between the chief and Kalala Ilunga, the founder of the Luba empire, was actively sought. Through such association the chief could claim *buvidye*, that is, supernatural power and links with dead chiefs. By virtue of such supernatural power, the grand chief was expected to provide fertility and prosperity to his subjects.

As in the Kongo and in the noncentralized societies, the Luba lineage structure and its underlying ideology greatly affected the broader society's ideological universe. The reliance on the ancestors and the postulate that almost all misfortune, bad luck, and death resulted from another person's action had several implications. Reliance on the ancestors and the dead was itself the source of many 'divination' and sorcery practices because both the sorcerer and the diviner drew their supernatural power from the dead. Reliance on the ancestors and the dead also explained the mushrooming of secret societies in Luba society. The dominance of the lineage structure was such that the culprit for every misfortune or death was almost always a fellow lineage member. Among the Songye, 'A witch may be a non-killer or a killer, and in the latter case, its power to kill *always* involves the sacrifice to the sorcerer of *a member of its family* who may be killed outright or changed into a *kisivikiswiki*.'[62]

The Kuba had the same practices as those found among the Luba. Their practices included ancestral cults and rituals as well as sorcery and witchcraft. Although sorcerers could harm individuals who had no lineage relationship with them, witches always acted upon fellow lineage members. The cult of the ancestors, which lost some of its vigor with the emergence of chieftainships, was revived during the Age of Kings. Kuba lineage elders also controlled the community, which was most likely the result of their closeness with the ancestors.

In their broad outline, the forces of production in the Luba and Kuba societies did not differ from those prevailing in the Kongo or the noncentralized societies. The Luba and the Kuba were devoted to the same types of economic activities: hunting, fishing, gathering, handicrafts, livestock, and agriculture. Agricultural cycles often determined the sexual division of labor, and the types of crops determined the forms of cooperation. Among the Luba-Songye, men took care of rice, bananas, pineapple, and sugarcane, whereas women tended corn, manioc, sweet potatoes, and beans.

Among the Luba and the Kuba, the institution of slavery was as well known as it was in the Kongo and in the noncentralized societies. Slaves were obtained from the same sources and for the same reasons: war and sale. Luba political expansion took place before the Atlantic slave trade, and so the Luba empire did not accumulate economic wealth through the sale of people. Some slaves were redeemed after war hostilities by the members of their lineage; those who were not became part of the lineage structure of their captors. For this reason, the Luba had special lineage subunits and villages for slaves. To be sure, slaves were not subjected on a day-to-day basis to the brutality that characterized New World merchant slavery. Nevertheless, slaves were used whenever there was a need for them, as in the ritual executions when they were buried alive with their owner/chief, or when they were recruited to provide labor at the royal court.[63] Among the Kuba, the condition of the slaves was also tolerable, but they performed a variety of labor services: fetching water or firewood or weeding the fields. There was also a special slave unit in the king's army.

As in the Kongo kingdom, there were intense trade activities in the Luba empire and the Kuba kingdom. The presence of a centralized state and its need for tribute in both cases helped stimulate these activities. In the Luba empire, 'the Pax Luba that had emerged in and around the Luba heartland before 1700' played a major supplementary role: 'As these states grew in size they promoted a degree of peace and order that encouraged people to seek subsistence and prestige goods from the near and distant neighbors. The greater the quantity of goods moved across the savanna and exchanged between villagers, the larger the quantity and the more varied was the tribute that flowed into royal courts.'[64] Trade was essentially regional, involving a network of exchanges among Luba villages and between the Luba and allied societies. It also consisted of a flow of goods between the Kasai and Shaba regions. But at the close of the eighteenth century, trade increasingly became international long-distance trade. The Luba used both raffia squares (cloth) and copper crosses as media of exchange in their trade transactions. The Kuba also used raffia squares as currency. Their trade activities were given a tremendous boost by the rule of King Shyaam. The Kuba seem to have taken advantage of the trade routes between the Kongo and the Kwilu regions by trading with the Ambuun. They also traded with the Lele, their closest neighbors. Among the items traded were mats, baskets, foodstuffs, salt, copper, and beads.

The combination of trade activities and the state's need for tribute had a major impact on the level of economic accumulation in both the Luba and Kuba states. In comparison to the noncentralized societies, the two boasted a higher level of economic wealth. Among the Kuba, new technology in agriculture imported from the Kwilu region spread with new techniques and methods of labor organization and crop rotation. Furthermore, the introduction of American crops – maize and cassava – allowed the accumulation of a surplus that was not possible with low-yield and easily perishable products such as yams. New crops required new methods, which increased the work load for women and men alike. The end result of this process was higher productivity, which, in turn, led to the accumulation of a surplus.

The relations of production also resembled those in the Kongo and in the noncentralized societies. The first similarity was recorded in the ownership of property, where land was collectively owned by the lineage. The Luba echoed the rationale behind the Kongo's pattern of land ownership, according to which the ancestors owned land and the living members simply exercised usufruct rights. It followed that what the ancestors owned could not be privately appropriated.[65] The exact modality of such collective ownership varied. The fusion between the lineage structure, on the one hand, and the village and the chieftainship, on the other, imposed variations from one case to another. In general, the village's lineage subunit, through its head, owned and managed the group's land.

Three situations presented themselves. In the first, the village was a single-lineage village that owned land; in this case, the village head as lineage head managed the collective land for the village/lineage members. In the second situation, the village was a multi-lineage village with a core lineage owning land and holding the political leadership of the village; the lineage head as the village chief managed the lineage's collective land. The modalities of the use of the land by other lineages were worked out with the core lineage. In the third, the village was a multi-lineage village with a core lineage owning lands but not controlling the political leadership of the village. This happened, for instance, when the king appointed a chief to represent him in the village. In this case, the village chief depended on the lineage head, who owned and controlled land in the name of his lineage. This explained the artificial lineage bond ('perpetual kinship') created between the two by rituals, which allowed the village chief to participate in the management of the village's lands.[66] As in the case of the village chief, control exercised by the grand chief (*mulopwe*) of a chieftainship over land also derived from his ties to the lineage structure.

In addition to land, the lineage also held a common trust for its members. As in the Kongo kingdom and in the noncentralized societies, such a trust was made up of funeral items, inherited goods, production instruments such as hoes, and bridewealth items such as salt and money. One could also add slaves because they belonged to the whole lineage group. Food products were included because they were the most shared items among lineage members. Among the Songye, the lineage head held monies that belonged to individual members.[67] In addition to being a form of extraction by the lineage head, this type of saving constituted cushion money for the lineage trust. The trust did not preclude any individual property; it only differed from it. Indeed, the Luba, like the Kongo, allowed individual property for lineage members, who owned their tools of production, houses, some livestock, planted trees, and any property that resulted from their personal labor. Such individual property did not prevent sharing. A lineage member had the obligation to share, within the limits of normal expectations, with other members of the lineage. Not doing so meant being treated as a sorcerer or witch.

The lineage head played a crucial role in the ownership of collective property because he represented the ancestors. For instance, the *mwine ntanda* (chief of land) allocated land to be cultivated; he also controlled and regulated its use at the village level. At a higher level, the chieftainship, the grand chief (*mulopwe*) played the same role. Both controlled the labor process and received tribute. The grand chief received double tribute – as a political figure and as the head of the senior lineage of the chieftainship.

At the lower level, owing to patrilineal descent reckoning among the Luba, the process of extracting was similar to the one that prevailed in imperial China.[68] The father played a major role in the extraction of the economic surplus. His authority was that of a *mfumwebe* or *mukelenge* (chief). His wife and children were subordinate to him; he could sell them.[69] This relationship allowed the father to extract a surplus from his children. Even those children who had split from their father's original lineage still owed him tribute in agricultural, hunting, or fishing products. Children's obligations were not limited to the father; they extended to the upper units of the lineage structure. Through the father, the lineage head extracted a surplus product from the children as lineage members. The lineage context facilitated the extraction of a surplus product from its junior members by applying the father–child relationship to each form of seniority and juniority. This explained the preeminence of eldest sons and their extractive capabilities vis-à-vis their juniors. The eldest brother (or the sons of the first wives in a polygamous family) could, at will, appropriate the younger brother's property. This included having, in theory, sexual intercourse with the younger brother's wife.[70] Senior sons were chiefs vis-à-vis juniors, whereas the juniors were 'things' (*mbintu*) vis-à-vis their seniors.[71]

Among the Kuba, rights over land were also held collectively by lineages, at least before the emergence of the kingdom. Later, as the role of the village increased, land seems to have been collectively held by the village. Even then, some villages were single-lineage, and what appeared to be the village's land was actually held by the lineage. In the more common multi-lineage villages, the collective ownership of land was arranged by the constituent lineages of the village.[72] Like the Luba, the Kuba held individual property. Lineage elders also dominated the relations of production among the Kuba. 'Elderly persons stayed in the village, tended the babies, and gave formal and informal advice. Elderly men generally ran the community. They also benefited most from the efforts of others, and in this sense the society was a gerontocracy, in which the relations of production were dominated by the elders.'[73] Because of their ability to extract a surplus product from their juniors, they were able to accumulate wealth, which allowed them to acquire numerous wives.

The State

Luba society was structured politically like the Kongo kingdom. Political organization differed in size and structure from that which prevailed in the non-centralized society. In size, the Luba polity was an empire; hence, it differed from small chieftainships. Although the historical record is very poor for the Luba Kasai (and only slightly better for the Luba–Shaba), there is evidence that the empire extended into some areas of today's Kasai and Shaba regions. The empire evolved in stages: the 'first empire' developed under rule of King Kongolo, and the 'second empire' coincided with the advent of King Kalala Ilunga. Structurally, the empire was centralized. To be sure, the Luba empire was not a unitary state; it was made up of more or less autonomous chieftainships. The major feature of the political and administrative organization of the empire was its reliance on a federated system. Nevertheless, the power of local political figures was overshadowed by that of the king, who dominated the power pyramid. The territorial organization was founded on the village, which was itself based on lineage. Above the village stood the chieftainships, the transmission belt between the royal court and the villages.

The Luba king used political and ideological means to dominate the chieftainships. He used the appointment of officials, such as the village chiefs, to keep the chieftainship under control. He had recourse to many other devices, including the institutionalization of lineage alliances between the royal court and the chieftainships. Thus, for instance, women of the royal lineage were married to some rulers in the constituent chieftainships. 'Offsprings of unions with client rulers frequently lived at the Luba king's court, and one of their number was likely to be chosen to rule over their father's domain after he died.'[74] Where matrilineal descent was still practiced, the offspring of these marriages were made legitimate successors through their mothers. A matrilineage rulership with links to a patrilineal system of royal succession was thus created. The end result was that the royal courts maintained control over the chieftainships of the empire even in matrilineal areas. Even though they were legitimate contenders to power in chieftainships, the offspring of these unions were still ineligible to challenge the king or his sons for the right to a patrilineal type of rule. These lineage alliances between the royal court and the chieftainships were further strengthened through the rites of investiture. The recognition of a lineage by the royal court was conditional upon its possessing delegated symbols of power (e.g., a royal shield and spear) from the king. 'Embers from the sacred fire were bestowed in a 'knocking off some of the holy fire' ceremony that transformed a candidate for client chiefship into a fire king (*mulopwe wa mudilo*) who became the symbolic son of the Luba king.'[75]

The royal court was a duplicate of the grand chief court at the chieftainship level in that its membership was selected on the basis of lineage affiliations. Most titleholders at the court were members of the king's lineage; others were members of allied and client lineages who paid heavily into the king's treasury in order to hold their positions. The royal court was, however, more impressive and imposing than that of the chieftainship. About fifty titleholders were directly subordinate to the king, including advisors, war generals, and petty functionaries responsible for the maintenance of court rituals and etiquette.

The Luba king was an imposing political figure. Like the Kongo king, he was venerated and quasi-divine. He provided rain and fertility to his subjects and was the source of prosperity for the whole empire. His supernatural power derived, as with chiefs at the lower levels, from the ancestors. In addition to ordinary ancestors, the king had contact with his departed predecessors, who were all sacred. Through secret societies, such as the *bambudye*, the king entertained the sacral nature of kingship and its supernatural attributes. His investiture and succession rituals, which resembled those of the chieftainship head, reflected this sacral and divine aspect of the kingship. A cooking fire was the primary symbol of the king's sacral rule. It was ignited during the investiture ceremony and not allowed to go out during his lifetime. Like the Kongo king, the Luba emperor had a tremendous amount of power that was tempered only by the members of his own lineage. He was, in principle, succeeded in the same way the leaders of the chieftainship were; his brothers and sons were first contenders to the throne. In practice, however, the succession was the outcome of a power struggle among the many contenders.

The Luba state, like the Kongo kingdom, depended on tribute. For this reason, territorial expansion of the empire targeted for the most part those fertile lands that were apt to increase the tax base of the state. Furthermore, the Luba developed an elaborate tribute system to increase the efficiency of tribute collection. Not only did the king have functionaries who collected tribute in the remotest areas of the empire, but 'royal women were also resident spies for the Luba king at the courts of clients [chieftainships], and they were responsible for supervising the collection and transportation of tribute from client states.'[76] Given the size of the empire, however, villages adjacent to the royal court were more affected by tributary policies than those on the periphery; they paid larger quantities of tribute than did the others. Similarly, the greater the dependency a chieftainship displayed vis-à-vis the royal court, the larger the size and the more frequent the payment of tribute it owed the king. Tribute was paid in salt, iron, raffia cloth, goats, chickens, dry fish, palm oil and wine, other food items, and luxury products. The state stimulated trade activities to increase the amount of taxable resources.

Lineage alliances, which made up the fabric of the Luba empire, combined with its federated character to determine the beneficiaries of the tribute. The delicate game of lineage alliances and power brokering was conveniently played through the manipulation of economic resources. A code of reciprocity was established between the king and the heads of chieftainships. Like his Kongo counterpart, the Luba king distributed tribute in the form of gifts to his allies and subordinates. In general, these gifts consisted of rare goods that were difficult to get in the receiver's region. As another way to distribute tribute, the king allowed the collecting functionaries to retain a portion of the tribute collected. At the royal court, granaries overflowing with grain, maize, beans, and manioc were built to supply state personnel, especially those working at the court.[77] As a center for resource control and allocation, the royal court regulated trade activities, which provided it with resources to redistribute to client chieftainships to hold their loyalty.

Like the Luba, the Kuba also developed a federated state. The kingdom was made up of several chieftainships, some of which consisted of a single village.

Territorial expansion and political domination, which culminated in the rise of the kingdom, were initiated by the Bushoong chieftainship after it had defeated other chieftainships. For this reason, the federated institutions of the state revolved around Bushoong, whose ruler was the king. The territorial organization of the kingdom was thus based on villages and chieftainships. Each constituent chieftainship maintained its autonomy; there was no centralized council for the whole kingdom, at least before the major push for centralization by the Bushoong rulers in the eighteenth century and after. Before this period, the recognition of a single king on top of the pyramid went arm-in-arm with the absence of a central executive council.[78] The king's representatives governed in the provinces and were assisted by regional officials appointed by the king but confirmed by each village council. Village representatives in the capital and members of the aristocracy in charge of territorial matters tempered the power of the provincial authorities.

The Bushoong-dominated councils at the capital were of two types: the Crown Council and the Kolm. The Crown Council was made up of eighteen members (*ngwoom incyaam*), who represented core lineages. All members were nominated by their lineage section at the capital and exercised collective responsibility. They installed the king and counterbalanced his power by deliberating and sometimes vetoing his proposals. The Kolm, or nobles, belonged to specific lineages: aristocratic lineages, the sons or grandsons of a king, or a combination of these. They wore different insignia, such as feathers, and each of them held a different title and office.

The Kuba king, like his Kongo and Luba counterparts, stood at the top of the pyramid. He was the supreme eagle feather on top of all other chiefs. He was divine and omnipotent, having the power to provide rain, fertility, and prosperity for his subjects. He was the priest of a nature spirit and a spirit himself. His subjects' lives so depended on him that they considered themselves 'people of the king.' Without the king there was no life. The king could not be deposed, but he could kill his subjects. The Kuba candidate to kingship also practiced the ritual incest that the Luba required for their kings. For his burial, the Kuba king was detached from common mortals and, like the Kongo and Luba kings, was buried with live slaves.

The king's power over his subjects was further displayed by his ability to extract tribute. The state maintained a large number of collecting agents throughout the kingdom. An extensive system of tax collecting contributed to a fairly high level of accumulation, which in turn had an impact on the overall Kuba forces of production. Both free and unfree villages paid tribute: unfree villages bore much of the tribute burden; free villages only paid tribute once a year. The same unequal treatment obtained between the Bushoong chieftainship and other chieftainships of the kingdom. In general, tribute was paid in food, maize, dried foodstuffs, yams, cassava, plantains, dried meat, raffia cloth, salt, iron, knives, hoes, and pottery. In addition, a noble tribute was levied, which consisted of leopard skins, eagle feathers, horns of buffalo, and tusks of elephants. Labor services and corvée were also imposed. Chores included the construction and maintenance of public buildings and enclosures, the building of bridges, and drum services. The collected tribute was distributed in many ways, but the bulk of it went to the maintenance of the state apparatus and functionaries. To that end, collecting agents were allowed to retain a portion of the tribute for themselves. Some tribute was used to import luxury goods for the royal court; some was distributed to royal and aristocratic lineages. The remainder was stored at the royal compound. The Kuba king gave to the masses only that portion of the tribute likely to perish in storage.

Conclusion

Fundamental similarities existed among the precolonial Ambuun, Bading, Basongo, Ngombe, Kongo, Kuba, and Luba. They shared roughly the same types of social and economic organizations. Because of their centralized state apparatus, centralized societies experienced greater economic accumulation than noncentralized societies. In all societies, however, lineage was the backbone of social life, permeating and regulating most social, political, and economic activities. This discussion will serve as the main empirical reference for the theoretical argument in chapter 4.

Notes

1. Lineage implies descent reckoning and differs from kinship reckoning. Descent is deeper and involves, generally, a corporate group reckoned by steps of filiation to a common ancestor. Kinship is shallow and emphasizes the distinction of proximate generations and the unity of the sibling group, which includes half-siblings. Kinship includes what is generally referred to as relatives and does not presuppose a common ancestor. The rights and obligations of its members differ from those of descent reckoning, which are deeper and more constraining. Rather than being largely nominal as it has become in contemporary Europe, descent relations create a network of relations in which the actors have very well-defined roles. Moreover, in descent reckoning a fictitious aspect coexists with reality, whereas kinship relations necessarily involve a real network of relations. Although kinship does exist in the West, descent reckoning does not. In non-Western societies, on the other hand, both kinship reckoning and descent reckoning exist, with descent reckoning dominating social relations. For a complete discussion on lineage and kinship, see Meyer Fortes, *Kinship and the Social Order* (Chicago: Aldine Publishing Co., 1963), pp. 276–310; Wyatt MacGaffey, *Custom and Government in the Lower Congo* (Berkeley: University of California Press, 1970), p.86; Jacques Maquet, *Power and Society in Africa* (New York: McGraw-Hill Book Co, 1971), p. 42; and I must thank Professor Grace Harris of the University of Rochester for suggesting these differences to me.
2. Alvin W. Wolfe, 'The Dynamics of the Ngombe Segmentary System,' in William Bascom and Melville Herskovits, eds. *Continuity and Change in African Cultures*, pp. 177–178.

3. Eugéne Biletsi, 'La Solidarité chez les Ambuun,' *Etudes Congolaises*, Vol XI, No. 1, 1968, p. 5.
4. Wolfe, *op. cit.*, p. 171.
5. Wolfe, Ibid., p. 173.
6. Joseph Mertens, *Les Badzing de la Kamtsha*, pp. 332–338.
7. See Biletsi, *op. cit.*; R. de Beaucorps, *Les Basongo de la Luniungu et de la Gobari*, pp. 7–20, 87–90; J. M. de Decker, *Les Clans Ambuun (Bambunda) d'après leur littérature orale.*
8. Biletsi, *op. cit.*, p. 5.
9. Jan Vansina, *The Children of Woot*, pp. 188–191.
10. de Beaucorps, *op. cit.*, p. 90; Mertens, *op. cit.*, p. 331.
11. Wolfe, *op. cit.*, p. 180; pp. 178–179; p. 174.
12. Biletsi, *op. cit.*, p. 16.
13. de Beaucorps, p. 73.
14. Jan Vansina, *Kingdoms of the Savanna*, pp. 20–21.
15. See Claude Meillassoux, *Anthropologie économique des Gouro de Côte d'Ivoire*; Emmanuel Terray, *Marxism and Primitive Societies*, pp. 109–110.
16. Wolfe, *op. cit.*, p. 185.
17. Some anthropologists and historians have disputed the notion of inalienability of land (see, for instance, Vansina, *Zaire*, Vol. X, 9, 1956, p. 903); I believe that the evidence does point to the inalienability of land.
18. Biletsi, *op. cit.*, p. 16–19, de Beaucorps, 75–76; Mertens, *op. cit.*, p. 340.
19. Vansina, *Kingdoms of the Savanna*, pp. 38–40.
20. See Anne Hilton, *The Kingdom of Kongo*, chapter 8.
21. J. Van Wing, *Etudes Bakongo*, p. 379.
22. Vansina, *Kingdoms of the Savanna*, pp. 152–154.
23. George Balandier, *La vie quotidienne au Royaume de Kongo du XVI\u1d49 au XVIII\u1d49 siècle.*, pp. 178 and 181–182; Hilton, *op. cit.*, p. 20; Bwakasa Tulu, *L'impensé du discours*, p. 13.
24. Hilton, *op. cit.*, p. 20.
25. Hilton, *op. cit.*, pp. 223–224; MacGaffey, *op. cit.*, pp. 238–244.
26. Balandier, *op. cit.*, pp. 132–133.
27. Ndongola Tadi Lewa, 'Quelques traits d'organisation économique Kongo au seuil de la colonisation Belge, vue au travers des 'Études Bakongo' du R. P. J. Van Wing,' in Ngimbi Nseka, ed., *Actualité et Inactualité 'Etudes Bakongo' du P. Van Wing*, p. 93.
28. Balandier, *op. cit.*, pp. 255–256; Hilton, p. 10.
29. Hilton, *op. cit.*, p. 12.
30. J. Van Wing, *op. cit.*, p. 379.
31. MacGaffey, *op. cit.*, pp. 229–238.
32. Ngimbi Nseka, *op. cit.*, pp. 170–171.
33. Hilton, *op. cit.*, p. 16.
34. Van Wing, *op. cit.*, pp. 131 ff; Balandier, *op. cit.*, pp. 86–87.
35. See Hilton, *op. cit.*, chapters 5, 6 and 7.
36. See Vansina, *Kingdoms of the Savanna*, pp. 41–53.
37. Ndongala, *op. cit.*, p. 97.
38. Hilton, *op. cit.*, pp. 20–21.

39. De Cleene, quoted by MacGaffey, *op. cit.*, p. 262. That De Cleene's statements were aimed at supporting indirect rule is undeniable. Nevertheless, the facts reported are accurate.
40. MacGaffey, *op. cit.*, p. 222; see also Balandier, *op. cit.*, pp. 173–183.
41. W. G. L. Randles, *L'ancien royaume du Congo des origines à la fin du XIXe siècle* (Civilisations et Sociétés Paris: Mouton, 1968), p. 75.
42. Hilton, p. 214.
43. For other forms of service extracted from juniors, see MacGaffey, *op. cit.*, pp. 136 and 154.
44. See Hilton, *op. cit.*, p. 32.
45. See the difference of opinions between Vansina, *Kingdoms* (p. 38) and Hilton, *op. cit.* (p. 33).
46. Balandier, *op. cit.*, p. 207.
47. Vansina, *Kingdoms of the Savanna*, p. 44.
48. See David Chandler, *A History of Cambodia*; John Taylor, *From Modernization to Modes of Production*, chapter 9.
49. Balandier, *op. cit.*, pp. 176, 191–198 and 201–203.
50. Hilton, *op. cit.*, pp. 36–39.
51. Lukoki Mavoka, 'Système et structures socio-politiques de l'ancien Kongo,' in Ngimbi Nseka, *op. cit.*, p. 71.
52. John Thornton, *The Kingdom of Kongo*, p. 46.
53. *Historio do Reino do Congo*, quoted by Balandier, *op. cit.*, p. 12.
54. Thornton, *op. cit.*, p. 46.
55. In addition to non-written sources, the discussion on the Kuba relies quite exclusively on Vansina's *The Children of Woot*.
56. P.T. Theuws, 'Outline of Luba Culture,' p. 9.
57. J. Vansina, 'Le Régime foncier dans la société Kuba,' *Zaire*, Vol. X–9, November 1956, p. 901.
58. See T. Kanyinda Lusanga, '*Pouvoir traditionnel*,' pp. 33–34; W. F. P. Burton, *Luba Religion and Magic in Custom and Belief*, pp, 20 and 62.
59. See Alan Merriam, *An African World*, p. 111; P. Tshimbombo Mudiba, 'La Famille Bantu-Luluwa et le Développement,' pp. 226–240.
60. Stephen A. Lucas, 'L'Etat traditionnel Luba,' (1967), pp. 86–90.
61. Kanyinda, *op. cit.*, pp. 36–38.
62. Merriam, *op. cit.*, p. 154.
63. Thomas Reefe, *The Rainbow and the Kings*, pp. 151–152.
64. Reefe, Ibid., pp. 201–202.
65. Tshimbombo, *op. cit.*, p. 157.
66. See Stephen Lucas, 'L'Etat traditionnel Luba' (1966), p. 96; Tshimbombo, *op. cit.*, pp. 154–157; and Merriam, *op. cit.*, pp. 57–58.
67. Merriam, *op. cit.*, pp. 98–99.
68. See Hugh D. R. Baker, *Chinese Family and Kinship* (New York: Columbia University Press, 1979).
69. Tshimbombo, *op. cit.*, pp. 189–190.
70. Theuws, *op. cit.*, pp. 20 and 29.
71. Kanyinda, *op. cit.*, p. 21.
72. See Vansina, 'Le Régime foncier dans la société Kuba.'
73. Vansina, *The Children of Woot*, p. 94.
74. Reefe, *op. cit.*, p. 133.

75. Ibid., pp. 126–127.
76. Ibid., p. 133.
77. Alexandre Delcommune, *Vingt années de vie Africaine*, p. 141.
78. I reach this conclusion on the basis of two apparently contradictory interpretations proposed by Vansina. In an earlier article (*Zaire*, Vol. XI, 5, 1957) he denied the existence of centralized institutions. This view is changed in *The Children of Woot*, p. 128.

4 Mode of production and the dynamism of precolonial societies

By developing a theoretical interpretation of the empirical description in chapter 3, one can define the constitutive elements of the dynamism of precolonial lineage societies. Such interpretation – crucial for understanding pseudocapitalism in the next chapter – requires comparisons with other societies through their modes of production and a critical reading of anthropological and historical insights.

1. The Primacy of Lineage over Class Ties

Despite some differences, such as mode of descent reckoning, noncentralized societies displayed remarkable similarities. In the four case studies in chapter 3, lineage remained the backbone of their relationships. Even in societies such as the Lega in the Kivu region in eastern Zaire,[1] where parallel structure seemed to overshadow lineage, lineage maintained its primacy. In centralized societies, these issues are not as clear-cut. Some historians and anthropologists explicitly or implicitly entertain the idea that societies were governed by class ties. According to Vansina, 'Social stratification developed into social classes among the Bushoong (Kuba) as a result of the prevailing strength of the capital against the village.'[2] John Thornton's analysis of the Kongo kingdom is more explicitly couched in class terms. Three major sets of relations buttress his class configuration: slaves and their town 'noble' owners; the town nobles and villagers; and, in the villages, the ruling class (*nkuluntu*) and the villagers. In the countryside, economic surplus consisted of rent in money or in kind and was appropriated by the elders (*nkuluntu*) as a ruling class: 'In short, a whole class had taken up the privileges normally only extended to the aged.'[3] In the towns, according to Thornton, the surplus was extracted by the nobles as a class. Two factors facilitated the extraction: control of the labor process by nobles via slavery and the larger concentration of the population in towns:

> In the towns ... the appropriation clearly stood outside of the village economy. No justification in terms of the household or lineage was provided for the town sector's appropriation of village surpluses or the labor of slaves. Here, the right of conquest, whether applied to the legendary conquest of the country by Nimi or Lukeni or to the forcible seizure of villagers for enslavement, was the only justification given. As for the fields which the slaves worked on behalf of the nobility, the distribution of their product was governed through the separate kinship system of the ruling class.[4]

In the class division between the towns and the villages, 'The towns dominated the country. Though the towns produced a surplus and the villages their own, smaller surplus, the town residents were able to demand a portion of the surplus from the villages. The nkuluntu, rulers of Kongo villages and the dominant social class within that world, were the link between sectors. ... They passed on a part of this surplus to the representatives of the towns, whom they recognized as political superiors.'[5] The class status of the town nobility was apparently facilitated not only by the lack of 'justification in terms of lineage,' but also 'because the nobility faced entirely different circumstances in their vast and centralized economic system; noble households became the center of the political system and were in turn formed into great political–familial alliances which we will term 'houses.'[6]

Vansina and Thornton further justify the use of class through their interpretation of the state and kingship. They conceptualize the state in the two centralized societies in terms consistent with the prevailing view that where there is a state, there is social class and exploitation. Thornton believes 'the right of conquest' by the king, and not lineage, was the only justification for exploitation. Because it resulted from the right of conquest alone, kingship was the embodiment of a network of class relations and not of lineage ties. Moreover, the king's divine qualities also derived from circumstances apparently devoid of any lineage influence. Vansina also advances these views. Thus, unlike noncentralized societies, the primacy of lineage in the network of social relations is contested in centralized societies by social class. Vansina and Thornton are not the only writers to espouse this view. It permeates most studies on tributary modes of production and is also found in other types of studies.[7] But to what extent was kingship an emanation of the right of conquest and territorial ties and, hence of class ties and not of lineage? Were the state and society sufficiently dominated by class relations to free themselves from lineage influence?

80

At the society level, on the whole, the evidence does not support the three-fold class characterization that Thornton proposes. It does not, in fact, support the existence of class relations. Instead, the lineage structure appears to have played the crucial role of organizing social relations. Thornton does not discuss the origin, mode of interacting, and social configuration of the class of nobles to establish their class base. Rather than unveiling their class nature, such a discussion would undoubtedly reveal the strong lineage ties of the Kongo nobles. The evidence for lineage ties – some of which has already been presented in chapter 3 – is overwhelming. Slavery in the Kongo, as in other African precolonial societies, defied the application of the concept of class to those relations that developed around the institution of slavery. Slaves were not 'more like medieval serfs in Europe,' as Thornton claims. First, most slaves imported into towns were actually serving the Catholic church and not the nobles. Second, the masters did not totally control the slaves' labor process. Although the slaves provided the labor rent, they fed themselves; more importantly, slaves were integrated into the families and lineage of their masters. Thornton himself speaks of 'slaves only in name.'[8] Third, it is true that slaves did work for the nobles and the king; they contributed to the empowerment of the elite and helped it acquire some sense of independence vis-à-vis the lineage structure. But a complete break with lineage was not a general occurrence. Slaves generally worked within the limits of lineage because in most cases they were the property of the lineage. Fourth, Thornton argues that the nobles' control over the slave labor process was evidenced by their ability to choose preferred foods (e.g. to choose millet over maize), thus providing themselves a more luxurious lifestyle.[9] This is scarcely evidence; the change in crops seems to have been general. Other societies, such as the Kuba, and even the noncentralized ones, such as the Ambuun, experienced advances in their forces of production that allowed them to become more selective about their foods. They ate millet without being a class society.

The evidence is not any more convincing about class relations involving town nobles and villagers on the one hand and rural dominant classes and villages on the other. As noted, Thornton's premise is that, in the towns, lineage did not have an influence on the appropriation of village surpluses but the right of conquest and the specificity of noble houses did. The latter two were conducive to class relations. This assertion is highly questionable, if not false. Class and lineage, as categories, are inseparable from production. To argue that the Kongo towns were class- and not lineage-based, one should be able to show that the town production system was different from that in the countryside; one cannot do so. Thornton recognizes this when he writes:

> While we have defined a lubata as a rural village, and set it aside from an mbanza, or town, in fact this distinction cannot be so clearly made when speaking of production. In seventeenth-century kikongo, *lubata* meant not only 'village,' but also 'quarter of a town.' Although rural mbanza were socially distinct from the rural villages (and somewhat larger), economically they functioned in very much the same way, the most important difference

lying in the career possibilities of the surplus-consuming classes of the rural mbanza. The major towns, Mbanza Nsoyo and São Salvador, the real operating centers of the town sector, were nothing more than a profusion of lubata.[10]

Given that the villages and towns shared the same type of production, it is doubtful that one would be governed by class relations and the other by lineage ties. To the extent that the town's nobles developed a 'separate kinship system,' or specific types of 'familial alliances' called 'houses,' how did these originate? How different was the village lineage structure from the nobles' 'separate kinship system?' Could the two be differentiated at all? That some core lineages in town formed political alliances resembling houses is scarcely evidence of a fundamental difference between town and village lineages in terms of their organizations, intrinsic goals, and roles. It supports even less the presence of class relations in town at the expense of lineage ones.

Thornton's argument is all the more surprising because the two factors that he proposes for the creation of noble houses were their descent from a common ancestor and marriage alliances; yet, he adds that relations by marriage and descent from a common ancestor also determined groupings in villages. Even more contradictorily, he writes, 'Among themselves (i.e., the nobles) they were still profoundly governed by the ethics that *applied in the villages*. Households and lineage, even though they no longer played a role in production, continued to govern consumption.'[11] If the nobles and villagers were governed by the same lineage ethics and practices, how can it be said that the nobles were under a different kinship system congruent with class exploitation? That the king and aristocrats belonged to different core lineages does not detract from the whole social organization's reliance on lineages.

Thornton also bases the existence of class relations between nobles and villagers on the size and organization of noble households. According to him, while the peasant household united various branches of production through the union of male and female labor in marriage, the noble household did not undertake any such productive activity. Moreover, noble households were larger because of the presence of many wives and servants; and the relationship among noble households was more complex because their lineages were far-reaching and hierarchical. This view is indefensible. True, the size of households can indicate class relations, but it is hardly a reliable indicator; it may simply reveal social inequalities, which always exist, with or without class relations. Kongo lineage had its share of inequalities, which Thornton blames on class exploitation and the market: 'While the 'republic' of lineages and households *in every village did not engender any inequality in the lives of the villages*, the two economic structures outside of the household, the dominant classes and the workings of the market, did foster inequalities in the village world. This is obvious in the case of the nkuluntu, but less obvious in the case of specialization and the market.'[12] Unfortunately, the evidence Thornton presents about these *nkuluntu*, the cornerstone of his model of class relations in the countryside, is weak; so much so that he admits that 'even

82

those who were rich by village standards, like the nkuluntu and his retinue, did not seem so terribly rich, being characterized by a few extra clothes, and perhaps a bit more food.'[13] This denotes more a situation of lineage inequality than one of class relations.

Whether town nobles' households were larger than villagers' is no proof of class relations between the two sectors. It simply reveals how society was stratified, especially around the apparatus of a centralized state. This situation was reinforced by the change that accompanied the disintegration of the kingdom by the seventeenth century. The town-based matrilineal-turned-patrilineal section of the lineage had easier access to politically distributed income.[14] Thornton recognizes this: 'The state machinery, from the king down to the lower ranks of the nobility, collected and distributed the rent, following closely the lines of power, all the more so since few Kongo possessed incomes *independent of their grants from the state*, such as might have been the case with commercial classes, or classes more actively involved in production.'[15] In the same vein, Anne Hilton writes: 'The establishment of the kingdom had an important effect upon the kanda (lineage), shifting them further towards the hierarchical pole of their structural continua. The provincial governorships constituted the most important sources of wealth and power available to the members of the Mwissikongo kanda at the centre, and competition for them within as well as between the kanda was intense.'[16]

This remark applies to Vansina's Kuba case as well. What he terms social class 'resulting from the prevailing strength of the capital against the villages' was a simple case of exacerbation of inequalities occurring around a centralizing state, which allowed the distribution of tribute in the form of incomes. The Kuba patricians, like their Kongo counterparts, depended on the state for whatever privilege they had: 'Their revenue stemmed from taxes and perhaps some trade. [They] could only have developed if there were means to sustain it. ... The wherewithal became available only as the result of a vigorous economic development that took place during the Age of Kings in a reciprocal relationship with the polity and its ideologies.'[17] At the societal, hence production, level, the patriciates' relations with the villagers were dominated by lineage alliances. In fact, as shown earlier, even their ties with the state apparatus took place via lineage. In these conditions, class relations could not govern their lives; lineage ties did.

Raising the issue of political power in precolonial centralized societies addresses the issue of kingship and the state apparatus that sustained it because the king stood massively at the top of the pyramid. The foregoing class versus lineage debate is further illuminated through the institution of kingship by inquiring about the social base of state power. The description in the preceding chapter pointed to the venerated status of the king and his control over nature and people. His power was such that historians and anthropologists have called him 'despotic.' For the discussion here, the leading question is: Why was the precolonial king an omnipotent ruler, with godlike, supernatural power?

Vansina answered this question in the case of the Kuba. His thesis for the 'Age of Chiefs,' that is, before full-fledged kingship emerged, revolves around the notion of territorial ties. Before the transition to matrilineage, chieftainship was 'based on control over territory and not derived from kinship seniority alone.'[18] However, during the transition itself and beyond, the influence of lineage was totally nonexistent: '[As] matrilinearity became the rule, chieftainship inevitably changed. From being a kum who was a particularly honored patriarch, the chief became a kum whose authority was *exclusively* based on territorial ties. No longer did he rule both because of his mpifo (Mongo: quality of senior in a lineage or clan) and his ekopo (Mongo: territorial tie). Only the ekopo counted.'[19] Given the weak or nonexistent influence of lineage on political power, the legitimation of the dynastic line was provided by a charter myth claiming the gift of ekopo.

Insofar as the notions of territorial ties and rights of conquest attempt to provide some insight into the Kuba (or other) chieftainships/kingships at the exclusion of lineage, they are questionable, even for the transitory period. Dynastic line and chartered myth suggest that the gift of ekopo belonged to a dynasty that the myth sought to revive. To eliminate the possibility of a stronger influence of lineage on political power, one needs to inquire about the types of relations on which the dynasty was founded. Unfortunately, Vansina says no more on this subject. Furthermore, he argues that the influence of lineage on political power was nonexistent during the period of transition to chieftainship and beyond. It is not clear what determined who was going to be *kumu* (chief) during this period. Territorial ties were acquired *after* political control was established, including via war. Conceivably, they could also *precede* the establishment of political control if a pattern for the division of the territorial lands was agreed upon. In the first case, where the Kuba chief relied on territorial ties after political power had been established, what factors contributed to his power? Because political power is never a one-man show, even in the most personalized form of authority, what was its social base? In the second case, where the holding of territorial rights preceded political power, what determined such territorial rights? The answer to all these questions may be war, but a war was never fought by one individual, no matter how skilled. One still needs to inquire about the social organization of the war.

It is, then, highly debatable, in light of these questions, that the authority of the *kum* was exclusively based on territorial, not lineage, ties. Vansina does recognize lineage as the base of political power, but only for the earlier period, that is, before the shift to matrilineage and to chieftainship. The questions raised, however, cannot be answered unless one recognizes the explicit or latent influence of lineage on political power, even during the transition period. It is symptomatic of the role of lineage that, according to Vansina, new 'unrelated groups' who came to support the chiefs and their matrilineages became known as the 'founding clans.' Why would their matrilineages be called founding clans if lineage did not play a role in political power? And why, for that matter, would they involve their matrilineages at all?

Contrary to Vansina's claim of exclusive reliance on territorial ties, his description of the relations between these founding clans and the chief amply demonstrates the reliance of chieftainship on lineage. Examples include the chief's council, which was made up of members of the founding clans, and the inheritance of the chief's wealth by his lineage successor. The chief received gifts from founding clans, and the succession to the throne was based on alliances between the ruling lineage and the founding clans. Indeed, the daughters of the ruling lineage's women were married to members of the *mbaangt* (founding) clans. The sons from these marriages were potential successors, and their fathers were members of *mbaangt* clans. These marriages created a web of kinship among all the matrilineages involved, which was limited only by the rule of exogamy. In this network of lineage relations, it is unlikely that only territorial ties sustained political power during the period of chieftainship.

In a modified version, Thornton shares Vansina's thesis. Not only does Thornton base his concept of class relations on the right of conquest but he also uses it to explain the omnipotence and aura of the king; according to Thornton, the invocation of the myth of conquest by an adventurer or king was enough to give him a mystical aura and his divine status.[20] This contention is questionable as well. If, during his tenure, a king invoked the right of conquest to justify his omnipotent rule, he invoked not necessarily his own conquest (not every king was a conqueror) but that of his predecessors, especially the founder of the kingdom. In other words, he invoked his descent reckoning. It follows that he did not gain his aura by virtue of the abstract rights of conquest, but by his descent to a conquering lineage. An attempt to link oneself to the founding lineage was at the very heart of political power in the Kongo kingdom.

Vansina's position on the role of lineage and of territorial ties in political power among the Kuba during the Age of Kings is not clearly stated. In an earlier article he seems to subscribe to the view that the king derived his political authority from his ownership of land,[21] which would be consistent with the territorial ties thesis. In his later work, he mentions that the cult of ancestors (hence lineage), which lost its role during the Age of Chiefs, was revived by the kings as they assumed supernatural powers. Moreover, his description of political power at the center of the Kuba kingdom seems to suggest the importance of lineage:

> What is surprising is that the clans, which did not form a very coherent front, were able to hold a position of strength and to embody the ideal of the titleholder to the extent that they did. This shows that force alone was not enough to explain the outcome of conflicts; ideology was equally important. After all, those clans were the guarantors of legitimacy, that of the king, that of the kingdom, and that of the status of kolm as well. To most if not all of the Bushoong, legitimacy of the system was essential: it conditioned their support for the regime and their participation in it.[22]

Yet, surprisingly, positive evaluation of lineage's relation to the legitimacy of the king is not evoked when Vansina explains the specific issues of the kingship's legitimacy and omnipotence. His explanations instead rely on variables that tend to support his territorial ties thesis. Four explanations of a king's legitimacy and aura are advanced: (1) he had been chosen by Ncyeem (the supreme creator), and he became a spirit when he assumed office; (2) he was the richest person and possessed the best charms; (3) he was an archsorcerer; and (4) he possessed intrinsic or inherent qualities of the kingship.[23] That the king was viewed as a spirit is imputed to the king's own proclamation. 'Shyaam introduced the notion that the king was a nature spirit, *ngesh*. This is the message, obvious to every Kuba, in the anecdotes about his madness and the invention of the *ncyeem ingesh* songs.'[24]

These four explanations rest on shaky ground. How did the king acquire the wealth that is linked to his power and legitimacy in the second explanation? He became wealthy because he was the king, but how did he become king in the first place? The answer ultimately raises the issue of core lineages, or founding clans; they not only stood at the center of power intrigues but contributed gifts that made the king rich. 'He [the chief/king] collected wealth from the mbaangt clans, since any new nomination to the council of the mbaangt clans (founding clans), whether a new clan section was added or whether a deceased incumbent was replaced, was accompanied by a gift to the kum.'[25] Whether under the rule of chiefs or kings, access to the royal throne depended on these clans.

That the king was an archsorcerer (third explanation) is highly plausible, but his sorcery was not unique. What role did sorcery play? In what context? For what purposes? These questions need to be answered because they will illuminate the broader social context of the king's position. The analysis in the preceding chapter underscored the importance of lineage in the flourishing of sorcery in all of the societies studied. It was not different among the Kuba. As part of Kuba 'religion,' sorcery was tightly linked to lineage because 'religious practice was so tied up with other institutions that it lacked sufficient autonomy and visibility to develop systematic traditions of its own.'[26] On the basis of the evidence presented in chapter 3, the link between sorcery and lineage was closer than that between lineage and other forms of religion. Under these conditions, the king's archsorcery did not develop in a vacuum; it was a reflection of the Kuba society, which rested on lineage.

The fourth explanation, which bases the king's aura on the intrinsic qualities of the kingship, strikes me as a tautology, and need not be addressed. The view that the king introduced the notion that he was a nature spirit is also highly debatable and is contradicted by Vansina himself when he writes, 'The abundance of the costume's imagery reflects the unfolding of a *collective dream* and shows that kingship stimulated the imagination of the Bushoong to the point of creating a fantasy world around the king.'[27] Because the dream was collective and the imagination of the Bushoong was stimulated to create a fantasy world around the king, it is not likely that the king was the creator of his own myth and aura. On the contrary, society at large (collective dream), which rested on lineage, created the aura.

In the first explanation about the kings' aura, Vansina links the king's omnipotence to the supreme creator and explains it by the king's rites of investiture. Vansina himself points out that the notion of Ncyeem (supreme

86

creator/God) may have been invented at the same time kingship developed; in this case, there can scarcely be a cause–effect relationship between the supreme creator and kingship. It would appear that both were dependent variables to be explained by something else. This point does not deny the possibility that the notion of the supreme creator was used at times to underscore the prevailing position of the king. And even if one subscribes to the idea that the supreme creator chose the king (which I do not), one still needs to ask: Why would God waste his time choosing the king? A possible answer is in the stiff competition for kingship, reason enough to accredit the idea of the intervention of the supreme creator on the side of the candidate who became king. The competition involved lineages: the founding lineages competed with the king's lineage, and potential heirs and successors of the king's lineage competed among themselves. Thus, even the ideological explanation the Kuba proposed about kingship does not escape the social base on which it rested – lineage.

The second part of the explanation, that the omnipotent and divine role of the king can be explained by his investiture, is shared by many writings in history and anthropology. Rites, such as the king's incestuous sexual relations with his niece and other rituals of enthronement, are used to explain why the king was expected to accomplish supernatural roles. Consider Randall Packard's study of the Bashu of the Kivu region. He argues that the Bashu chief was expected by his subjects to produce rain and fertility and that such expectations formed a cosmological view about the actions of the chief among the Bashu. Investiture, more than social and economic forces, influenced these perceptions about the supernatural power of the king. 'Through his accession to office, [the chief, because of investiture] acquires a permanent position between the homestead and the bush. This position, combined with his control of local ritual activity, permits him to insure the demonstration of potentially beneficial forces of the bush and periodically to cleanse the chiefdom of chaotic forces of nature.'[28]

The rituals of investiture were undoubtedly important ideological components of kingship, but they did not create the supernatural power of the king or chief. If they did, how does one explain the simplicity of those rites that accompanied the succession of a simple lineage head who was also expected to mediate between the homstead and nature in noncentralized societies? The need for mediation with supernatural forces in noncentralized societies did not lead to the investiture of a king with elaborate rituals. The accompaniment of succession ceremonies by rituals in both noncentralized and centralized societies indicates clearly enough that the mediating role was not an exclusive attribute of the king or grand chief. Even a simple lineage head was expected to do the same. Expectations about their role of mediation differed, as did the rituals accompanying investitures; but this was not because rituals related to the king gave him his supernatural powers and those accompanying the investiture of the lineage head did not. They varied simply because one was a king and the other was not. The rituals of investiture only *formalized* their respective positions in the social hierarchy; they did not create mediating, supernatural power. After all, a modern head of state does not control state power because he takes the oath of office with a hand on the Bible, or goes to Mass, or rides in a convertible limousine on inauguration day. These rituals simply formalize position and power. It is essential to look at the social origin of the ideology to explain the king's aura. In this context, one needs to ask the questions of why and how the king, the chief, and the lineage head were all expected to play a mediating role with supernatural forces. The answers lie in the description in chapter 3. Their position within the lineage organization and the overall lineage ideology constituted the source of their supernatural power. The mediating role they played with the forces of nature was a reflection of this situation. Despite Placide Tempels' scholarly flaws concerning 'Bantu philosophy,' he was quite right when he stated, 'A man does not become a lineage head and a patriarch just because he succeeds his forebears and by virtue of his being now the eldest of the group, but because the primogeniture involves an internal secretion of vital power, which elevates the foresaid eldest's *muntu* to the rank of intermediary between the clan ancestors, on the one hand, and the living members, on the other.'[29]

Lineage was the framework – the social base – for political power in precolonial societies. The evidence presented so far is overwhelming, but supplementary evidence further strengthens the argument. Most striking about the Kongo kingdom was its dual, self-reinforcing structure. The state structure, at every level, rested on the lineage structure, and a system of equivalency was thus in action. State structure was represented by the political title of *mani*, whereas the corresponding lineage title was *mbuta* or *mfumu*. The *mbuta* (elder) was the landowner upon whom the political title depended, because state power was a delegated power; lineage power, on the other hand, emanated directly from the ancestors. As W. G. L. Randles correctly points out: 'The kingdom can decline due to the weakening of the king; the clan, on the other hand, can only strengthen itself, since it is formed by the living and the dead; the king's role is to conserve the clan in conformity with the model established by its founding heroes, for in the Kongo kingdom, the king is above all the head of the clan.'[30]

That the king and kingship reflected the lineage was further confirmed by the characterization of the king. He was God-king because he remained the chief of the initial Kongo clan; he was the 'eldest' of all lineages, hence of the whole kingdom, which explained his venerated persona. This dual structure endured even after Christian influence was felt by the Kongo polity. No doubt, in the fifteenth century, by virtue of his 'absolute' power, the king stood above the lineages. Despite this, however, he relied on lineage for the exercise of power. The organization of state power offers the best illustration. The king was a representative of the *mwissikongo*, the ruling corporate group, consisting of the core lineages; the core lineage, in turn, had twelve representatives at the royal court. The king's succession, although not automatic, set in motion a competitive system in which candidates derived their credentials from their lineage affiliations. What was called constitutional monarchy in the Kongo reflected the crucial role played by lineage in shaping political power. One manifestation of this constitutional monarchy was the *mani-mwivi* (claimant to

the kingdom), the designation of the king's successor among many competitors and the submission of his candidacy to the approval of a lineage-based
electoral college. Another manifestation was the approval of the king's decisions by his lineage-based council. Evidence is also ample of the importance
of lineage in the Luba empire at various levels of political organization (see
chap. 3).

The critical remarks in this section do not detract from the depth with which
Vansina approaches the study of these precolonial societies; his insights into
many of the issues are remarkable. My comments are aimed at the specific
issues of class and kingship. I argue that no class relations existed in the
precolonial societies discussed here; rather social relations revolved around
lineage and did not display the type of domination, exploitation, and class
struggles present in class relations. Social classes can be analyzed only
through the relations they involve, which, in turn, are indissociable from
production. Therefore, class relations involve exploitation that production
relations generate. More specifically, one class appropriates a part of the
surplus product that is produced by another class and also controls the conditions under which this (exploited) class works. Such control involves: (1)
controlling the means of production; (2) determining what portion of the
production generated by the exploited people/ class goes where and for what
purpose; (3) lowering or raising at will the portion of the product allocated to
producers; and (4) the inability, except under capitalism, of the producers or
the exploited class to 'withdraw' from the exploiting class because the
producers cannot subsist unless the exploiting class ('lord/master') allows
them access to land.[31]

Lineage was a deterrent to this type of class control. The collective ownership of the major means of production – land – despite the dominant position
of the lineage head, the dual control over the labor process whereby lineage
and the producer *qua* lineage member owned different categories of the means
of production, and the loophole that allowed lineage members to own property
were all incongruous with class exploitation. Thus, for instance, in theory and
in practice, lineage juniors could rebel against their seniors, constituting a
'withdrawal' from the dominant relations. Yet this did not cut off their means
of subsistence because they still had access to land. (There were, of course,
sanctions imposed, such as curses, but they differed from class sanctions. I
shall return to this point later in this chapter.) Undoubtedly, some lineage
leaders extracted a high level of surplus product. However, what distinguished
this relation of extraction from a class relation was the modality of the distribution of the surplus product.

Although I have argued that social groups associated with the state in
precolonial societies were not classes, I do not suggest that social classes
cannot be associated with the state. Nor do I suggest that the state apparatus
cannot reproduce social classes; it can and does help reproduce social classes
(e.g., in feudal and capitalist states). However, the state does so only where
society is dominated by class relations, which is not the case in societies
discussed here. Given that the fundamental social relations were structured

around and by lineage, the king's ownership of the lands of the kingdom and territorial ties were governed by lineage prescriptions; so were his policies of extraction and redistribution. For example, lineage heads were in charge of tribute collection for the state/king and benefited from the policies of redistribution.

I have maintained that the explanations generally proposed about the king's aura and kingship are not convincing; lineage – not territorial ties, rights of conquest, and class ties – was the basis of a king's power. No doubt, some of the explanations proposed by the authors reviewed here partly address the issue by invoking the ideology of kingship. However, missing from their explanations is the very social matrix on which kingship and the state rested that would help explain the ideology. One runs the risk of imputing the ideology of kingship to metaphysics or to gods and unexplainable beliefs or myths. The result is a misinterpretation of the precolonial state. Ideology has a social base; so does the state. Neither can be explained unless placed in the social context. As already noted, the people of the Kongo were aware of this fundamental reality:

> to this day few Congolese comprehend the idea of a state or other political unit based primarily on territoriality rather than on descent. For Kongo villagers in particular, government is not something established to govern a limited territory; a government is the representative of a particular power. . . . Investiture entitles the chief to use insignia that represent the particular power and authority conferred upon him, *according to the particular source whence they come, perhaps the ancestors of his group or such and such an n'kisi*.[32]

For the Kongo, then, political power was first a socially based power. The state was the representation of the fundamental relations that governed their lives in society. And without doubt, lineage ties were at the center of social relations. Failure to recognize this reality explains some misinterpretations of the precolonial state.[33] The mere presence of the state apparatus and state functionaries is confused with the presence of class relations.

2. Lineage mode and Ideological Routinization

I have refuted the idea of class relations even in centralized ('tributary') societies by demonstrating the centrality of lineage. The primacy of of lineage is shown, but what is its theoretical meaning? In other words, how does one derive from it an understanding of the dynamism of precolonial societies? To answer this question one must bring together the concepts of lineage and mode of production. In chapter 1, I suggested that, as a formal model, a mode of production is best defined by its core relations: the relations of production and the means by which the extraction of surplus product takes place. From the evidence presented in chapter 3, it is clear that the relations of production of precolonial societies were characterized by a nonseparation of the producers (members of the lineage) from their means of production. On the one hand, the ownership, control, and coordination of land by the lineage as a whole and, on the other, the effective possession of the tools of labor by lineage members during the productive process prevented the separation. This nonseparation distinguished these societies from capitalist ones. As in other noncapitalist modes, an extraeconomic means (physical or ideological coercion) intervened to ensure the extraction of surplus product. Was the extraction in the non-European societies under discussion here realized by ideological or physical coercion?

To answer this question, one must explain the primacy of lineage in these societies. According to Marc Block, the great invasions that preceded the emergence of feudalism stifled lineage ties in Europe and caused them to disappear. Feudalism was, in a sense, a response to this situation.[34] One may infer from this explanation that no specific historical circumstances acted to weaken such ties in Africa and other non-European societies. But this historical explanation does not really explain the primacy of lineage in non-European societies; moreover, it does not shed light on the means of extraction of the surplus product.

Emmanuel Terray has proposed a theoretical explanation. He argues that the centrality of lineage in African societies resulted from the absence of the exploitation of labor, that is, from the absence of class relations. Such an absence had the effect of reproducing lineage ties.[35] Although consistent with the view I proposed in the first section, Terray fails to explain what exactly in this mode realizes the extraction of surplus product. This, in turn, prevents him from convincingly explaining why lineage ties are reproduced. Arguing that 'a lineage often appears to be a production unit, a political body, and a sort of religious congregation,' he suggests that 'only after close examination of these various determinations and their combinations can it be decided which of them is the dominant determination.'[36] This is not a solution. The extraction could not be done by economic means because this is possible only under capitalism, where a purely economic means (wage) is used to extract surplus product. And, despite claims to the contrary, there is no evidence to suggest that physical coercion was used to extract surplus product in African societies.

The failure to specify. and especially to explain, the means of extraction in 'primitive' societies is at the basis of the misinterpretation of the leading role played by lineage elders. Claude Meillassoux sees the elders' role as the result of the sum of 'technical' knowledge acquired by them.[37] Terray thinks of the 'power of the elders as essentially a functional power derived from their office.'[38] For Pierre-Philippe Rey, the role of the elders is a reflection of their class position vis-à-vis their juniors.[39] None of these interpretations is convincing. The accumulation of knowledge thesis is contradicted by Meillassoux himself: 'In this kind of society the sum of essential technical knowledge is limited and can be acquired in a relatively short time. It tends to put all men above a certain age on an equal footing.'[40] If one can join the club of 'knowledgeable people' easily, it can scarcely grant its members the kind of privilege they enjoy. In the functional power thesis, Terray argues that production relations determine the office of the elders. True, relations of

91

production determine the office of the elders by endowing them with the power to organize production and to extract surplus. But what in production relations gives them the power? By what means do they organize and extract surplus product? The class thesis supported by Rey, I have already shown to be untenable, even in centralized states. That these authors later retreated from the concept of lineage mode of production reveals their failure to grasp the secrets of its explanatory power.

It is precisely the lack of class relations in lineage societies that offers a clue to the role of lineage elders; it, too, helps explain the means of extraction in these societies, their dynamism, and, ultimately (in chap. 5), why lineage ties were reproduced at the expense of capitalism. The following proposition can be advanced to that end: Given the absence of class relations in lineage societies, only via ideological coercion could material production be organized and surplus product extracted because the absence of class exploitation and domination excluded class-based means of organization and extraction that relied on the use or threat of physical coercion. Stronger reliance on ideological coercion than in other types of society constituted the dynamism of these societies. To support this proposition, some preliminary remarks about ideology are in order.

Ideology: A Definition

The literature on ideology and its role in social change is vast.[41] Mustafa Rejai has proposed a matrix in which ideology has five dimensions: the cognitive, affective, evaluative, programmatic, and social base dimensions. Cognitively, ideology is both a concept and a belief. As a concept, if refers to knowledge by opposing itself to truth and science. As belief, it fulfills a function in politics by relying on notions and attitudes about society and politics that are accepted on faith. The affective dimension refers to the call on emotions. In its evaluative dimension, ideology makes value judgments: negatively, it denounces the existing system of social relationships; positively, it puts forth a set of norms according to which social reconstruction is to take place. Given its programmatic dimension, ideology involves action directed toward the maintenance and perpetuation of the status quo or, more characteristically, toward the transformation of the existing social order. The program of ideology sets forth priorities specifying immediate, intermediate, and ultimate goals. Finally, the social base dimension of ideology refers to social groups, classes, collectivities, or nations that are associated with it.[42] Other writers have proposed a similar characterization.[43]

Yet crucial, unanswered questions remain. Rejai concedes that 'ideologies embrace deliberate elements of distortion or myth. This, in fact, is one of the few points on which most writers on ideology agree.'[44] But how is the myth formed? By equating myth with beliefs Rejai answers that it is accepted on faith without any necessary foundation in reality. Maybe so, and this is the mainstream explanation of beliefs in ideology. But, then, distortion is also equated with myth. How is the process of distortion accomplished, and why?

Obviously, the answer here cannot be 'on faith' because distortion implies an active process or, as Fernand Dumond puts it, a praxis.[45]

Answers to these questions are the sine qua non for a definition of ideology. Some elements of the answers are provided by Louis Althusser and his associates.[46] Althusser's fundamental thesis is that ideology represents the imaginary relationship of individuals to their real conditions of existence. By imaginary he means that it does not correspond to reality, but constitutes an illusion and an allusion to the reality. This formulation is not far removed from Marx and Engels' notion of false consciousness. However, according to Althusser and contrary to the orthodox Marxist interpretation, ideology does not represent the 'system of the real relations which govern the existence of individuals;'[47] rather, it represents the imaginary relations of individuals to the real relations in which they live by transforming individuals into 'subjects.' Individuals recognize their status as subjects through rituals (the practice of ideology) that relate them to a bigger Subject (e.g., God, the state, etc.). This imaginary relationship created by ideology, in turn, distorts and conceals the real relations of existence of individuals/subjects by elevating itself.

Althusser's first contribution is his treatment of the imaginary relationships by modifying the classic Marxist interpretation. He does not reject the link between ideology and the social/material relations of existence; he adds to it a new dimension, making the link two-tiered instead of one-tiered. His second contribution, closely related and embedded in the first, is the notion of the subject as a creation of ideology. 'Individuals not only imagine their relations to each other to be those of interacting subjects. They also treat their conditions of existence as subjects with which they interact.'[48] As a result, Althusser is able to provide ways to answer questions about myths, beliefs, and distortions in ideology and about ideological praxis. For Althusser, myths, beliefs, and their connected rituals are by-products of the imaginary relationships created by ideology. Action or praxis is the direct by-product of these ideological rituals and apparatuses.[49] This explains the evaluative and programmatic dimensions of ideology.

One can draw some important conclusions to make the concept of ideology operational. First, ideology is a set of cognitive, affective, evaluative, and programmatic propositions that allude to a concrete social reality. By simplifying the complex, ideology often conceals and distorts reality, setting forth its own truth through a two-tiered process. One of the main outcomes of this process is the reproduction/perpetuation of the real (prevailing) conditions of existence. Second, ideology does not exist only in a class society, and it is not only associated with a social class. Social groups, organizations, movements, and larger units, such as nations, have ideologies. Class is not a sine qua non for ideology's existence; it is a sufficient condition, but not a necessary one.

Third, the notions of imaginary relationship and real relations of existence are theoretically more useful than false consciousness is. By helping to explain myths, beliefs, and distortions on the one hand, and action and praxis on the other, they illuminate another crucial ideological category: 'ideological routinization.' By this term I suggest that ideological practices and rituals are taken so much for granted by individuals that they become routine. Individuals are unaware of their involvement in these practices because, at the extreme, they are identical with real political, economic and social practices. The distinction that Franz Schurmann makes, for example, between 'pure' ideology and 'practical' ideology becomes irrelevant[50] because practical ideology is nothing more than ideological practices and rituals.

Ideological routinization is a theoretical derivative of both imaginary relationships and real conditions/relations of existence. The real conditions of existence are those economic, social, and political relations ('social order') that govern the concrete existence of individuals, groups, or classes. They are reproduced by ideology, which makes them depend on ideology and its imaginary relationships. In this sense, the conditions of existence cannot stand on their own; their reproduction by ideology is accompanied by the secretion of ideological practices, symbols, rituals, and beliefs that become, in the long run, almost the same as the real conditions of existence. The dependence of the concrete conditions of existence on ideology's imaginary relationships places individuals in contact with ideology that is too close; they cannot separate themselves from it. Ideological routinization is accompanied by automatic recognition and obviousness. That is, as ideology creates the imaginary relationship of individuals to their real conditions of existence, it converts individuals into subjects (s) interacting with a bigger subject (S). As a result of the obviousness and its accompanying rituals of automatic recognition, the individuals breathe ideology as they breathe air (see figures 4.1 and 4.2 in this section).

What, then, is the relationship between ideology and societal change? Given that ideology implies real conditions of existence, what is the fate of ideology and its routinization when these conditions of existence no longer exist? Does the routinization disappear, or does it endure? The answer is possible only by viewing ideological routinization as a structural characteristic. Despite the important role of individuals in routinization, it is only within a network of social relations that they become affected by it. Ideological recognition and obviousness only express these relations. One needs to analyze a whole set of relationships to show the prevalence of ideology. Even beliefs imply a set of relationships that involve all or part of society. Three important consequences follow for societal change. First, whenever individual actors choose to sever their ties within the broad network of relationships, the impact is likely to be minimal. Ideological routinization is apt to be carried on by the prevailing relationships. Second, whenever a part of the relationships making up the initial social order is lost, the remaining part is likely to perpetuate the ideology and its rituals and be imbricated with new types of relationships. Third, whenever the initial social order itself disintegrates or disappears, ideology can and is likely to survive because its routinization is the result of the imaginary relationships and rituals created by ideology. Once they have been generated, they can survive without the real relations that generated them. Thus, for instance, the slave and Nazi social orders have disappeared, but their ideology of racism has endured. In the two-way dependence between the real conditions of existence and ideology, reality needs ideology more than ideology needs reality.

Core Relations and Society's Dynamism

These remarks about ideology shed light on my earlier proposition about the extraction of surplus product and the role of ideological coercion/routinization in the dynamism of precolonial societies. As in any other society, the accumulation of resources (hence surplus product) and material survival were at the very heart of lineage societies' existence. Ideological coercion constituted the means of its organization and extraction. As stated earlier, all precapitalist societies relied on either physical/political coercion or ideological coercion for extracting surplus; lineage societies chose ideological coercion because *class domination was absent*. The reliance on ideological coercion meant that the threat that hangs over the producers in a feudal or capitalist society (i.e., fear of losing wages, of going to jail, or of being repressed by the police), which allows the extraction of surplus from them, was replaced in lineage societies by the fear of being cursed or of being struck by unknown disasters (see the analysis in chapter 3). Recourse by society to ideological coercion for extraction purposes explained the exceptionally high number of ideological rituals in lineage societies (see chap.3).

To elaborate, a lineage is a network of social relations: real relations of existence and imaginary relations created by ideology. Its specificity in precolonial societies resided in its ability to secrete, more than other social orders, an exceptionally high dose of imaginary relations at two different levels. The first level, well covered in the anthropological literature, consists of ideological reconstructions of the origin and transformations of lineage ties. An example of this is the reconstruction through genealogical accounts using charters. Not only did charters create fictitious descent filiations beside real ones, they were also rewritten to depict a positive picture of the lineage founders, their deeds, and their descent lines. Furthermore, in its mode of descent reckoning, the choice between patrilineage and matrilineage was highly ideological. There was no scientific justification for children to 'belong' to the mother's side or father's side. Finally, the shift from matrilineage to patrilineage took place when there was a need to rationalize and reproduce real political and socioeconomic conditions of existence.

The societies discussed offer many examples of such ideological reconstruction. In the Kongo, where, in spite of its benign character, slavery was feared by all, the need to belong to a lineage was high; slavery meant lack of freedom, whereas belonging to a lineage helped one obtain it. The result was the expansion of lineage ties through assimilation or distortion of genealogical accounts. Among the Kongo, 'Any informant asked to describe his own origin, quotes tradition [ideology]; asked to describe the origin of his competitors, he recites history [reality].'[51] In the Luba empire, 'Every chief profess[ed] to trace his line ... back to an original kingly aristocracy in the dimly distant past, beyond which ignorance [made] his position unassailable.'[52] In most of the societies, a shift in the mode of descent reckoning took place, thus confirming its 'artificiality.' The Kongo went, albeit temporarily and partially, from matrilineage to patrilineage by the sixteenth and seventeenth centuries. The Kuba shifted from patrilineage to matrilineage; the Luba probably were matrilineal before settling for patrilineage.

Lineage's real conditions of existence included the relations of extraction, economic ownership, distribution of economic resources, political relations and conflicts. For instance, the incompatibility between the matrilineal form of descent reckoning and the virilocal form of residence often caused quarrels and broken relationships between 'fathers' and 'sons.' Other conflicts occurred over matrimonial compensations and brideprice. Women given in marriages were 'produced' by women and their husbands, yet they were controlled (as production) by men, that is, the lineage heads. In other words, maternal uncles owned their nieces without 'producing' them, which led to conflict. Lineage seniors opposed their juniors. These real conditions of existence, conflictual or consensual, were then maintained, reinforced, or amended by lineage depending on the prevailing interests. The first level of ideological reconstruction (i.e., genealogy and charter) alone was insufficient to compensate for the absence of physical/political coercion and to cause individuals to face up to the task of reinforcing or amending the real conditions of existence. A second, more elaborate level backed up the first.

At this second level, lineage secreted an even higher dose of imaginary relationships at different levels. Three types of imaginary relationships were present: (1) between the dead ancestors and living lineage members; (2) between lineage heads/seniors as representatives of the ancestors, on the one hand, and lineage members, on the other hand; and (3) between lineage members and the lineage itself. Each type formed a subject–Subject (s–S) relationship. They explain the rituals, ancestral cults, and such practices as the deep respect for elders, sorcery, initiation, and witchcraft. The lineage leadership maintained the real relations of existence within a lineage through such practices. In type number 3, a lineage was presented as the bastion of freedom (as opposed to slavery), peace, security, and harmony. Lineage members were subjects (s), whereas the lineage was the Subject (S). For instance, in the Kongo the *kinkimba* was an initiation ritual that helped teach boys how to despise noninitiates who lacked a clan to protect them. The relationship between a lineage and its members was imaginarily recreated through initiation rites by focusing on the opposition of freedom (lineage) and the lack thereof (slavery). This strengthened the lineage structure and its membership. The same held true in the Lega society, where the initiation practice, the *bwami*, dominated social life. The unity of the lineage was strongly affirmed by the possession of two *musagi wa kindi* (ritual objects). One *musagi* was shared by two core lineages and the other by five other core lineages. Lineage bonds were also strengthened by the ownership of a single large male figurine kept by the most senior of all living members of the lineage.

The practice of sorcery manifested the imaginary relationship between a lineage and its membership. By presenting itself as a bastion of security and harmony, the lineage ideology created a set of oppositions: sorcerer versus

96

good lineage members. Whenever peace and harmony were disrupted, affecting lineage members (e.g., disease or mishaps), sorcery was blamed because, as ritual, it represented the imaginary relationship between a lineage and its membership. Through it, the lineage reinforced its postulates about peace and harmony by despising and rejecting the sorcerer, who was opposed to harmony and peace. This rejection took many forms. It involved ordinary lineage members, as manifested in their frequent accusations against fellow lineage members; it also often involved the lineage head/senior. On the one hand, as the representative of the lineage, the lineage head generally led the rejection movement, for 'the true chief is one who can see who is a witch at heart and can restore order by frustrating deceit.'[53] On the other hand, by being the intermediary between the ancestors and the living members, the lineage head/senior was himself from time to time the object of rejection. The rejection movement involved antisorcery practices and rituals, such as divination. Not all imaginary relationships had a clear and direct link to lineage. In many cases, the link was indirect.[54]

Thus, as the direct result of the absence of class relations, the primacy of lineage ties led to an exceptionally high number of ideological rituals to offset the nonuse of physical/political (and economic) coercion; these rituals served as coercive means to organize material production and extract surplus product in lineage societies. It follows, then, that the ideologically played role of the lineage head as the representative of the ancestors in the extraction of surplus product made the persona of the elder prominent, not his 'knowledge,' 'office,' or 'class position' as wrongly claimed by French anthropologists. Rather than being an attempt to conceal the elders' class position, the persona of the elder reflected, on the contrary, the absence of class relations. In short, precolonial societies relied on ideological core relations.

The State, Politics, and Ideology

Was the state in centralized societies the same as that in noncentralized societies, or was it similar to, say, the capitalist or feudal state? If one holds to the Marxist characterization of the state, there was no state at all; centralized societies, like noncentralized ones, did not rest on class relations. From a non-Marxist view, according to which the state is a neutral organization, there was a state that resembled its capitalist or feudal counterparts. The only difference, of course, is that one (capitalist) is 'modern' and sophisticated whereas the other is 'primitive.' In this view, however, noncentralized societies were 'stateless' because they lacked organized state apparatuses.

The truth lies somewhere in between. As detailed in chapters 1, the state is a relationship that represents the fundamental relations in society. Politics, on the other hand, is the expression of competitive interests of actors, groups, or classes making up society. Politics implies the state because the state is that relationship formed by competing social actors as they are regulated by political power in its coercive form. The state, in turn, gives politics its form. As competition, politics aims to distribute the social product by controlling or influencing state (or political) power ; hence, political power is the nodal point between the state and politics. Consequently, the state and politics are not the exclusive attributes of a particular type of society, or class society. The notion of 'stateless' societies is untenable. That specialized roles with clearly defined political authority are less easy to find in some societies reflects the form of the political organization, not the lack thereof. Arguing the opposite collapses into evolutionism because this would mean that only evolution toward a class society can lead to the formation of a state. The position is also functionalist because institutions and functions are posited as the basis of analysis; the form is confused with the reality. Yet this does not mean that the state is a neutral organization, some kind of one-size-fits-all thing in all societies. Precisely because it is a relationship embodying other fundamental relations in society, it is inextricably shaped by them. In this sense, the capitalist state is a class-based state, as was the feudal state. In precolonial societies, centralized and noncentralized, social relations were not class-based, and the state reflected this. Centralized states did not resemble capitalist or feudal ones; they represented nonclass societies and bore their own specificity. They differed from states in noncentralized societies *only in form*, the result of their policies of conquest and expansion.

What is true of state and politics holds true also for ideology. All societies have some kind of ideology. In most situations, ideology is used in and by politics. The association of politics and ideology means that all kinds of state do use ideology because politics is played within the state. Despite this association, ideology is not politics. The definitions of both concepts given clarify this difference. That ideology is part of politics is undeniable, but only in the sense that ideology is a tool of politics; it maintains its separate identity.

This distinction helps one to grasp another important point about politics in precolonial societies. State power and politics in all societies rely on coercion. Yet not all societies and states use the same type of coercion. Their choice is between physical/political coercion and ideological coercion (see chap. 1). The choice of one type of coercion over the other is dictated by the type of society and mode of production. Only by relying on the core relations of the mode of production can one specify the form of coercion at the center of state power and politics. As the nodal point of social relations, the state in a class society embodies and reflects the type of class domination and exploitation present in the core relations of the mode of production. Such a domination is ineluctably congruent with physical coercion. This explains why under feudalism and capitalism state power and politics rely on physical/political coercion. By contrast, given the absence of class relations and the preeminence of ideological core relations at the society level, state power and politics in lineage-based societies rely not on physical/political coercion but on ideological coercion. The absence of class domination and exploitation dictates that the exercise of state power and politics rely on nonphysical means of control. The reliance of the state and politics on ideological coercion means that whenever the state extracted resources or prepared the framework for extraction, it did so through ideological coercion (even tax/tribute was collected through ideological coercion). This is not to suggest that physical repression is never used. As class-based societies do not always use physical coercion, choosing instead ideological manipulation, so, too, lineage-based societies do not completely reject physical coercion. In both situations, the legitimacy of state power is at stake. In a class society, where coercion is mostly physical, legitimacy results from the subjects/citizens constantly assuming and fearing the use of force by the holders of state power. Ideological manipulation and other factors (e.g., 'trust in the efficiency of the institutions') come second. In societies governed by ideological coercion, on the other hand, legitimacy results first from the subjects' ideology-inspired fear of the holders of state power; the fear of force comes second.

It now becomes clear that it was the ideological coercion that explained why the king's 'despotism' was divine and kingship venerated. What appeared to be the excess of political power on the surface was actually ideological coercion, ritually expressed by the king. The earlier empirical statement (chap. 3) that the king's power reflected lineage can be substituted by a theoretical one: *the lineage mode and its ideological core relations and coercion explained the king's aura and divine nature.* The statement runs counter to those that explain ancient despotism in Africa and Asia by hydraulic works,[55] conquests, prolonged wars, or internal security.[56] Ideological coercion also explains the puzzling fact that 'the African despot exploited less his own subjects than the neighboring tribes.'[57] To 'exploit less' means that expansionist states (e.g. Menelik's Ethiopia, the M'siri state in today's Zaire/Tanzania borders and others) did use physical coercion, but much of it was directed against foreign states/tribes. Indeed, given that internal coercion was applied ideologically, the king often used his army (hence, physical coercion) for plundering and destructive incursions against other states. And finally, the use of ideological coercion in politics explains why African rulers devoted much time in building elaborate 'religious'/ideological structures.[58] They did so not because they were particularly religious; 'religious' structures were an expression of political power that relied on ideological coercion.

As noted earlier, ideological rituals are not an exclusive attribute of the lineage societies. Their role in any society is to reproduce the real conditions of existence by concealing them. This point needs to be emphasized especially in the case of capitalist societies to avoid misunderstanding. Ideology is important and routinized under capitalism; it is expressed in the form of commodity fetishism and mystification whereby relations among people take the form of relations among things[59] and in the form of equal opportunity that sustains liberal democracy and its attendant 'hegemonic consensus.' Under these conditions, ideological rituals do help reproduce the real conditions of existence (i.e., relations of ownership and extraction, distribution of resources, political relations/domination and competition). Ideology does not, however, intervene *directly* in the *daily functioning* of these conditions of existence, especially the extraction of the surplus product; such functioning relies on *physical (and economic) coercion.* For instance, physical/political coercion, or the threat of its use, regulates daily the distribution of resources among competing interests and the relationship between the rulers and the ruled; in capitalism specifically, physical coercion protects the relations of ownership while the extraction of the surplus product is realized through an economic means (wage). The pervasiveness and higher number of ideological rituals in lineage societies (direct involvement at both society and state levels) distinguished them from other societies. As in capitalist and feudal societies, ideological rituals helped to reproduce the real conditions of existence. Unlike in capitalist and feudal societies, however, the *daily functioning* of the real conditions of existence *relied also on ideological coercion* rather than on physical or economic coercion. Ideology and ideological coercion regulated daily and directly the relations of ownership and the extraction of the surplus product, the relationship between the rulers and the ruled, and competing individual or group interests.

The lineage mode was, thus, specific; it relied on ideological core relations. Ideological rituals played the double role of reproducing *and* governing the real conditions of existence daily. The double reliance and dependence on ideology had important consequences. By being reproduced by ideological rituals and by relying on them daily for the organization/extraction of surplus product, the real conditions of existence of lineage societies were made *doubly* and inextricably dependent on these rituals. As in other societies, this led to ideological routinization. However, unlike in feudal or capitalist societies where physical coercion intervenes, the level of ideological routinization was higher in lineage societies because of the double dependence on ideology. The result was structural indistinguishability between the real conditions of existence of individuals and ideological practices and rituals. For people in lineage societies, the reality and ideology were (are) indistinguishable; ideological practices and rituals became interchangeable with real life, more so than under feudalism and capitalism. Lineage members did not consciously create this situation because no 'consciousness' is involved here. For this reason, ancestral cults, rituals, sorcery, or witchcraft must not be seen as superstition, tricks, or lies; nor should these practices be reduced to characteristic features of 'backward' societies. They constituted 'real life' for the people involved. The discussion in this section is summarized in figures 4.1 and 4.2.

Figure 4.1. Lineage Mode, Imaginary Relationships, and Ideological Routinization

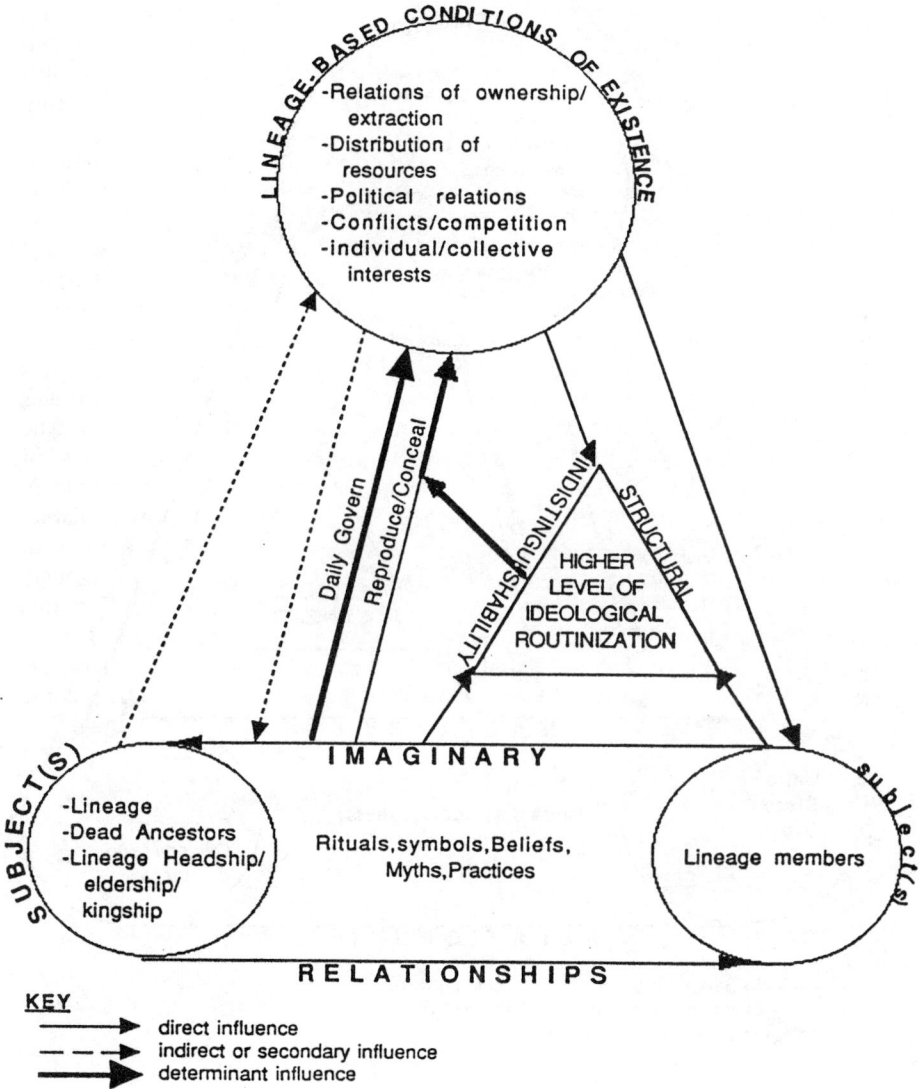

Figure 4.2. Capitalist and Feudal Modes, Imaginary Relationships, and Ideological Routinization

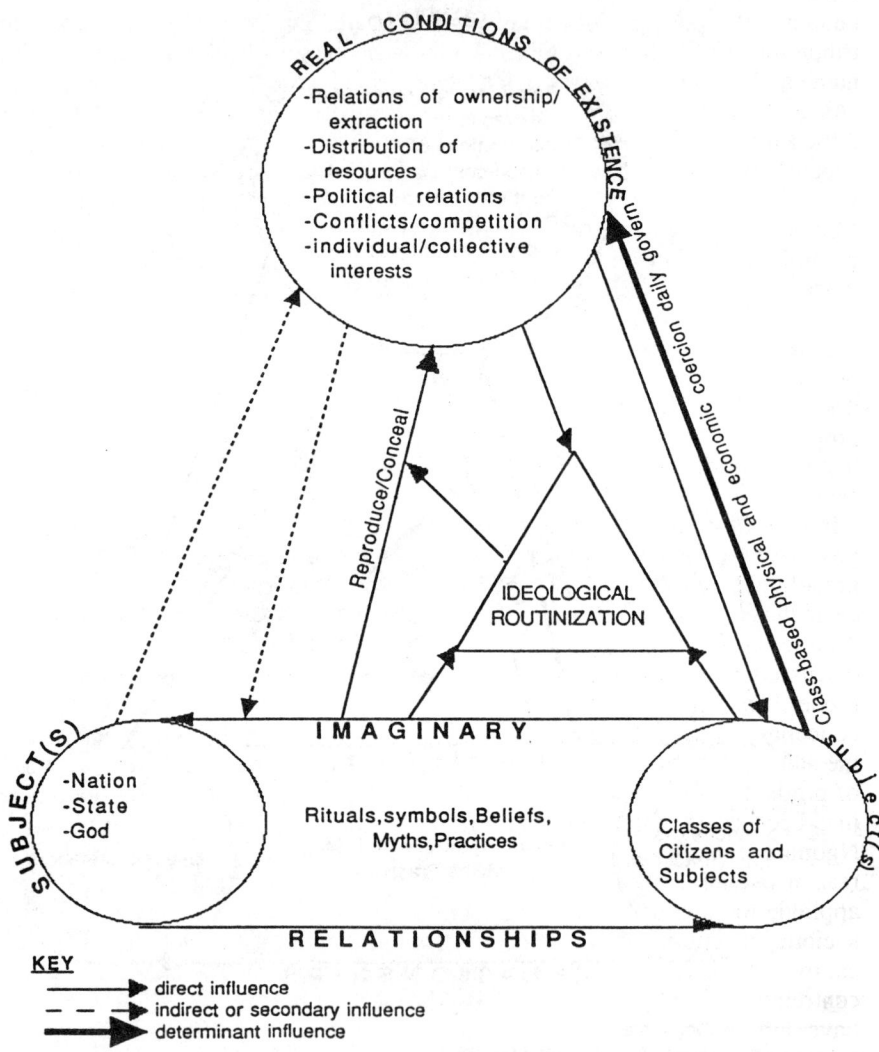

Conclusion

For some authors the notion of the Asiatic mode is inaccurate because it seems to suggest the existence of a single mode of production. Moreover, it is an inaccurate characterization of the tribute-paying mode of production because the latter existed not only in Asia but also in Europe (Crete and Etruria), pre-Columbian America, and in Africa. Calling it the Asiatic mode is, therefore, tantamount to suggesting wrongly that it existed only in Asia. As a result, the tribute-paying mode is substituted for the Asiatic mode.[60] Rather than change the name and extend it geographically, other writers have sought to restrict the term 'Asiatic mode' to specific societies other than African ones because 'Nowhere in Africa do we find generalized slavery, which made the state an entrepreneur, capable, despite the low level of technology, of carrying out enormous public works – hydraulic (the irrigation systems of the river states of the Near and Middle East), military (the Great Wall of China) or prestigious (the Egyptian pyramids).'[61] Other observers reject the notion in toto on other grounds. Perry Anderson argues that neither hydraulic works nor communal property, on which Marx based his views (of the Asiatic mode), were to be found in all Asiatic societies. Whereas Turkey, Persia, and India were marked by the absence of private property in land and important public irrigation works, China had both private property in land and major irrigation systems. Anderson does not propose a substitute for the notion of the Asiatic mode, but suggests that historical studies be undertaken to determine the type of mode of production in each society.[62]

In light of the evidence presented here, public works, tribute, or small private property are not enough to justify a typology of modes of production in the precolonial societies discussed. By concentrating on core relations, it becomes clear that the distinction made between the lineage mode and the tributary (or Asiatic) mode is false. The evidence reveals that the precolonial societies discussed here were governed by a single mode of production: the lineage mode. This stand implies a rejection of the tributary or Asiatic mode. The concept of mode of production rests on its core relations, and society makes the state and not the opposite. It follows that there is no reason why the mode of production of the Kongo kingdom or Luba empire would be tribute-paying just because they had centralized states whereas those of the Ambuun or Ngombe would be referred to as lineage mode or communal mode. There is no reason even for Southeast Asian societies, to which the Asiatic mode was applied, to have modes of production different from those in the African societies discussed in this work. The reasons behind the elevation of ideological means to the position of core relations were the same in noncentralized and centralized societies. They were also the same in Southeast Asian societies.[63] I have argued that this reliance on ideological core relations reflected the primacy of lineage ties over class relations; in the absence of class exploitation, political power and the extraction of surplus product relied on ideological coercion rather than on class-based physical coercion. For this reason, lineage societies secreted a higher dose of ideological rituals than other types of society. The pervasiveness of ideology led to a higher level of ideological routinization; the latter manifested itself in the structural indistinguishability between imaginary relationships (ideological rituals) and real conditions of existence. The higher level of ideological routinization and its attendant structural indistinguishability were the constitutive elements of the dynamism of precolonial societies.

Notes

1. See Daniel Biebuyck, *Lega Culture*, pp. 66, 120–123, 132.
2. Vansina, *The Children of Woot*, p. 165.
3. J. Thornton, *op. cit.*, p. 17.
4. Ibid., p. 32. Emphasis added.
5. Ibid., p. 16.
6. Ibid., p. 38.
7. See, for instance, Walter Rodney, *How Europe Underdeveloped Africa*, pp. 38–48; S. A. Dange, *India: From Primitive Communism to Slavery* (New Delhi: People's Publishing House, 1972).
8. Thornton, *op. cit.*, p. 22.
9. Ibid., p. 23.
10. Ibid., p. 28.
11. Ibid., p. 57. Emphasis added.
12. Ibid., p. 34. Emphasis added.
13. Ibid., p. 35.
14. A. Hilton, *op. cit.*, p. 201.
15. Ibid., p. 46. Emphasis added.
16. A. Hilton, *op. cit.*, p. 43.
17. Vansina, *The Children of Woot*, pp. 169, 171.
18. Vansina, *The Children of Woot*, p. 97.
19. Ibid., p. 115. Emphasis added.
20. Thornton, *op. cit.*, p. 57.
21. Vansina, 'Le Régime foncier dans la société Kuba,' p. 924.
22. Vansina, *The Children of Woot*, p. 160.
23. Ibid., pp. 208–209.
24. Ibid., p. 129.
25. Ibid., p. 117.
26. Ibid., p. 197.
27. Ibid., p. 130.
28. R. Packard, *Chiefship and Cosmology*, p. 4.
29. Placide Tempels, *Bantu Philosophy* (Paris: Présence Africaine, 1959), pp. 67–68.
30. W. G. L. Randles, *op. cit.*, pp. 42–43, 50.
31. I have borrowed this characterization from Gavin Kitching; see his *Class and Economic Change in Kenya*, pp. 443–444.
32. MacGaffey, *op. cit.*, p. 263. Emphasis added.

33. According to Jewsiewicki ('Lineage Mode of Production,' in Crummey and Stewart, *op. cit.*, pp.101–102) the changes in the organization of labor and technology explained the formation of the state in the nineteenth century, because labor and technology allowed the autonomy of political organization vis-a-vis lineage. There is no doubt that the state enjoys some autonomy in its relationship with society; and the precolonial state was no exception. It is debatable, however, whether this autonomy can be posited as the prerequisite to state formation. Jewsiewicki even talks of these states being based on the 'progressive destruction' of lineage and on dependents and slaves. One wonders how a state based on simple dependents and slaves was possible in a society deeply shaped by lineages. Unless the state was identical and reducible to the capital city, the argument is questionable. The attempt to dissociate the state from society explains why, for Jewsiewicki, state formation occurred only in the nineteenth century; in his view, the presence of strong lineage ties would not explain the presence of a state before then. Contrary to this view, the tension between the lineage structure and the state structure, recorded in other African societies (see L. Fallers, *Bantu Bureaucracy*, pp.227–238) reveals that lineage was the backbone of society on which political power rested.
34. Marc Block, *Feudal Society*, Vol. 1, p. 142.
35. See E. Terray, *op. cit.*, pp. 137–156.
36. Ibid., p. 151.
37. C. Meillassoux, 'Essai d'interpretation de phénomène économique dans les sociétés traditionnelles d'auto-subsistence,' *Cahiers d'Etudes Africaines*, No. 4 (December 1960): p. 47.
38. Terray, *op. cit.*, p. 131.
39. See P. P. Rey, *Colonialisme, néo-colonialisme et transition au capitalisme*.
40. Meillassoux, 'Essai d'interpretation ...,' p. 47.
41. See, for instance, Franz Schurmann, *ideology and Organization in Communist China* (Berkeley: University of California Press, 1968); Crawford Young, *Ideology and Development in Africa* (New Haven: Yale University Press, 1982); Theda Skocpol, *States and Revolutions: A Comparative Analysis of France, Russia, and China* (Cambridge: Cambridge University Press, 1979), pp. 168 ff.; Martin Seliger, *The Marxist Conception of Ideology*; Fernand Dumont, *Les Ideologies* (Paris: PUF, 1969); G. Luckas, *History and Class Consciousness* (London, 1971); V. Lenin, *What Is To Be Done?* (Moscow: Progress Publishers); L. Dumont, *Homo Hierarchicus: The Caste System and Its Implications* (London, 1970), pp. ff.; Karl Manheim, *Ideology and Utopia*, HBJ, 1985; Clifford Geertz, *The Interpretation of Cultures* (New York: Basic Books, 1973), pp.193–233.
42. M. Rejai, *Comparative Political Ideologies*, pp. 3–9.
43. See Roy Macridis, *Contemporary Political Ideologies*, Chapter 1.
44. Rejai, *op. cit.*, p. 5.
45. See F. Dumond, *op. cit.*
46. See Althusser, *Lenin and Philosophy and Other Essays*; and Poulantzas, *Political Power and Social Classes*, pp. 206 ff.
47. Althusser, Ibid., p. 165.
48. Stephan Feuchtwang, 'Investigating Religion' (Mimeo, 1975, p. 68.
49. Althusser, *op. cit.*, pp. 168–169.

50. Schurmann, op. cit., chap. 1.

51. MacGaffey, *op. cit.*, p. 82.

52. Burton, *op. cit.*, p. 62.

53. MacGaffey, *op. cit.*, p. 249.

54. This is the case with the 'cult of spirits,' which was not part of the ancestral cult or ordinary arsenal of sorcery practices. But this does not mean that the spirits remain in the realm of 'unexplainable myths.' An interesting hypothesis, to help interpret these spirits in light of the theoretical guidelines discussed, has been advanced by Buakasa Tulu (*L'impensé du discours*, pp. 294). He suggests that the cult of spirits, which affected the whole village (as opposed to a given lineage), was the result of guilt on the part of new occupants of the village, who may have occupied the land of their predecessors by force. To calm these vanquished predecessors, who could breed hatred against them, the new occupants of the land organized rituals and cults. On the surface, these rituals and cults do not appear to be a by-product of an imaginary relationship between a lineage and its membership, but rather one between the villagers and the dead. A closer examination, however, reveals otherwise. Indeed, the collective cult of the spirits was not actually collective, since each village had a core lineage. It is plausible to assume that the guilt, hence the cult, was organized under the leadership of the core lineage of the village. In this case, the notion of imaginary relationship applies. This hypothesis helps explain non-African societies where rituals were not explicitly lineage-based, or where ancestral cults were not practiced, as in many African societies.

55. See K. A. Wittfogel, *Oriental Despotism* (New Haven: Yale University Press, 1963).

56. See Roland Mousnier, 'Quelques remarques pour une comparaison des monarchies absolues en Europe et en Asie,' Revue Historique, no. 551 (July–September 1984): 29–43.

57. Coquery-Vidrovitch, 'The Political Economy of the Peasantry,' p. 105.

58. Vansina, *Introduction à l'ethnographie du Congo*, p. 4.

59. K. Marx, *A Contribution to the Critique of Political Economy* (Chicago: Charles H. Kerr, 1904), p. 30.

60. S. Amin, *Unequal Development*, Chapter 1.

61. Coquery-Vidrovitch, 'The Political Economy of the African Peasantry and Modes of Production,' p. 105.

62. See P. Anderson, *op. cit.*, pp. 403–491.

63. See Nguyen Khac Kham, *An Introduction to Vietnamese Culture*; David Chandler, *A History of Cambodia*. Boulder, CO: Westview Press, 1983 ; Paul Chao, *Chinese Kinship* (London: Kegan Paul International, 1983).

5 Explaining pseudocapitalism

In chapter 4, I argued that precolonial lineage societies were characterized by higher levels of ideological routinization than other societies. The consequence was the structural indistinguishability between the real conditions of existence and ideological rituals, which constituted the dynamism of these societies. I argue here, in an attempt to propose an alternative explanation of society in Zaire, that the higher level of ideological routinization and its attendant noncapitalist path of development neutralized the implantation of capitalism. As a result, capitalism adopted contradictory policies, which led to pseudocapitalism in colonial and postcolonial societies.

1. The Precolonial Noncapitalist Path of Development

In chapter 2, I argued against the stagnation thesis by recognizing the development of the forces of production in precolonial societies. Refuting the stagnation thesis and recognizing that there was change in precolonial societies breeds its own danger. One may easily be tempted to connect such a change with capitalism. With respect to Zaire's societies proper, such a danger is present in the use, if ambiguous, of some phrases. For instance, Harms writes: 'African traders could not have undertaken this initiative had not the basic institutions and concepts necessary for trade and capitalistic activity already existed in equatorial African society. Trade had existed for a long time, and so had the practices of renting out capital goods and paying wages in kind. The international economy provides opportunities for expanding and strengthening the mercantile and capitalistic elements that already existed in riverine society; it did not create them.'[1]

It is true that capital, in its broader sense, does not necessarily imply capitalism. Unless 'capitalistic' is used in this broad sense, it can scarcely be consistent with both theoretical and empirical evidence. For example, working for wages in kind was generally done by sons working with their fathers or nephews working with their uncles, but any child could work for any adult and any poor person could work for any rich one.[2] If the practice took place generally between a father and a son, an uncle and a nephew, or even between an adult and a child, it cannot be thought of as a class-induced or capitalist wage. The prevalence of the lineage structure is obvious. For capitalist relations to take place, a change would have been necessary to make the basic relations of production of society resemble capitalist ones. Obviously, this did not happen, as Harms himself points out: 'These changes did not occur smoothly. ... Activities changed rapidly, institutions changed more slowly, and ideology changed little or not at all. ... Despite the tremendous changes that accompanied the expansion of the market, certain fundamental structures remained intact.'[3]

What was this ideology? Why did it not change? Why did the basic relations of production ('fundamental structures') remain intact? In other words, why were precolonial societies not capitalist? (This question differs from the evolutionary one: Why did they not become capitalist?) Bogumil Jewsiewicki has argued that 'the appropriation of collective surplus in the form of men, both by the elders and by the political structures, weakened potential demographic pressures and limited the internal dynamic of the mode of production, thus ensuring a greater stability of the basic structures.'[4] This explanation is only slightly different from the stagnation thesis; I reject it. Others have insisted that the abhorrence of exploitation and profit in these societies go arm in arm with the rejection of wage labor. The motto was 'to each according to his need' (not 'according to his capacities').[5] No one worked as an agrarian laborer, no one worked by the day, and no one wished to be someone else's servant for a wage.[6] Moreover, accumulation of wealth by one individual at the expense of the others was equated with sorcery and condemned by all lineage members: 'An individual who displayed more entrepreneurship and was willing to take advantage of possible gaps between supply and demand was hated by all. One's advancement and good fortune caused in them [the Kongo people] a fit of anger. ... They fabricated lies to oppose and wreck him, till he fell in disgrace vis-à-vis the king and other authorities.'[7]

This does not mean that the people of precolonial Zaire/Africa did not 'by nature' like exploitation, wage, or profit. It does not imply 'primitive communism' either because private property and competition were allowed. Wage, exploitation, and profit were despised within the social context provided by lineage. Therefore, the answer to the central question of why these societies were not capitalist is found only through a comparison of capitalism, as a mode of production, with the lineage mode (see chaps. 1 and 4). Capitalism is characterized first by the separation of the producer from the means of production at both the ownership and productive process levels. However important, private ownership and commodity markets are simple appendages to this core relationship. By relying on wage, capitalism reflects this double separation; the separation is consistent with relations of production based on the extraction of surplus product from one class by another class. Wage (an economic form of coercion) and physical coercion govern daily this separation and form of extraction. The most important definitional element of the lineage mode, on the other hand, is its ideological core relations that led to the structural indistinguishability between ideology and the real conditions of existence. For it to make a 'transition' to the capitalist mode, a fundamental prerequisite would have to be met; the lineage mode would have to offer the possibility for a double separation similar to that under capitalism to occur. The lineage mode was intrinsically incongruent with this double separation. The ideological core relations, their attendant higher level of routinization, and, hence, the structural indistinguishability of lineage societies prevented the separation.

To elaborate: because of the double role played by ideology in lineage societies, ideological rituals became almost the same as real life; this perpetuated the intrinsically noncapitalist relations. It must be recalled that ideology reproduces the real conditions of existence of individuals by subordinating these conditions to its imaginary relationships and rituals; as noted, these conditions (social order) cannot stand on their own. In lineage societies this dependence was stronger because of the double role of ideology. Unlike in other societies, the very pervasiveness of ideological rituals almost totally controlled the reproduction conditions of the social order, especially its relations. For social individuals, rituals and their real conditions of existence were more indistinguishable than in other types of society. This higher level of routinization could not allow capitalist-like change in their basic production relations or core relations; for these relations themselves became ritualized and rituals (see figs 4.1 and 4.2). Changes in forces of production, tensions, and conflicts did take place, but they did not alter core relations so highly routinized. These were reproduced over time in a consistently noncapitalist way. The reproduction affected the collective ownership of the major means of production, land; dual control over the labor process whereby lineage and the worker qua lineage member owned different categories of the means of labor; and the extraction and redistribution of surplus product. The state reflected society, and its reliance on ideological coercion also perpetuated the noncapitalist relations. The best illustration of this is provided by the king's intervention in reinforcing and legitimizing lineage-based relations/competition among his subjects and clients. The perpetuation of the noncapitalist path of development in Central Africa closely resembled that in Southeast Asia: 'The determinancy of the ideological, embodied in the actions of the state, places severe restrictions on the processes of capital accumulation, the private ownership of land or capital, and, of course, on any separation of direct producers from their means of production (except for occasional seasonal or cyclical labour in the state 'factories' or mines.'[8]

In short, the higher level of ideological routinization in lineage societies had two results. First, it reproduced their fundamental socioeconomic relationships. Second, this reproduction perpetuated these relationships in a way inconsistent with capitalist relations. The result was a noncapitalist path of development. Because they were not capitalist, these precolonial societies appeared 'stagnant' to dualist and transition theorists.

2. Capitalism Neutralized

Pseudocapitalism does not imply that capitalism did not expand in Zaire. Nor does it suggest that capitalism did not affect society. My thesis that the lineage mode neutralized capitalism does not write off the responsibility for the colonial policies that contributed to pseudocapitalism. I do not completely dismiss the imperialism-inspired argument; my point is that it is overblown. To put my thesis in its proper perspective, some preliminary remarks about the points made by imperialism-inspired theories are in order. I will comment on economic growth, the exploitative impact of imperialism, the degree of success of capitalist expansion, and the role of colonial policies as they apply to Zaire before discussing how the lineage mode neutralized capitalism.

A Case for Imperialism-Inspired Theories

Accumulation and economic growth defined by indicators such as national product, sectoral growth, or gross investment were not lacking in colonial Zaire. Its rate of capital investments was undoubtedly one of the highest in developing countries. The average ratio between gross investment and national revenue considerably exceeded the minimum 15 percent required to sustain reasonable economic growth, according to most macroeconomists. Its average ratio was 34 percent for the 1950–60 period, which was higher than that of South Africa, Argentina, or Brazil.[9] The industrial infrastructure was one of the most advanced in developing areas as well, with one of the highest rates of increase in industrial production (14 percent per year). By 1958 the rate of contribution of the industrial sector to the national product was the highest in Africa: 8 percent as compared with a mere 2 percent in all French West Africa and Nigeria.[10] Zaire's mineral production was among the highest in the world.

The role of imperialism in the exploitation of the Third World is recognized. In colonial Zaire, the rate of profit extracted by metropolitan companies offers a clear illustration. The rate was far higher than that obtained in Belgium (table 5.1).

Moreover, capitalism did expand in African societies. Infiltration in the specific case of colonial Zaire was not identical to that obtained elsewhere in the Third World because capitalism itself underwent phased transformations. In some cases, penetration took place under mercantilist capitalism (Latin America and Indonesia). In other cases, capitalism expanded during its competitive stage or later. Given the different patterns of capitalist expansion, the effects in different colonies were not the same. These differences notwithstanding, capitalist expansion in Zaire shares crucial similarities with that in other Third World countries. In addition to the strong involvement of the colonial state, attempts at capitalist expansion took place through new forms of taxation, which caused Africans to sell their labor power as wage earners; through the policy of land expropriation and redistribution to private interests; and through infrastructural projects, forced labor, and recruitment. These policies often coercively prepared the conditions for displacing workers from the lineage mode and for separating them from the means of labor. Attempts at capitalist expansion were accompanied by the eclosion of class relations.

Table 5.1: Net income of industrial enterprises in Belgium and in the colony (percentage of invested capital), 1936-57

Year	Enterprises in Belgium	Enterprises in the colony
1936–39	7.00%	10.10%
1947–50	6.88%	15.00%
1951–54	8.20%	21.48%
1955	8.19%	18.47%
1956	9.40%	20.16%
19 57	9.49%	21.00%

Source: P. Joyce and R. Lewin, *Les trusts au Congo* (Brussels: Société Populaire d'Editions, 1961), p. 57

In the case of industrial workers, for instance, one has to examine state-sponsored campaigns of recruitment, which first involved recruiting free labor. Recruitment agencies (*bourse du travail*) were established in the Katanga (Shaba), Léopoldville (Kinshasa), and Kasai provinces and were given full support by the colonial state. Throughout the colony, state agents worked in close collaboration with indigenous chiefs to turn peasants into workers. However, 'free labor was quickly to give way to forced labor which was a brutal process which soon generated serious concern among some missionary and administration circles but was not altered until the depression, when massive short-term recruitment was gradually superseded by a manpower stabilization program.'[11] Recruitment was not limited to manufacturing and mining industries; in the rural areas, concessionary companies and other medium-sized agro-industrial enterprises also used state power to satisfy their labor needs.

Although the depression years significantly decreased the number of workers recruited, the war effort, by contrast, helped increase the number of workers in industry. Nationally, according to 1959 figures, there were 1,097,000 workers, most of whom were hired by the mining, agricultural, building, and manufacturing industries. Katanga province prevailed in the distribution of the wage-earning population in the mining sector. Although its share of African workers was somewhat smaller than that of Kivu Province, the number of European wage earners was the highest in the colony. Katanga Province, the locus of the leading mining industry, had 32.3 percent of the African wage-earners in mining and 71 percent of the European wage earners in the same sector. The evolution of the working class on a national scale was influenced by the economic ups and downs of the depression and World War II. The number of workers declined in 1930 and 1932 before jumping to a high during the war and the post-war expansion period. On the whole, the Belgian Congo had the third largest number of African wage earners, behind South Africa and Egypt.[12] Owing to stabilization programs, the working class was also one of the most stable on the continent (table 5.2).

Table 5.2: Wage labor in selected African colonies, 1952–54

Country	Year	Number in wage employment (in 000s)	Total population (in 000s)	% of population engaged in wage labor
Kenya	1953	453	4,644	8.0
Tanganyika	1954	439	8,084	5.4
Nigeria	1952	300	31,170	1.0
Northern Rhodesia	1954	265	2,010	13.2
Uganda	1954	225	5,365	4.2
Ghana	1952	216	4,478	4.8
French West Africa	1952	318	15,996	2.0
Madagascar	1952	195	4,150	4.7
French Equatorial Africa	1952	155	4,131	3.9
Cameroons	1952	112	2,854	3.8
Angola	1961	156	4,037	3.9
Ruanda-Urundi	1954	129	4,263	3.0
Belgian Congo	1954	1,146	12,317	9.3

Source: F. Bézy, *Problèmes Structurels de l'Economie Congolaise* (Louvain: Institut de Recherches Economiques et Sociales, 1957), p. 102.

Social categories other than wage workers were affected by the expansion of capitalism. Perhaps the best known attempt to propose a class nomenclature for the Belgian Congo is that by Nzongola-Ntalaja.[13] Although Nzongola has retracted some of his earlier views, his basic nomenclature can serve as a point of departure here. In addition to workers and the multi-layered European bourgeoisie, he includes the traditional ruling class (chiefs), peasants, lumpenproletariat, and petty bourgeoisie. Each of these categories was affected by the expansion of capitalism. Land and fiscal policies of the colonial state were instrumental in increasing peasants' contact with capitalism and led to the 'widening and depersonalization of market relations consequent to the introduction of a pervasive cash economy and a colonial state.'[14] The process was uneven across the regions of the colony. Because compulsory cultivation affected each region differently, involvement of the peasants in a 'depersonalized market' varied from one region to another.

The lumpenproletariat's link to capitalism was indirect. The industrialization process and higher wages in urban areas affected rural areas, stimulating rural exodus and feeding a preexisting country-to-town movement triggered by exactions by the colonial state. In urban centers the job market did not follow the demographic increase. The result was unemployment, which was exacerbated by the depression years. Displaced workers and migrants from rural areas were later joined by young school dropouts. They all formed a specific category of city dwellers, the lumpenproletariat. It can be estimated that by 1958 one million were unemployed in the cities. The lumpenproletariat also held a classlike position. Nzongola argued that 'economically and socially, the lumpenproletariat was clearly distinguishable from the other African social classes, by the manner in which its members earned their living and by the behavioral patterns associated with their adventurous and parasitical mode of life.' He adds that the common discourse opposed this class to other classes by identifying them as *chomeurs* (the unemployed) as opposed to those doing useful work.[15]

Capitalism affected the development of the petty bourgeoisie through a whole range of factors. Because of the introduction of a unified means of exchange (money), some formerly long-distance traders managed to prosper in spite of serious setbacks by colonial policies. In a study devoted to southwestern Katanga (Shaba), Jean-Luc Vellut shows this relationship between trade and wealth accumulated by chiefs and traders:

> Agricultural produce also entered the early colonial market economy. In some cases trading in foodstuffs was actually an expansion of former regional bartering. For example the trade in palm oil, which by 1905 had made the fortune of Chief Lumpungu, had linked for many years the oil-consuming and fish-producing areas of the Lualaba with the complementary economies of the Luba-Songe country farther north. In the immediate neighbourhood of European settlements, administrative and military coercion played some part in bringing agricultural produce to the market, but at least by the 1910's small-scale private entrepreneurs were playing a more important role. African and European petty traders, recruiters, sub-contractors, etc., roamed villages to purchase foodstuffs and to entice men to seek employment with Europeans.[16]

Trade encouraged new forms of rural oppression through the more widespread use of slaves and the exploitation of women. Through their economic influence, indigenous traders challenged the existing traditional political power. Chiefs, locally recruited soldiers, and African supervisors (*capitas*) became pillars of the colonial state as it strove to implement its policies; they made fortunes that contributed to their economic and political power. Under colonial rule the chiefs/kings not only received tribute from their subjects but also were on the payroll of the colonial administration. Some of them became involved in the trading business. Auxiliary agents, such as *capitas*, increased their power by extracting for themselves additional surplus from the peasants. Compared with a country like Côte d'Ivoire, where 'commercial agriculture fostered the growth of a stratum of Africans who shared similar concerns and who were affected in the same way by colonial policies, competition with European *Colons*, and cyclical fluctuations in the world market for primary commodities,'[17] colonial Zaire was far from displaying a large stratum of entrepreneurs. However, as colonial rule proceeded, chiefs, capitas, and traders were joined by other self-employed elements of the indigenous population. In 1959, there were about 2,481 planters, 3,567 artisans, 11,113 traders, 1,576 small businessmen, and 29 liberal professionals.[18] Their total share of invested capital amounted to only 5 percent of the total invested capital in 1958.

The colonial ideology of 'civilization,' the need for economic accumulation, and the increasing bureaucratization of colonial society set in motion two separate but complementary mechanisms. On the one hand, indigenous populations had to meet fixed standards of so-called civilization through school attendance or church enrollment. Such devices as the *carte de mérite civique* were instituted as certificates verifying one's compliance with the stated norm of civilization. On the other hand, through the establishment of on-the-job training and religious and educational programs, Africans were trained to fill the lower positions in the colonial bureaucracy, in business, and in the service sector, and to become schoolteachers and gospel preachers. It was estimated that on the eve of independence there were 11,550 African civil servants, most of whom were lower level clerks; the number of teachers was estimated at 44,069 in 1959.[19] Along with traders, chiefs, capitas, planters, and small businessmen, they formed a distinct social category – Nzongola's petty bourgeoisie. The highly elitist process that led to their selection contributed greatly to 'class consciousness' among members of the petty bourgeoisie. Nzongola has shown their troubled yet enduring unity through political practices, especially in the postindependence period.

As will be seen in the final section of this chapter, the economic dislocation that prevailed in colonial Zaire had three aspects: absence of capitalist links at the input/output, sectoral, and geographical levels. The role of colonial policies cannot be denied. The case of the dependence on exports is a good illustration. There were policies designed to increase export revenues in order to remunerate invested capital and to contribute to the state's budget. By 1950 Zaire had become the leading African and world producer of cobalt (86 percent of African production, 60 percent of world production), the world's leading producer of industrial diamonds (64 percent of the world's supply), and an important world producer of copper (7 percent of the supply). It produced 70 percent of African tin, 53 percent of its zinc, 51 percent of its silver, and also became an important producer of gold.[20] On the average, the export of mineral products was highest, with about 60 percent of the total value of exports; agricultural products came second (30 percent), and manufactured goods stood at about 10 percent. In spite of the huge profit margin accumulated in the colony by investing companies, colonial policies made it difficult for the profit to contribute to a viable self-sustained capitalist economy. The assumption that the distribution pattern favorable to the upper-income strata would induce savings for further investments did not hold true in the Belgian Congo. The consumption of luxury goods absorbed an important share of high incomes. In addition, much of the private savings was transferred to Europe, as was a substantial portion of the profits realized by private enterprises (table 5.3).

Table 5.3: The utilization of surplus by private companies (in billions of francs at 1950 value)

Year	Divi-dends	Amortiz-ations	Reserves	Taxes	Transfer of Profits	Private transfer	Outside private expendi-tures	Trans-port and insur-ance
1950	3.2	1.8	4.7	1.2	−1.2	−0.9	–	−1.1
1951	3.6	2.2	6.7	1.3	−1.3	−0.5	–	−2.5
1952	3.7	2.9	7.1	1.4	−1.7	−0.4	–	−2.8
1953	4.0	3.8	4.8	2.0	−2.2	−0.5	−0.6	−3.5
1954	5.0	4.4	4.2	2.1	−2.4	−0.6	−0.8	−4.5
1955	6.2	4.9	3.7	2.2	−3.2	−0.7	−1.0	−5.3
1956	6.3	5.3	4.4	2.2	−4.4	−1.0	−1.3	−6.4
1957	4.8	5.5	1.7	3.3	−3.5	−1.3	−1.5	−6.8
1958	5.0	5.9	1.2	2.0	−3.4	−1.4	−1.7	−5.4
1959	–	–	–	–	−4.0	−3.5	−1.7	−5.9

Source: J. P. Peemans, 'Capital Accumulation in the Congo under Colonialism: The Role of the State,' in *Colonialism in Africa 1870–1960*, ed. P. Duignan and L. H. Gann (Cambridge: Cambridge University Press, 1975), pp. 197 and 198.(–) in the last four columns indicates the transfer of surplus from the colony to the metropolis.

The high rate of profit in the colony and its easy transfer caused new investments to flow into the most profitable sectors of the economy, that is, into the already dislocated sectors. Although reliance on exports helped remunerate invested capital, it allowed the colonial state to draw, through taxation, on invested capital's revenues. Tax on exports contributed more to the state budget than any other source of revenue. The more a sector (e.g. mineral products) contributed to colonial exports, the more revenues it provided to the colonial state. In 1958, for instance, exit tax on mineral products was 1,241 million francs; on agricultural products, 613 million francs, and on other products 1 million francs, which is 0.05 percent of the total exit tax.[21]

The role of colonial policies is also evident in social dislocation, that is, in the lack of capitalist implantation among various social categories or groups in the colony. State policies of capitalist reproduction were instrumental in distorting the pattern of involvement of social actors in the process of production. The system of violence used to extract compulsory work, the suppression of free trade, and the substantial reduction by 1925 of the rights of the African population to develop small trade eliminated incentives for economic development within the normal framework of capitalism. It suppressed the profit motive in the process of production; the corollary was the elimination of the necessary conditions for the development of a viable internal market. The structure of the economy was so much shaped by the relationship between the colonial state and large- and medium-sized corporations that African small enterprises could not play a role in the diversification and interdependence of the sectors of the economy. But more importantly, the process of accumulation based on coercion of the rural producers reduced them to passive economic actors who produced first to satisfy tax requirements.

Even though the simple act of privatizing land does not make capitalism, the more interventionist Belgian policies in this and other areas somewhat differentiated the Belgian Congo from French or British colonies. Indeed, in the latter cases, peasant agriculture benefited greatly from the policies of the colonial state. French and British colonial officials put obstacles in the way of foreign small traders in rural areas to encourage the development of local small traders or farmers.[22] This encouragement had the effect of 'privatizing' the rural economy for the benefit of the African populations. This was the case in such countries as Côte d'Ivoire and Ghana, where local populations succeeded in developing a rural economy based on big plantations of coffee and cacao. On some of these plantations, immigrant or local labor was hired by the African owners.[23] In the Belgian Congo, on the other hand, the marginal role assigned to the African populations in the process of capitalist accumulation resulted in their exclusion from capital ownership. In 1958, two years before independence, indigenous populations, who made up 99 percent of the colonial population, shared only 5 percent of the total invested capital, and controlled only 18 percent of the means of production and 30 percent of the material production.[24]

The quasi-total exclusion of the African populations from influencing the process of production and reproduction contributed to the dislocated character of capitalism. Exclusion limited its relations of production socially. The foreign private sector and the colonial state dominated the structure of ownership. On the private side, the structure of ownership was dominated by some powerful financial groups, such as the *Société Générale*, the Empain Group, the Brufina Group, and the Cominière Group. In 1932, these four groups controlled 75 percent of the invested capital in the colony. Small- and medium-sized entrepreneurs in service, agriculture, mining, and manufacturing shared the remaining private foreign capital. The colonial state's participation in capital ownership took place through direct and indirect investments, through which the colonial state held assets, shares, and rights in a variety of companies – public, semipublic, and private – totaling about two hundred. At the same time it had exclusive rights on mining and forest reserves and other types of land properties. During 1950–59 the average revenue drawn from the state was 1.1 billion francs. In 1920 those revenues made up 35 percent of the colonial state budget.

In short, then, I do not deny economic growth, imperialist exploitation, capitalist expansion, and the role of colonial policies. Yet, they do not attest to the implantation of capitalism. Neither commodity exchange nor exploitation is an exclusive attribute of capitalism. If this were the case, by virtue of its extensive commodity exchanges ancient Rome would have been capitalist. And if exploitation defined capitalism, then ancient forms of slavery or feudalism would have been capitalist systems. These features are important aspects of capitalism, but they are not sufficient conditions for its existence.[25] If anything, they, along with the empirical evidence on agrarian and industrial pseudocapitalism in the next two sections, only reveal the specificity of the colonial and postcolonial society; they denote the nonimplantation of capitalism, whose striking manifestation is the persistence of precolonial, noncapitalist relations. This interpretation raises the question of why capitalism did not implant itself (as opposed to simple expansion). This question was asked by Ernesto Laclau in 'almighty capitalism' terms: 'Why does [Western] capitalism maintain precapitalist relations of production in the third world?' His answer, predictably, is that it is necessary for capitalism to increase its rate of profit.[26] Here again, capitalism is credited with omnipotence in the face of 'passive' Third World societies. Capitalist/ imperialist exploitation or deliberate decisions by colonial authorities only partially, if at all, answer this question.

The Primacy of the Neutralization Thesis

Capitalism's efficiency is indissociable from its means of action. In pursuing its goal of exploitation and accumulation in Zaire/Third world, it arranged its means according to its requirements as a mode of production. (This holds true even if one bears in mind the much-stressed point that the influence of capitalism differed according to its phases – merchant, commodity, competitive, or monopoly). Racial prejudices or 'primitive accumulation' notwithstanding, it is difficult to imagine European entrepreneurs of the nineteenth and early twentieth centuries completely changing their ways of doing business just because they dealt with 'primitive' people whom they loved to exploit. As non-European societies were colonized, the probability for European entrepreneurs to use means congruent with capitalism was high. Moreover, even if one takes into account the notion of 'exploitation colony' and various payments and transfers to the metropolis, there is no evidence that the colonial powers and conquerors were prepared to exploit their colonies and leave. Most did not foresee the end of colonial rule; also, the frequent turnover in European colonial personnel never created a shortage of European settlers in the colonies. There is no reason why capitalism would not have had recourse to its normal means and implanted itself.

Yet, the evidence points to the lack of congruence between capitalism's requirements and the means used in its exploitation of Central African socie-ties/Zaire and in its attempt to establish itself there. Why? The reproduction of the intrinsically noncapitalist relations and path of development by the lineage mode *neutralized* the means of implantation of capitalism (see chap. 4 and the previous section). The neutralization resulted in contradictory and anti-capital-ist colonial policies; it also allowed – contrary to Laclau's claims – precapital-ist relations to persist.

There was a link between the noncapitalist path of development and contra-dictory colonial policies. As noted in chapter 1, capitalist convergence implies capitalism's social extension. The position taken is not that everyone should become a worker or a capitalist; it means that the capitalist core relations between these two actors ought to affect most, if not all, other social relations. The latter, in turn, strengthen capitalism. As seen in the previous section, in colonial Zaire the confrontation between capitalist core relations and ideologi-cal core relations (of the lineage mode) gave the edge to the lineage mode; blocked, capitalist core relations could not affect all other social relations. Social relations, in turn, could not strengthen capitalism, *forcing capitalism to retreat and adopt policies with grave disintegration consequences.*

One such policy was the development of enclave capitalist economies, the so-called development poles of which the Katanga region was the best illus-tration. Another major policy dictated by the limits imposed on capitalist implantation was a strong dependence on the world market. Indeed, the repro-duction of noncapitalist relations by the lineage mode severely limited the ability of the capitalist sector to create linkages with the noncapitalist sector, especially peasant agriculture. Because an integrative structure-induced demand was lacking and because the local industrial sector could absorb only a minimal quantity of locally produced raw materials, two processes were set in motion. Primacy was given to those resources (mineral and agricultural) that could provide the colonial state with revenues and, at the same time, suffi-ciently remunerate invested capital; however, only an external market suffi-ciently developed to absorb those raw materials could provide such revenue. The result was the emergence of an export-oriented economic structure subject to fluctuations of the world market. Even the massive transfer of profits from the colony was the direct outcome of the limits imposed on capitalism; inves-tors realized an uneven rate of profit realized by investors in a disintegrated economic structure. 'The exceptional rate of profit in certain sectors could not be reproduced in others because of the limited size of the internal market and the unequal distribution of income.'[27] Companies did not reinvest their net profit in new economic sectors that could have contributed to the production of intermediary goods or to the integration of isolated economic sectors. The intractability of the lineage mode explained the massive use of compulsion by the colonial state in its attempt to break noncapitalist relations and to justify expanded capitalism. In the same vein, it justified the opposite policy of accommodating Africans in the name of the '*spécificité de l'indigène*' (specificity of the natives).

The lineage mode, its higher ideological routinization, and the attendant noncapitalist path also determined colonial policies about social dislocation. The failure of the policy of land privatization (see the next section on agrarian pseudocapitalism) amply demonstrates this, as does the distribution of the means of production. Although the pattern of distribution of property and other means of production was, in most instances, a colonial policy decision, the very lack of implantation of capitalism prevented the extension of capitalist property relations among the African populations. Differently put, given the maintenance of noncapitalist relations, ownership of capitalist means of production was inescapably limited. It would be unrealistic to expect the pattern of the distribution of capitalist production to favor the African populations marked by noncapitalist relations. This view does not absolve the Belgians of their responsibility, especially in view of the more 'positive' stand of the French and British in West Africa. But it does show that the Belgian experience in colonial Zaire was not unique in this respect. The higher proportion of Africans owning plantations in West Africa or elsewhere was not by itself proof of capitalist implantation. It did not denote a distribution pattern of invested capital, capitalist means of production, and material production skewed in their favor. The proportion allocated to the African populations was in all cases smaller than that allocated to Europeans. Reasons causing the limitation of these capitalist property relations among Africans in colonial Zaire applied to other colonies as well. Even if one considers only the sheer number of Africans owning plantations in British or French colonies, the impact of the lineage mode there was as crucial as in the Belgian colony. Thus in Senegal, Nigeria, and Sudan, the chief planter extracted labor from workers not as a capitalist but as a traditional chief who used ideological coercion.[28]

The neutralization of capitalism by the lineage mode can be gauged further by considering the various social categories that were marked by the expansion of capitalism. As shown, owing to this expansion, some of them displayed class-like behavior. However, this behavior did not necessarily attest to their intrinsically capitalist character. Character can only be determined by investigating their role and place in the specific types of production relations introduced by capitalism. Not only did capitalist core relations not become established, they did not make the various social categories 'capitalist' or classes that depended on the capitalist core relations. To be sure, under colonial rule, the specific class character of some of these social categories could no longer be denied; they were not, however, under the exclusive influence of capitalist core relations as it would have been under capitalism. The reproduction of noncapitalist relations by the higher level of ideological routinization in the lineage mode prevented this from occurring.

Let us consider first those at the very core of capitalist relations. Speaking of Africa in general, some authors have distinguished between proletarianization and semi-proletarianization. Giovanni Arrighi and John Saul distinguished between the 'proletariat proper' and the 'semi-proletarianized peasantry.' The proletariat is 'generally a very small minority [who] receive incomes sufficiently high . . . . to justify a total break of their links with the peasantry. As for the semi-proletarianized peasants, they are only marginally or partially

119

proletarianized as, over their life cycle, they derive the bulk of the means of subsistence for their families from outside the wage economy.'[29] It has been argued that the distinction is misleading because it negates the relationship existing between the two in their common struggle.[30] No doubt, in many situations of class domination the distinction is useless because no such distinction is made about who should be repressed and who should not be. Likewise, when responding to the exploiting or dominating class, workers and peasants, proletarianized or semi-proletarianized, are likely to attempt to form a common front, even though such is not always the case. Considerations about the unity of the masses, however, sidetrack my point; at issue here is the position of these 'working masses' vis-à-vis the capitalist means of production, on the one hand, and the lineage mode on the other. Although the distinction – proletariat proper or semi-proletarianized peasantry – is questionable, it does point to the problematic character of capitalist core relations established under colonial rule. In colonial Zaire, various indices demonstrated this; for example, the seasonal and migrant labor that took place in the mining zones before the stabilization policy and in other regions and sectors of activities. To this one must add the compulsory cultivation that caused peasants to work temporarily for concessionary companies. In each of these instances, the relationship between African workers and the capitalist class was peculiar ; the separation of the workers from the means of production was affected temporarily. Caught between two modes of production, workers acted under two contradictory requirements imposed on them by the capitalist mode and by the lineage mode. In the lineage mode their position was one of nonseparation from the means of production.

Not all workers were in this situation. In colonial Zaire, after the stabilization policy, a category of proletariat proper, urban-based workers, lived outside the traditional milieu. Although colonial Zaire had one of the most stabilized working classes in colonial Africa, the lineage mode also neutralized the 'capitalist' character of this proletariat proper. First, the stabilization of the working population in urban centers did not necessarily mean that the whole population worked in capitalist industries. The presence of a lumpenproletariat confirms this fact; establishing residence in an urban center was not proof of proletarianization. Second, those workers who lost their jobs, or elected to quit them, and returned home were more often than not easily reabsorbed by the lineage mode. No longer characterized by separation from their means of production, they fell back on the nonseparation defining the relations of production in the lineage mode. Third, workers in industrial centers remained attached to the lineage mode: they sent a portion of their wages to lineage elders; they contributed to or paid the brideprice, and they depended on the requirements of sorcery and ancestral cult. In a study of Thysville (now Mbanza Ngungu), L. Baeck concluded that:

the African wage worker does not want to cut his ties with his traditional past now since he is not yet convinced of the social solvency of our [European] society. It is for this reason that many city dwellers keep sending traditional family subsidies to their fellow clan members who had stayed in the villages. It is a transaction which insures the donor of solid ties in the traditional milieu so as to make sure that the latter still considers him as one of its members whenever he needs assistance, and which allows him to live on the clan's land whenever his city life becomes untenable.[31]

Fourth, the 'tribal consciousness' that workers developed in towns was the result of their rather unconscious attachment to the lineage mode. As one author has remarked, by withdrawing individuals from rural communities, the partial proletarianization caused them to seek in the artificial social space of the towns a new principle of cohesion and solidarity.[32] Fifth, capitalism is based on the integration of its sectors of production. One of the characteristics of capitalism, as indicated in chapter 1, is the establishment of department 2, that is, enterprises that produce means of subsistence for workers and capitalists. In colonial Zaire this condition did not obtain, at least with the workers. They relied, not on department 2, but on productive units associated with the lineage mode. This was true whether one takes into account the flow of consumer goods from the workers' own lineages or the flow of commercialized subsistence goods from the villages to the industrial centers. Empirical data on the Katanga industrial zone (see section four) confirms this.

Perhaps more obvious is the lack of imprint of capitalist core relations on colonial social groups other than workers. Although capitalism did affect the peasants, capitalist core relations did not govern their lives. In most cases, peasants produced according to the requirements of the lineage mode. Even though they became involved in the network of commodity exchange via the market, monetary values and the rest of production fulfilled the requirements of the lineage mode: 'The African still considers the clan as the orbit of all his family, economic, social and religious interests; in short, it is his social order, the only one he has interest to protect. The European system has not replaced it. It has brought some beneficial improvements which have led to the weakening of the clan without replacing it.'[33] J.M. Domont spoke of the planters' 'prestige' and professional abilities, which were equal to those of a European artisan, but deplored their unbreakable ties to 'tradition.'[34] As will be seen in the next section, debates between direct rule and indirect rule and between the privatization and nonprivatization of land (and the defeat of the privatization policy) only revealed the intractable hold of the lineage mode on peasants. Even production of cash crops, in most cases, took place under the auspices of the lineage mode because it took place on lineage-owned lands. Moreover, a cash-crop economy underscored the limitations imposed on capitalism; reliance on the international market for the sale of peasant-produced crops was the result of the lack of internal integration of the peasant economy into capitalism.

A look at such social categories as traders, artisans, and bureaucrats also reveals the lack of imprint of capitalist core relations. Speaking of artisans and merchants in Léopoldville (Kinshasa), Van Couwenbergh pointed to the 'progress' they had made; yet, he argued that their dependence on the lineage's obligations resulted in their lack of 'respect' for the fundamental principles of capitalism, freedom of the market, and individual initiative.[35] The hold of the lineage mode on these various social categories took different forms; it ranged from priests and intellectuals relying on the dictates of the lineage mode (e.g. practicing ancestral cult)[36] to the priority accorded tribal alliances by clerks, bureaucrats, and intellectuals in their struggle for independence.

Thus, the society that emerged under colonial rule was specific. This in itself is not a big discovery. The importance of the foregoing analysis lies in its attempt to explain this specificity. The analysis reveals that the lack of solid imprint of capitalist core relations on the discussed social categories results from the neutralization of capitalism by the lineage mode. The higher level of ideological routinization had three effects on these social categories. First, the severance of 'traditional' ties by some Africans had only a minimum impact; the routinization of the prevailing relationships made the 'loss' marginal. Second, where new (capitalist) relations succeeded in destroying some precolonial relations, the remaining ones were perpetuated; being highly routinized, they reproduced themselves while being imbricated with new types of relationships. Third, even those Africans, who considered the 'traditional order dead,' were still affected by the lineage mode because imaginary relationships that allowed the routinization did not need the original lineage organization to survive. Empirical evidence on the two specific aspects of pseudocapitalism, agrarian and industrial, further supports the neutralization argument.

3. Capitalism Neutralized: Agrarian Pseudocapitalism

The inquiry into capitalist infiltration in the colonies cuts deeply into the issue of types of colonial rule. In colonial Zaire and elsewhere, the two major options opened to colonial authorities were direct and indirect rules. Depending on which was adopted, there were some variations in the way capitalism attempted to establish itself. Beyond these variations, however, capitalist infiltration faced similar obstacles in the colonies. Belgian colonial rule attested to the limits imposed on the establishment of capitalism in both types of rule. The Belgians debated throughout their tenure as colonial authorities the merits of both types of rule without formally opting for either one. This 'mixed system' reflected their indecision and lack of commitment. But here, perhaps better than elsewhere, the indecision and the debate revealed clearly the contradictory patterns of the coexistence between the capitalist mode and the lineage mode.

The debate between supporters of direct rule and those of indirect rule began earlier with the emergence of the EIC (Congo Free State, 1885–1908). It lasted until about the year of independence. A series of legislations, reflecting both ends of the spectrum, superseded each other. Most legislations dealt with the status and place of 'customs' and 'traditional rule' in the colonial society. Article 1 of the decree of October 6, 1891, stipulated that '*chefferies* [chieftainships] are recognized as long as their chiefs are recognized by the

Governor-General. Their exercise of power is accepted insofar as it is not contrary to public order.'[37]

The January 29, 1892, and May 2, 1910, decrees reaffirmed the 1891 decree by insisting on respect for traditional authority and went as far as to require that African subjects obtain authorization from their chiefs before traveling. At the same time, these pieces of legislation and others supported also direct rule. For instance, the June 3, 1906, decree made recognition of the chiefs conditional upon their collecting taxes for the colonial administration, recruiting labor power on behalf of the colonial state and companies, and directing infrastructural works among their subjects. The December 5, 1933, decree, although attempting through the creation of *secteurs* to strengthen traditional constituencies, actually created an administrative structure supportive of colonial direct rule; for the *secteur* was often under the direct supervision of the colonial authority. More often than not, application of these various decrees leaning toward direct rule was, in fact, applied in favor of indirect rule and vice versa. For instance, the colonial district commissioner often intervened to appoint the traditional chief, a task that was supposed to be the exclusive right of the chieftainships. On the other hand, matters related to taxation, justice, and the building of colonial society, which normally fell under the authority of colonial officials, were transferred to native chiefs. Most colonial policies were a mixture of direct and indirect rule.

Those who favored direct rule did not lack arguments. Monsignor J. de Hemptine, the archbishop of Katanga, argued that direct rule was the only viable means to bring about 'civilization' in the political and social conditions of the native population. He added that indirect rule leads to hybrid and counterproductive results for the colony:

> The civilizing nation means to bring the black race, cautiously, slowly and surely, to a more exalted conceptualization of human existence; it believes in the perfectibility of natives and invites them to take part in its endeavors, its labors, its civilization, and in the general progress of humanity. ... As a transition and in order not to skip the stages of a normal process, the structures of traditional systems will be maintained, but with the determined intention of causing this traditional authority to evolve in our direction and of eliminating it wherever it might become ossified or stand in the way of the civilizing process.[38]

Direct rule generally coincided with assimilation of the native population; through assimilation of the educated elite (*evolués*), the colonial administration could prevent their isolation, hence the likelihood of their inciting the 'uneducated' masses to revolt.[39] Still others maintained that direct rule and assimilation gave coherence to Belgian colonial thought and demarcated it from British rule.[40] By imitating the British in applying indirect rule, the argument went, the Belgians simply displayed their lack of a coherent colonial policy.

In support of indirect rule, the minister of the colonies contended that it was impossible for Europeans to exercise direct control over the natives because they did not know the native personality. Only through indigenous political entities and their chiefs could the European authorities exercise their power.[41] Furthermore, indirect rule was justified on the grounds that 'in most African societies the control over individuals was exercised either by the family head, the head of the clan or of the tribe, or by an aristocracy. Therefore, to destroy that authority in the present circumstances could only lead to chaos and anarchy, which would frustrate the utilitarian goals of the colonial rule.'[42] Others argued that the colonial society was in crisis because, by applying direct rule and assimilationist policies, colonial officials did not reflect 'the genius, traditions, customs and the political and social organization of the [black] race.'[43]

It is a given that, in the era of capitalism, colonial rule was predicated upon the implantation of the capitalist mode of production. Establishing capitalist relations required a fundamental restructuring, that is, destruction, of those relations that buttressed the lineage mode. Indirect rule could not offer such destruction possibilities. How, then, can the debate and the openness to indirect rule be explained? One might say that even direct rule never lived up to expectations; indirect rule offered an alternative. But, by definition, indirect rule could not be an alternative because it could not destroy traditional rule and customs. It could be an alternative only to the extent that failure of direct rule to implant capitalism revealed contradictory patterns that only indirect rule could resolve. In other words, recourse to indirect rule was justified because the limitations imposed on the success of capitalist implantation via direct rule were embedded in traditional rule and customs. The colonial strategy was, therefore, to 'join them' (i.e., tradition and customs) because it could not 'beat them.'

Taking into account different colonial powers, this formulation leads to the following hypotheses:

- Colonial direct rule was, as a matter of logic, the best option for the implantation of capitalism.
- In reality, contradictory factors stifled such implantation and raised doubts about direct rule itself.
- To the extent that most of these contradictory patterns were embedded in traditional rule and customs, indirect rule was imposed as an alternative by all colonial powers.
- However, the actual choice or contemplation of the rule itself was a function of each individual colonial power's ideological, economic, and socioeconomic constraints.

An analysis of colonial policies reveals such contradictory patterns of capitalist expansion, which resulted from the neutralization of capitalism by the lineage mode and the noncapitalist path of development associated with it.

The policy adopted toward the chieftainships, for example, aimed to create conditions conducive to improving the socioeconomic conditions of the native populations. Capitalism offered the framework within which the task was to be undertaken, and direct rule was consistent with the goal. The June 3, 1910, decree, in a rather convoluted way, established de facto direct rule over the chieftainships by appointing an advisory board that guided and, in fact, replaced the chief in the decision-making process. The October 6, 1891, decree, allowed the colonial district commissioner not only to preside over investiture of chiefs but also to appoint them where needed. De Hemptine's strong support for direct rule extended to this legislation.

These attempts to control the chieftainships directly led to contradictory outcomes. Direct control over the chiefs and their appointments was inconsistent with the expectations that they would order their subjects to execute the policies of the colonial state. Once the traditional chief was appointed by the colonial authority and, hence, became subordinate to it, and once he was on the colonial payroll and susceptible to punishment, imprisonment, or fines by the colonial authority, he lost the aura that characterized his rule in the precolonial era. Consequently, his subjects were no longer bound to obey him as they had in precolonial times. This disobedience negatively affected colonial policies of capitalist implantation. Colonial officials soon discovered that dismissing a chief was not in itself a solution unless his successor, no matter how docile, possessed enough authority to secure the villagers' compliance with the objectives set by the administration. For example, although 'every one of the four Cokwe chiefs was replaced at least once during the 1930s, the quality of their successors' administrations did not substantially improve, and a report written in 1934 concluded somewhat despondently that lack of authority seems to be endemic among the Cokwe.'[44] Under these conditions, only recourse to physical coercion could bring the subjects to compliance; the result was frequent use of force in the process of capitalist expansion.

What does this suggest? Obviously, the lack of compliance by the subjects to the traditional chiefs' orders during colonial rule did not result from the absence of physical coercion; the colonial state used plenty of it. Moreover, as I argued in chapter 4, by virtue of its subordination to the lineage mode, the precolonial state had recourse to ideological coercion. Combined, these two factors suggest that by (artificially) repudiating the ideological conditions on which the chiefs' aura rested, direct rule (appointment of the chiefs) created conditions for nonobedience by their subjects. In their eyes, the chiefs no longer fulfilled the ideological requirements that created their power in the precolonial era. Such noncompliance shows the contradictory patterns that hampered the execution of policies and frustrated the implantation of capitalism; they resulted from the ability of the lineage mode to neutralize the implantation by reproducing itself thanks to its higher level of ideological routinization.

A good illustration of this conclusion is provided by the Bashu. As in many other regions, the colonial authorities attempted capitalist implantation among the Bashu through direct control over the traditional chiefs. In the early 1930s, the Belgians, bypassing the rules of succession for chieftainship, appointed a *grand chef* who did not have the approval of the Bashu aristocracy and population. As the colony faced the depression years, its socioeconomic conditions were bleak. Among the Bashu the situation was exacerbated by ecological and other factors. Economic decline was accompanied by sickness and death. Compulsory cultivation and taxation increased at a time when there was a shortage of food and a great fear of sorcery. The Belgian-appointed grand chief took office in a period of social and economic upheaval (1932–35). As indicated in chapter 4, in the precolonial era the Bashu chief was the source of fertility and economic productivity, hence of life, for his people. He mediated between them and the forces of nature to bring peace and prosperity in times of trouble. Such supernatural power was of utmost importance, for its use pacified each homestead. The legitimacy of the chief and his ability to control the forces of nature were a function of his fulfillment of the ideological qualifications imposed by the lineage mode (e.g. rituals.). By ignoring the rules of succession, Belgian colonial officials transgressed these prescriptions. Therefore, the newly appointed chief lacked legitimacy and, hence, the supernatural power to control the forces of nature. For the Bashu, 'declining productivity of the land, tne destruction of crops by locusts, wild animals and hail-storms, and increases in sorcery, sickness, and death, were a product of Belgian interference in the Bashu political system, the removal of a central chief, and the consequent disruption of ritual control over the land. To restore the well-being of the land, it was necessary to reestablish ritual control. This required the investiture of a new *mwami w'embita*.'[45] Calls for the removal of the Belgian-appointed chief were answered by the reappointment of the legitimate chief. Highly routinized and ritualized noncapitalist relations alerted the Bashu to the illegitimacy of an appointed chief. The alert was triggered by colonial attempts to directly control them and establish capitalism. The revolt set the limits of such an implantation. On the other hand, the call for a more legitimate chief strengthened noncapitalist relations.

To be sure, under colonial rule not all chiefs were appointed by colonial authorities. Although they were under the control of the colonial state, many chiefs derived their legitimacy from tradition, that is, from the lineage mode. Opposition and contradictions generated by attempts at direct rule further helped their status. As opposition to direct rule mounted, new decrees were issued to shift toward indirect rule or, at least, to mitigate the effects of direct rule. A 1926 colonial convention advocated a greater role for the traditional chiefs in colonial affairs; it urged their subjects to recognize the chiefs as their 'natural defenders.' The chiefs' double status was revealed by these recurrent calls for indirect rule. They collected taxes from their subjects for both the colonial administration and themselves. This double role made it possible for the colonial administration to punish those subjects who failed to execute its orders by claiming that they had disobeyed the orders of their chiefs. For whatever it was worth, however, the flirtation with indirect rule could not help colonial policies of capitalist implantation any more than direct rule did. If anything, it revealed the inability of direct rule to help establish capitalism and the ability of the lineage mode to stifle capitalism and to make it retreat, via the colonial administration, into the pretenses of indirect rule.

Colonial land policy illustrates better this last point. One major land issue the Belgians dealt with was 'privatization' of lineage-owned lands, a major component of which was the *paysannat indigène*. One of the policy goals assigned to the colonial state by the colonial charter of 1885 was the elimination of lineage ownership of land; it sought to replace it by private property. The 1906 decree elaborated further on the idea. A June 3, 1914, memorandum expressed even more strongly the need for private property in land for the African population. In spite of these legislative and administrative acts, the policy's real boost came from the heir to the Belgian Crown, the Duke of Brabant. In a 1933 speech to the Senate he forcefully argued in favor of private property in land and the establishment of the *paysannat indigène*:

> The post-war economic circumstances and the exceptionally low cost of labor have caused the maintenance in the Congo of an agricultural system which has been condemned everywhere else; we generally limit ourselves to collecting products in their raw state as they appear in nature. ... A new method, based on a two-pronged policy, is needed. The first policy, the main one, consists of establishing a paysannat in its most complete form, allowing the native populations to obtain [private] property and to enjoy economic freedom which is recognized [to] them by the colonial charter.[46]

To acquire private ownership of land applicants had to go through two stages. They were given a certificate after three years of tenure and then obtained full rights of landownership after ten more years of satisfactory tenure.

General and particular reasons lay behind the policy of privatization of land and *paysannat*. Among the general reasons is that Belgium sought to imitate Britain, France, and Holland, which had applied similar policies of privatization in their colonies with different results. Belgian colonial authorities feared that migrations toward industrial zones were a sure path toward peasant proletarianization. Only by curbing the migrations could it be avoided. The first step toward this goal was the system of compulsory cultivation, which would stabilize the population on the land. Yet conditions in the countryside – the rural exodus, the lack of fertile soil, low revenues for peasants, and the use of 'traditional' methods by peasants – were specified as obstacles to the stabilization of peasant agriculture. To avoid these obstacles, the colonial state recommended privatization of lineage land and establishment of the *paysannat indigène*. The rationale behind the recommendation was that the *paysannat indigène* would allow more efficient coordination, control, and assistance by the state.

Three specific reasons, consistent with the goal of capitalist implantation, were advanced to justify the privatization of land property. (1)áPrivate property was an impetus to economic productivity and growth because it allowed the owners-workers to enjoy the fruits of their own labor. (2)áPrivate property in land would strike a blow to the authority of lineage heads and traditional chiefs and would, therefore, pave the way for capitalism. (3) Privatization of land would allow for capitalistic transactions, such as loans because privately owned land could be used as collateral in loan transactions.[47]

Implementation of the policy thus conceived was marred and stifled by

127

contradictions inherent in the colonial rule itself and those imposed by the lineage mode. Various kinds of contradictory patterns resulted from colonial rule itself. First, the claim for economic freedom for the indigenous populations and their access to the financial market was contradicted by the actual refusal to allow such freedom and access. The declaration of support for the increase in productivity for the peasants was contradicted by lopsided support for and increase in the production of European farmers. In 1958, European sector production increased 68 percent as opposed to only an increase of 12 percent in the African sector.[48] Second, the claim for privatizing land for native populations was, in actuality, contradicted by the elitist character of the assimilation policy; private land property was to benefit only the small number of educated elite (*evolués*) from whose property noneducated fellow lineage members were to be kept away.[49] A committee sent to examine the issue of land privatization in the Katanga province revealed the reason why the elitist policy was favored. 'It is the committee's opinion that the policy be applied only to paratraditional centers (*centres extra-coutumiers*) and to agrarian settlements or groupings of *evolués* peasants since we fear that the settlement of individual landowners on state lands would free them from political and administrative control.'[50] One understands why one critic of the policy saw in it a demonstration of an incoherent system giving to a small group of elite what was supposed to be given to the masses.[51]

The third set of contradictions affected more directly the policy of *paysannat indigène*. Not only were plots concentrated on unfertile lands but an overall program to buy peasant crops was absent. Although cash crops such as cotton fared well, other crops such as cassava and rice often remained unsold because of the vast influence exercised by corporations with a vested interest in cash crops. But more importantly, coercion was still practiced to organize the plots, which greatly reduced peasant free participation. Furthermore, European settlers (*colons*), who feared competition from African 'rural capitalists,' mobilized themselves against the policy, thus immensely contributing to its failure. As one colonial official pointed out, 'There exists now a real psychosis among European settlers, who oppose directly the *paysannat indigène*. In the Ituri region, agricultural centers which were founded to help the peasants have been sold off and given to settlers or European agencies, thus suppressing all progress made after ten years of work. In the Kivu region, the interests of the native cultivators have been entirely subordinated to European settlers.'[52]

These contradictory policies were initiated by the colonial state or individual Europeans. However, as already noted, many of them were the outcome of the neutralizing power of the lineage mode. For instance, there is no doubt that the lopsided support for European settlers was sometimes dictated by prejudice; in most cases, however, it resulted from the degree of unreceptiveness of Africans to capitalist private property. The use of compulsion, I have already shown, was often the result of noncompliance to the orders of the colonial authorities, itself an effect of the reproduction of noncapitalist relations. The challenge by the lineage mode is better argued through a discussion of the three specific reasons that the colonial state advanced to justify capitalism and the counterarguments offered by the opponents of the policy.[53]

The first reason advanced by the colonial administration in favor of land privatization was that private property would increase productivity by allowing peasants to enjoy the fruits of their labor. It was faulted by opponents on several grounds. First, the attempt to provide a surplus to the producers was superfluous because this was already being accomplished by the lineage itself through the distribution of the surplus. Second, collective ownership of lands never meant the absence of private ownership of goods within the lineage. The assumption that the relations of production within the lineage were an expression of primitive communism was a false one. As one critic wrote: 'Rather than finding the cause [of the failure of the policy] in the inability of colonial officers to understand the native mentality, they held to their view of the collectivist mind of the black population and ... blamed altogether the indigenous land tenure system, seeing it as a detestable economic formula lacking viability.'[54] Third, the view that lineage ownership of land did not cause peasants to take care of the land, but rather led them to practice extensive agriculture could not be supported. For one thing, opponents argued, private property is not synonymous with, or a result of, intensive agriculture; for another, within the lineage, peasants already had property because they were masters of their own fields, even those left fallow, and did protect their fields. Given that, in most cases, environmental constraints did not permit intensive agriculture, recourse to such a practice would not have been successful; Africans practiced extensive agriculture as a response to ecological constraints. Fourth, land privatization by a simple juridical decree was an artificial way to create private property. In Europe, land privatization resulted from class conflicts and not from intensive agriculture. Juridical codification of land relations followed the outcome of class conflicts and not the other way around. An abstract juridical notion of private property, opponents added, did less to protect individual peasants than the lineage land tenure system. Fifth, and most importantly, raising the issue of the appropriation of surplus in conjunction with private property, while significant, missed the point; opponents argued that in traditional society the extraction of surplus took place through ideological means ('superstition'), and private property would not change the situation.

Although the colonial state advanced a second reason to justify the policy – that private property in land would prevent the role of lineage elders and chiefs – the counterargument was also as persuasive. Opponents of the policy argued that the authority of the chiefs was limited in precolonial times by a whole range of superstitious (hence, ideological) means. In fact, they maintained, the chiefs appointed by the colonial administration were the ones most likely to commit abuses against peasants because they were not bound by the types of prescriptions that limited the actions of the legitimate chiefs. Moreover, in the precolonial era the chiefs collected tribute as an expression of their political authority; this practice would not cease to exist simply because of land privatization. At any rate, the chiefs' 'arbitrary rule' was not always visible; it was invisible and feared, hence it was ideological. Private property would not easily modify the situation.

The third reason justifying land privatization – that it would allow capitalistic transaction – was opposed as well. Opponents countered that within the lineage notions of profit and exploitation did not exist. Tribute paid to the chiefs was never perceived as profit but rather as tax. Therefore, attempts to turn land into a capitalistic venture were doomed to failure. Furthermore, using land as collateral in loan transactions would most likely benefit financial usurers, who would take advantage of the peasants and turn them into landless beggars, as was the case in India.

The counterarguments to the policy of land privatization did not imply that their proponents opposed capitalism; on the contrary, ample evidence strongly suggests their commitment to its establishment. How does one explain, then, their rejection of the policy? Given their commitment to the establishment of capitalism, it cannot be because of their 'concern' or 'respect' for 'African tradition.' Such respect would be antithetical to colonialism. The answer is provided by a careful reading of their arguments. It is obvious that factors inherent in lineage organization dictated the position of the opponents. Dissatisfied with direct rule, they advocated indirect rule. The opponents' call for indirect rule revealed the limits of direct rule and its inability to implant capitalism. By contrast, it demonstrated the ability of factors inherent in 'tradition' to force both opponents and the colonial administration to retreat from the policy of capitalist implantation. Unable to beat tradition, they had to join it. The Belgian colonial 'mixed system' was a concession to tradition. It was tradition that provided opponents with ammunition to mount their attacks against the policy of privatization. As one of the opponents put it: 'To a society which is based on blood ties, no other system [of property rights] can be proposed unless it takes these ties as its point of reference. ... Any system which is based on individual initiative and freedom is infeasible.'[55] He was right, although not because of 'blood ties.' The failure of agrarian capitalism was vividly shown by the failure of the *paysannat indigène*.

Why and how did the factors inherent in tradition, which caused the failure of agrarian capitalism, endure? The answer lies in the analysis undertaken in chapter 4 and in the preceding sections of this chapter. By reproducing the intrinsically noncapitalist relations and developmental path, the lineage mode, its higher level of ideological routinization, and the attendant structural indistinguishability in these societies neutralized the means of implantation of capitalism. It was ideological routinization through its reproduction power that alerted the colonial subjects to the illegitimacy of the colonial state's policies; it, too, by reproducing 'traditional' social relations, dictated the position of the opponents to the policy of privatizing land. In practically every point raised by the opponents of the policy, the role of ideological routinization in maintaining a set of actively (as opposed to stagnantly) different social relations was acknowledged (consider the use of the term superstition). Many studies undertaken by Belgian scholars during colonial rule, although supportive of the implantation of capitalism, were equally convinced of the intractable challenge presented by the ideological core relations of the lineage mode.

This intractable challenge led to agrarian pseudocapitalism; this further set the limits within which industrial capitalism could operate by preventing the necessary linkages between peasant agriculture and capitalist core relations in industry. The result was industrial pseudocapitalism.

4. Industrial Pseudocapitalism

The Katanga Enclave Economy

Under Belgian King Leopold's rule (1885–1908), holdings were set up to prospect and exploit mineral resources. As colonial rule proceeded, the mining sector expanded. By 1950, more than fifty companies were engaged in prospecting and producing mineral resources in colonial Zaire. Various minerals were discovered and were concentrated in three major geographical areas: the northeastern part of the country (gold), the central region of Kasai (diamonds), and the southeastern region of Katanga (copper, cobalt, manganese, tin, etc.). In Katanga, the formulation and implementation of investment policies took place under the aegis of the *Comité Spécial du Katanga* (CSK). Apart from leasing its estates to private developers, the CSK signed many investment agreements with international banks and cartels, most of which were Belgian. By 1910, investments flowed into the mining sector. From 1910 to 1952, seventeen holdings were created to support investment efforts in mining zones, while fifteen corporations to produce mineral resources were founded.[56]

As early as 1901 the CSK had worked out an agreement with private interests, including Tanganyka Concessions, a British corporation. Under this agreement, the CSK and Tanganyka Concessions were to share equally all investment expenses related to prospecting in mining zones, while 80 percent of investment returns were to be appropriated by the CSK. The most important outcome of the agreement was the creation, on October 30, 1906, of the giant corporation *Union Minière du Haut Katanga* (UMHK), whose initial capital was valued at 10 million Belgian francs. Apart from its main objective, the production of copper, cobalt, zinc, gold, silver, and other mineral resources, the UMHK founded a variety of subsidiaries. Its major initial shareholders included the *Société Générale*, Tanganyka Concessions, and the CSK. The colonial state and the *Compagnie du Katanga* held shares in the new corporation by virtue of their control over the CSK. Because of the importance of the UMHK, its capital stock was increased on several occasions. By 1950, it was valued at 3 billion Belgian francs, made up of 1,242,000 shares representing 414,000 votes. Out of those shares the CSK held 315,825 shares (25 percent). Out of 200,000 bonds valued at 100 francs each, the CSK held 99,093, entitling it to 248,400 voting rights (60 percent) in the UMHK.[57] CSK's shares in the company were paid for by its partners, the Société Générale and Tanganyka Concessions, which increased the power of these two corporations on the board of directors of the UMHK.

Well before 1960, the UMHK had become the world's leading producer of cobalt and the world's third largest producer of copper after Kennecot and Anaconda, two U.S. companies. Its copper production was about 300,000 metric tons, and it produced about 8,000 tons of cobalt. It was capitalized at 8 billion Belgian francs, its capital assets totaled nearly 20 billion francs, and the overall value of its capital stock was 1,875 billion francs.[58] The peripheral position of the colonial government (the principal shareholder) was reflected on the board of the UMHK as well; the CSK de facto dominated by private interests, represented the colonial state in both voting rights and stockholding.

As the 'leading industry,' the UMHK dominated the colonial economic structure and was able to turn the Katanga (Shaba) region into a 'development pole.' Owing to the number of people that it drew and the economic activities that it involved, new manufacturing industries were established in the Katanga region. From 1885 to 1950, Katanga Province absorbed about 80 percent of the investments in the mining sector and shared with the Léopoldville (today's Kinshasa–Bas–Zaire) pole the largest share of capital investment in manufacturing. By African (and Third World) standards, colonial Zaire as a whole enjoyed a privileged economy between 1947 and 1957, with U.S. $148 invested per inhabitant; over the same period, in Katanga Province the amount invested per inhabitant amounted to U.S. $319.

This concentration of economic activities impacted activities in other parts of the country. Goods produced by industries in the Katanga development pole were sold in other regions of the colony; and some manufacturing industries in Katanga used inputs from other regions and sectors of the economy. For instance, industries from Katanga exported manufactured products such as cigarettes, confections, biscuits, beer, textiles, and metal and wood products to the rest of the country. In turn, the Katanga development pole imported consumer goods and inputs such as maize, groundnuts, and tobacco from Kasai; manioc and rice from Kasai and Kivu; palm oil from Kasai, Oriental Province (today's Haut-Zaire), and Léopoldville; sugar from Kivu; wood from Kasai and Kivu; and coffee and cotton from the northern provinces.

In spite of these exchanges, the UMHK and its attendant manufacturing sector did not lead to an integrated economy. Unless the economic structure is based on some kind of autarky, economic exchanges such as those just mentioned are not uncommon in any type of economic structure. At a minimum, the economy is a matter of production, exchange, and consumption; therefore, these exchanges were not by themselves enough to establish an integrated, let alone capitalist, economy. This contention is further supported because products such as maize, manioc, rice, palm oil, millet, and groundnuts imported from other regions of the colony were for direct consumption by the African population, especially the UMHK's workers living in Katanga Province. From 1920 to 1933 the increase in the work force in the mining zones and other connected industrial zones in Katanga Province was accompanied by an increase in the importation of agricultural goods from other regions of the colony. Any decrease in the number of workers recruited was also accompanied by a decrease in the importation of goods from other regions (table 5.4).

Table 5.4: Food* and Labor supply in Katanga, 1920–33

	1920	1921	1922	1923	1924	1925	1926
Total imported food (in tons)	4,361	11,588	7,846	11,312	10,506	13,338	13,085
Total labor force	35,825	38,098	35,573	39,000	?	64,133	?

	1927	1928	1929	1930	1931	1932	1933
Total imported food (in tons)	18,000	17,021	18,540	18,336	13,548	11,091	11,854
Total labor force	55,165	54,010	71,486	72,947	40,010	28,530	21,879

Source: B. Jewsiewicki, 'Unequal Development: Capitalism and the Katanga Economy,' in *The Roots of Rural Poverty in Central and Southern Africa*, eds. R. Palmer and N. Parsons (Berkeley: University of California Press, 1977), p.á334.
* Maize/millet, cassava (manioc), rice, beans, ground nuts, and palm oil.

The relationship between goods imported from other regions of the colony and direct consumption suggests that the quantity of goods imported from other regions and integrated as inputs by the manufacturing sector in the Katanga region was minimal; the integration affected less than 5 percent of the 26 percent of agriculture's share of gross domestic commercialized production in 1957.[59] In other words, the capitalist commodification of the agricultural sector by the Katanga development pole, itself the by-product of the mining industry, was minimal. The capitalist commodification of agriculture does not suppose only the monetarization of the exchanges of products; more important is the stimulation of the agricultural sector itself. Such stimulation is possible whenever the integration of the agricultural sector by the manufacturing sector imposes some requirements (e.g. capitalist relations) on the former. In fact, such a capitalist transformation is essential for 'normal' capitalist reproduction in the manufacturing sector itself because noncapitalist relations in agriculture are likely to stand in the way of its expansion. The penetration of capitalist relations in agriculture leads to change in the organization of labor and technology and in the acquisition of such intermediary goods as equipment for stocking agricultural goods. All of these factors expand the internal market by expanding production. They stimulate competition, hence the quality of the goods; they expand, in turn, the manufacturing sector insofar as they lead to the manufacture of intermediary and capital goods (e.g. equipment for stocking and agrarian technology).

In exchanges between the manufacturing sector in the Katanga development pole and the colonial agricultural sector, the minimal integration of agricultural goods in the manufacturing sector could not help fulfill these requirements. Furthermore, the settlers' plantation agriculture, which was likely to contribute to helping the economy as a whole to meet them, was primarily for export to the world market; it stood almost completely detached from the internal market. During the 1920–40 period the export of agricultural products was, on the average, 40 percent of the total exports value; during the period 1950–59 it was, on the average, 30 percent of total colonial exports, second to exports of mineral resources. The settlers' plantations produced coffee, palm nuts/oil, cotton, wood, rubber, and tea. By comparing figures for the export and local consumption of four (industrial) agricultural products, one can easily detect both the lack of integration with the manufacturing sector and the imbalance in favor of exports. Only wood relied heavily on the internal market, with 70–71 percent of the local consumption (table 5.5).

Table 5.5: Export and local consumption of some agricultural products, 1958–59 (in tons and in percentage of total production)

	Export				Local Consumption			
	1958	%a	1959	%	1958	%	1959	%
Palm products	284,000	85	313,000	84	50,000	15	59,000	16
Coffee	51,900	97	56,600	91	1,500	3	5,700	9
Cotton	63,300	78	86,400	89	18,300	22	10,400	11
Wood (lumber)	100,300	29	106,800	30	250,000	71	250,000	70

Source: Adapted from F. Bézy et al., *Accumulation et sous-développement au Zaire* (Louvain-la-Neuve: Presses Universitaires de Louvain, 1981), p. 219. Annex 4 A and B.
* Percentages were calculated by the author.

The Katanga manufacturing sector was not the exclusive user of this minimal quantity of inputs; the Léopoldville development pole also used it, which further reveals the lack of integration of agriculture with the Katanga manufacturing sector. The lack of integration between agriculture and the manufacturing sector supports Adam Przeworski's observation about pseudocapitalism in Latin America: 'The development of capitalist production in one sector or several sectors does not lead automatically to the commodification of production in other sectors, notably in agricultural production; and ... the capitalist activities, whatever they are, do not become integrated with each other by means of the market. ... Hence, reproduction of the particular activities is *serially*, that is, each independently, conditioned by the world system.[60]

Figure 5.1.   UHMK's inputs/outputs' self-centered linkage effects.

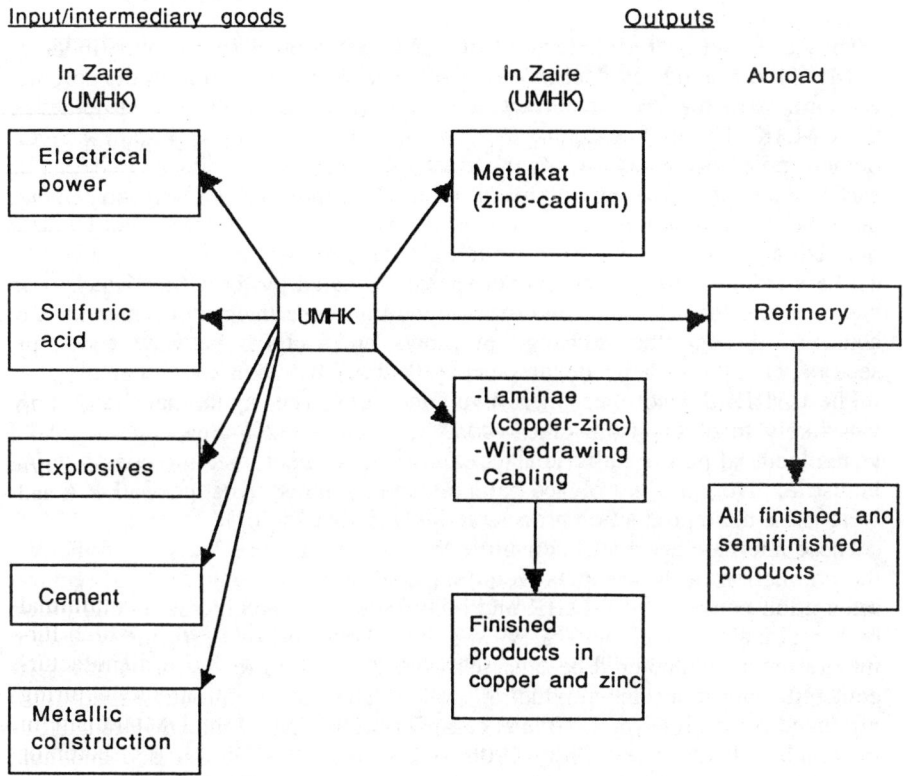

SOURCE:Adapted from J.L. Lacroix, Industrialisation au Congo, (Paris: Mouton,1967),pg.99

That the manufacturing sector around the UMHK was thus only marginally integrated indicates yet another more serious aspect of dislocation. In spite of its almost total domestic orientation, the Katanga manufacturing sector did not integrate, either through capital or intermediary goods, with the manufacturing sector in the Léopoldville development pole nor with the UMHK itself. On the basis of the trends in the interprovincial trade, a UN study established that exchanges between the two development poles were limited to services and to manufactured goods sold on their respective markets. Integration at the production level was almost nonexistent; these exchanges mainly involved banking services, transport of capital and intermediary goods (imported from abroad), and dealerships offered to the Katanga-based industries by Léopold-ville-based companies.

Thus the manufacturing sector that developed around the leading industry (UMHK) in Katanga evidenced important aspects of dislocation in the colonial economic structure. But the effects are further revealed within the structure of the UMHK. The importance of the economic activities in the Katanga development pole was based on, for the most part, the copper industry. Given the earlier dependence of the colony on mineral exports, particularly on copper, the UMHK became not only a crucial means of revenue for the colonial state but also a major instrument of capitalist expansion for the colony as a whole. To be viable, the role of capitalist expansion played by the UMHK had to be based on the fulfillment of two major conditions: the integration of economic activities through the exchange of inputs and outputs between economic sectors (1) in the Katanga development pole and (2) on a national scale.

The UMHK did not meet these two conditions. The inputs that the UMHK was likely to obtain from other economic sectors (excluding capital goods) were electrical power, sulfuric acid, explosives, cement, metallic construction, industrial glycerine, hydrolyzed palm oil, and compressed oxygen, all of which were used in the production process at the UMHK (fig. 5.1).

These intermediary goods constitute 'backward linkage effects.' In principle, the production of these inputs would have stimulated a long chain of sectoral integration between the UMHK and other sectors of the colonial economy on both regional and national scales. In reality, however, this propensity toward integration was hampered because the UMHK operated on the basis of a self-centered investment and production policy. The aforementioned inputs were produced by satellite (or auxiliary) companies founded by the UMHK itself or in which it held shares. From 1906 to 1960 the UMHK founded and held shares in about twenty companies, most of which were in the manufacturing and service sectors (table 5.6).

The emergence of the UMHK as a leading industry did very little for integration. All the companies were concentrated in the Katanga development pole, which led to geographical dislocation. The major, if not exclusive, beneficiary and producer was the UMHK itself. Capitalist reproduction by intermediary goods thus became impossible. Because they were vertically produced (by the UMHK itself) as opposed to horizontally produced (by independent units), intermediary goods used by the UMHK did not stimulate demand for outside products. In the absence of demand from the UMHK, the manufacturing sector, in Katanga and nationally, remained without any link with the leading industry. Because capital goods were entirely imported from foreign countries, it can be reasonably concluded that at the input level the emergence of the UMHK as a leading industry did not lead to capitalist integration but to disarticulating effects instead. Linkage factors, such as railroads, did have some integrative effects between different regions of the country, but, because they emerged parallel with the leading industry, they were tailored to respond exclusively to its requirements (to increase production, reduce production costs, and improve the means of export of products). This response was facilitated by the UMHK, which often held shares in the transportation companies.

At the output level, the UMHK produced copper and other semifinished and finished allied products, such as electrolytic zinc, electrolytic cadmium, germanium, cobalt, lead, and copper and zinc wires (Fig. 5.1). Most of the semifinished or finished allied products were partly refined or chemically treated by the UMHK itself or its auxiliary enterprises (see table 5.6 for zinc, cadmium, and germanium). The result here was also the nonextension of economic activities to other sectors or branches of the economy. More importantly, these finished or semifinished products were almost all exported. In 1959 (the year for which data on allied products are available), the UMHK produced 117,000 tons of crude zinc and 54,810 tons of refined zinc and exported about that amount; it produced and exported 475 tons of cadmium; it produced 13,643 tons of germanium and exported about 95 percent; finally, it produced about 8,000 tons of cobalt and exported about the same amount.61 Only one product had 5 percent of its total production locally consumed. All the others were exported in toto.

Data on colonial exports are not specific about the exact amount of copper, produced and refined in Zaire and exported. However, by using the 1959–60 production and refinery figures and the 1970 export figures, one can approximately determine the distribution of the UMHK output during the colonial period (Table 5.7). In 1959 the UMHK produced 282,320 tons of copper; in 1960 it refined 145,000 tons of the total production of 302,297 tons; in 1970 it produced 386,000 tons of copper and refined 189,000 tons (49 percent) locally. From this, 99.7 percent of total production and 99.4 percent of refined production was exported.62

These figures suggest that (1) under colonial rule the UMHK refined locally about the same amount of its copper as in 1970 (45–50 percent); (2) the amount of exported copper as a percentage of total production and of refined copper was about the same as in 1970, if not higher (99 percent). Technological change at the UMHK was progressive, and the use of copper output by local industries could not be higher during the colonial period than it was in 1970. In fact, only one industry (Laminoir, Trefilerie et Cablerie du Zaire, LATRECA) used UMHK-produced copper. Overall, only 0.6 percent of the total refined output and 0.3 percent of the crude output was consumed locally. Because of this outward-oriented structure, the UMHK was, as in inputs, cut

Table 5.6: Companies founded by the UMHK as the result of its self-centered production process

Company	Capital share	Object	Beneficiary	Location
Sogefor	340t	electrical power	UMHK & Katanga cities	Zaire/Katanga
Sogelec	234t	idem	idem	idem
Sofichim	100t	sulfuric acid	UMHK	Belgium/Zaire/Katanga
Sogechim	100t	idem	idem	Zaire/Katanga
Métallurgique de Katanga	750t	zinc-cadmium germanium	idem	idem
Metalkat	–	idem	idem	idem
Minoteries du Katanga	100t	maize, cassava/wheat	UMHK & Katanga	idem
Le Charbonnage de la Lwena	100t	coal	–	idem
Cofoka	385t	real estate	Katanga	idem
SudKat	46t	manganese	–	idem
Mindsut Kat	50t	copper (ended 1960)	–	idem
Chimexplo/ Afridex	20%p	explosives	UMHK & other industries	idem
Ciment de L'Afrique Centrale	20%p	cement	UMHK & general consumption	idem
Elvaluilu	30%p	animal breeding	general consumption	idem
Bauxicongo	20%p	bauxite	UMHK & general consumption	idem
Exforka	17.5%p	forest	general consumption	idem
KDL	–	railway	UMHK & others	Katanga & other regions
Métallurgie	47%p	refinery/copper and cobalt marketing	–	Belgium
Société Générale des Minerais	–	UMHK products	–	Belgium

Sources: Hauzeur de Fooz, *Un demi-siècle avec l'économie du Congo Belge* (Brussels: Imprimerie Mondiale, 1957), p. 40; J. Gerard-Libois, 'L'Affaire de l'Union Minière du Haut-Katanga,' *Etudes Congolaises*, no. 2 (March–April 1967): 1–3.

t = total ownership   p = participation (shares)

off from other sectors of the economy. This structure was coupled with the UMHK's reliance on foreign-based refinery plants, which refined the remaining 50 percent of the UMHK's mineral output. For this reason, the UMHK held shares (47 percent) in the Hoboken refinery plant in Belgium. Like the UMHK, other colonial mining industries exported almost all of their production. The exception, the coal industry, sold a small part of its output to the cement industry. The UMHK, which used a large volume of coal-serviced products, did not use the locally produced, low-quality, coal derivatives. Instead, it imported its coal products from Zimbabwe (then Rhodesia).

Table 5.7: Exports and local consumption of UMHK's output, 1959–60 (production and refined product in tons)

	Production	Refined locally	Exports (in % of total output) Crude	Refined	Exports (in % of total output) Crude	Refined
Zinc	117,000	54,810	100%	100%	0%	0%
Cadmium	475	475	–	1 00%	–	0%
Germanium	13,643	13,643	–	95%	–	0%
Cobalt	8,00 0	–	100%	–	0%	–
Copper	302,297	145,000	99.7%	99.4% (of 157.297 remaining crude)	0.3% (of 145,000 refined output)	0.6%

Sources: Nyembo, *L'industrie du cuivre dans le monde et le progrès économique du Copperbelt Africain* (Brussels: La Renaissance du Livre, 1975), pp. 106–108, 191–195; IRES, *Indépendance, inflation, développement* (Paris: Mouton, 1968), p. 642; World Bank/IBRD, GCM Expansion Project, p. 7, Annex 2–3.

Because linkage effects at the input and output levels were not only concentrated in the Katanga region but centered around the UMHK itself, the effects were reflected in the pattern of proletarianization. In 1959, Katanga Province had about 31 percent of the total wage earners in the mining industry and shared with the Léopoldville development pole about 60 percent of the total wage earners in manufacture, commerce, and transport.[63]

Thus, the UMHK and the industrial structure that developed around it failed to satisfy conditions conducive to an integrated capitalist economy. The economic structure was marked by geographical and sectoral dislocation, which blocked the reproduction and extension of capitalist relations. In spite of the pronouncement of the Ten-Year Plan (1949–59) to correct it, this dislocated structure persisted and, in some cases, was exacerbated by the plan's policies. For instance, Katanga Province's share of investments related to power infrastructure, transportation, and agriculture was far more important than in the other provinces (except the Léopoldville pole). Although it was third in the distribution of private investments during the 1950–59 period, its 13.8 percent share added to an already privileged and disarticulated economic infrastructure.

Dislocation on a National Scale

One of the characteristics of an export-oriented economy is a concentration of private investments in the export sector. In colonial Zaire, private investments flowed by priority to the mining regions but were not limited to the mining industry. They extended to the manufacturing and agricultural sectors. In some instances, as in the case of the UMHK, manufacturing industries emerged as auxiliary industries to the leading industry. In other cases, they were the result of an independent decision by investors. Other industries were implanted in conformity to the Ten-Year Plan. It is not easy to accurately and comprehensively establish the value of private capital invested in colonial Zaire from 1885 to 1960. Such value can be determined only partially by dividing the colonial period into different economic phases.

According to Jean Louis Lacroix, there were two major flows of investments in manufacturing industries.[64] The first flow of investments, between 1920 and 1930, was caused by two major factors: (1) a well-devised fiscal policy and high import duties imposed by the colonial government and (2) the need of Belgian steel and heavy industries for a growing consumer goods industry that could absorb their products. Thus the colony's economic structure became complementary to that of the metropolis and led to the implantation of consumer manufacturing industries in the colony. The second flow of investments in the manufacturing sector took place between 1948 and 1952 and was also caused by two factors. On the one hand, Europeans predicted the outbreak of the Third World War, and Africa was seen as a refuge for capital. On the other hand, the demand for the colony's export goods, propped up by the Korean War, increased export revenues, which, in turn, eased the import of new equipment and machinery and, hence, internal demand for goods. Although the bulk of colonial private investments was basically made up of Belgian private capital, other Western private capital was invested as well through joint ventures and indirect participation.

Although there are some differences in data,[65] strictly new investments (taking into consideration only initial capital) in the 1950–60 period were valued at about 15 billion francs and devoted to the creation of 2,924 companies. The investments were distributed geographically among the six provinces that made up the colony. Léopoldville Province (today divided into two rural provinces and the capital city) obtained 33 percent of the investment; Katanga Province, 13 percent; Oriental Province (Haut-Zaire) 16 percent; Kivu province 10.4 percent; Equateur province, 6.1 percent; and Kasai province (today divided into two provinces) 0.03 percent of the investments. Almost 20 percent of remaining investment spending went to Rwanda-Burundi (then a Belgian protectorate) or were unspecified.[66] Apart from reinforcing the Katanga development pole, this structure of private investments led to the

Table 5.8: Origin of inputs/raw material and intermediary and inputs/capital goods used by Belgian Congo's industries, 1950-58 (in million of francs, 1950 value)

	1950	1951	1952	1953	1954	1955	1956	1957	1958	Total 1950-58[a]	% of total 1950-58[a]
A. *Inputs/raw materials & intermediary goods*											
- from local industries	1,083	1,569	1,953	2,713	2,450	2,740	2,645	2,490	2,320	19,963	30%
- from imports	2,077	3,672	4,951	4,752	5,434	6,176	6,631	7,137	5,686	46,516	70%
- total	3,160	5,241	6,904	7,465	7,884	8,916	9,276	9,627	8,006	66,479	100%
- % local industries/ total	34.2%	29.9%	28.2%	36.3%	31.0%	30.7%	28.5%	25.8%	28.9%		
B. *Inputs/ capital goods*											
- from local industries	275	366	434	670	579	613	664	495	567	4,663	7%
- from imports	3,902	5,937	8,962	8,064	6,790	6,636	7,328	7,528	6,425	61,572	93%
- total	4,177	6,303	9,396	8,734	7,369	7,249	7,992	8,023	6,992	66,235	100%
- % local industries/ total	6.5%	5.8%	4.6%	7.6%	7.8%	8.4%	8.3%	6.1%	8.1%		

Source: Adapted from J. L. Lacroix, *Industrialisation au Congo* (Paris: Mouton, 1967), p. 309, Annex.
[a] 1950-58 total and 1950-58 percentage of total were calculated by the author

emergence (reinforcement) of the Léopoldville development pole. Unlike the Katanga pole, the Léopoldville development pole did not develop around a leading industry. Geographical factors played an important role. The capital city (Léopoldville, today Kinshasa) is located on the Zaire River approximately 400 km from Matadi, a port on the Atlantic Ocean. This particularly strategic position made it a major export-import center, which contributed, in turn, to the manufacturing and commerce-oriented nature of investments made in the Léopoldville region.

There are no reliable data to determine if investments were unbalanced in favor of the Léopoldville pole before 1950. However, of the total number of companies that existed in the colony by 1950, about one-half of them had their headquarters or main plants in the Léopoldville (Kinshasa–Bas–Zaire) pole. This unbalanced structure was reinforced during the 1951–59 period and coincided with the Ten-Year Plan. With 33 percent of the capital invested, the Léopoldville pole came first on the distribution scale of private investments. In 1957, contributions of industries in this pole to the gross domestic product were: 10.5 percent for agriculture, 53.7 percent for manufacturing, 26.8 percent for construction, 25 percent for transportation, and 37.4 percent for commerce.[67] Although the Ten-Year Plan did not particularly exacerbate the imbalance in public investments, it reinforced it in public infrastructure such as power, telecommunication, and transportation.

This geographical imbalance reinforced the existing sectoral imbalance. Indeed, colonial companies operated on a self-centered productive process. As Lacroix points out, 'starting in 1920, the industrial network was set up through progressive agglomeration at a location with industrial enterprises which did not exchange their products. Each enterprise had implanted [its own] production line perfectly integrated from the reception of raw materials to the delivery of a finished product aimed at satisfying the final demand of consuming goods: from the start, several enterprises themselves produced their [own] power, designed and manufactured their spare parts, and undertook their own construction and carpentry works.'[68] Such an economic structure prevented the development of an intermediary sector of production because it did not allow industrial exchanges between sectors or branches of the economy. New industries that could be integrated into other sectors of the economy on a national scale were implanted in development poles where each industry was self-reliant. To produce, new industries also had to apply a policy of self-reliance, thus exacerbating the sectoral dislocation. Even if the geographical imbalance had allowed some sectoral integration, it would have remained confined within the limits of the development pole itself, as shown by the case of the UMHK and the Katanga pole.

The manufacturing sector in colonial Zaire, unlike the mining or agricultural sectors, directed almost its total output toward the internal market. By satisfying the needs of the African population with consumer goods, the manufacturing sector drew the peasants into the market economy. Peasants were stimulated to produce more cash crops, which helped them to earn enough money for their taxes and for purchasing manufactured goods. The link between the manufacturing sector and the peasant sector at the exchange level, rather than production level, occurred mainly in those cases where the manufactured good was produced at a distance close enough to the peasants to interfere with their consuming behavior. For example, by 1959 there were twelve brewing plants in the colony – a least one plant in each of its six provinces. Roughly, this meant a ratio of one plant per 2 million people. Even in the immediate post-independence period, despite deteriorating conditions in cash agriculture (the result of political crises), some peasants reluctantly devoted their time to the production of cash crops in order to buy beer rather than other manufactured goods.[69]

This suggests that the less the branch of the manufacturing sector was influenced by the geographical imbalance of investments, the more its effects were integrative on the economic structure (even though this integration remained at the simple exchange level), and vice versa. Unfortunately, the distribution of the 1950–59 investments led to the concentration of most branches of the manufacturing sector in the two major development poles; as a result, most manufactured goods were not close enough to the population to strongly interfere with its consuming behavior, let alone its production. Goods such as beer were the exception to the rule.[70] Because they were not readily accessible to peasants, manufactured goods did not establish enough of a capitalist link between the manufacturing sector and peasant agriculture. Geographical imbalance reinforced sectoral disarticulation of the colonial economy, thus blocking implantation of capitalist relations.

I do not argue here that there was a total lack of integration between economic activities. As stated earlier, no economy is made of completely separate sectors and branches. Because its output was almost totally oriented toward the internal market, the manufacturing sector did reach some level of input/output exchange among industrial branches and between the manufacturing sector and local raw materials. At the input level, some manufacturing industries used some of the local raw materials. For instance, the textile industry partly used locally produced cotton, the shoe and rubber industry used local rubber, and the food industry used inputs such as palm oil for the manufacture of margarine and cooking oil. However, these exchanges could scarcely lead to capitalist integration of the economy by capitalist relations. By comparison, there were more inputs from foreign countries than from local producers, even in cases where the same inputs could be found locally. Thus the cement industry in the Bas-Zaire region, metallic construction in Kinshasa, the shoe, tobacco, beer, and chemical industries all imported, in part or in toto, their inputs. This dependence on foreign inputs had serious adverse consequences in the postcolonial period. Because they lacked foreign earnings, some industries could not import their inputs and were forced to close.[71]

As in the Katanga manufacturing sector, the marginal use of local inputs could not lead to viable capitalist integration between the manufacturing sector and the most dynamic branch of agriculture, that is, plantation agriculture. Plantation agriculture was export-bound. Its exchange with the local manufacturing sector remained very marginal, and its production was not conditioned by the demand in the manufacturing industry. Consequently, whenever conditions for export (e.g., low demand on the world market) did not allow a high level of production in export agriculture, the manufacturing industries that partly depended on local raw materials produced by export plantations experienced serious shortages of those particular inputs/raw materials. This was particularly true in the food industry for such inputs as palm oil or groundnuts. Lack of integration between the manufacturing, that is, capitalist sector and lineage agriculture was even more striking. The reliance of manufacturing industries on foreign inputs and the competitive edge that settlers had over peasants attested to this situation. Attempts to infuse capitalist relations into peasant agriculture were made through the policy land privatization. As argued in the previous section, the policy was a failure.

At the input/intermediary goods level, some industries produced goods used by other manufacturing industries: the beverage industry, which used locally produced sugar; the shoe industry, which used leather produced by local industries; and the clothing industry, which used textile fabric made by local spinning mills. In spite of these isolated cases, the integration of sectors of the economy at the intermediary goods level was not conducive to capitalist integration. First, the manufactured goods used by these industries as intermediary goods were not intended to play that role; these goods were not produced because other manufacturing branches demanded them. Most of these goods were aimed at general direct market consumption. Those industries that needed to use some goods as inputs purchased them on the regular market. Therefore, some integration between branches of the manufacturing sector was coincidental. Second, because of geographical imbalance, these isolated and accidental instances of integration remained confined within the limits of the Léopoldville and Katanga development poles. Exchanges involved only branches of the same sector, that is, the manufacturing sector. They were nonexistent between manufacturing and other sectors, especially lineage agriculture. The pattern found between the Katanga manufacturing industry and the UMHK repeated itself in the Léopoldville pole. Third, by comparison, manufacturing industries used far more imported inputs/intermediary goods than those locally produced. Table 5.8 summarizes the imbalance between exchanges of inputs/raw materials and intermediary goods and inputs/capital goods among industries in colonial Zaire.

During the 1950–58 period the yearly value of local inputs (raw materials and intermediary goods) used by local industries in their productive processes fluctuated between 36.3 percent and 25.8 percent. This contrasted with imported inputs, whose yearly value fluctuated between 74.2 percent and 63.7 percent. Overall, throughout 1950–58, manufacturing industries in colonial Zaire used only 30 percent of local inputs as opposed to 70 percent of imported inputs. As for inputs/capital goods, manufacturing industries in the colony used a mere 7 percent of local inputs as compared to 93 percent of imported goods. Even if one agrees that at its initial stage of development colonial Zaire had to depend on imported capital goods, the use of only 7 percent of local inputs after almost sixty years of capitalist expansion suggests the presence of strong dislocating effects. The suggestion is even stronger in inputs (raw materials/intermediary goods), which could have been purchased from local industries had the economic structure not been dislocated.

Thus, industrial pseudocapitalism was best illustrated by the Katanga enclave economy and a dislocated economic at the national level. A lack of capitalist integration from geographical, input–output, and sectoral points of view is apparent from the data. Because it was neutralized, capitalism failed not only to link its isolated sectors to each other but, more importantly, to extend its core relations to the noncapitalist sector.

Conclusion

Marx wrote that 'when the shift to bourgeois methods of production is initiated from above [and not from within as in feudalism], then the process of transition is apt to stop half-way, and the old mode of production is preserved rather than supplanted.'[72] One would easily be tempted to apply this remark to Zaire and, indeed, to the Third World in general. Yet, such an application would be misleading. The coexistence of the capitalist mode and the lineage mode, hence pseudocapitalism, was not the result of bourgeois methods being imposed from above – even though they were, in fact, imposed from above. Marx's view entails acceptance of the transition theory, which I have rejected. The 'old mode of production' (in this case, the lineage mode) was preserved not so much because of the way bourgeois methods were imposed, but because the old mode of production followed a path of its own; it was inconsistent, unlike feudalism, with capitalism. It is this difference, revealed by resilient noncapitalist relations and maintained by a high level of ideological routinization, that neutralized bourgeois methods; it caused the latter to generate distorted policies of exploitation, growth, and expansion whose effects made colonial and postcolonial society in Zaire fundamentally different from capitalist societies of the West. The neutralization explains agrarian and industrial pseudocapitalism and the detachment of the various colonial and postcolonial social groups and classes from the capitalist core relations. I have referred to the specificity of this society as pseudocapitalism because, as argued in chapter 1, it does not meet the definitional requirements of capitalism or meets them only partially. The traits of pseudocapitalism defined in chapter 1 – and they need not be repeated here – are very consistent with the empirical and theoretical evidence of this chapter.

The neutralization argument is not meant to deny that some of the policies undertaken in the process of capitalist expansion were deliberate, 'anticapitalist' policies, consistent with the colonial interests of those involved. Rather, I have argued that, on balance, the neutralization thesis prevails over the almighty capitalism explanation. (This type of explanation leads to the rejection of the term 'peripheral capitalism,' which is the by-product of the almighty capitalism explanation.) The primacy of the neutralization thesis over the almighty capitalism explanation does not absolve capitalism/imperialism of its exploitative responsibilities; this is not to 'blame the victim,' as may be objected. Rather, the explanation gives to precolonial societies what is owed them: they followed a different developmental path with different dynamics; capitalism was not the converging point for all civilizations. In the next three chapters, I will draw the implications of this analysis of society for the post-colonial state, the central issue of this book.

Notes

1. Harms, *River of Wealth, River of Sorrow*, p. 234.
2. Ibid.
3. Ibid., p. 235.
4. B. Jewsiewicki, 'Lineage Mode of Production . . . ,' p. 104.
5. Ndongala, op. cit., pp. 104–105; Lukoki, op. cit., p. 82.
6. Ba landier, op. cit., p. 190.
7. Randles, op. cit., p. 173.
8. Taylor, op. cit., p. 184.
9. Federation of Congolese Enterprises, *The Congolese Economy on the Eve of Independence* (Brussels, 1960), p. 19.
10. Lacroix, *Industrialisation*, p. 191.
11. Bustin, *Lunda under Belgian Rule*, p. 85.
12. Nzongola-Ntalaja, 'Class Struggle and National Liberation in Zaire,' in Bernard Mugubane and Nzongola-Ntalaja, eds. *Proletarianization and Class Struggle in Africa*, p. 69.
13. See Nzongola, *Journal of Modern African Studies* 8:4 (December 1970): 511–530; Proletarianization, pp. 57–94; *Class Struggle and National Liberation in Africa; Revolution and Counter-Revolution in Africa.*
14. Robin Cohen, 'From Peasants to Workers in Africa,' in Gutkind and Wallerstein, *The Political Economy of Comtemporary Africa*, p. 156.
15. Nz ongola-Ntalaja, *Proletarianization*, p. 73.
16. Jean-Luc Vellut, 'Rural Poverty in Western Shaba, 1890–1930,' in Palmer and Parsons, eds, *The Roots of Rural Poverty in Central and Southern Africa*, p. 300.
17. Zolberg, *One-Party Government in the Ivory Coast*, p. 26.
18. INCDI, *Staff Problems in Tropical and Subtropical Countries* (Brussels, 1961).
19. Young, *Politics in the Congo*, p. 200; Gerard Dupriez, 'L'Etat et le marché du travail,' in IRES, *Indépendance, inflation, dévelopement*, pp. 340–341.
20. Martelli, *Leopold to Lumumba*, p. 204.
21. Hugues Leclercq, 'L'inflation, sa cause: le désordre des finances publiques,' in IRES, *Indépendance, inflation, développement*, p. 147.
22. Gann and Duignan, *Burden of Empire*, pp. 258–266.
23. Samir Amin, *Le développement du capitalisme en Côte d'Ivoire* (Paris: Edition de Minuit, 1967), pp. 14–18.
24. J.P. Peemans, *Diffusion du progres economique et convergence des prix: le cas Congo Belge 1900–1960* (Louvain: Nauvelaert, 1968), p.386.
25. For the debate on this, see Ernesto Laclau, *Politics and Ideology in Marxist Theory*, Chap. 1; Immanuel Wallerstein, *The Modern World-System*, T1; Dale L. Johnson, 'Class Analysis and Dependency,' in Ronald Chilcote and Dale Johnson, *Theories of Development*, pp. 231–255.
26. Laclau, op. cit., pp.37–38

27. Jean Philippe Peemans, 'Capital Accumulation in the Congo under Colonialism: The Role of the State,' in Duignan and Gann, eds., *Colonialism in Africa 1870–1960*, 4 (Cambridge: Cambridge University Press, 1975), pp. 169–177.
28. Amin, *Unequal Development*, p. 334.
29. G. Arrighi and J. Saul, *Essays in the Political Economy of Africa*, p. 69.
30. Peter Waterman, 'The Concept of the 'Semiproletarianized Peasantry': An Empirical and Theoretical Note' in Mugubane and Nzongola, op. cit., pp. 172–180.
31. L. Baeck, 'Une société rurale en transition: Etude socio-économique de la Région de Thysville', *Zaire*, Vol. XI, 2: 115–186.
32. Bogumil Jewsiewicki, 'Political Consciousness Among African Peasants in the Belgian Congo' in *The Review of African Political Economy* 19 (September–December 1980): 23–31.
33. V. Gelders, op. cit., p. 29.
34. J. M. Domont, *La Prise de Conscience de l'individu en milieu rural Kongo*, Academie royale des sciences coloniales, T XIII, fasc 1, 1957, p. 42.
35. A Van Couwenbergh, 'Le Développement du commerce et de l'Artisanat indigènes à Léopoldville', *Zaire*, Vol. X, No. 6 (June 1956), pp. 636–664.
36. Kanyinda, op. cit., p. 118 discusses the case of Luba ex-priests and intellectuals who did so.
37. B.O de l'EIC, Décret du 6 Octobre, 1891, pp. 259–261.
38. Quoted by E. Bustin, *Lunda Under Belgian Rule*, p. 97.
39. See A. Sohier, 'Le problème des indigènes evolués et la commission du statut des Congolais Civilisés,' *Zaire*, Vol III (October 1949): 843–880.
40. Michel Wiste, 'La politique indigène au Congo Belge et l'exemple du Portugal,' *Zaire*, Vol. IV, no. 6 (June 1950): 651–658.
41. See de Hemptine, 'La politique indigène du Congo Belge,' *Congo*, T2, no. 2 (Oct. 1928): 359–374.
42. G. Van Der Kerken, 'Notre politique indigène au Congo Belge,' *Congo* (July 1949): 250.
43. Congres Colonial Belge, *Comptes Rendus et Rapports*, Brussels, February 6 & 7, 1926, pp. 196–197.
44. Bustin, op. cit., pp. 168–180.
45. Packard, op. cit., pp. 168–180.
46. 'Discours de S.A.R. le Duc de Brabant au Sénat de Belgique,' July 15, 1933.
47. This summary of privatization of land is based on Guy Malengreau, 'De l'accession des indigènes à la propriété foncière individuelle du code civil' Zaire (March 1947): 235–270; and G. Malengreau, *Vers un paysannat indigène: Les lotissements agricole au Congo Belge* (Institut Royal Colonial Belge, Memoires) TXIX, Fasc. 2, 1949.
48. G. Peeters, 'L'agriculture Congolaise et ses problèmes,' *Zaire*, Vol XII, 5 (1958): 451–478.
49. See A. Sohier, 'Le problème des indigènes evolués et la Commission du statut des Congolais Civilises, *Zaire*, Vol. III, no. 8 (October 1949): 843–880.
50. Quoted by Malengreau, 'De l'accession des indigènes . . . ', op. cit., p. 251.
51. Michel Wiste, 'Assimilation des indigènes ou ségrégation,' *Zaire*, Vol V, no. 8 (Oct. 1951): 829–838.
52. Moulaert, 'Colonisation européenne au Congo,' *Congo*, Tome II, no. 4, (Nov. 1939): 370.
53. The argument here is borrowed from Malengreau, 'De l'accession des indigènes

...', and 'Vers un paysannat; also L. Baeck,, 'Une société rurale en transition: Etude socio-économique de la Region de Thysville,' *Zaire*, Vol XI, 2: 115–186; J. M. Domont, *La prise de Conscience de l'individu en milieu rural Kongo* (Académie Royale des sciences Coloniales, 1957), T XIII, fasc. 1.

54. G. Malengreau, De l'accession des indigènes ...', p. 256.
55. V. Gelders, *Le Clan dans la société indigène* (Institut Royal Colonial Belge, 1943), T. XI, fasc. 2, p. 36.
56. Hauzeur de Fooz, *Un demi-siècle avec l'économie du Congo Belge*, pp. 34–35; CSK: Comité Spécial du Katanga 1900–1950 (Brussels: Editions Cuypers, 1950), pp. 122–125.
57. CSK:*Comité Spécial du Katanga*, pp. 60–61.
58. J. Gerard-Libois, *Katanga Secession* (Madison: Wisconsin University Press, 1966), p. 322.
59. United Nations, *Economic Bulletin for Africa*, 1, no. 2 (June 1961): 72.
60. A. Przeworski, 'Class Compromise and the State: Western Europe and Latin America,' 1980 (mimeographed).
61. Nyembo Shabani, *L'industrie du cuivre dans le monde et le progrés économique du Copperbelt Africain* pp. 191–195.
62. IRES, *Indépendance, inflation, développement*, p. 642; World Bank/IBRD, GCM Expansion Project, p. 7, Annex 2–3; and Nyembo, l'industrie du cuivre dans le monde et le progrés économique du Copperbelt Africain, pp. 106–108.
63. United Nations, *Economic Bulletin for Africa*, p. 70.
64. Jean-Louis Lacroix, *Industrialisation au Congo: La transformation des structures économiques* (Paris: Mouton, 1967), pp. 16–21.
65. Thus, for instance, the Federation of Congolese Enterprises estimated that in global terms from 1950 to 1957 nearly 130 billion francs were invested in Zaire, of which 62%, that is about 80 billion francs, were invested by private enterprises.
66. Percentages calculated from Belgium, Ministère des Colonies, La situation économique du Congo Belge et du Ruanda-Urundi (1959 issue), pp. 14ff.
67. La croix, *Industrialisation au Congo*, p. 106.
68. Ibid., p. 96.
69. Ibid., p. 263.
70. It may not be totally inaccurate to suggest that colonial officials used beer as a means to divert the attention of the indigenous populations.
71. See F. Bezy and J. L. Lacroix, *L'industrie manufacturière à Léopoldville et dans le Bas-Congo et ses problèmes d'approvisionnement 1960–1961* (Leopoldville: IRES, 1962).
72. Quoted by Maurice Dobb, 'From Feudalism to Capitalism,' in Rodney Hilton, et al., op. cit., p. 168.

6 Pseudocapitalism and overpoliticization: Competitive rule

The analysis in chapter 5 revealed the specificity of society in Zaire. I have argued that this specificity – pseudocapitalism – is explained by the neutralization of capitalism by the dynamism of the lineage mode. The analysis of pseudocapitalism leads to the central issue of this study: the overpoliticized postcolonial state. Before explaining in chapter 8 why pseudocapitalism led to an overpoliticized state, I discuss first in this chapter (and the next one) the empirical manifestations of overpoliticization under the 1960–65 competitive rule. Contrary to various explanations proposed about the 'Congo Crisis' of the 1960s, I show that the crisis highlighted the overpoliticization of the allocation of the social product in pseudocapitalism and was not the result of Belgium's lack of decolonization policy. To place the discussion in its proper context, an outline of the events surrounding the 1960–65 competitive rule follows.

1. Competitive Rule and the Congo Crisis

For tactical reasons, the Belgians sought in the fifties to create a solid alliance with the Zairian *évolués* (educated elite). Manipulated by the ideology of 'civilization,' the *évolués* forcefully worked toward such an alliance and demanded full integration with the Europeans. At first these demands did not threaten the colonial system because they were aimed at simply enhancing the status of the *évolués*. This elite sought to separate itself from the peasants and workers and to play an increasing role in colonial public affairs. Even such people as Patrice Lumumba, who later displayed a radical anticolonial stand, strongly subscribed to these petty bourgeois integrationist views: 'The native elite [évolués] whose loyalty has been officially acknowledged by a decision of the High Court, should be regarded as a genuine ally of the Belgians; it should form with them a united and dynamic team in order to continue the work of civilizing [the Congolese]. The elite must be closely associated to the goals of the Belgo–Congolese Community and act as an intermediary between their people and the colonizer by taking an adequate share in the conduct of public affairs.'[1]

Several decisions were made by the colonial government to progressively meet the goal of integration, among them the *carte de mérite civique*. However, the slowness of the integration process, exacerbated by a mutual racial suspicion and the growing frictions within the Belgian establishment on integration policy, convinced the Zairian *évolués* that full integration into the colonial system was impossible. Consequently, the *évolués* adopted a radical stand against colonial rule. They became convinced that only by assuming political power would they satisfy their socioeconomic interests. By 1956 the *Manifeste de la Conscience Africaine* was published, which raised grievances against colonial rule on socioeconomic issues; but the major part of the manifesto was devoted to emancipation issues of the African populations. Although it agreed with the Bilsen Thirty-Year Plan for independence, the manifesto rejected the idea of the Belgo–Congolese Community that was being advocated in Belgium. A countermanifesto was published in the same year by the *Association de Bakongo* (ABAKO), an ethnic sociocultural organization. ABAKO's countermanifesto espoused a more radical tone and, unlike the *Manifeste de la Conscience Africaine*, advocated political rights and total and immediate independence.

Although by Belgian rule standards these two documents were revolutionary, they did not have an immediate effect on the colonial system. The real signs of change occurred from 1957 onward as international events reinforced the radical stand of the *évolués*. De Gaulle's speech on the autodetermination of the French colonies in neighboring Congo-Brazaville in 1958, the All-African Conference organized by Kwame N'Krumah in Accra (Ghana) in 1959, in which Lumumba and other delegates participated, and the whole issue of 'self-determination' forcefully advocated by the then-emerging Third World countries were the major stimuli. These events combined with increasing tensions in the colony itself to precipitate the demise of colonial rule. In 1957, municipal elections were allowed in three major cities (Léopoldville, Elizabethville, and Jadotville) in which there were large indigenous populations. ABAKO, turned political party, was the big winner of the elections. From this victory, ABAKO was able to mobilize – if only on an ethnic basis – the unemployed in the cities and the peasants against the colonial rule. On January 4, 1959, in its attempt to contain ABAKO's influence, the colonial government banned a popular rally organized by the party. The ban generated one of the worst preindependence mass riots, causing 42 deaths and 250 injured. ABAKO's leaders, including Joseph Kasa-Vubu, were jailed.

The January 4 incident set into motion two processes. On the one hand, the Belgian and colonial governments faced a fait accompli; they had to take action in favor of emancipatory options, which was contrary to their long-held views about the political emancipation of the colony. King Baudouin announced on January 13, 1959, the organization of popular elections in other cities and the formation of a bicameral parliament for the colony. On the other hand, the Africans organized themselves institutionally to force the colonial government further toward accepting the idea of total independence. The success and prestige – assumed or real – obtained by ABAKO caused politicians to found a multitude of political parties.

There were 31 political parties as of September 1, 1959. This number increased to 51 by January 11, 1960 and reached about 120 by May 1960.[2] These political parties drew their followers primarily on the basis of ethnic allegiance. The ethnic orientation of the party system made most of these political parties nothing more than local organizations aimed at defending parochial and local interests; only a few were known on a national scale. Among the latter were those parties that based their support on large ethnic groups or coalitions with other parties, such as *Parti Solidaire Africain* (PSA), ABAKO, or *Conféderation des Associations Tribales du Katanga* (CONAKAT). The *Mouvement National Congolais* (MNC/Lumumba), on the other hand, was able to secure a wider popular base than the more ethnically oriented political parties because of its unitary and nationalist appeal.

The haste with which political parties were formed led to anticolonial and interethnic violence. For instance, in October 1959 anticolonial violence erupted in Stanleyville (Kisangani) after a congress held by the MNC/ Lumumba, during which twenty-one people were killed. In Kasai Province, the two major ethnic groups, the Lulua and Luba, fought one of the worst interethnic wars in Zaire's history; thousands of people were killed. Pressured by the emergence of a multitude of political parties and the mounting violence, the Belgian and colonial governments accepted a proposal by the Zairian political parties to organize a round table to set a date for independence.

The round table was held from January 20 to February 20, 1960, in Belgium. Fourteen political parties were represented. The delegates discussed both political/institutional and economic matters of the independent-to-be country. From a political/institutional point of view, they decided that general elections would be held in May 1960, from which the first government of independent Zaire would be formed. June 30, 1960, was chosen as the date for independence. The round table delegates also established the constitutional and institutional guidelines of the state. The *Loi Fondamentale* was worked out to guide the colony after independence. It advocated the establishment of a parliamentary regime and maintained unchanged the administrative structure of the country with its six provinces. The transfer of colonial assets to the independent-to-be state was also discussed.

The May 1960 general elections handed a sweeping victory to Lumumba's party, the MNC. It obtained 41 seats (out of 137) in the House, 19 seats in the Senate, and 113 seats in the provincial assemblies, thus placing it ahead of the

ten major political parties. As a result, Lumumba was appointed prime minister and Kasa-Vubu, the leader of ABAKO, was elected president by the parliament. On June 30, 1960, colonial rule gave way, and an independent state was
born.

However formal it may have been, independence modified social relations:
Africans became the ruling class as they assumed political power. This modification held implications for institutional change. Similarities with the *Charte
Colonial* notwithstanding, the *Loi Fondamentale* expressed the new relationship between social forces by organizing the legislative, executive, and
judiciary powers according to existing social forces. The May 1960 elections,
the appointment by the prime minister of more than twenty representatives of
different political parties to ministerial offices, and the 'Africanization' of the
bureaucracy reflected the new social relationship within the state apparatus. In
addition to the state institutions, other institutions influenced and were
influenced by the new relationships. Of these, the most important were the
trade unions, the church, the universities, and the media.

Competitive institutions were established at both the central and local levels.
At the central level, state power was shared by the head of state, a cabinet led
by a prime minister, and a two-house parliament. The election of the president
was not specified by the *Loi Fondamentale*. Rather than being a simple
constitutional figurehead in a parliamentary system, the president exercised
some executive powers as long as actions were cosigned by a minister.
Furthermore, the president was given the power to sign executive orders and
ordinances aimed at the execution of laws and could exercise legislative
powers collectively with the parliament. The cabinet, led by the prime
minister, exercised full executive powers and was responsible to the parliament. The prime minister was to be appointed by and could be fired by the
president. However, this stipulation did not apply to the Lumumba government
because Lumumba was not appointed by the president; he became prime
minister on the basis of his electoral majority in the House of Representatives.

Legislative powers were exercised mainly by the two houses of the parliament. Members of the House of Representatives were elected by direct universal suffrage and those of the Senate by provincial assemblies. Each province
was represented by fourteen senators, at least three of whom were traditional
chiefs or notables. At the local level, each province had an assembly whose
members were elected either by direct universal suffrage or by indirect vote.
The assembly elected a government either from among its own members or
from outside.

It was agreed during the 1960 round table that the *Loi Fondamentale* was to
be temporary and was to give way to another constitution after independence.
The new constitution, voted into law in 1964, radically modified some of the
main articles of the *Loi Fondamentale*. The president was given wider executive powers at the expense of the prime minister. The president was also
endowed with broader legislative powers. He was to be elected for a five-year
term and could seek reelection only once. The prime minister and the cabinet
were appointed by and could be fired by the president. The 1964 constitution

adopted a federalist stand toward local governments. Provinces were given broad autonomy, and each was led by a governor, who was elected by the provincial assembly.

The newly established social relations and political institutions soon faced a harsh reality. Only five days after independence, on July 5, 1960, army units mutinied in several cities where they were stationed,[3] triggering a series of political crises. The rebellion led to the intervention of Belgian paratroops on July 10 and 11 on the soil of this 'independent' country without the consent of the Lumumba government. Belgium argued that its intervention was aimed at 'protecting Belgian citizens.' Because it considered Belgian intervention a violation of Zaire's sovereignty, the Lumumba government requested the interposition of the United Nations to restore peace and oust Belgian troops. Amidst this troubled situation, Moïse Tshombe, the leader of the Katanga-based CONAKAT, proclaimed the independence of Katanga Province on July 11, 1960; this led to what came to be known as the Katanga Secession and lasted until 1963. Following suit, the leader of Kasai-based MNC/Kalonji, Albert Kalonji, also seceded Kasai, one of the richest regions, from the central government on August 8, 1960. Thus, within two months of its existence, the new state was torn by three major crises, and these generated a chain of other crises that lasted up to 1965.

The Belgian intervention led to the death of several innocent civilians at a time when the mutiny had subsided and no Belgian life was in real danger. Upon the Lumumba government's request, UN troops were sent to Zaire on July 15, 1960. However, because of the principle of 'noninterference in the internal affairs of a sovereign state,' the United Nations, in the first months of its intervention, could not eradicate the secession or drive the Belgian forces out. Lumumba and his closest allies sought help from the Soviet Union, while anti-Lumumbist forces strengthened, via the United Nations, their ties with the United States and Belgium. This polarization was intensified by the Katanga and Kasai secessions.

Rather than restoring peace and ousting Belgian troops, the presence of the United Nations exacerbated the struggle for state power between competing forces and internationalized the crisis. The Lumumbist forces deplored the United Nations's inertia and its complicity and appealed for help to the Soviet Union. Other local political forces directly or indirectly backed UN actions through which they could get support from the United States. As Stephen Weissman put it, 'The United Nations was the transmission belt for American policy.'[4] In fact, the crisis offered fertile ground to increase the Cold War between the East and the West. Through material assistance and political advice, both the Soviet Union and the United States and their allies took sides in the struggle for state power between national competing forces. The Soviet Union, although on a more limited basis, supported the pro-Lumumbist forces with military and political advisors, civil aircraft, and motor vehicles. The United States' high contribution to the UN operations increased its influence among the 'moderate' anti-Lumumbist forces, especially the Binza Group.[5]

N'Krumah, one of the few African leaders closely involved in the 'Congo Crisis,' stigmatized US–UN connections :

> The United Nations is, on behalf of all its members, in control of the finances of the Congo. It is now two months ago since I personally wrote to Mr. Hammarskjold to ask him where the money came from which is being used to pay the soldiers in Mobutu's illegal army. I am still awaiting an answer. One thing is certain, however, this money does not come from the revenue of the Congo. It is supplied from outside by those who wish to restore colonialism in practice by maintaining in office a puppet regime entirely financially dependent upon them.[6]

United States' support for the anti-Lumumbist forces consisted of economic, military, and political assistance. From 1960 to 1964, Zaire was the major African beneficiary of American assistance; about $178.6 million was given in economic aid.[7] Because of its support for the Katanga Secession, Belgium's attitude vis-à-vis the Léopoldville-based anti-Lumumbist forces (themselves opposed to the secession) was ambiguous.

The polarization of political forces and the internationalization of the power struggle totally split the ruling class. Three major factions emerged: the pro-Lumumbist forces, the Léopoldville-based anti-Lumumbist forces, and the secessionist forces. Because they were radically opposed to each other in a cold war fashion, both the pro-Lumumbist forces and the Léopoldville-based pro-Western forces could not agree on the strategy likely to help eradicate the secession. On the contrary, the Kasai and Katanga Secessions exacerbated their differences. On September 5, 1960, President Kasa-Vubu fired Lumumba as prime minister. Because the action was constitutionally questionable, Lumumba retaliated by firing President Kasa-Vubu. In the ensuing show of force, the then Colonel Joseph Mobutu 'neutralized' both the president and the prime minister. He set up a *Collège des Commissaires*, a provisional governent made up of college graduates, some of whom were still studying in Belgium.

The Mobutu coup and the *Collège des Commissaires* constituted a victory for the pro-Western forces. All the evidence indicates that the coup, the *Collège des Commissaires*, and the *Collège*'s subsequent policies were aimed at eliminating Lumumbist forces. Furthermore, these policies were supported and financed by the United States and Belgium.[8] The most obvious proof, perhaps, was that although both Lumumba and Kasa-Vubu were supposed to be 'neutralized,' KasaVubu resurfaced shortly after and was able to perform his tasks as the head of state while Lumumba remained under arrest. After an attempt to escape, Lumumba was recaptured by Mobutu's forces. He was eventually transferred to the secessionist forces in Katanga (in an effort to appease them), where he was killed in January 1961.

Lumumba's death compounded the crisis and triggered more radical centrifugal forces. Following the death of their leader, pro-Lumumbist forces proclaimed an 'independent state' in the northeastern part of the country where they commanded strong popular support. Their government was recognized by several Eastern bloc countries and some African countries, such as Ghana, Guinea, and Egypt. Thus, by 1961 there were three centers of power (the Kasai Secession having been eliminated), each claiming the legitimacy of state power.

The existence of three independent centers of power was advantageous for both the Katanga secessionist and the Lumumbist forces. For the Lumumbist forces, an 'independent state' of their own helped to protect them against increasing hostility toward them at the center of the power structure, that is, in the capital city. It also gave them a base from which they could launch military and diplomatic offensives against the moderates in the capital city and against the secessionist forces in Katanga Province in an attempt to regain state power on a national scale. The perceived or real advantages for the centrifugal forces were at the expense of the central government led by pro-Western forces. Deprived of Katanga Province, the central government ran out of revenues crucial for its survival; also, it faced a permanent military and political threat from the Stanleyville (Kisangani)-based Lumumbist forces. Centrifugal forces were detrimental to the interests of the Western countries that supported the 'moderates.' As a result, the pro-Western forces who controlled the central government sought a compromise with both the secessionists in Katanga and the Lumumbist forces.

The search for compromise began in a series of conferences held from January to May 1961, leading to the demise of the Stanleyville-based Lumumbist 'independent state.' The result was a national union government led by Cyrille Adoula, which lasted until 1964. Under the Adoula government, the Katanga Secession was ended militarily in January 1963 because of increased US support for UN operations against the secessionist forces. To prevent further 'unlawful' centrifugal tendencies, the Adoula government created new provinces in accordance with the expectations of the competing centrifugal forces. From six, the number of provinces increased to twenty-two in 1962. But the effect was to further Balkanize the state. The amount of autonomy granted to each of the twenty-two provinces parceled the highly sought-after state power. Competing political forces used to individual best advantage their portions of state power. The result was the appropriation of public offices and political and territorial fragmentation.

Because politics took place in a fragmented power structure, it directly affected the peasants and the unemployed, and added to their colonial frustrations. Benoît Verhaegen vividly described these frustrations:

Administrative coercion and political repression became so unbearable that they completely stood in contrast with both promises which were made (during the struggle for independence) and the masses' expectations about independence. The rural masses could not understand nor could they accept the brutal deterioration of their conditions of life and the maintenance of the administrative coercive system. In contrast with their misery, they realized that certain strata of the population had widely benefited from independence. Thus they expressed their resentment against this new bureaucratic bourgeoisie in the same way as they did against the Belgians during colonization.[9]

In their effort to eliminate the still-impetuous Lumumbist forces, the pro-Western forces used the Adoula government to silence and repress any Lumumbist opposition. The United States and other Western powers increased their influence over the Binza Group. Such influential Lumumbist leaders as Antoine Gizenga and Christophe Gbenye were either arrested or fired from the national union government. By 1962, fifteen Lumumbist ministers previously incorporated into the national union government had left the Adoula government. In the face of pervasive repression, the Lumumbist forces fled the country and organized an opposition movement (the *Comité National de Libération*) in neighboring Congo-Brazaville.

Thus, by 1962, the masses and Lumumbist forces were engaged in political struggle; having a common enemy, they combined their efforts in a series of popular rebellions. Starting in Kwilu Province in 1963 under the leadership of Lumumbist Pierre Mulele and in the Northeast, these rebellions spread rapidly throughout the country; and by 1964 rebels controlled almost three-quarters of it. On June 30, 1964, in the face of spreading popular rebellions, the Adoula government resigned. Tshombe, the former leader of the Katanga Secession, became prime minister. The major task facing his government was the eradication of popular rebellions, which was partially achieved by using mercenaries and the support of Western countries. A major blow to the rebel forces came in November 1964, when Belgian paratroops supported by the United States intervened in Stanleyville (Kisangani) and ended the rebellions in the Northeast.[10] With the end of the rebellions, a power struggle erupted among the pro-Western forces. To control state power, the Binza Group, via General Mobutu, ended the five-year competitive rule by means of a coup d'état on November 24, 1965.

2. The Katanga Secession as Overpoliticization

With good reason, the Katanga Secession has been viewed by many observers as the backbone of the 'Congo Crisis' because it set off a chain of events that dominated the 1960–65 period. The secession justified foreign interventions and precipitated the fall and death of Lumumba. Attempts to eradicate it led to the Adoula government, which tried to curb secessionist threats by Balkanizing the country. This, in turn, triggered popular uprisings, and so forth. The secession can thus be viewed as a prime manifestation of overpoliticization.

At the Brussels round table, CONAKAT, Tshombe's party, expressed views that already reflected secessionist tendencies. Politically, one of the main problems confronting the participants was the territorial form of the independent-to-be state. Three options were open. According to the first, the unitary option, power would not be divided between the central government and the provinces. Even though local authorities could make decisions on their own initiatives, the central government would be able, in all matters, to overrule them. In the second option, a federal system, the provinces would be given broader autonomy and powers while agreeing to surrender some power to the central government. A two-chamber parliament would ensure such a distribution of power, having its house representing the people at large and its senate representing the interests of the provinces. In the third option, a confederation, each of the provinces would become a separate sovereign state. The states would be linked by some kind of consultative assembly and would have certain services in common. Each state would voluntarily apply the decisions of the assembly.[11] Whereas the position of most participating parties oscillated between the unitary and the federalist systems, CONAKAT was the only party that advocated the confederal system. It also sought, contrary to most parties, to maintain a union with Belgium.

On the economic plane, CONAKAT's position was made known not only at the political round table, but also at the economic conference, which was held on April 20, 1960. The Katanga delegation argued that all natural resources are the property of the province where they are found and should be controlled by it. Furthermore, it maintained that holdings in the colony's portfolio had to be divided among the provincial governments in whose territories the companies were located. In Tshombe's own words: 'We want a relationship between development and people, a share on the basis of the contribution to the development and to the needs created by it.'[12] On most economic issues, CONAKAT's position was opposed and rejected by other political parties, especially Lumumba's MNC. Most of these parties resented the often open influence of the Katanga settlers acting as advisors to Tshombe.

The outcome of the conference was a compromise between CONAKAT's views and those expressed by other delegates. In political matters, the solution, which was finally adopted and embedded in the *Loi Fondamentale*, was neither a pure unitary system nor a federation. Although the confederal system was rejected, the compromise struck between the unitary and federal systems more or less satisfied CONAKAT's demands. The power to legislate on the exploitation of mineral deposits was vested in the central authority, which undertook to ensure the provinces a fair share of the revenues collected. The central government would also guarantee to any expropriated companies an equitable prior reimbursement and would permit the provinces to exercise the right to allocate concessions under certain constitutional rules. On the whole, the Katanga delegation expressed satisfaction with the outcome of the conference. 'We are also very satisfied,' Tshombe said, that an end has been put to the excessive centralization under which the Congo was labouring and that the Round Table Conference has resulted in the recognition of the former provinces as political entities. ... Thanks to this basic reform the independent Congo of tomorrow will escape the dislocation which threatened it.'[13] This satisfaction runs counter to the prevailing view that the Katanga Secession resulted from a constitutional crisis linked to the rejection of Katanga's call for a federalist system.

The round table set the stage for the general elections of May 1960. Because the elections were aimed at both central and provincial institutions, political parties had to concentrate their efforts on both fronts. In Katanga, Tshombe's party faced the challenge of other parties, such as the Fedeka, Atcan, MNC/Lumumba, MNC/Kalonji, and the *Union Congolaise* (the settlers' party). Despite its satisfaction with the outcome of the round table conference, CONAKAT played its old drum in Katanga. Its leadership sought during the elections to run its separatist platform, invariably playing federalist, confederalist, independentist, or separatist tunes. CONAKAT's separatist platform, in the pre-round table period, had polarized forces along ethnic lines. Out of this ethnic polarization emerged Katanga's political parties, including the Balubakat, Atcar, and Fedeka, which later joined forces to oppose the separatist stand of CONAKAT by forming the Balubakat-Cartel. Because of its separatism, CONAKAT concentrated during the general elections on provincial elections rather than on national ones.

To keep alive its separatist claims, CONAKAT's leadership relied on anticommunist and tribalist themes. Lumumba and those associated with him or his party were called Communists. To the extent that the Balubakat-Cartel shared Lumumba's unitarist views, it was an easy target for the attacks. But more importantly, perhaps, CONAKAT's separatist stand rested on the manipulation of ethnic differences. A distinction was made between 'authentic' Katangese and 'foreigners.' Foreigners referred to those ethnic groups, mostly the Luba Kasai, who had populated Katanga as labor immigrants. Even though Balubakat was originally made up of 'authentic' Luba Katanga, their ethnic bonds with the Luba Kasai differentiated them from CONAKAT. Moreover, Balubakat's association with those parties whose members were considered foreigners (Luba Kasai and Tshokwe) could not shield it from CONAKAT's attacks.

At the time of the 1957 municipal elections CONAKAT and Balubakat were yet to be constituted as political parties. Although Balubakat was already organized as an ethnic association on January 26, 1957, CONAKAT was not formed until October 25, 1958. Like Balubakat before it, CONAKAT assigned to itself the goal of organizing 'all the existing tribal associations of Katanga in order to coordinate and intensify their activities.'[14] It was, in fact, their identical goal that caused Balubakat to become a member of CONAKAT. Under the circumstances, the race for municipal offices in Elizabethville (Katanga) in 1957 was not organized by political parties as such. In the absence of CONAKAT, those who later became its core nucleus ran as individuals. However, Balubakat, which was organized a few months earlier, was able to present, if only on a purely ethnic basis, an organized front; and its members fared better than other candidates who ran as individuals.

Unlike the 1957 elections, the 1959 and 1960 general elections were characterized by a high level of antagonism created by CONAKAT's separatist stand and ethnic polarization. The outcome of the 1960 general elections at the national level has been discussed. At the provincial level in Katanga proper, sixty seats were at stake for the provincial assembly and sixteen for the

158

national House of Representatives. Two factors made provincial elections particularly crucial for Katanga's political parties. The first was the separatist stand taken by CONAKAT, which had the effect of galvanizing the opposition. The second was the constitutional requirement set by the *Loi Fondamentale* according to which a provincial government can be formed by the majority party only if two-thirds of the members of the assembly are present. For Tshombe's CONAKAT to form a homogenous government open to its secessionist ideas, the party had to ensure a solid majority in the provincial assembly. Opposition parties, however, sought to gain the edge to block any attempt at secession. They also ran hard for the national assembly slots to defeat CONAKAT's separatist claims.

In absolute numbers of votes the Balubakat-Cartel obtained more votes (110,091) than CONAKAT (104,871). Jason Sendwe, the leader of Balubakat, obtained 20,283 preferential votes as opposed to 2,200 for Tshombe.[15] In terms of seats, however, CONAKAT obtained a relative majority: 25 seats out of 60 as opposed to 23 seats for the Balubakat-Cartel. MNC/Lumumba obtained 1 seat; MNC/Kalonji, 1 seat; *Union Congolaise*, 1 seat; and independents, 9 seats.[16] This discrepancy was the result of the carving up of electoral districts. This distribution still did not ensure the majority in the assembly for CONAKAT. Through political maneuvering and payoffs, it got the majority by bringing into its camp the MNC/Kalonji and the independents. The Balubakat-Cartel claimed that the elections were characterized by massive fraud and requested an investigation; pending the investigation, it would not participate in the vote designed to form the provincial government.

The boycott of the assembly's sessions by the Balubakat-Cartel made itself felt. Unable to reach the two-thirds quorum in the assembly for the formation of the government, CONAKAT sought to amend the *Loi Fondamentale*'s proviso for the two-thirds quorum to a simple majority. The request for the amendment was flawed, because for it to be valid, the request had to come from all the participants at the round table. Despite this, the Belgian Parliament voted for the amendment by a vote of 98 votes in the House and 66 votes in the Senate. The vote for the amendment was the result of strong pressures: CONAKAT's leadership threatened to secede if the amendment was not voted through. One of the top leaders of CONAKAT warned: 'Tell the minister [of the colonies] that we give him 48 hours to have the amendment voted, and once the deadline is passed, and nothing is done, we will officially ... engage in talks with Rhodesia. Tell him simply that and do not waste your time with useless discussions.'[17] Another leader raised the specter of a coup d'état. Jules Chomé has argued that the then deputy governor-general in charge of Katanga, Scholler, strongly favored secession and played a major role in having the amendment passed.[18] In addition to threats, the Katanga transitional government strongly repressed the opposition.

The amendment to the constitution paved the way for the formation of the provincial government. Now enjoying the majority in the assembly, CONAKAT could afford to do without the vote of the Balubakat-Cartel. A homogenous government made up only of CONAKAT's members and its allies was formed on June 16, 1960. Tshombe was elected president of the provincial government, and the stage was thus sct for the secession. CONAKAT and the provincial government sought to secede from the central government on June 28, two days before independence day, June 30, 1960. Attempts to secede before independence were dictated by the false assumption made by the Katanga government that the colonial government would not intervene against secessionist forces. The favorable attitude of the settlers and of some Belgian officials, including the king, vis-à-vis Katanga's claim for separation, explained the assumption. However, to CONAKAT's surprise, once the colonial government discovered the plot, it threatened to use force against secessionist leaders. The secessionists had no choice but to call off the plan and wait for a more propitious occasion.

The army's mutiny on July 5, 1960, five days after independence, offered such an occasion. The mutiny accomplished two things for the CONAKAT leaders. First, they became convinced that, faced with the mutiny crisis, the Lumumba government was in no position to squash the secession. Second, the mutiny served to support their claims that the central government was unreliable and prone to anarchy, whereas Katanga was an oasis of peace. Six days after the mutiny, Tshombe proclaimed the independence of Katanga and with it the beginning of a three-year armed confrontation.

The Belgian government never recognized officially the 'independent state of Katanga.' But, at the time of the secession, the Belgian government was at odds with the Lumumba government over the mutiny issue; its policy actions were strongly influenced by the perception of 'Lumumba's communism.' Therefore, 'now Belgium hoped that Katanga, which had the most important investments and a third of the European population, could be insulated from the disorder and militant nationalism sweeping other provinces. Rapidly, a new image of Independence took form in government and business circles: friendly Katanga would be built up as a strong counterweight to the Lumumbist center, and would serve as a pole around which the Congo could eventually be reorganized on confederal lines.'[19] The King of Belgium himself made this clear on July 21, 1960: 'Entire ethnic groups, the leadership of which is assumed by honest and worthy men, have kept their friendship with us and ask us to help them in building their independence amidst chaos which characterizes the Belgian Congo. Our duty is to respond to all those who loyally request our collaboration.'[20] This collaboration took various forms. Politically, the Belgians advised the secessionist forces to sign an agreement with another secessionist province, the Kasai 'independent state.' The strategy to make the two secessionist provinces 'confederal states' was designed to give credibility to the idea of a 'confederal union' and to tempt other provinces to follow suit, thus weakening the Lumumbist 'unitary state.'

Belgian unofficial support for the secession took the form of administrative, economic, and military assistance. Administratively, the secessionist government benefited from the Belgian *Mission Technique*'s efforts to maintain Belgian civil servants on the job. In economic and technical matters, the *Mission Technique* stepped up its operations by increasing the number of technical personnel; the number of Belgian personnel in Katanga increased from 700 to 1,500. Militarily, Belgian support extended to disarming those members of the *Force Publique* who were hostile to the secession and to the constitution of a new military force, the *gendarmerie Katangaise*. 'Between 11 July and 8 September, more than 100 tons of arms and ammunition were flown from Brussels to Katanga, including mortars, sub-machine guns, and FN–38 automatic rifles. Twenty-five Belgian Air Force planes were repainted with Katanga's colors. Eighty-nine Belgian officers and NCOs, serving with the *Force Publique* were seconded to Tshombe's army in addition to 326 Belgian NCOs and technicians who [were] serving as volunteers.'[21] The Katanga Secession was scarcely a Belgian private affair. As the crisis intensified, the secession became an international issue. In addition to the Afro-Asian countries, Western powers were also involved in one way or another. The secessionist leaders benefited from some support from most Western countries. In the United States pro-Katanga lobbies were set up to mobilize political and financial support for the secessionist government. Influential political figures, such as Herbert Hoover, Richard Nixon, and Barry Goldwater, took an open pro-secessionist stand.[22]

However, a pro-secessionist stand, which, in fact, meant the Balkanization of the former Belgian colony, was antithetical to US long-term interests. For one thing, in spite of his anticommunism, Tshombe relied more on the Belgians than on the Americans, and there is no evidence that his government would have shifted from its pro-Belgian stand to a pro-American position. From the point of view of American long-term interests, to be efficient, the system of alliance with internal anti-Communist and pro-American forces needed to be supported by a strong, broad power basis, including such factors as territory, economic infrastructure, population, and legitimacy of the holders of state power. Any attempt at secession eroded such a base. Furthermore, in the Cold War context, centrifugal tendencies were detrimental to the United States, for they could be 'won over' by the Soviet Union. This concern was expressed by George Ball, the US under secretary of state: 'If Prime Minister Adoula should prove unable to deal effectively with the Katanga Secession of Mr. Tshombe, militant extremists such as the Communists' chosen instrument, Mr. Gizenga, would bid to take over the central government in the name of Congolese unity. In the resulting civil war our main objectives in Central Africa would be drowned in blood.'[23] The result of all these factors, as Stewart Smith put it, was that 'American imperialism came into hostile confrontation with [Belgium] and found greater opportunity to conduct its own aggressive strategy.'[24] Part of this strategy was stronger US involvement in UN operations against the secession by 1962 in spite of Belgium's protests and Britain's passive resistance. After three years of bloody confrontations and thousands of deaths, the secessionists were finally defeated by UN forces in 1963.

Interpretation and Discussion

The conclusion reached in most studies on the 'Congo crisis' has been that the crisis occurred because Belgium lacked a decolonization policy. In the Katanga Secession, an extra factor – constitutional crisis – was added. In fact, the particularity of Belgian colonial rule has often been cited as the cause of the crisis. Although the argument bears some truth, it can be disposed of easily. Undoubtedly, Belgian colonial rule was specific, as seen in the foregoing analysis. Peculiar to the rule were the extremely small number of indigenous petty bourgeoisie by independence day, including those in agriculture; the relatively low level of formal education for the elite and the elite's lack of political and managerial experience; the higher level of economic growth than in most colonies; and the enormous crude wealth of the colony. The consequential effects of these particularities were the *earlier* eruption of the crisis than in most newly independent countries and the sheer *magnitude* of it. However, neither the earlier eruption of the crisis nor its magnitude made the crisis specifically a Belgian Congo phenomenon. Would the crisis have occurred at some point in Zaire had the Belgians had a decolonization policy? The answer is yes. This by no means suggests the teleological inevitability of the crisis in the former Belgian Congo or elsewhere but makes two crucial points. First, a body of comparative empirical evidence supports the claim. Second, the 1960–65 crisis in the former Belgian Congo shared structural similarities with those in other Third World countries, whether colonized or not.

That the crisis was not specific to the Belgian Congo has been supported by ample evidence from the Third World for the last four decades in African and Asian countries and longer in Latin America. But for a comparison with the immediate postcolonial period, a quick survey of some cases will suffice to back the claim. In Indonesia, a 'commonwealth' with the colonial power – Holland (one is reminded of the Belgo–Congolese Union) – was envisaged by 1942. With the onset of World War II and the ensuing Japanese occupation, the project was halted. In spite of a 1946 agreement (Linggadjati Accord), which recognized the Republic of Indonesia, the Dutch waged war against Indonesian nationalists until 1949, when they finally recognized Indonesia's independence. Sukarno, who had become chairman of a Japanese-sponsored All-Indonesian Independence Preparatory Committee in 1945, emerged as one of the major postwar Indonesian leaders. In 1950, a new constitution was enacted, and the Sukarno government wanted to establish a unitary state. The new constitution concentrated authority in the parliament and made the cabinet responsible to the parliament. The result was a proliferation of political parties, leading to a pattern of political instability and crises. Sukarno's undermining of the democratic institutions by bypassing them and the anticonstitutional behavior of some political parties led to political disorder and bureaucratic ineptness. The result of this pattern was open armed confrontation expressed in guerilla warfare, military coup attempts, rebellions, civil war, the imposition of martial law, and, finally, the decisive coup that led to the overthrow of Sukarno in 1966.[25]

In Burma, independence was declared from Britain on January 4, 1948. General chaos prevailed in the postindependence period as political factions waged war against each other. Civil war, rebellions, secessionist movements by ethnic groups such as the Karens and the Shans, and an incurable wave of banditry often dominated Burma's immediate postindependence political scene. The countryside formed a maquis populated by Communist partisans, dissidents, autonomists, those who had lost power, and fanatic students, not to mention groups of bandits.[26]

Whether in India, Indo-China, Latin America, or Africa, the postindependence period was characterized by a protracted crisis. One recalls the crises of 'national consolidation' in the first half of the nineteenth century in Latin America, the Hindu–Muslim confrontation in India in 1947–48, or the circumstances surrounding the origins of the Vietnam War. These cases reveal convincingly that the 'Congo Crisis' was not in essence a by-product of Belgian colonial rule. Belgian rule only gave it its specific form.

Another thesis about the 'Congo Crisis' in general, just as questionable, was proposed by Jean-Claude Willame. While attempting to explain the centrifugal relationship that characterized the crisis by using Weber's concept of patrimonialism, Willame argued that it resulted from the elite's reliance on personal loyalties. It is this type of loyalty, wherein 'the person exercising authority is not a superior but a personal chief,' that led to centrifugal tendencies among the elite: 'Weber further asserts that patrimonial rulership is an inherently decentralized system of government. Indeed, in the Congo the rush to appropriate public offices coincided with a process of centrifugal fragmentation that totally undermined the coherence and primacy of the central government. The only real centers of political power were various competing paramount suzerains backed by shifting clientele of local followers and personal retainers.'[27] This explanation, which would be outdated today were it not for the resurgence of Weberian analyses as seen in chapter 2, is deceptive for two reasons. First, in an attempt to apply the concept of patrimonialism, Willame unjustifiably personalizes all relationships even where they are obviously group-based. According to him, 'The new provinces [in 1962] resulted neither from ethnic imperatives nor from a rational political process. They were the product of arduous discussion between *powerful individuals*, and so did not necessarily exhibit tribal uniformity.'[28]

The evidence presented by Willame himself does not support this claim. Concerning the reasons given for creating new provinces, the debates in both parliamentary houses contradict the patrimonial argument. In the House of Representatives, 49.2 percent of the members favored the creation of the new provinces on the ground of 'tribal homogeneity.' In the Senate, 28.4 percent of the members argued in favor of the new provinces for the same reason. Members of the parliament also supported the creation of the new provinces on the grounds that it fostered the representativeness of regional leaders: 34.9 percent of the members of the House of Representatives and 43.2 percent in the Senate. On the whole, then, 84.1 percent of the members of the House of Representatives voted in favor of Balkanization for ethnic and regional

163

reasons; in the Senate, 71.6 percent of the members favored Balkanization for the same reasons. Clearly, Balkanization resulted from 'ethnic/regional' imperatives rather than from the dictates of 'powerful individuals.' No doubt, some powerful politicians played a major role in determining the outcome of the policy. But how could it be otherwise? Rarely, if at all, can an ethnic or regional movement be successful without a leader.

To further strengthen his patrimonial claims, Willame maintains that these powerful patrimonial leaders did not always operate within the confines of their ethnic groups. Many extended their 'suzerainty' over other ethnic groups and regions. This is scarcely a convincing argument in support of patrimonialism. That political leaders cross party lines to appeal to others does not mean that their association with their own party has ended. In the same vein, that politicians appeal to other ethnic groups is not evidence of their patrimonial character and their lack of association with their ethnic groups. This is not to reduce everything politicians did to 'tribal politics' but to show that the evidence in favor of personalized and patrimonial relationships is unpersuasive.

Willame also justified the notion of patrimonialism by arguing that Balkanization was not based on 'rational' (economic) reasons because 'the economic survival of many new provinces was uncertain. Seven of the twenty-one provinces had no real economic resources. And some provincial capitals faced the loss of hinterland areas necessary to their continued commercial and industrial development.'[29] This may be true; but by the same token, patrimonial leaders, who obviously needed as many resources as the provinces did to maintain patrimonial links, also faced the same economic hardship. Why, then, would patrimonial relationships flourish while group- or region-based ones did not? Furthermore, if seven out of twenty-one provinces did not have a sound economic base, fourteen did. One cannot, therefore, minimize the important role played by economic factors in the Balkanization.

In his attempt to apply Weber's concept of private armies, Willame reduces the Katanga and Kasai secessions and the Lumumbist government that was established in the Northeast to patrimonial relations. He reduces their armies to 'private armies.' The Katanga Secession was, without doubt, a broad regional movement. The Lumumbist government in the Northeast part of the country, on the other hand, was genuinely a national movement. How could their armies be private, that is, organized in the sole interest of the individual leaders? That secessionist or Lumumbist leaders were prominent in these movements and had real control over the armed forces was to be expected, but this scarcely made the armies private instruments of the leaders. If anything, they were the coercive instruments of what the movements stood for. Again, the point is not that the Balkanization of the territory was a regional or tribal movement – even though in many respects it was. What is being underscored is the fact that centrifugal forces were not the result of patrimonial, personalized relationships.

Even if these relationships were personalized, patrimonialism fails to explain them – the second major weakness of the patrimonial thesis. At best it describes the form these relationships took: appropriation of public offices as the elite's prime source of status, prestige, and reward; political and territorial fragmentation through the development of relationships based on primordial and personal loyalties; and the use of private armies, militias, and mercenaries as chief instruments of rule.[30] A question remains: Why did centrifugal forces take the form (Balkanization, secession) they did? In other words, why were these relationships patrimonial? Here, Willame, like most protagonists of patrimonialism, provides a tautological answer: They were patrimonial because they fit the description of patrimonialism. Differently put, they were patrimonial because Max Weber said so. In the given definition of patrimonialism, it appears that the 'elite's quest for status, prestige and reward' is an implicit explanation. But, then, why does the elite in Western democracies not seek reward through the same patrimonial means? Willame answers this by saying that in Western countries the effects of patrimonialism are diffused by established political and governmental hierarchies. In the Third World, the effects of patrimonialism are felt because authority is dispersed, the scope of government activity limited, and intense power politics often the only channel of social mobility.[31]

Two things transpire from this explanation. First, patrimonial relations are subordinated to a causal variable, that is, intense power politics. Second, the causal variable itself is compared to that prevailing in Western countries and is said to differ from it. It follows that Balkanization and centrifugal forces did not result from patrimonial ties but from 'intense power politics.' It also follows that the causal variable – intense power politics – needs to be explained and its difference from Western countries accounted for. The concept of patrimonialism cannot help fulfill this task. The Balkanization of the territory and centrifugal movements such as secession were the expression of intense power politics, that is, overpoliticization. As such, they revealed the specificity of the competition over the social product under pseudocapitalism. Power holders, centrifugal forces, and insurgents fought for power control to ensure an advantageous position in the competition. For example, centrifugal movements allowed politicians to strengthen their economic and financial bases. In 1962, their wages rose by 400 percent, causing the wage and salary budget to average 82 percent of the state spending. Owing to this accumulation of wealth and the appropriation of public offices, 36.8 percent of Provincial Assemblymen, 33.3 percent of Provincial Ministers, 47.8 percent of House Representatives, and 47.8 percent of senators invested in private businesses.[32]

For the Katanga Secession itself, the evidence in support of the constitutional/institutional failure argument is shaky as well. First, as pointed out earlier, by his own admission, Tshombe and his party were satisfied with the resolutions of the round table. Most of their concerns and requests had been met. The many declarations they made after the conference attested to this. Even such die-hard unitarists as Lumumba conceded to some of CONAKAT's demands by allowing a greater level of decentralization within a unitary framework. Second, and perhaps most important, the *Loi Fondamentale* itself embraced the concepts of a federalist state, which was in tune with Tshombe's options. There is, therefore, no reason to believe that an institutional vacuum triggered the secession. Nor can it be imputed to the mutiny of July 5 because Tshombe and his party had sought to secede (but failed) two days before independence and before the mutiny became a reality.

Having thus eliminated the institutional, patrimonial, and lack-of-Belgian-decolonization-policy arguments, four other reasons have been advanced to explain the Katanga Secession: economic grievances, the role of the settlers, the role of foreign-based actors, and ethnic rivalries. René Lemarchand has summed up the first three; it is worth quoting at length.

> Among the several factors which predisposed the Katangese leaders to claim self-determination, at least three deserve emphasis. One is the sense of economic grievance which shaped the attitude of the Katangese toward the inhabitants of the other provinces. ... Regional differences in the distribution of economic resources operated to aggravate latent tensions among ethnic groups, so that economic stratification tended to coincide with tribal divisions. In a sense, therefore, sectional and tribal antagonisms must be viewed as symptoms of economic grievances. The fact that the Conakat succeeded in rallying the support of otherwise unrelated entities (Lunda, Bayeke, Batabwa, etc.) suggests indeed that these grievances were an important source of solidarity among its members.
>
> A second determinative factor was the part played by the white settlers in making the idea of secession both economically attractive and politically meaningful. The alliance between settler interests and 'genuine' Katangese, prompted by the decision of the Belgian government to grant the Congo its independence, did not imply a fundamental change in their objectives. On the contrary, the tactics employed by the colonat consisted in communicating its political conceptions to the Conakat without in any way attempting to exercise exclusive control over the affairs of the party. By a process like osmosis, the Conakat identified itself with the ideas and attitudes which gave the settler community of the Katanga its distinctive outlook.
>
> A third explanatory factor lies in the outside support accorded by Belgian metropolitan interests to the advocates of the secession. This support by itself did not provoke the emergence of separatist claims, but it provided the external stimulus that made the prospects of a secession increasingly attractive. And it was the external stimulus that made the secession feasible.[33]

In some writings, the focus on external support, Lemarchand's third explanatory factor, reduces CONAKAT's leaders to simple puppets of the Belgians. No doubt, foreign actors, especially the Belgians, played an important role in the secession. The support ranged from that of the Belgian king to the economic and financial package provided by the UMHK to the *Mission Technique*'s managerial and military assistance. Considering the central position of the UMHK in Katanga's economy, it came as no surprise that its local and Belgium-based officials played a major role in the secession. 'The UMHK's direct contribution to the Katangan state was vital to Elizabethville not only because of its size, but also because of its 'demonstrated value' for all the other Belgian companies. During the 2½ years preceding January 1963, when Tshombe's government capitulated, they had obtained roughly 240 million dollars from the Union Minière in payment of royalties, taxes and other assessments.'[34]

Despite the support of foreign-based actors, external support did not create the secession. Lemarchand correctly argued that it only provided the stimulus and made secession feasible. Had it not been for the delay tactics used by the Belgian government at the United Nations while organizing the secessionist armed forces in the first months of the secession, the Lumumba government would have been able to crush the secession. The Belgian role here was to make the secession feasible. Another good argument against an overemphasis on foreign actors has been provided by Jules Gerard-Libois. One issue advanced to support the claim of a secession 'made in Belgium' has been the scheme for division of the CSK portfolio and the agreement concluded by the Belgian authority on the eve of independence with the *Compagnie du Katanga*. Against this, Gerard-Libois has argued that the antisecessionist Balubakat's signing of the agreement with other Katangese delegations, including the secessionist CONAKAT, contradicts the claim. To see the agreement as a Belgian attempt to foster secession would be tantamount to viewing Balubakat as a secessionist movement, which it was not. Gerard-Libois put the role of the UMHK, which has also been seen as the foremost secession maker, into perspective. He admits that in July 1960 Katanga could not secede without the support of the UMHK, which had to provide it with essential resources, directly or indirectly, and that 'the Union Minière and Tshombe were inseparable and lived in direct symbiosis for several months.' Nevertheless, the active role of CONAKAT's leaders themselves and the dilemma of the UMHK shows that the UMHK was not the incurable secession maker it was purported to be: 'That explains why, after November, 1961, when the Katangans thought they could detect a desire on the part of the UMHK management in Brussels to review relations with Leopoldville, Tshombe, his ministers, and his advisers let the UMHK understand that they would not tolerate negotiations by the company alone with the UN or with the Congolese Monetary Council.'[35]

Caution is also required in assessing the role of the settlers in the secession. This role has generally been presented as a self-regulating process detached from African influence. In reality, their role and that of the Katangese influenced each other. The result was mutual influence between the settlers and the Katangese leaders. The role of the European settlers in the secession antedated 1960; one has to go back to 1956 to detect the first signs of secessionist tendencies. In the aftermath of ABAKO's 'radical' manifesto, the mood among Katanga settlers was one of defiance and panic. The manifesto's unequivocal demand for immediate independence and basic freedom was seen by the settlers as a veritable call for war by a 'group of deranged people.' As a result, the settlers' pre-1956 call for increased settlement by Europeans in Katanga became even more urgent. To channel these efforts toward increased settlement, the settlers founded the Union for the Settlement (UCOL). The call for increased European settlement aimed to defend the settlers' economic interests by demanding internal autonomy for Katanga. Ample evidence shows that the settlers' claims for Katanga's autonomy did influence CONAKAT's leaders, some of whom acknowledged it.[36] There is also evidence that the settlers financially supported CONAKAT.

Yet CONAKAT's leaders were no more a creation of the settlers than they were of foreign-based actors. CONAKAT was at the very outset tailored along tribal lines. Among its constitutive groups was the *Groupement des Associations Mutuelles de l'Empire Lunda*, which by itself was indicative enough of the need to capitalize on the fame of the precolonial Lunda empire. Before taking an antisecessionist stand, the Balubakat was a constitutive group of CONAKAT. The concerns these groups sought to express when organizing themselves were not inspired by the settlers. Moreover, even when taking into account the settlers' later influence on CONAKAT's leaders, such an influence was successful only because these leaders were open to it. Although they may have become more conscious of secessionist claims through their association with the settlers, there is no evidence that the settlers created that consciousness. Some earlier references to the autonomy of Katanga by CONAKAT's leaders can be found in speeches before their collusion with the settlers. The creation of CONAKAT was partly the result of antisettler sentiments among the Katangese. Thus Evariste Kimba, one of CONAKAT's leaders, maintained that CONAKAT was founded 'to demonstrate to the settlers that Katanga was not a desert before the arrival of the Europeans and that this province could not be made to serve (as some settlers had hoped, for reasons abundantly clear) as a region for massive European settlement.'[37] Such sentiments against the settlers were justified, for the settlers had early on 'a very poor opinion of the 'authentic' Katangese (the core membership of Conakat). They were considered especially incompetent, and, because of this alleged lack of ability, the UMHK recruited 'stranger' workers.'[38] In short, the collusion between the settlers and the Katangese was not complete; it does not in itself explain the secession. Gerard-Libois' observation on the complex relationship between the settlers and the Katangese is to the point: 'We are sometimes tempted to explain totally the Conakat phenomenon by the strongly felt need of the Europeans to have at their disposal a transmission belt into African circles. The reality is more complex. ... Elsewhere another phenomenon was developing. Ethnic groups in Katanga – the very same who proclaimed themselves 'authentic Katangans' – had the more or less spontaneous feeling that industrialization and urbanization were benefiting them less than 'stranger' Africans, especially Kasai immigrants.'[39]

There is no doubt that ethnic claims figured prominently in the secessionist discourse. But such claims were not exclusive to the African Katangese; they also pervaded the secessionist discourse of the settlers and foreign-based actors. As early as 1956, in the aftermath of the ABAKO manifesto, the settlers' attempt to speed up the process of European settlement in Katanga and to ensure an alliance with the Katangese was based on the 'respect of the traditions and customs' of the Katangese natives, whom they contrasted to those in other 'dangerous' provinces. Such a respect for traditions, they maintained, was needed to further and protect investments in Katanga. At the same time, these traditions were said to prevent the African Katangese from practicing political democracy and managing Katanga's economy. The 1957 municipal elections and the electoral success of the Balubakat were major turning points for the settlers in their manipulation of tribalist claims. In the face of Balubakat's unitary views, the settlers' discourse more closely identified with the more particularistic and tribalist views of CONAKAT. To 'authentic' Katangese, they opposed 'strangers' and claimed the right to share the fruits of development of Katanga with its 'authentic' sons. They were given a boost by King Baudouin of Belgium, who insisted on the cultural, ethnic, and economic particularities of Katanga. Ethnic claims were made in the name of traditional chiefs, whose subjects were said to be the prime beneficiaries of Katanga's immense wealth.[40]

Claims of ethnic and economic particularities were also made by the Africans. The year 1957 marked a turning point in Katanga's ethnic polarization. In that year Balubakat, whose goal was to insure mutual assistance among all the Luba people and to protect any aspect of their traditions and customs, was formed. In a chain reaction, CONAKAT was founded in 1958 with the goal to unite 'all tribal associations of Katanga,' including Balubakat. However, signs of strains between CONAKAT and Balubakat appeared in early 1959. Citing the increasing influence of the Luba Kasai in Katanga's affairs and economy at the expense of the 'authentic' Katangese, CONAKAT openly adopted an anti-Luba stand. Its leaders relied increasingly on the ethnic and economic particularities of Katanga. They wrote: 'We are a tribal movement, since beside us there are no other interlocutors whose claims are based on concrete facts: land, history, population, in short, Katanga's heritage.'[41] Traditions, customs, and traditional chiefs became catchwords expressing ethnic identity.

The reliance on traditions and tribes brought into sharper focus the role of traditional chiefs, who were seen as 'sovereign authorities' from whom all decisions emanated. According to CONAKAT, 'Having always recognized and respected the authority of the traditional chiefs before the arrival of the Europeans, Katanga would not allow it to be otherwise.' The traditional chiefs, in addition to history, the dead and living populations, and land, ensured the legitimacy of CONAKAT and its claims for separation. To these chiefs CONAKAT promised 'unlimited authority,' contrary to what happened during colonial rule. The chiefs responded in kind and strongly subscribed to the secessionist theses. For example, Luhinda Mwenda Munongo, the grand chief of the Yeke, maintained that 'our Confederation (CONAKAT) will only make progress. If it is prosperous, it will be much happiness for all this country and the Bayeke.' Mwat Yamv, the Lunda grand chief, supported the idea of development based on cultural, ethnic, and economic particularities.[42] As the date of independence approached, traditional chiefs opposed a united country, claiming that their subjects, who were profoundly attached to them, did the same. Recall that it was with the support of the traditional chiefs in the provincial assembly that CONAKAT was able to obtain a majority of the seats and thus to form a homogenous government. Support by the traditional chiefs was also crucial in Katanga's armed confrontation against the central government and UN forces.

The prominence of ethnic claims did not, however, explain the secession. First, recourse to such claims by the settlers and foreign actors amply demonstrated that 'tribalism' was a mere instrument used by them to advance other specific interests. The settlers were not 'tribesmen' owing allegiance to a tribe. Commitment to the tribe could not be the reason why they advocated secession. Second, the 'authentic' Katangese were not made of a homogenous 'tribe.' They were an assortment of different groups led by the Lunda. On strictly tribal grounds, these groups were as much 'strangers' to the Lunda as the Luba were. Therefore, their alliance with the Lunda could not have been based on tribal allegiances. There is no reason why the Lunda would be allied with other groups that were not part of their tribe but be opposed to Luba-Katanga on 'tribal' grounds. Nor could the alliance be explained by regional affinities because both the Balubakat and the 'authentic' Katangese were from the same Katanga region. Clearly, CONAKAT's opposition to the Balubakat stemmed from the latter's control over and claims to socioeconomic resources.

Thus, as explanations of the secession, foreign actors, the settlers, and ethnic rivalries do not fare well; they cannot stand on their own. They were determined by the competition over the social product ('economic grievances'). Foreign actors and the settlers were not the secession makers, but they were part of the competition. By standing as the 'engine of development' for the newly independent country while being controlled by foreign interests, the Katanga economy was at the center of competition (see the discussion about pseudocapitalism in chap. 5). The role of foreign actors in the secession was, therefore, explained by their attempt to compete over economic resources provided by the enclave economy. This held true also for the settlers. Unlike the Africans, the settlers controlled the major means of production and held a prevailing position in the Katanga pseudocapitalist economy. The secession constituted for them a form of competition over resources that their prevailing position afforded them.

Competition over the social product was also the determinant factor behind the secessionist stand of the Katangese, the main secessionist force. It must be borne in mind that the continual development of mining was conditional upon an increase in labor, which could not be found in Haut Katanga itself. Efforts were made to recruit workers from the northern regions of Katanga, especially from the Lomami district. After the railroad leading to Port Francqui was opened, workers were recruited from the Kasai region where the Luba live, resulting in more migrant workers from the Luba region than Katangese workers. In 1958 and 1959 unemployment grew severe, especially among unskilled workers. The unemployment issue caused CONAKAT's leaders to express their grievances against the Luba. These grievances stemmed from the undisputed fact that Katanga as an enclave capitalist economy was the provider of goods and services for the whole country. The dislocated, hence, pseudocapitalist nature of this economy had made those originally from

Katanga its 'proud owners.' Grievances were expressed not only against the Luba but also against other regions of the country through attacks against the central government. CONAKAT's leaders made the point aptly: 'We want more fairness in the distribution of resources. ... We insist on the fact that Katanga, which provides the biggest share of the Congolese budget, should not be deprived of its share of the cake.'[43] Comparing the central government to the biblical pigs, the secessionist leaders claimed that it did not deserve the larger share of the cake.[44] Here also, the secession constituted the means of competition for the larger share of the social product.

Conclusion

The conventional explanations advanced to account for the Katanga secession and the 'Congo Crisis' do not stand up well under close scrutiny. For the Belgian rule and institutional arguments to be convincing, one needs to show that the two also obtained in other Third World countries where crises have occurred; institutional weakness is not sufficient. Patrimonialism does not fare any better, limited as it is to describing rather than explaining. I have argued that the roles of foreign actors and settlers and ethnic rivalries in the secession were indissociable from the competition over the social product in pseudocapitalism. Because the competition relied on overpoliticization, it manifested itself in the form of secession and 'crisis.' The manifestations were consistent with the definition of overpoliticization in chapter 1. Reliance on overpoliticization distinguished the 1960–65 competitive rule from capitalist democratic rule; this, in turn, suggests that their respective types of state are different.

Yet this discussion does not advance the argument that much. The Katangese did not deserve pride of place for economic grievances. Even if one takes into account the auxiliary role of ethnicity, the discussion would remain incomplete.[45] The Belgians themselves were (and are) confronted with socioeconomic grievances against the background of the Walloon–Flemish ethnic problem; so are Canadians with the issue of French-Canadians. If economic grievances along ethnic rivalries explained secession, then we would expect the Walloons to secede from Belgium or the French Canadians to secede (or succeed in seceding) from Canada because they, too, have grievances along ethnic lines. Because this is not the case, the crucial question becomes: Why did competition over the social product in Katanga result in overpoliticization (secession) resembling that which prevails in other Third World countries? In other words, why was it necessary for the Katangese and other social forces to rely on overpoliticization when, as part of a 'democratic rule,' they could have solved their economic grievances through democratic means? (The question still holds even if one takes into account CONAKAT's leaders' threat to secede before democratic rule was actually established; the round table-generated constitution, to which they subscribed well before independence, guaranteed the democratic rule to come.) Because it is central to this study, this question can be answered well only in comparative and theoretical terms (see chap.

8). Before doing so, however, I show in the next chapter that Mobutu's authoritarian rule was also an expression of overpoliticization in the competition for the social product in pseudocapitalism.

Notes

1. P. Lumumba, *Congo, My Country* (New York: Praeger, 1962), p. 9.
2. Alan Merriam, *Congo: Background of Conflict* (Evanston, IL: Northwestern University Press, 1961), p. 114.
3. On the causes of the mutiny, see R. Cornevin, *Histoire du Congo*, p. 263.
4. Weissman, *American Foreign Policy in the Congo 1960–1964*, p. 75.
5. The Binza Group was a group of pro-Western politicians associated with the US CIA and who displayed a strong anti-Lumumbist feelings.
6. N'Krumah, *Challenge of the Congo*, p. 131.
7. Weissman, *op. cit.*, p. 205.
8. See Cornevin, *op. cit.*, p. 274 and Weissman, *op. cit.*, pp. 85–99.
9. Verhaegen, *Rébellions au Congo*, T1, pp. 62–63.
10. On Northeastern rebellions, see B. V. Verhaegen, *Rébellions au Congo*, T2 (CRISP, 1968).
11. See Catherine Hoskyns, *The Congo since Independence* (London: Oxford University Pres, 1967), p. 43.
12. Economic Round Table 1960, Document 17.
13. Infor Congo, 'The Belgo–Congolese Round Table,' p. 18.
14. *Essor du Congo*, October 29, 1958.
15. J. Chomé, *Moise Tshombe et l'escroquerie Katangaise*, pp. 201–203.
16. *Congo 1960* (Brussels: CRISP, 1961), p. 243.
17. *Essor du Congo*, June 12, 1960.
18. Chomé, *op. cit.*, pp. 207–218.
19. Weissman, *op. cit.*, p. 69.
20. Quoted in Chomé, *op. cit.*, p. 266.
21. *Daily Mail* quoted by Colin Legun, *Congo Disaster* (Baltimore, Penguin Books, 1961), p. 159.
22. J. Gerard-Libois, *Katanga Secession*, pp. 181–182.
23. US Department of State Bulletin (January 1, 1962), pp. 47–48.
24. Stewart Smith, *US Neocolonialism in Africa* (Moscow: Progress Publishers, 1974), p. 39.
25. See E. Kim and L. Ziring, *An Introduction to Asian Politics*, pp. 311–333; Institute Royal des Relations Internationales (Brussels), *Chronique de politique étrangère*, Vol. XIII, no. 4–6 (July–November 1960): 422–423.
26. *Chronique de politique étrangère*, p. 427.
27. J. C. Willame, *Patrimonialism and Political Change in the Congo*, p. 34.
28. Ibid., p. 43 (Emphasis added.)
29. Ibid., pp. 46–47.
30. Ibid., p. 2.
31. Ibid., p. 3.
32. Willame, *Patrimonialism and Political Change in the Congo*, pp. 32, 177.
33. R. Lemarchand, *Political Awakening in the Belgian Congo*, p. 247.

34. Mugur Valahu, *The Katanga Circus* (New York: Robert Speller and Sons, 1964), p. 142.
35. Gerard-Libois, *Katanga Secession*, pp. 207–208.
36. *Essor du Congo*, February 1, 1956.
37. Chomé, *op. cit.*, p. 80.
38. Gerard-Libois, *Katanga Secession*, p. 17 and note 21 on the same page.
39. Ibid., pp. 278–79.
40. *Chronique de politique étrangère*, pp. 1153–1156; *Europe Magazine*, January 12, 1960.
41. *Essor du Congo*, April 25, 1959.
42. See Chomé, *op. cit.*, pp. 101 and 137, 142–143.
43. *Essor du Congo*, May 30, 1959.
44. Uhaki, no. 37, November 13, 1961.
45. In the Appendix I explain why ethnic claims are prominent in the Third World.

7 Pseudocapitalism and overpoliticization: Authoritarian rule

The 1965 *coup d'état* by General Mobutu ended the five-year competitive rule and consolidated the hitherto fractionalized state power. The consolidation incurred a clearly defined course of action, within an authoritarian framework, for the role of the state in organizing national unity and in promoting the economic well-being of the country. One month after the takeover, General Mobutu gave a speech in which he identified these different features, including the essentially civilian form of the government.

> With your accord I will take necessary measures. Owing to the exceptional nature of the situation, the measures ought to be exceptional too, in every aspect [of the state's life]. Thus, since November 24, 1965 I have ended the stupidly intense power struggle among political parties. For five years no political party will be allowed to exist in this country. Politicians had harmed the country so badly that they should not be allowed to do it again. My government is not made of politicians. The appointed ministers represent no political party but only and strictly their provinces. ... As such, their activities will be kept in check and supervised by another military officer whom I am appointing as Prime Minister, namely Colonel Mulamba, this courageous and honest man whom you all know. Were it ever to happen that one of them [i.e., ministers] fails to fulfill his duties as a civil servant, aware of our military role, Colonel Mulamba and myself would act and take our responsibility. I have told you that no political party will be allowed to exist in this country. As a matter of fact the situation is so urgent that we should

not allow any political debate, however short, among politicians. ... And finally, I realize that the social, economic, and financial situation of the country is catastrophic. ... No one works in the Congo anymore, no one produces anymore. Before 1960 the Congo produced 120,000 tons of corn; today it produces only 20,000 tons; before 1960 it produced 5 million tons of manioc; today it produces 900,000 tons.[1]

Policies under the Mobutu regime were to be formulated against this authoritarian background. Authoritarian rule became the other side of the same coin, the overpoliticized state; the other end was the 1960–65 competitive rule. Like the 1960–65 competitive rule, authoritarian rule meant reliance on overpolitcization in the competition for the social product in pseudocapitalism. It differed from the 1960–65 competitive rule only by its form of coalitions and the more rigid elimination of interest articulation by power holders. Overpoliticization had a corollary: by serving as a means of accumulation and allocation of the social product, it reinforced pseudocapitalism. The result was the exacerbation of socioeconomic deprivation and more overpoliticization in the form of political crisis. As in the previous chapter, I do not intend to explain here why overpoliticization took place under Mobutu, a task I will perform in the next chapter. My intention in this chapter is to simply describe the manifestations of overpolicization under authoritarian rule.

The literature on authoritarian rule in Zaire is abundant. An outline of the rule will be enough here. The data in support of the discussion that follows are mostly related to the 1965–80 period; change and evolution in the post-1980 period scarcely altered the basic tenets of the rule established during the earlier period.

1. Authoritarianism and Capital Investments

General Mobutu revealed in his speech that a sharply authoritarian move was needed to achieve the stability of the new regime. After the coup d'état, the new regime emasculated the parliament by removing its legislative powers; physically or legally eliminated the opposition; and finally, in 1967, created a new constitution. The new constitution drastically reduced the number of provinces from twenty-one to nine, eliminated all competing political parties, and formed a single state-supported political party, the *Mouvement Populaire de la Révolution* (MPR). After the post of Prime Minister was eliminated in 1966, the president's power was increased.

The MPR arose from a national youth organization called *Corps des volontaires de la République* (CVR), which was formed in 1966 as a means to prop up the new regime through political rallies and denunciation of all opponents. The new regime, eager to absorb all political and administrative institutions into a monolithic structure, abolished the CVR and created the MPR on May 20, 1967. Juan Linz calls regimes' attempts to mobilize citizens to participate in well-defined, more or less monopolistic channels through a single or dominant party mobilizational authoritarianism.[2] The MPR, in many respects, played that mobilizational role. It emerged with a manifesto of its own, *Manifeste de la Nsele*, containing some of its main ideological postulates. Among these, three particularly revealed the authoritarian and 'developmentalist' nature of the new regime.

- The MPR sees to the establishment of a political structure that favors the economic development of the nation and the emancipation of the people.
- The MPR is opposed to any attempt to contest the national state's authority.
- The MPR is opposed to any kind of economic domination and proclaims the necessity to free the people from economic exploitation.

In spite of their inclusion in the manifesto, these postulates remained vague and without any real internal coherence. The *Manifeste de la Nsele* enunciated such generic values as patriotism, nationalism, and social justice. Attempts to give them some coherence were made later when *authenticité* (authenticity) became the official ideology of the state. Nationalism was redefined in terms of authenticity, both fusing within the catchphrase 'authentic nationalism.' And authenticity was defined as 'a movement tending to revive the moral, cultural, philosophic, social and economic values distinct to the Zairian nation. Such a movement repudiates contradictory foreign ideas. It proceeds from a consciousness of the particularity of Zairians ... who have no reason to abase themselves before European culture.[3]

In May 1970, the first party congress was held, during which the MPR was designated the sole party and supreme institution of the country. The party's political bureau grew in importance, and so did its members, the political commissioners. At the same time, party membership was awarded de facto to all Zairians. In the same year a parliament was established, whose members were chosen by the party. Presidential elections were held in which General Mobutu was the sole candidate. On August 15, 1974, the constitution was revised; the president of the republic, the MPR, and its political bureau became even more powerful. Instead of being the supreme institution as was decided in 1970, the MPR became the *sole* political institution, thus subordinating all other political and administrative institutions. Its political bureau, as an 'organ of conception, inspiration, orientation, and decision,' was to play an increasingly ideological role. As president of the MPR, the president of the republic increased his power tremendously. Through various reforms, public administration, trade unions, the university, the army, and the church were to follow the dictates of the party–state.

At the territorial level, the tendency toward centralization culminated in law no. 73/015 of January 1973, whose main characteristics were (1) the suppression of 'administrative duality' to avoid the 'conflicts of power'; (2) state intervention in formulating and implementing the budgetary policies of those administrative entities (*secteurs* and *villes*) that had financial autonomy before the 1973 law; (3) the establishment of a 'uniform administration' within which no administrative entity would be autonomous; and (4) the introduction of a new administrative vocabulary that reflected the five hierarchical divisions of the state (*région, sous-région, zone, collectivité,* and *localité*), which were headed by appointees of the president or of the minister of the interior, acting respectively as chair and member of the party political bureau.[4] An important aspect of the law was the emasculation of the traditional chieftainships by the removal of their powers. This was contradictory in light of the policies of authenticity that were being promoted at the same time (see chap. 8).

This trend toward total centralization was designed to increase the role of the party. By 1970, the party had entered into conflict with provincial political and administrative institutions; several times before the 1973 law, attempts had been made to give primacy to the party and to 'avoid conflicts.' For instance, in 1970 regional commissioners were required to become members of the party and to implement their administrative duties according to the prescriptions of the MPR. In the absence of a formal law, however, this effort did not prevent recurrent conflicts between the party and other administrative and political bodies. With the 1973 law and the 1974 revision of the constitution, the party's interference and supremacy passed from their informal status to a legal and constitutional reality. Article 28 of the new constitution defined the party as the 'nation politically organized.'

The civilian nature of the new regime was revealed by its position vis-à-vis the army. Far from being a military dictatorship, the regime managed to keep the army outside the arena of power; but at the same time, it manipulated the army to maintain military loyalty whenever needed. David Gould's observation is particularly appropriate: 'It is true that President Mobutu, the chief representative of the patron class, is and remains a military man, who used the Army to come to power and relies on certain military units to protect himself. But it is no less true that, with the arguable exception of November 1965–December 1966 at which period General Mulamba served as Prime Minister and Defense Minister, with Mobutu serving as Chief of State, the Army has never ruled the country.'[5] After the creation of a single party an effort was made to integrate the military into it. Command structure and personnel were modified. With the increasing role of the party political bureau, some military officers were appointed to it. The national police force was transformed into a *gendarmerie* and integrated into the military structure. Political and civic education was inculcated in soldiers. The integration of army officers into the political bureau of the party may suggest a trend toward the militarization of the party. In reality, this did not happen, nor could it happen. The state personnel were mostly civilian. Besides, at the time of the appointment of these officers, the politcal bureau of the party had thirty-two members, of whom only five were military officers. To further consolidate party control of the army, nine top officers who participated in the 1965 coup d'état were named *compagnons de la révolution* and were forced into early retirement after granting them, in exchange, substantial material rewards.

Other autonomous centers of power that were affected included the trade unions, the church, the university, and the press. The trade unions and the universities were forced to merge into one state-owned union, the *Union des*

177

Travailleurs du Zaire (UNTZA) and one state-owned university, the *Université Nationale du Zaire* (UNAZA). In each of these merged institutions a member of the political bureau of the party was appointed president. The press was also attacked. It was reorganized and drastically reduced from thirteen weeklies to four in the capital city and from twenty to two in the interior. In fact, the press became a vehicle for the ideas of the party and its president–founder. As with the universities and the trade unions, the party exercised its control over the press by appointing members of the party's political bureau to oversee the decisions of the newspapers. In some cases newspapers became mixed enterprises owned and run conjointly by the state and 'militant' individuals. The state and the party found it difficult to control the church's power channels, especially those of the Catholic church. After a long struggle, they overcame the church. The theological faculty at the university was abolished; all religious instruction in the schools was banned and was replaced by courses in *Mobutisme* (the ideology of the party); the state took control of the church's school system throughout the country. (Later some of these stringent policies were relaxed.)

Authoritarian institutionalization and power consolidation went hand in hand. The authoritarian context was to facilitate the 'developmental options' of the new regime and the types of class coalitions involved. It resulted in internal stability (as opposed to the 1960–65 crisis period) for about ten years. No curfew was imposed from 1965 to 1977, contrary to frequent recourse to them during 1960–65. No military coup was attempted until 1975; no major ethnic rivalry was reported; street murders were almost completely eliminated; and very few cases of murder were reported in the whole country. All these factors enhanced the new regime's prestige. The 1967 OAU annual meeting was held in Kinshasa, and diplomatic relations were established with more than fifty countries by 1970. Above all, authoritarianism-generated stability and prestige gave a boost to the holders of state power.

While the political conditions conducive to instability were being eradicated by the new regime's recourse to sharply authoritarian means, on the economic plane the situation remained hopelessly shaky. The budget deficit was 12 billion Congolese francs for the first semester of 1967 as opposed to 6 billion in 1966. State borrowing went from 3.9 billion francs on June 30, 1960, to 80 billion francs in June 1967. Because most of the borrowing came from the national bank, this meant that there was more printed money on the market. With manufacturing companies running out of supplies as the result of restrictions on imports (themselves the result of lack of foreign exchange), the scarcity of consumer goods on the market and high volume of printed money raised the price index from 476 (1960 = 100) in 1966 to 584 in 1967.[6] The gap between the official exchange rate and that on the black market went from 115 percent in 1965 to 193 percent in 1966, thus adding to the scarcity of foreign earnings for the state. Moreover, the overvalued official exchange rate for the Zairian currency (the then-Congolese Franc) prevented any accumulation of revenues for the state, which would have been possible through fiscal imposition on import and export of goods. Price increases also meant increases in state spending, thus reducing resources that could have been available for investment purposes. These combined elements hampered the formulation and implementation of a coherent policy of investments by the new regime.

But the economic overtone in General Mobutu's 1965 speech and the party's ideological charter left no doubt about the role authoritarianism was to play in the formulation and implementation of economic policies. On June 24, 1967, assisted by the IMF's provision of US $27 million stand-by credit in a guarantee, the Zairian government undertook a series of monetary reforms with fiscal and budgetary implications. The Congolese franc was devalued, and a new currency, the *zaire*, was created to replace it. The new currency was pegged to the US dollar; one zaire was worth US $2 and 1,000 old Congolese francs. From a fiscal point of view the tax increase was substantial. For instance, from 12 percent the tax rate on exported mineral goods jumped to an average of 30 percent. It stood at 40 percent for copper and diamonds, and at 30 percent for cobalt. Budgetary measures involved basically an effort to reduce public spending and to balance the budget. Restrictions on imports were eased. Most companies established in the country were allowed to transfer their profits abroad. A policy of price stabilization was forcefully pursued.[7] Although these measures were aimed at substantially increasing state revenues and improving the economy in general, their main effect was to create an atmosphere conducive to a flow of both private and public investments.

These measures required, if not a sophisticated development plan, at least a number of sectoral guidelines embodied in a short- and medium-range development strategy. This task was undertaken by the Zairian government assisted by a variety of international bodies, of which the World Bank group and the IMF were the most influential.[8] By 1969, policy makers had come up with development guidelines on which Zaire was going to base its economic policies over a ten-year period (1970–80). This period was divided into two subperiods, with 1970–75 the first target subperiod. Development guidelines defined, on the one hand, broad goals for the decade, and, on the other hand, some quantitatively specified objectives for the subperiod 1970–75.[9] Among the defined broad goals were (1) national control over the country's resources without prejudice to foreign investments – a mixed economy in which the state had the crucial role of partner; (2) sectoral and geographical equilibrium of investments, which implied diversification of the economy; (3) promotion of local entrepreneurs; (4) increase of peasants' income; (5) modernization of the transportation infrastructure; and (6) substantial increase of production in mining and manufacturing industries and of the country's exports.

To reach these goals some quantitative objectives were specified for the five-year subperiod (1970–75). It was estimated that from 1970 to 1975 the gross domestic product would increase from Z757.8 million (1Z = $2, 1970 value), to Z1 billion. This growth rate supposed, in turn, an average rate of 5 percent for mining, 6 percent for commerce, and 7 percent for agriculture, energy, transport and communication, and services. Assuming a capital coefficient of 4.4 (K/Y = 4.4), it was estimated that a total of at least Z1.4 billion had to be invested over this period to reach the growth rate target. in spite of differences in data, the sectoral distribution of the invested capital was approximately 18 percent (+Z252 million) for agriculture; 18 percent (about Z252 million) for mining; 4 percent (+Z56 million) for manufacturing industry; 4 percent (Z56 million) for construction and public works; 3 percent (about Z42 million) for energy; 16 percent (about Z224 million) for banking and services; 33 percent (about Z462 million) for transportation and communication; and 3 percent (+Z42 million) for commerce. Of the target figure of Z1.4 billion to be devoted to investment spending, the state was to contribute about Z500 million (US $1 billion) in direct investments, whereas the remainder was to be spent by private and public corporations.[10]

To accumulate the needed capital in accordance with the projected capital/output ratio, the Zairian government offered incentives to private (foreign) would-be investors by promulgating a highly liberal investment code in 1969. Thus, for instance, profits of newly established enterprises were exempt from tax on profit for five years; and new enterprises were exempted from the special tax on expatriates' salaries until production began and from property tax for five years. Because of colonial pseudocapitalist conditions, national private entrepreneurs could not take advantage of the investment code. Two major actors – the state and foreign investors – shared most of the investment deals, as was the case under colonial rule.

The state's role as an investor and the leading economic actor was inaugurated by a June 7, 1966, law (the *Loi Bakajika*),[11] which abrogated all concession rights given by the colonial state to chartered companies. In addition, a mining law was promulgated on May 11, 1967, stating that 'mines belong to the nation and constitute part of the public domain.' Claims for ownership by the state paved the way for and culminated in the nationalization of the UMHK, the main copper producer, on December 31, 1966. It was renamed and became *Générale des Carrières et des Mines* (GECAMINES). The nationalization of the UMHK provided the state with increased capital shares and portfolio value. In addition to GECAMINES' expansion projects,[12] the state established capital stock through new ventures. In the energy sector the most important investment venture was the Inga Dam on the Zaire River in the Bas Zaire region and its auxiliary, the Inga–Shaba Transmission Line.[13] The state also invested in the Maluku Steel Plant, located about fifty miles from Kinshasa, as well as in transportation and communication ventures. Energy, transportation/communication, and manufacturing were given 45 percent of the state's investment spending from 1968 to 1975. This represented about Z300 million ($600 million at the 1975 exchange rate) out of the Z669.1 million total capital spending[14] devoted to nonmining investments. By taking into account the mining sector, the state's total investment spending was estimated at $2.458 billion for the entire 1968–75 period.[15] About 3 percent was devoted to shareholdings in private concerns.

Foreign investments set a postcolonial record during 1969–75. Although Belgian colonial investments remained by far the most important, American, Japanese, and European investments also dominated. In the mining sector, two major investments need to be mentioned. The first is the *Société de*

180

Développement Industriel et des Mines du Zaire (SODIMIZA), whose major shareholders were Japanese companies. The Zairian state held 15 percent of the shares. The second is the *Société Minière de Tenke-Fungurume* (SMTF), in which the Zairian state held 20 percent of the shares. Its other major shareholders included American, British/South African, Japanese, and French companies.[16] On the whole, for the 1969–75 period, 139 investment projects were approved for a total value of about Z250 million (US \$500 million at 1975 exchange rates).[17]

Financing for these investments came from various sources. The state's direct investments were financed by its own tax revenues and especially by foreign banks and credit agencies on which the state came to rely heavily by 1974. Financing for private investments was provided by the investors themselves and by foreign financial institutions. In 1974 local financing declined 60 percent from the 1970 level. This change reached its highest level in 1976 when foreign borrowing made up 71 percent of investment financing. From 1970 to 1974, the state's share of financing averaged a mere 9.2 percent. From 1975 to 1977, the state's share was negative. The result of this pattern of financing was the debt burden. For the origin of investment financing for the 1970–77 period see table 7.1.

Table 7.1: Origin of financing of investments 1970–1977 (in percentage of total financing)

	1970	1971	1972	1973	1974	1975	1976	1977
National saving	81.7[a]	58.9	49.8	63.4	21.8	32.9	10.5	30.0
–Government	21.2	3.5	5.0	8.8	7.6	–[b]	–	–
–Private	60.5	55.4	44.8	54.6	14.2	–	–	–
Foreign borrowing	18.3	41.1	50.2	37.0	78.2	68.1	89.5	70.0

Source: Calculated by using data from IMF, *Zaire: Recent Economic Development* (March 30, 1979): 12; IMF, *Zaire: Recent Economic Developments*, SM/77/113 (May 18, 1977): 11.
[a] Figures rounded off to the nearest tenth of a percent.
[b] Percentages were not calculated for these years since the government's share of saving was negative.

2. Overpoliticization and Distribution of the Social Product

Under authoritarianism the state's revenues and resources are both accumulated and distributed by authoritarian means. The state's almost total control over most organizations and institutions results in many social actors depending on the state for their income and material survival. Compliance with authoritarian requirements is the sine qua non for claims to budget revenues. As an expression of overpoliticization in the distribution of the social product following the 1965 coup d'état, authoritarianism involved stringent requirements. Potential beneficiaries of the social product owed verbal support to the party–state. Loyalty and commitment consisted, in part, of expressing verbal *militantisme*. As used by the party leaders, *militantisme* sometimes meant adherence by the militants to the guidelines of the party; it could also mean the militants' awareness of doing correctly what was required of them. It became the militant bureaucrat's, merchant's, and intellectual's watchword, forcefully expressed by the 1972–73 administrative reforms. As stated by the then-chairman of the Civil Service Commission, when summarizing the law: 'Special emphasis, among the conditions required for recruitment, is placed on party militancy and Zairian nationality.'[18] Verbal *militantisme* was expressed through the *animation populaire*, a combination of dancing and cheerleading that involved songs or chants in praise of the regime, or through the repetition of such phrases as *'le MPR avant tout et le reste immédiatement après'* (MPR comes first, the rest immediately after). With respect to the *animation populaire*, the state commissioner for the interior and member of the political bureau wrote:

> One should not think of 'animation' as simple spectacle. The animation is a political act of adhesion to the Revolution and of faith in our Guide [Mobutu]. ... The militant who participates in an animation session proclaims by other ways than words his obedience to the Guide and his attachment to the ideals of the Revolution. He expresses his faith in Mobutism. Through animation, the militant learns the slogans and the watchwords of the Party. He learns how to magnify the MPR and its founder's merits.[19]

Intellectuals' support consisted basically of expertise. Knowledge was put in the service of the 'revolution.' This move caused some to suggest that Zaire exemplified a bureaucratic–technocratic authoritarianism.[20] Through opportunism, fear, or fanaticism, intellectuals expressed their support in newspaper and popular journal articles or in zeal for party activities. This was summed up meaningfully by a former vice-chancellor of the National University: 'The role of the Zairian intellectual cannot be reduced to the production of inapplicable theories, rather it should consist of applying and reinterpreting the party's guidelines.'[21] In many instances, university professors were threatened with dismissal (or were actually fired) when suspected of coolness toward the party. Whether verbal or practical, *militantisme* played a tremendously mobilizing role; it popularized the party and the regime, that is, legitimized them.

Support and loyalty for the party also involved domination of 'outsiders,' that is, peasants, workers, the unemployed, and students. Mystified by the intellectuals' or bureaucrats' *militantisme*, these classes or groups became vulnerable; this facilitated gaining their support of the party. Workers, students, peasants, and soldiers were required to organize into groups for the *animation populaire* under the supervision of party officials, who also mobilized them for forced collective work. Peasant oppression was high. Given the poverty level in the Zairian countryside, rural inhabitants were generally unable to pay the required *contribution personnelle minimum* (CPM), a state-imposed income tax. (The CPM averaged, by 1972, $8 per individual, while in real terms the income of most peasants was less than $100 a year.) Because of their refusal to pay the CPM, peasants were either incarcerated or forced by local bureaucrats to cultivate. While peasants were forced to cultivate crops, the merchants decreased, in the name of economic efficacy and with full knowledge of the government, minimum producer prices. In a study conducted in the northern part of the country, Michael Schatzberg summed up the situation:

> Because of low prices and unmarketed harvests, the villagers have no incentive to produce and agricultural output declines; unmarketed crops means there will be no money to pay the CPM; collectivities depend on the CPM for about one-half of their monetary intake; the chiefs and their associates will appropriate funds for their own use. This bureaucratic capitalism results in a shortage of money for other employees. ... These employees will then extract what they can from the people in their jurisdictions often resorting to violence.[22]

State-controlled organizations for the masses also exacerbated the domination of the lower classes while facilitating support for power holders. At the head of these organizations were top party and state officials. In the early years of authoritarism rule, the national trade union (UNTZA), the board of trustees of the National University, and the youth organization (JMPR) were all headed by members of the political bureau of the party. Within these organizations a host of officials acting as intermediaries between power holders and the lower classes and groups fulfilled their requirements of loyalty and support to the party by resorting to repression of the lower classes. In addition to various repressive moves against students,[23] peasants were repressed as in the Kwilu/Idiofa district: 'Angered by the rapid deterioration of their standard of living, the villagers (cutters of palm fruits), had attacked ... local officials of MPR (Mobutu's single party) at Imbongo village and in the Kanga sector, located between Kikwit and Idiofa in the Bandundu Region. All the villagers in Aten, Mulembe, and Lukamba were killed, and their villages were burnt by Zaire's special troops. ... The number of killed persons reached 500 in Aten village alone.'[24] Worker compliance with authoritarian requirements meant no strikes and strict adherence to the guidelines of the state-controlled UNTZA. In all these instances of domination of the masses, lower party officials, acting as intermediaries, played a crucial role of support, either by denouncing the *anti-révolutionnaires* or by assuming a direct role in the repressive process.

Compliance with authoritarian requirements made one a recipient of the social product in indirect or direct ways. The newly reformed and centralized political institutions could be joined only by those who expressed their *militantisme* and loyalty to the party. The 1977 party-controlled parliamentary elections, for example, gave 50 percent of the seats to merchants, 30 percent to bureaucrats, almost 15 percent to intellectuals, and 5 percent to members of the political bureau of the party.[25] The discretionary power enjoyed by some power holders (e.g., the president and the commissioner for party affairs) enabled them to appoint to government and top public and bureaucratic offices only those who had displayed a *militantisme agissant*. For example, faculty members at the university who had demonstrated their militancy by praising the Mobutu regime in articles were appointed to top ministerial positions. University graduates who had proven their attachment to the regime were also appointed to high bureaucratic and political positions. Within the bureaucracy itself, promotion was a function of one's degree of militancy and commitment to the party.

Much has been written and documented about corruption and the appropriation of offices by officials in Zaire.[26] One of the characteristic features of the allocation of the social product in its indirect form was a tolerated pattern of bureaucratic corruption. In 1973, a director in the Department of Finance misused public funds (estimated at $100,000) for his own needs; rather than being prosecuted, he was removed, one year later, and appointed as director in another public office. At the Lubumbashi campus, funds intended for students were misused by the vice-chancellor of the university in 1974; after students protested, he was removed, one year later, and appointed as director of a teachers' college before being promoted to the rank of director-general of the Department of Education. In many regional and local administrative services, bureaucrats and local officials were cited in cases of public funds' mismanagement, but they were neither fired nor prosecuted. Pressured by public opinion, President Mobutu had to twice acknowledge the tolerated character of bureaucratic corruption. In an oft-cited public rally in 1975, he pleaded with bureaucrats to steal with moderation and to invest in the country. In 1977, in another oft-quoted address to the party congress, after summing up the pervasiveness of corruption, President Mobutu went on to recognize the degree of tolerance to it:

> In a word, everything is for sale, anything can be bought in our country. And in this flow, he who holds the slightest cover of public authority uses it illegally to acquire money, goods, prestige, or to avoid all kinds of obligations. Even worse, the citizen who simply asks for his most legitimate rights to be respected is subjected to an invisible tax, which is then openly pocketed by officials. Thus the right to be heard by a public servant, to register one's children in school or to obtain their report cards at the end of the year, to obtain medical care, a seat on an airplane, a diploma – and I could go on – are all subject to this tax which, though invisible, is known and expected by all. ... In the face of all these evils, we must acknowledge that, all too often, *the State and the Party have not discouraged the bad and encouraged the good.*[27]

David Gould analyzed twenty-two different techniques used in different public services by bureaucrats to get material resources within the authoritarian context. He shows, for instance, that the Shaba regional commissioner was grossing $100,000 per month in 1975, of which only 2 percent was his nominal salary.[28]

To be sure, corruption practices are not an exclusive attribute of Third World countries; they exist in Western countries as well. What characterized corruption in the Third World is its pervasiveness and the often high rate of tolerance for it. (This is not to suggest that in the Third World everyone accepts corruption.)[29] In capitalist democracies, corruption, when revealed, is viewed as scandal and is subject to political and juridical repression. The reason for this is not that 'the system works' but that corruption breaks the rules of the game at the center of the democratic compromise based on opportunities and not guarantees. Corruption injects an element of certainty and guarantees in the allocation of the social product for some actors in a system of competition that otherwise grants equal opportunities to all. The pervasiveness and higher rate of tolerance of corruption in the Third World, on the other hand, is consistent with a system in which overpolitization is used to compete over the social product – a system in which guarantees, not equal opportunities, govern such a distribution. This reliance on overpoliticization rests, in turn, on a specific form of support and coalitions. By requiring an extremely high level of manipulation of resources, these coalitions are, in turn, congruent with a pattern of corruption tolerance. The authoritarian context under the Mobutu regime identifies with such a system. Compliance with authoritarian requirements and their attendant coalitions ensured a share of the social product, including a tolerated pattern of corruption and office appropriation.

The link between authoritarian requirements and allocation of the social product is even more clearly established by the skewed pattern of allocation of state revenues. In broad terms, state expenses are twofold: capital expenses aim at productive or social investment, and ordinary expenses include all other routine expenses, such as wages and salaries and the functioning of the bureaucracy and other government apparatus. With respect to capital expenses, the role played by the state's tax revenues was minimal. From 1970 to 1974, the period during which the state contributed to the financing of public investments, its share of financing was a mere average of 9.2 percent of total financing. From 1975 to 1979, the state's share of financing was negative; the bulk of financing for both private and public investments came from the private sector and especially from borrowing. From 1966 to 1977, the state's ordinary expenses were on the average 104.6 percent of total state tax revenues, fluctuating between 84.1 percent in 1970 and 146 percent in 1977. The conclusion is clear. State tax revenues were not used for capital spending.

Granted that the state's tax revenues were almost totally devoted to ordinary expenses, what was the distribution pattern they followed? One can answer this by analyzing budgetary data related to three types of state ordinary expenses: political endowments, wages and salaries, and health during the 1972–78 period (table 7.2).

The three budgetary categories of spending are representative of the functions assumed by the budget and have some kind of impact on the country as a whole. Only 1.7 percent of the state's total budgetary expenses was allocated to health for a total population of about 30 million. In other words, from 1972 to 1978, on the average only Z0.3 (US $0.60 at 1975 exchange rates) was spent per year per inhabitant for health purposes. State expenses in health did not, by any standard, respond to the needs of the 'nation.' In real terms the picture was even more gloomy. For instance, 'in Kinshasa of the 55% of the population falling into the lowest socioeconomic category, only 19% had access to medical facilities in contrast to 100% of those in the highest socioeconomic group having such access.'[30] If health is representative of social services, evidence clearly shows that state expenses were not devoted to social services, or by implication, to the masses.

Table 7.2: Ordinary budgetary expenses in political endowments, wages and salaries, and health, 1972–78 (value in millions of zaires; percentage of total ordinary expenses)

	1972	1973	1974	1975	1976[a]	1977[a]	1978[a]
Political Endowments							
value	47.7	64.3	93.2	77.8	103.5	114.4	–
percent	17	18	16	15	17	14	–
Wages and salaries							
value	149.2	170.0	180.3	280.8	285.2	380.1	428.7
percent	54.4	46	39	42	43	47	55
Health							
value	9.93	13.88	3.7	3.7	8.1	11.7	8.9
percent	3.6	3.8	0.7	0.7	1.2	1.4	1.1

Source: Calculated from World Bank/IBRD, *The Economy of Zaire* 3 (1975), Tables 5.7 and 5.9; IMF, *Zaire: Use of Fund Resources–Stand-By Arrangements*, EBS/76/129 (March 13, 1976): 28; IMF, *Zaire: Recent Economic Developments*, SM/79/85 (March 30, 1979), Tables 13 and 14.
[a] Values for these years were nominal. In real terms they were inferior to those of 1972 to 1975 because of monetary readjustments from devaluations and inflation.

The bulk of state expenses was drained by both political endowments (uncontrolled and discretionary expenses by the office of the president, its auxiliary agencies, the political bureau of the party, and the party-controlled parliament) and wages and salaries. They made up more than 50 percent of the state's ordinary expenses over the entire 1972–78 period. Because of sociodemographic divisions holding 70 percent of the population in the countryside, more than one-half of state ordinary expenses (about 20 percent of GNP) were allocated to less than 30 percent of the total population. The 30 percent of the urban population included workers who received their wages from the private sector and the unemployed, which suggest that the real percentage of the beneficiaries was less than 30 percent.

To argue that the 62 percent of state expenses was used to foster coalitions by authoritarian means, one needs to show that in fact many of these wage-related expenses were concentrated in the hands of those who formed the coalitions. The budgetary category of political endowments offers such proof. That it constituted a means by which budgetary resources could be distributed by power holders is revealed by its discretionary character. Its very denomination of 'political endowment' (*dotations*) suggests that expenses related to this category served political purposes. In other words, they were used to create political coalitions by authoritarian means. Revenues in this category were spent for various payoffs, such as providing houses and cars for newly appointed officials. No control was exerted over the spending. Mobutu's now well known and documented wealth is the result of this form of overpoliticized resource allocation.

It is quite clear that state expenses for wages and salaries were (and are) devoted to state bureaucracy personnel. Without raising here the long debate about class categories in the bureaucracy,[31] the state bureaucracy personnel are not only made up of elements of the ruling class. There is also a low-level category of personnel, whose monthly wage is not any higher than that of the workers. Therefore, to have a more accurate view of the distribution of wages and salaries, one needs to know the share of this lower-level personnel of the bureaucracy and that of members of the upper categories. The Zairian Civil Service Commission (the *Commission Permanente de l'Administration Publique*) divides civil servants into three major categories, each with several subcategories: positions of command (*grades de commandement*), positions of collaboration (*emplois de collaboration*), and positions of implementation (*emplois d'exécution*). For this discussion, those civil servants who occupy the command and collaboration positions are high-level state officials and potentially members of the ruling class. The lower-level personnel in the third category, by contrast, are part of the lower classes.

In 1974, there were 2,513 (23.17 percent) state personnel occupying command and collaboration positions, and 8,318 (76.7 percent) state personnel occupying implementation positions. The monthly total amount of salaries of command and collaboration personnel amounted to Z4,812,143, whereas that of implementation personnel was Z2,175,988. This meant that 68.8 percent (about 70 percent) of total state expenses devoted to wages and salaries was allocated to command and collaboration personnel, who made up only 23.1 percent of state. The positions of implementation, making up 76.7 percent of state personnel, were given only 31 percent of state expenses devoted to wages and salaries (table 7.3). As in health and social services, state expenses in wages and salaries were not focused on classes and groups other than high-level state officials. For example, in 1974 the director of the political bureau of the party earned Z26,000 (US $52,000) a month; members of the political bureau of the party earned $2,000 a month but were given *in manu* $8,000, giving them a monthly income of $10,000.[32] In 1979, the political bureau of the party was downgraded, and the Central Committee of 106 members instituted. Their monthly salaries are shown in table 7.4. By comparison, a peasant earned less than $100 and a worker about $200 per year.

Table 7.3: Salary/wage gap among state/bureaucracy personnel, before 1979 (monetary value expressed in zaires)

Category	Number (1)	Monthly unit wage/category (2)	Monthly total wage/category (3)=(i) x (2)	Percentage share of total wages
Command and Collaboration (A)	N = 2,513 % = 23.1	1,914.9	4,812,143.7	68.8
Implementation (B)	N = 8,318 % = 76.7	261.6	2,175,988.0	31.2
Total average gap index =(A) (B)		7.3[a]		

Source: Calculated by using data from *Commission Permanente de l'Administration Publique du Zaire* (COPAP), (October 24, 1974); Kikkassa Mwanalessa, 'La Révision de l'échelle des salaires au Zaire,' *Zaire–Afrique*, no. 135 (May 1979): 264.
[a] This gap inndex was 34 if one compares the top salary in the command category and the lowest position in the implementation category.

Table 7.4: Monthly salaries of the members of the Central Committee of the party in zaires (1979: 1Z = $.33)

Dean of the Central Committee	Z28,000 x 1 = 28,000
First vice-president	26,000 x 1 = 26,000
Second vice-president	24,000 x 1 = 24,000
First secretary-reporter	22,000 x 1 = 22,000
Second secretary-reporter	22,000 x 1 = 22,000
Permanent secretary	20,000 x 1 = 20,000
Presidents of committees	21,000 x 3 = 63,000
Vice-Presidents of committees	20,000 x 5 = 100,000
Committee reporters	18,000 x 5 = 90,000
Presidents of subcommittees	20,000 x 11 = 220,000
Vice-Presidents of subcommittees	18,000 x 11 = 198,000
Subcommittee reporters	16,500 x 11 = 181,500
Members of the Central Committee	15,000 x 63 = 945,000
Total	Z1,939,500

Source: Hearing before the Subcommittee on Africa, House of Representatives, Washington, DC (September 15, 1981), p. 52.

To be sure, with the rate of inflation as high as 90 percent, these salaries did not provide their beneficiaries with viable purchasing power. But most members held other positions in the bureaucracy, academia, and business. Their cumulated salaries allowed them to withstand any inflationary pressure and to live an easy life. Furthermore, when compared to workers' wages, these salaries were scandalous. The monthly wage of a skilled worker was, in 1979, 0.5 percent of the monthly salary of an ordinary member of the Central Committee. As in the case of Mobutu's wealth, the equally well documented wealth of state officials in Zaire resulted from this overpoliticized competition over the social product.

The Zairianization Measures

The best evidence of the relationship between the distribution of the social product and overpoliticization, perhaps, is provided by the politics of nationalization and expropriation of colonial and pre-1969 investments. On November 30, 1973, in pursuit of authentic nationalism, President Mobutu gave a long speech before the parliament in which he raised serious grievances against Belgian colonization. He announced a series of measures designed to 'definitely free the Zairian economy from foreign domination.' These measures were to be known as the 1973 Zairianization measures. They were enacted in two phases: 'Zairianization' and 'radicalization.'

In 1973 the Zairianization phase instituted a series of measures:

- complete transfer of ownership of land from foreigners to the state;
- in addition to small-and medium-sized businesses, which a previous (January 5,1973) law stipulated were to go to Zairian citizens, transfer of all foreign-owned agricultural, artisan, and service industries to the state;
- total or partial (no less than 50 percent) control by the state over mining, shipping, insurance, and construction industries;
- complete transfer to the state of all outdated industrial enterprises whose plant and equipment had not been updated for thirty years.[33]

The sole exception to these measures was foreign investments made in conformity with the 1969 investment code.

On December 26, 1973, a joint meeting of the cabinet (*Conseil Exécutif*), political bureau of the party, and the top leadership of the parliament (*Bureau du Conseil Législatif*) set out guidelines for the implementation of the measures:

- The state was given the largest agro-industrial and commercial businesses, that is, those considered 'strategic.'
- Plantations, ranches, and certain (types of) businesses, the President intended to experiment with by entrusting them to his closest aides, that is, Political Bureau members, Cabinet members and Parliament members.

189

- Military officers, judges, ambassadors, regional commissioners, and civil servants were disqualified from running such expropriated businesses.

On December 31,1973, President Mobutu announced the transferral of ownership of category 2 to the state. Implementation of these measures was to follow a threefold pattern: (1) state ownership, (2) exclusion of a category of high officials as potential beneficiaries, and (3) no restriction as to the acquisition of expropriated small business; 'vocation for business' and 'means of running businesses' were specified as the sole objective criteria.[34]

A totally different pattern of distribution actually took place, in flagrant contradiction of the official guidelines. The December 27 and December 31 clarification measures resulted in a de facto three-dimensional distributional pattern: (1) State ownership actually meant ownership by the ruling class. Thus, President Mobutu's roving ambassador since 1965 received large export and import businesses, a soft drink factory, and a large commercial office. A long-time former finance minister under President Mobutu acquired a series of groceries and food-processing businesses as well as a number of (colonial) Cominier Company subsidiaries, including Okapi Hotel, Vici-Zaire, Comuele, Pantadem, Cometric, and Imoaf, most of which provided services.[35] (2) In spite of the nominal disqualification of a certain category of civil servants from the privilege of acquiring businesses, a policy of 'silent tolerance' was used to provide civil servants with booty. (3) Many Zairianized businesses were acquired by merchants, members of the parliament, and other auxiliary groups such as mass media leaders.

The capital of Shaba (Katanga) region, Lubumbashi, for example, contained some highly desirable Zairianized businesses. The distribution pattern there was 35 percent of the Zairianized businesses to merchants-businessmen and 21 percent to bureaucrats. Almost 30 percent were allotted to sixteen members of the parliament; the editor of *Mwanga*, a Lubumbashi-based newspaper; the editor of *Elima*, a Kinshasa-based newspaper; the director of *AZAP*, the Zairian press agency; the regional director of UNTZA; two ambassadors; one former chief of police; two local JMPR officials; one collectivity chief; the deputy assistant regional commissioner; the head of the regional agricultural division; the head of regional veterinary services; two regional judicial officials; one magistrate; one official of the economic affairs division; a teacher; the chief justice of the supreme court; and the vice-chancellor of the university. And 14 percent of the businesses were given to two retired generals of the army (*compagnons de la révolution*), one active general, the president's chief of staff; and two members of the political bureau of the party.[36]

This incompletely drawn but, nonetheless, illustrative pattern of distribution suggest that 86 percent of the businesses in Lubumbashi were given to those close to state power, and 14 percent were appropriated those at the center of political power. Given that the distribution of these businesses was not made, in many cases, according to officially established criteria, the distributional pattern provided by the Lubumbashi sample is necessarily incomplete. Table

7.5, summarizing data collected three years after the Zairianization measures, gives a more complete distribution.

Because distribution of the businesses was subordinated to authoritarian means, the ultimate implementation outcome of these measures was threefold: (1) the consolidation of political power through new economic acquisitions and through new and strengthened loyalty ties that were owed holders of state power by the new acquirers of businesses (widely known with opprobrium as the *nouveaux acquéreurs*), who demonstrated a new form of zeal and assiduity for party activities (*militantisme agissant*); (2) a new form of material and social security for the *acquéreurs*; and (3) the impoverishment and domination of the masses in a more extreme form than heretofore.

In a study of Cameroon, Jean Francois Bayart pointed out that 'no political process, be it as manifestly oppressive or conservative as the clientelist relations or one-candidate elections ... escapes completely the political influence of lower social groups, nor is the process outside the social struggle.'[37] The impact of the Zairianization measures on the masses, that is, peasants, students, workers, and the unemployed, produced major socioeconomic disruptions and suffering. The conditions of the masses deteriorated dramatically. Not only did the *acquéreurs* display signs of wealth after the Zairianization measures, but the measures led to acute shortages of consumer goods, hence price increases. The shortage resulted from most of the new *acquéreurs'* lack of experience in business and from the blockade imposed on Zaire by European import-export dealers who did not want to do business with the *acquéreurs*. But the shortage of consumer goods was also a result of the deliberate attempt by some *acquéreurs* to liquefy the capital stock of the acquired businesses to satisfy their personal cash needs. In any case, faced with an acute shortage on the local markets, the masses resorted to some kind of violence. In Lubumbashi, students threw stones on the new *acquéreurs*. They threatened to take over businesses acquired by the vice-chancellor of the university. The military was sent in to protect them from students. In the Bas-Zaire region peasants attacked some *acquéreurs* in Matadi City.[38]

Faced with this threat raised by the masses, the power holders had recourse to ideologically charged policy language. In a dramatic move, President Mobutu expressed his concern over the well-being of the lower classes. He declared in a speech: 'It is unthinkable that I, who have fiercely fought three hundred Belgian families who were exploiting our country, can tolerate their replacement by three hundred Zairian families. ... As to the question whether Mr. Mobutu is working for the people or the officials (les cadres), I reply that I am working for the people and not for the officials. ... To be precise, I tell you nothing new when I say that I have declared war on the bourgeoisie in our country.'[39] In policy terms, this meant that the state would take back businesses given to the *acquéreurs* under the 1973 Zairianization measures. The logic behind this move – apart from 'declaring war on the bourgeoisie' – was that the state would manage the expropriated businesses better than the *acquéreurs* and would thus prevent the shortage of consumer goods on the market. Because it was radical in its intent, this phase of the Zairianization of

Table 7.5: Largest businesses in Lubumbashi distributed under Zairianization measures of November 30, 1973

Rank of *acquéreur*	Name of company	Type of business
Regional commissioner	Soco	Wholesale
	Hasson	Wholesale
	Mercado	Wholesale
	Boutique France	Retail luxury
Director, executive office of president	VAP	Bakery
Political bureau member and state commissioner	Covema	Hardware
	Mobiza	Furniture
State commissioner for orientation	Marberie du Shaba	Quarry
Assistant regional commissioner	Keshav Vital	Food
Subregional commissioner	Bernstein	Jewelry
Ex-Ambassador	Angevan	Wholesale
State commissioner for justice	Franco	Wholesale
Eighteen congressmen	18 businesses	Wholesale/Retail
Regional military commander	Tarica	Wholesale
	Menasche Velo	Bicycles
Assistant military commander	–	
Retired general	Alimenza	Wholesale
Retired general	Maessart	Retail
Leading company director	Vendome	Boutique
	DeReusch	Jewelry
Leading company director	Danon	Wholesale
	Schlitz	Spare parts
Air Zaire pilot	Sporville	Men's wear
Tribal chief	Sideris	Hardware
Brother of tribal chief	Stanzos	Bakery
Assistant tribal chief	–	Wholesale
University vice-chancellor	P. Stanzos	Bakery
	Mme. Toilette	Women's wear
Newspaper editor	Atadji, Paraytos	Wholesale
Established businessperson	Levico	Wholesale
	Bata	Shoes
Bank director	–	Retail
Director, CND (Secret Service)	Deftersos	Wholesale
Ex-Minister	Piesauto	Body Shop
Ex-Minister	Jannaza	Supermarket
Ex-Minister	Blackwood/Hodge	Wholesale/Retail
President, Journalists Association	–	Wholesale
Ex-Mayor, subregion	Selected bars	
Head, youth organization	–	Retail shops

Source: David Gould, 'Underdevelopment Administration: Systemic Corruption in the Public Administration of Mobutu's Zaire.' (Paper presented at Bellagio Conference, Italy, August 7–11, 1978), pp. 60–61.

private investments was known as the 'radicalization' measures of December 30, 1974.

On December 30, 1974, after a three-day meeting held on the president's yacht, the MPR political bureau expressed its deep concern about the 'ten plagues' that afflicted Zairian society, including, inter alia, the agricultural crisis, unemployment, excessive consumption of luxury goods, social injustice, and individualism. As remedies for the ten plagues, the political bureau took steps to transfer to state ownership all large means of production and distribution including those owned by Zairians. As a result, as of January 1, 1975, the state would take over all construction companies, large production units, large distribution units, companies manufacturing construction materials, and big transportation companies. Once again, 1969 investment code-protected foreign investments were not affected. Members of the political bureau and all party officials (cadres) were to give up all their businesses, both those acquired under Zairianization measures and those they had previously owned. Some Zairian-owned big businesses, such as *Société Générale d'Alimentation, African Lux, Société des transports en Commun de Kinshasa-STK, Banque de Kinshasa, Usine Zairoise des Meubles-Uzam* and *Zaire-Prestige*, were also nationalized. By presidential ordinances, President Mobutu named the chief executive officers *(délégués généraux)* of the more than one hundred 'radicalized' companies (tables 7.6 and 7.7). The *délégués* were for the most part former politicians and high officials in the bureaucracy and the party. Other *délégués généraux* were bureaucrats or intellectuals.

Table 7.6: Number of firms radicalized by sector, 1974–75[a]

Commerce, distribution and banking	19
Construction and construction materials	14
Manufacturing	62
Public transport	6
Others[b]	5
Total	106

Source: World Bank, *The Manufacturing Sector of Zaire* (1979), p. 106.
[a] Excluding firms already in the state portfolio.
[b] Includes firms for which it was not possible to identify the sector to which they belonged.

The radicalization measures, overall, changed little in the sufferings of the masses. On the contrary, they provided the appointed executive officers with new economic power bases. As a reflection of the overpoliticization of the competition for the social product, these measures reinforced compliance of the *délégués* to authoritarian requirements. By further precipitating the collapse of the economy, the radicalization measures exacerbated the impoverishment of the masses. In an attempt to reverse the trend and, thereby, avoid political consequences, a third wave of measures, called 'retrocession,' was announced in 1976; they consisted of giving back many important businesses to their former owners, who, in some cases, declined the offer.

Table 7.7: Distribution of radicalized firms in the manufacturing sector by branch

Branch	Number of firms	% of total branch sales 1974
Agro-industry and food processing	15	50
Beverages and tobacco	9	95
Wood (including furniture)	2	50
Textiles and leather	10	90
Metal products	4	46
Paper and printing	4	50
Chemical industry	6	56
Rubber industry	0	–
Transport equipment	1	30
Electrical equipment	1	52
Nonmetallic minerals	8	82
Miscellaneous	1	61
Total	61	67 (average)

Source: World Bank, *The Manufacturing Sector of Zaire* (1979), p. 107.

3. Overpoliticization and the Reinforcement of Pseudocapitalism

The above discussion reveals that recourse to overpoliticization in the competition for the social product required a high level of resource manipulation by the power holders. To accumulate badly needed resources, they reinforced the colonial unbalanced structure of state revenues. The situation is summed up by the World Bank: 'The government of Zaire has given high priority to the development of the copper sector. ... The authorities consider that in the medium term an increase in mining would be the fastest, most reliable way to increase exchange earnings and raise government revenues. This policy is directed toward the expansion of GECAMINES, the attraction of foreign private investment for new mining ventures, and the construction of additional copper refining capacity in Zaire.'[40]

As noted, one of the first measures taken by the Mobutu regime was to increase the tax base for exportable goods; from 12 percent the tax rate on exported mineral goods jumped to an average of 30 percent, on copper and diamonds to 40 percent and on cobalt to 30 percent. From 1966 onward, percentages in all tax categories related to the export sector increased dramatically. From 1966 to 1973, export revenues for mineral products averaged 85.6 percent of total export revenues. From 1975 to 1979, they averaged 78.1 percent of total export revenues. The post- 1965 period represented, on the average, an increase of 25 percent of total export revenues for mineral products during the colonial period, 6 percent over the 1960–65 crisis-ridden period. Export revenues for agricultural products for 1966–79 averaged 16 percent. In comparison with the colonial period, this represented an average decrease of 24 percent; and a decrease of 8 percent from the 1960–65 period (table 7.8).

A sectoral analysis of both public and private investments from 1965 to 1980 reveals that, combined with other imperatives of overpoliticization, reliance on an unbalanced structure of revenues reinforced pseudocapitalism. By using data on the total spending by the state (i.e., total public investments) during 1968–1975, one can calculate the sectoral distribution for the major sectors of public investments, that is, mining, energy, transportation/communication, manufacturing, and agriculture (table 7.9). From 1968 to 1975, both public and private sectors invested a total of Z1,482,697,000 (twice that amount if converted into dollars at the 1975 exchange rate). The five sectors were given 75 percent of the total capital spending (private and public). All other remaining sectors had 25 percent of total capital investments during the 1968–75 period (Table 7.10).

The 26.5 percent of total investment spending (32 percent of state investments) obtained by the energy sector was almost totally devoted to the Inga Dam project and the Inga–Shaba Transmission Line project. These projects, in turn, were aimed at increasing copper production in the Shaba (Katanga) region. The Inga–Shaba Transmission Line, which crosses the country over 1,700 km, does not affect local populations in their productive activities or otherwise; nor does it relate to sectors of the economy other than mining. The line was built as a continuous line, that is without any extra converter, to avoid the loss of electricity. It runs west to east from the Inga Dam directly to the mining zones in the Katanga (Shaba) region. This strategy reduced the possibility of linkage between the energy sector and the agricultural sector even though the line crosses four predominantly agricultural regions. In other words, investments in energy were part of investments in the mining sector. As a result, the actual share of mining was 49 percent of the total investment spending.

This distribution exhibits striking similarities with colonial investment strategy. Colonial investments in infrastructure were realized as auxiliary investments to the mining sector. This was the case for infrastructure (transportation and energy) in Katanga Province around the UMHK. This was also true of the Ten-Year Plan, whose 50 percent of capital spending was devoted to transportation and energy, which in turn were basically established in the mining zones or in areas adjacent to them as support for the mining industry. By subordinating investment in energy to the mining industry, investment policies under the Mobutu regime repeated colonial patterns of investment and reinforced the colonial economic structure.

195

Table 7.8: Export and tax revenues: comparative table for contributing categories 1958/59, 1960–65, and 1968–79 (in percentage average of total of each category)

	1958/9	1960–5	1968–79				
			1968–74	1975–79	1968–79	Change from 1958/9	Change from 1960–5
	(1)	(2)	(3)	(4)	(5)	(5)–(1)	(5)–(2)
Export revenues							
– Mineral products	55	74	81.8	78.1	80	+25	+6
– Agricul. products	40	24	–	–	16	–24	–8
Indirect tax	43	63.3	73	56	63.4	+20 (+30)[a]	+0.1 (+10)
Tax on foreign trade	31.2	56	65	41	53	+22 (+34)	–3 (+9)
UMHK (GECAMINES)							
– to export revenues	20[b]	43	68	59	63	+43 (+48)	+20 (+25)
– to state revenues	16.4[c]	33.7[c]	46	24	35	+19 (+30)	+2 (+13)

Source: Banque du Zaire, *Rapports annuels 1968/69* (Table 6) and *Rapports annuels 1969/70* (Tables 52 & 97); Bezy et al., *Accumulation et sous-developpement au Zaire*, pp.78,84, tables 23A and B, Annex 5, 5B and 6B, 9; Vanderlinden et al., *Du Congo au Zaire*, p.305; H. Leclercq, 'L'inflation, sa cause: le desordre des finances publiques,' IRES, *Independance, Inflation, Developpement*, pp.133, 169.
[a] Values in ( ) indicate the change from the 1968–74 period, which yielded high returns for all the categories.
[b] Estimates.
[c] Not average but percentage for one year only; data not available for other years.

The dominant role of the mining sector illustrates another striking similarity with the colonial economic structure. Because data on pre-1950 colonial investments are sketchy, one cannot determine accurately the exact value of investments in mining before 1950. From 1951 to 1959 capital investments in mining amounted to only 3 percent of total capital spending. However, one does not need an exact figure to be convinced of high value of investments in mining during the colonial period (see chap.5). That the amount of investment capital devoted to the mining sector from 1951–1959 was only 3 percent merely suggests that most investments in mining were made before 1950. So whether one looks only at the capital value devoted to mining in the strict sense (22.5 percent) or considers its combined actual value of 49 percent, investment capital devoted to mining during the 1968–75 period repeats and reinforces colonial investment patterns. It reinforced and repeated colonial patterns not only because the mining sector had 49 percent (which is convincing enough) but also because under colonial rule the mining sector dominated other sectors; its share of investment capital, the expectations of investment returns, and its impact on economic activities were higher than for other sectors of the economy. In 1958, the mining sector produced 28.8 percent of commercialized goods, and during the 1970–80 period, it produced 35–40 percent.[41]

Table 7.9: State capital spending in five major sectors (in thousands of zaire, and in percentage of total state capital spending), 1968–75

Sector	Value	Percent
Energy	393,901	32.0
Mining	286,729	23.0
Transportation/Communication	95,471	7.7
Manufacture	91,080	7.3
Agriculture	23,242	1.8
Other	339,274	28.2
TOTAL	1,229,697	100.0

Source: Calculated from data in IBRD, *The Economy of Zaire* (1975), table 5–1; Banque du Zaire, *Rapport annuel 1975*, p. 117; ibid, *Rapport annuel 1971/72*; World Bank/IBRD, *GECAMINES Expansion Project* (December 26, 1974); EXIMBANK, *Inga–Shaba Transmission Line*, Background Memorandum, May 8, 1979.

The state relied strongly on revenues from mineral resource exports. As already seen, in 1959 the mining sector generated 55 percent of export revenues; in 1970, it was 81 percent. To be sure, raising government revenues through the mining/copper sector is not by itself aberrant. Through the budgetary process, the state can reinvest mining-derived revenues in other sectors of the economy. In Zaire, however, revenues from the mining/copper sector fell victim to the vicious circle of pseudocapitalism. Because of the high priority attached to the mining sector, a major portion of the state's revenues was reinvested in the mining sector itself. At the implementation level of the investment code (as opposed to its theoretical guidelines), the sectoral and geographical distribution of investments from 1968 to 1980 followed the colonial pattern. The result was that even if some revenues from the mining/copper sector were transferred via investment to other sectors (which they were not), they only could have exacerbated the colonial economic structure.

Three sectors were likely to benefit from capital transfer from the mining sector-derived revenues: agriculture, manufacturing, and transportation/communication. The manufacturing sector came second with 14.5 percent of the total capital spending. The state's share of capital spending for the sector was 42 percent, as compared to 58 percent for the private sector. To the extent that revenues from the mining/copper sector were mainly appropriated by the state, one may reasonably assume that some of these revenues were transferred to the manufacturing sector. To verify this assumption, one needs to demonstrate (1) that such a transfer corrected the colonial dislocated economic structure and (2) that the transferred investment capital was indeed provided by ming-generated revenues.

Table 7.10: Sectoral distribution of total investment spending: public *and* private, 1968–75 (in thousands of zaires)

Total investment value		Sectoral Distribution		
		Sector	Value	% of total capital spending
Private	253,000	Agriculture	53,080	3.5
Public	1,229,697	Transportation/ Communication	125,390	8.0
		Manufacture	215,947	14.5
		Mining	334,554	22.5
		Energy	393,201	26.5
		Others	360,525	25.0
TOTAL	1,482,697		1,482,697	100.0

Source: World Bank/IBRD, *GECAMINES Expansion Project*; Banque du Zaire, *Rapport Annuel 1975*, pp. 71 and 117; ibid., *Rapport 1971/72*, p. 122; Mulumba Lukoji, 'Investir au Zaire,' *Zaire-Afrique*, no. 103 (March 1976): 148; Table 7–1.

Evidence shows that neither of these two conditions was met. State-sponsored investment projects in manufacturing consisted basically of a steel mill, the Maluku Steel Plant. It alone absorbed Z80 million (US $160 million at the 1975 exchange rate) out of the state's total capital spending in manufacturing of Z91 million. This amounted to 88 percent of the state's total capital spending in the manufacturing sector. The remaining 12 percent consisted of state participation in ventures with private partners. Assuming, momentarily, that investment capital for the Maluku Steel Plant was provided by revenues from the mining/copper sector, did such a transfer lead to the integration of the economy? The answer is no. The raw material (iron) used by the plant was (and is) imported because the plant was built before any serious feasibility study about the exploitation of local iron ore. As a result, the unit cost of the final output of the plant has been kept high, making its chance of expanding the local market of steel, hence, its capitalist integration with the overall economy, nonexistent. The point about the disintegrative character of the plant was made by Fernand Bézy and others:

In 1972, SOSIDER [the *Société d'Exploitation Sidéurgique*] was established offshore, 80 km from Kinshasa. Up to now, and this is likely to last, it is not a steel mill, but simply an electrical steelwork, which is supplied with imported

198

scrap-iron [*mitraille*] and which runs a flowing tapping [*coulée*] of a hot and cold rolling-mill, Its capacity: 150,000 tons of iron betons and 100,000 tons of sheet-iron. But the rolling-mills have been shut since 1976, and no more than 100,000 tons of both betons and sheet-iron have been produced per year. Worst of all, this firm, in spite of its deteriorating state due to its total idleness, was able to accumulate a gross profit of 27 millions in 1978 and 16 millions in 1979. This is so because if it cannot produce, at least it can sell. One would end up believing that the building of the plant, for which 60% of financing was provided by Italian and German capital, was a simple pretext to obtain a license for imports, not to mention the super profits derived from the contract to build with keys at the door (as soon as the door is opened, it is shut).[42]

Therefore, the first of the two conditions mentioned (i.e., correcting the colonial economic structure by expanding capitalist core relations) was not met by 88 percent of the state's capital spending in manufacturing. Capitalist integration could not be met with the remaining 12 percent of the state's spending in manufacturing, which consisted mainly of joint ventures, such as the *Societé Textile de Kisangani* (SOTESKI) or the *Cimentereie Nationale* (CINAT). SOTEXKI, a textile plant in the northeastern part of the country, imports its inputs, even though northeastern Zaire produces cotton that could be used in manufacturing clothes. CINAT, a joint venture in which a German company held 50 percent of the shares, posed similar problems. It was established in the Kinshasa–Bas-Zaire region, which already produced 80 percent of the cement output, although its establishment in the Northeast would have allowed more linkage effects with a nascent construction sector.

Thus even were one to assume – as I did – that investment capital used b the state in the manufacturing sector was provided by mining revenues, such a transfer did not correct the colonial economic structure. But did financing for these state's investments in manufacturing actually originate from the mining sector? Here also the answer is negative. As Bézy and others have indicated, 60 percent of the financing for SOSIDER, which runs the Maluku steel plant, was provided by outside sources, namely Germany and Italy. The state contributed 40 percent of the financing. Although there are no specific data on the origin of the state's 40 percent share of financing for the plant and other manufacturing investments, the bulk of investment capital did *not* come from the mining/copper sector. As already shown, the state relied heavily on foreign borrowing for its investment projects and, partly because of the easy borrowing conditions prevailing from 1969 to 1974, used tax revenues from the mining/copper sector mainly for ordinary budgetary expenses.[43] In 1966 the state's ordinary expenses amounted to 98.4 percent of its ordinary revenues; in 1974, 104.2 percent. On the average, ordinary expenses during the 1966–77 period were 104.6 percent. These data further support the contention that the state's investment projects in manufacturing were not financed by state ordinary revenues (e.g. from mining), which in turn suggests reliance on foreign borrowing or, at least, no transfer from the mining/copper sector to the manufacturing sector.

The mere 3.5 percent of capital spending devoted to the agricultural sector left it the most neglected sector of the economy. As I indicated earlier, under colonial rule the agricultural sector (export branch) provided the state with substantial indirect tax revenues, second to those of the mining sector. Because of the high priority given the mining sector under the Mobutu regime, agriculture lost its competitive position. The loss of indirect tax revenues from agriculture was to be offset by a substantial increase of capital spending in the mining industry. But more importantly, the low level of capital spending in agriculture indicates the lack of transfer of revenues from the mining sector to the agriculture sector. The state spent only 1.8 percent of its total capital commitments on agriculture, that is, 1.5 percent of total capital spending (public and private), during the 1968–75 period. The private sector invested the remaining 2 percent of capital in agriculture. Because of its private origin, the 2 percent did not represent a transfer from the mining sector. Even if one were to assume that the state's share of capital was made up of revenues from the mining/copper sector, 1.5 percent is too minimal to talk of transfer. Yet because of the state's high level of ordinary spending and high level of foreign borrowing, not all the liquid capital making up the state's share of 1.5 percent came from ordinary state revenues. The very low priority given agriculture prevented this sector from expanding capitalist core relations in peasant agriculture.

Transportation/communication did not benefit from mining revenues either. Financing in most cases came from foreign sources. For instance, the satellite communication network and the ultramodern broadcasting system valued at Z52.6 million (US $105.2 million, 1975 exchange rate), that is, about 42 percent of total capital spending in transportation/communication, were financed by French and American capital. The remaining 58 percent of capital spending in transportation/communication was shared by the state and private entrepreneurs. As with the agriculture and manufacturing sectors, the state's high level of ordinary expenses and foreign borrowing precluded any transfer from the mining/copper sector to transportation/ communication. Whatever capital the state contributed to communication came from borrowing.

To sum up the discussion so far: the sectoral distribution of investments from 1968 to 1980 reflected the high priority assigned to the mining sector. The importance of mining derived from its ability to provide the state with revenues. Investments in the manufacturing, agriculture, and transportation/communication sectors did not benefit from investment transfers from revenues accumulated in the mining sector. Nor did these investments help correct the dislocated colonial economic structure, that is, pseudocapitalism. They only exacerbated it, as will be apparent from supplemental geographical and input–output analyses of 1968–80 investments.

200

As analyzed in chapter 5, the geographical distribution of colonial investments revealed the leading roles played by the Katanga (Shaba), the Léopoldville (Kinshasa–Bas-Zaire), and, to a lesser extent, the Haut-Zaire development poles. From 1885 to 1950, Katanga absorbed 80 percent of the investments in mining and shared with the Léopoldville pole the higher portion of investment in manufacturing. During the 1951–59 period, the leading position of the Katanga pole was reinforced with 13 percent of new investments; that of the Léopoldville pole was also reinforced with 33.1 percent of new investments over the same period. In short, the colonial economy was based on a bipolar structure – a structure reinforced by 1968–80 investments, as is demonstrated by their geographical distribution. Although the percentage decreased relatively for some regions and increased dramatically for the Léopoldville pole, in general, the similarities with the colonial period are striking (table 7.11).

Under colonial rule, sectoral and geographical disarticulation culminated in the input/output disintegration of the economy. One of the salient characteristics of the colonial economy was its lack of interindustrial and intersectoral exchanges. Outputs from some industries were not transformed into inputs for other industries. Production in some sectors of the economy or branches of the economy did not stimulate the demand for intermediary goods in other sectors or branches. Capital goods were mainly imported, as were inputs for many industries. Outputs produced by local industries, especially the mining industry, relied heavily on the world market. In the postcolonial period under the Mobutu regime, this pattern was repeated and reinforced.

Unlike the mining sector, the manufacturing sector under colonial rule had its final output almost totally directed toward the internal market. This was the result of an industry based on import-substitution rationale. In the post-1965 period the manufacturing sector operated under the same conditions. As a result, the domestic market absorbed about 60 percent of manufactured consumer goods and about 39 percent of intermediary and capital goods produced by manufacturing industries. But, as I showed in chapter 5, the reliance of the colonial manufacturing sector on the internal market did not by any means integrate the sectors of the economy. Given that investments for 1968–80 sectorally and geographically followed the colonial pattern, they did nothing to alter this disarticulated structure of exchange. Rather they maintained and reinforced it. Although aimed at the internal market, final output was not directed as inputs to other sectors of the economy, such as the mining and agricultural sectors. Locally manufactured intermediary and capital goods were almost totally consumed by a few industries concentrated in the Kinshasa and Shaba regions. Most local firms imported a high proportion of their intermediary and capital goods (see tables 7.12 and 7.13). These firms' reliance on imports for their inputs clearly shows the low integration of local firms in different sectors of the economy with the manufacturing sector. But the data also indicate that over this period the manufacturing sector itself depended heavily on imports for its inputs. In general, the input/output dislocation under the Mobutu regime remained almost the same as under colonial rule (table 7.14).[44]

The structure of the exchange of inputs and outputs between sectors of the economy and the direction of economic outputs from 1966 to 1980 remained about the same as under colonial rule. Sectorally, however, dependence increased on imported inputs and exported outputs of mineral resources. First, everything being equal, because the colonial economic structure was maintained and reinforced, the extra demand generated by investments in the leading sectors during the 1968–80 period necessarily followed the colonial outward-oriented structure of exchange. As a result, this extra demand meant a higher level of input imports in some sectors, such as manufacturing and mining. Second, everything also being equal, extra investments in sectors such as mining during the 1968–80 period helped increase the production of mineral outputs, which meant an increase in outputs exported compared to the colonial period.

Thus, as in their sectoral and geographical distributions, the structure of exchanges between the inputs and outputs of investments under the Mobutu regime repeated and reinforced pseudocapitalism. Lack of integration between sectors led to a lack of linkage effects in the economy as a whole. Reinforcement of the disarticulation at the input/output level meant a reinforcement of the scanty internal market. Investments during the 1968–80 period contrasted with such goals as the 'sectoral and geographical equilibrium of investments' and the 'importance of the linkage effects to other sectors of the economy,' which served as criteria for approval of investment projects. They reinforced the enclave capitalist economy, which blocked the expansion of capitalist relations to other sectors of the economy where such relations were absent or only partially present.

Agriculture, for example, was given low priority in the sectoral distribution of investment spending. With state and private investments almost nonexistent, the structure of agriculture remained as it was under colonial rule; subsistence agriculture dominated and was not integrated with other sectors by means of capitalist relations. It also remained outward oriented, hence, unable to expand capitalist core relations inside Zaire. This tendency was reinforced by the sociogeographical distribution of investments and the rural exodus. As under colonial rule, the geographical and sectoral distribution of investments helped block the extension of capitalist core relations. The twin consequences of rural exodus, that is, redundant labor supply in towns and abundant land in depopulated areas, revealed the extent of such a blockade. The pricing policy of the state, which fixed a minimum of producer price for peasant agriculture, helped further to block the implantation of capitalist relations in agriculture. Because their purchasing power was shrinking, the peasants withdrew from commercialized agriculture and were even more confined to subsistence agriculture.[45]

Table 7.11: The geographical distribution of investments 1968–75 and 1951–59 (in percentage of total number of investment projects)

Region	No of projects 1968–75	%	No of projects 1951–9	%
Kinshasa/Bas-Zaire/Bandundu (Leopoldville)	97	69.7	900	33.1
Shaba (Katanga)	18[a]	12.9[a]	377[a]	13.0[a]
Haut-Zaire (Orientale)	9	6.4	462	16.0
Equateur	7	5.0	167	6.1
Kivu	5	3.5	284	10.4
Kasai Orientale	1	0.7		
Kasai Occidental	1	0.7	135	0.03
Nonspecified	1	0.7		20.0
Total	139	100.0	2,325	100.0

Source: For 1968–75: calculated from Mulumba, 'Investir au Zaire,' op. cit., pp. 149–150; for 1951–59: Belgium, Ministère des Colonies, *La Situation economique du Congo Belge et du Rwanda–Urundi* (1951 to 1959).
[a] As was the case for the 1951–59 colonial investments, investments for the 1968–75 period came to add to an already unbalanced industrial base.

Table 7.12: Imports of primary (raw materials) and intermediary goods by Zairian firms in selected economic sectors, 1969–72 (in percentage of total inputs)

Sector	1969	1970	1971	1972
Agriculture	14.7[a]	9.9	18.6	16.0
Mining	66.6	68.9	63.6	68.7
Manufacture	67.5	67.4	65.3	64.5
Construction	26.5	28.1	30.6	10.3
Transportation/Communication	32.5	23.4	35.2	37.7

Source: Département de l'Économie Nationale, *Enquête sur les entreprises* 1971/72. (Kinshasa, 1972) n.p. [a] The low level of imports of inputs for agriculture (1969–72) is not indicative of a greater use of locally produced inputs, but rather reflects the very low priority given the agricultural sector.

Table 7.13: Capital goods imported and locally produced, 1966–75 (in percentage of total utilized capital goods)

	1966	1970	1974	1975
Locally produced	7	6	9	9
Imported	93	94	91	91

Source: D. Van der Steen, 'Echanges économiques extérieurs du Zaire: dépendance et développement,' *Les Cahiers du CEDAF*, no. 4–5 (1977): 25.

Table 7.14: Origin of inputs 1950–59 and 1966–75 (in average percentages of total inputs)

	1950–59		1966–75	
	Local	Import	Local	Import
Capital goods	7	93	7	93
Raw material/intermediary goods[a]	30	70	33[b]	67

Source: Tables 5.8, 7.12, and 7.13.
[a] Percentages reflect the situation only up to 1972.
[b] The percentages calculated for local and imported raw material/intermediary goods are for 1969–72, the period for which data are available.

4. Overpoliticization as Crisis

The subordination of the allocation of the social product to overpoliticication had a chain of consequences. First, the deepening of pseudocapitalism had an immediate effect on major economic activities. The reinforcement of the export sector meant reliance on fluctuations of the world market. Because of the fall in copper prices, the state's revenues from international trade shrank from an average of 65 percent in 1970–74 to about 41 percent during 1975–79 and resulted in negative terms of trade from Zaire. In 1975, whereas its average import prices rose by 19 percent, its average export prices declined by 27 percent. The shrinking purchasing power for the state brought about the collapse in every import category. In 1975, the quantity of food that could be imported with a given quantity of exports was only 40 percent of the 1970 level, that of energy was 29 percent, intermediate goods, 55 percent, and capital goods, 60 percent. On the average, the terms of trade fell to 51 percent of their 1970 levels. Second, decline in aggregate output was exacerbated by the policies of Zairian-ization and radicalization. These policies were, on the economic front, a total failure: 'Zairianization led in many instances to the destruction or dispersion of the capital stock; it disrupted marketing by causing an exodus of small expatriate intermediaries who traditionally played a vital role in the distribution of inputs and consumer goods; but more importantly perhaps it led to the neglect of maintenance and repair, the discouragement of private investments and financial mismanagement in both the manufacturing and agro-industrial sectors.'[46] Third, these problems were compounded by the budget-supported political expenses that led to a serious waste of crucial resources. These three factors combined to precipitate a regressive tendency in economic activities and growth. Almost all sectors of the economy were hard hit. From 1975 to 1979 aggregate output (marketed GDP) declined steadily. By 1977, it had declined by 13.5 percent. The sharp decline in aggregate output had serious repercussions on prices. As the fall in aggregate output settled in, the profitability of most economic activities could be maintained at their previous levels only through an increase in domestic prices. This brought about a hyperinflationary trend that reached 100 percent by 1978 and seriously affected nutrition, health, and other basic social services as their costs climbed uncontrollably.

Foreign debt was another consequence of the policies that deepened pseudo-capitalism. Because they were highly capital intensive, investments required substantial financial capital, which could not be provided by the private or public sectors in Zaire. Both the state and the private sector had recourse mostly to foreign capital in realizing their investments under the state's liability. The state borrowed heavily for its own direct investments, and it guaranteed loans received by private and public enterprises for investment purposes. Because of budgetary expenses, on the one hand, and reliance on one main source of revenue, that is, mineral resources, on the other, the state's budget faced a chronic deficit. From 1970 to 1976, the average budgetary deficit stood at 11 percent of GDP. To make up for the deficit, the state had to borrow from foreign banks and credit agencies. In addition, loans or grants under 'advantageous conditions' from foreign-based sources increased Zaire's indebtedness. These three factors made Zaire one of the most indebted countries in Africa. From US $492 million at the end of 1970, total external debt rose to US $2.724 billion at the end of 1975 (about 41 percent per year).[47] From 1975 to 1980, this total almost doubled to about US $5 billion; by 1989, it was US $7 billion. From 70 percent in 1973, the total debt/GDP ratio reached 102.4 percent in 1976. On the one hand, the increase was the result of more borrowing and grants as the state's deficit grew steadily by 1975; on the other hand, the budgetary deficit and lack of revenues made it difficult for the state to repay both the debt principal and the interest owed its creditors.

Rescheduling of the unpaid interest and principal had serious political and economic side effects. To obtain rescheduling of its debts, Zaire subscribed to several requirements of its creditors and of the IMF. Institutionally, the requirements consisted of having a team of IMF and expatriate personnel head Zaire's national bank, the Department of Finance, and the customs service. Economically, the IMF and Zaire's creditors requested drastic cuts in state spending; they also requested that a percentage of export revenues be set aside by the Zairian government and be automatically allotted to debt repayment. From 1973 to 1977, Zaire used, on average, 11 percent of its export revenues for debt service. In 1981 it was 27 percent. Finally, the IMF urged Zaire to devaluate its currency to accumulate export revenues that would help repay the debt. From 1976 to 1980, the *zaire* was devalued seven times.

These requirements did not improve the situation as the IMF had anticipated; if anything, they created a vicious circle. The requirements were set up to help reestablish Zaire's creditworthiness among its creditors by creating institutional and economic conditions conducive to accumulating revenues that would help to pay the debt; this, in turn, was the sine qua non for getting more loans to pay debts or for further rescheduling of the debts, which had the effect of increasing debt volume without an actual positive effect on the economy. In a confidential letter to the managing director of the IMF on September 5, 1980, President Mobutu wrote: 'The Executive Council [i.e., the Zairian government] has established as a priority the re-establishment of the creditworthiness of Zaire in the international community. As a result, the Executive Council will continue to honor all the external debt service obligations of Zaire; it also intends to observe all the performance criteria established for September 30 and December 31, 1980.'[48] The reestablishment of creditworthiness meant serious economic hardships for the common people. The drastic reduction of state expenditures further reduced already poorly run social services. Successive devaluations generated a hyperinflationary rate, which seriously weakened the purchasing power of consumers. Using a percentage of export revenues for debt repayment decreased the amount of resources available to the state, thus preventing it from undertaking new economic projects. And finally, the debt service worsened Zaire's balance of payments.

The deterioration of agriculture was another major effect of overpoliticization. The relationship between the reinforcement of pseudocapitalism and the fate of the agricultural sector has already been shown. To reiterate, four policies exacerbated the state of agriculture: (1) the low priority given agriculture in the sectoral distribution of investment spending; (2) the socio-geographical distribution of investments that, by favoring the urban areas, led to a massive rural exodus; (3) the Zairianization measures, which disrupted the channnels of production in agriculture; and (4) the producer minimum price (the peasants' equivalent of minimum wage). These factors combined with the more structural conditions of pseudocapitalism to precipitate a dramatic decline of agricultural output. Thus in 1959 (the colonial period), agriculture's share of GDP was estimated at about 26 percent; from 1970 to 1977 it was only 16.6 percent. Commercialized agriculture contributed only 40 percent of agriculture's share of GDP.[49] The contribution of agriculture to total exports also declined dramatically. As noted earlier, in 1959 the share of agriculture in total exports was about 40 percent; from 1968 to 1979 it was only 16 percent.

The result of all these processes was the exacerbation of socioeconomic deprivation for the masses manifested by the brutal degradation of their standard of living and the deterioration of education, health, nutrition and other social services. In a spiral movement, scarcity triggered many illicit and survival activities. These included parallel economy, self-enclosure, and pervasive corruption, activities that proponents of the 'soft state' paradigm wrongly impute to the 'softness' of the state.

In an overpoliticized state, response to the impact of the distribution of the social product is likely to be through overpoliticization rather than the type of response that prevails in a capitalist democratic state. As in the Katanga Secession, the response is generally given outside existing institutional and procedural limits. During the early years of Mobutu's rule, this pattern of responses manifested itself in many crises. The first was the weakened resistance by the remnants of the 1964–65 popular rebellions. Although much of the resistance was ended by 1968, some pockets remained in the Northeast. The second was the double mutiny (1966 and 1967) of the former Katanga gendarmes (who were incorporated into the national army) along with mercenary units hired to assist the government in its campaigns against popular insurgencies. The third was a number of attempted coups or alleged coup attempts designed to overthrow the newly established regime; an illustration of this is the 'Pentecost Plot,' which led to the public hanging of four prominent politicians (the alleged plotters) in 1966.

During the later years of Mobutu's rule, the response of the opposition was also through overpoliticization. The effects of subordinating the allocation of the social product to authoritarian means were felt in many ways. The fallouts were felt first and foremost by peasants, workers, and the unemployed. The result was a response to power holders through overpoliticization. In defiance of the ban on strikes, by 1976, workers began wildcat strikes to voice their grievances against the regime. In addition to various skirmishes with security forces or party officials, peasants engaged, on three major occasions, in open conflicts against power holders. In 1977 and again in 1978, the *Front National de libération du Congo* (FNLC), an Angola-based opposition movement partly made up of recruited unemployed, invaded the Shaba (Katanga) region. Peasants and the unemployed joined the invaders and provided them with logistical, material, moral and human support. Both instances of armed conflict were ended by the joint intervention of Belgian, French, and Moroccan troops. In the Kwilu district in the Bandundu region, peasants attacked in 1978 the party's representatives and security forces before being subjugated by the elite division of the Zairian army. Peasants also joined small insurgent groups in the northern Shaba and Kivu regions.

As a means of distribution of the social product, authoritarian rule revealed serious contradictions at two levels. At the policy-making level, the consolidation of the relationship with foreign-based actors and the responsive policies of the state in favor of the lower classes, whenever the latter threatened the regime, hurt members of the upper classes; these policies decreased the amount of material or political goods that otherwise would have been manipulated in their favor. The politics of Zairianization is a good illustration. The 1973 Zairianization measures were devised in attempt to consolidate internal coalitions among upper classes and groups. As already noted, these measures constituted a serious blow to foreign-based businesses and states. They also led to acute shortages of consumer goods on the market, to the dramatic deterioration of the conditions of peasants, workers, and the unemployed, and to the consequent violent reactions by the masses. The state responded to the masses' grievances by 'radicalizing' Zairianized businesses in 1974, transferring businesses owned by members of the upper classes to the state. State ownership meant, in fact, that the power holders and their closest allies were to become managers of the state-owned businesses.

Rather than solving the problem of economic deprivation caused by the 1973 Zairianization measures, the 1974 radicalization measures aggravated it. But more importantly, they concentrated wealth in the hands of top power holders and some of their closest allies. For the expropriated members of the upper classes the radicalization measures constituted a major loss of resources; by 1975, they began to show signs of disenchantment with top power holders. Furthermore, pressure from foreign-based expropriated businesses and states and the impoverished masses caused the state in 1976 to give back many of the Zairianized and radicalized businesses to their former owners (the 'retrocession' measures). Some top power holders were allowed to keep the businesses they had acquired under the Zairianization and radicalization measures. The attempt to be responsive to foreign-based actors through the retrocession measures further hurt many *acquéreurs*. From their point of view, this constituted another major loss of resources and exacerbated emerging tensions within existing coalitions.

Contradictions were also revealed at the policy outcome level. The material base that sustained coalitions crumbled, decreasing the amount of distributable goods. The decrease caused top power holders to withhold some crucial resources for themselves and to become more selective about coalition building. As a result, the bulk of the members of the upper classes no longer had the material security that they had come to enjoy, which caused them to seek a modification of the political coalitions. To be sure, the effects of economic deprivation were more damaging for peasants, workers, and the unemployed. Nevertheless, the crumbling of the material base left many members of upper classes with material uncertainty as wealth and prestige concentrated in the hands of top power holders and some of their closest allies. The conflict took the form of ethnic and regional polarization, if a little more circumscribed than under the competitive rule of 1960–65.

The result of the recurrent conflicts among the members of the upper class was political crisis. Like the masses, their response to the power holders took place outside established constitutional limits. The disenchantment already occurring by 1975 because of the radicalization measures continued in the post-1975 period. Party and state officials denounced, paradoxically, corruption and mismanagement. They began to appeal more and more to such groups as peasants, workers, the unemployed, and students. In Kinshasa, for the first time since 1965, workers went on strike in 1976 to improve their materials conditions; for the first time, officials of UNTZA were accused by the regime of collusion with the workers. Strikes took place even though they were illegal. In Lumbumbashi, for the first time since 1965, university professors backed up students and workers who went on strike in 1977. In an open letter addressed to the Commissioner for Education, they wrote, 'We, Senior Professors (*Professeurs Ordinaires*) of Zairian nationality have approved as of

Tuesday, December 6, the deliberate and collective cessation of work decided upon by the wage-earners in order to obtain material and moral advantages.'[50] Such an appeal of the intellectuals and bureaucrats to the lower classes may have been more a tactical stand than anything else, but it did reveal the type for response given by these groups. Although the church's position had been ambiguous, and despite manipulation of resources in its favor by power holders, its actions strengthened the position of the discontented classes and groups. Some prominent church representatives read pastoral messages in which they expressed their dissatisfaction with the regime. For instance, the archbishop of Lubumbashi denounced in 1975 corruption, oppressiveness, and the regime's injustice in an open letter to Christians entitled *'Je suis un homme'* (I am a human being).

In February 1977, the legislative council, then composed of party-appointed members, refused to approve the budget and denounced presidential overspending and the oppressiveness of the regional administration. In 1980, a group of its prominent members wrote a fifty-one-page open letter to President Mobutu, in which they vigorously denounced the policies of the regime and their effects on the Zairian population. (The group later was instrumental in the process of 'democratization' that weakened the Mobutu regime.) About the concentration of economic and political power in the hands of power holders, they wrote:

> It is common for you to argue that there are no little and big guys in Zaire. But out of a population of 25 million, only fifty (50) individuals occupy the most lucrative jobs and control the whole political apparatus. This is tantamount to saying that in the Zairian 'authentic' society, the percentage of those who control the economy and the political amounts to 0.00002%! To our knowledge there is no country in the world which displays an economic and political power concentration as scandalous.[51]

Tensions culminated in the defection of some of the prominent members of the party. Monguya Mbenge, a former regional commissioner, and the Zairian ambassador to Iran fled to Belgium, where they formed two opposition movements. Most conspicuous was Nguza Karl i Bond, a long-time foreign minister, a one-time secretary general of the political bureau of the party, and prime minister until 1981. He was accused of collusion with invading forces from Angola in 1977, was tried, sentenced to death, and then freed; he defected in 1981 to Belgium, where he took a hostile stand against the Mobutu regime before being co-opted by the regime in 1985.

Tensions also occurred in the army. As I pointed out earlier, in spite of the influence exercised by the army through General Mobutu, the regime did not resemble a military dictatorship. Few top officers, such as some *compagnons de la révolution*, stood at the top of political power. The bulk of officers and junior officers owed loyalty to the party. For coalition building, the military, for obvious reasons, was crucial. The authoritarian distribution of the social product also affect it. Although construed in patrimonial terms, the following quote reveals this reality.

> Mobutu ... provided the money senior officers (need) to acquire almost anything. ... Senior officers in Zaire are (thus) like any other elites and appointed members of the Mobutu regime. Since Mobutu controls both the money and the power to appoint everybody, army officers live in a permanent fear of losing their priviledged status in the regime. Thus, Mobutu insures the support of the officers by buying them, appointing and promoting them to posts in both the army and the (political bureau) of the MPR, and making them believe that their loyal support to him guarantees them their position, status, and material advantages.[52]

It follows, then, that in terms of policy formulation and policy outcome, the contradictions of the overpolicized state were also felt by the military and eroded military loyalty and support for the party–state. In 1975 some military officers staged an abortive coup. Generally referred to as *coup monté et manqué*, that coup attempt was, according to President Mobutu, backed by the United States. As a result, the American ambassador in Zaire was expelled, and nine military officers were tried and some sentenced to death. The tendency toward disloyalty culminated in 1977 when high and junior officers conspired with invaders from Angola and revealed, according to military sources, the defense strategies of the Zairian army to the enemy. Colonel Mampa, chief of staff of ground army units, was accused of high treason and sentenced to death. In 1978, a year after the first invasion and almost concomitantly with the second invasion by the same opposition group, a group of ninety-one high and junior officers 'set a plot to overthrow the regime.' During the trial these officers blamed the high concentration of wealth in the hands of power holders.[53] Military dissatisfaction also took the form of a pervasive lack of discipline among the military on the battlefield, not only in the Shaba wars but also in Angola, where Zaire supported Holden Roberto's FNLA against Agostino Neto's MPLA.

It is important to underscore that these oppositions and defections are not by themselves unusual; they are not specific to the Third World. What is peculiar and specific to the overpoliticized state is that they took place outside the established institutional and procedural framework. Unable to express themselves through a process of compromise (legal opposition), opposition groups did so outside the established rules of the game. Likewise, whether the coup attempts were real or imaginary is beside the point; coup attempts, or the fear thereof, denote the kind of response prevailing in an overpoliticized state. The overpoliticization of the allocation of the social product and coalition building triggers the military's response, which is also an expression of overpoliticization.

The foregoing analysis has amply demonstrated the role of foreign actors in the competition for the social product. However, one must examine this role with caution. In the post-1965 authoritarian rule, competition over distribution of the social product reveals the primacy of internal classes and groups.

Foreign actors faced overpoliticization by both holders of state power (authoritarianism) and by classes and groups outside or on the fringe of state power (crisis, insurgency). Given that the internal competition for the social product called for reliance on overpoliticization, they faced a *fait accompli*; they were influenced by the prevailing type of political competition. Whether they were beneficiaries or victims of overpoliticization, foreign actors' behavior was dictated by it rather than vice versa. This general situation explains the relations between foreign-based actors and Zaire (or the Third World in general). Forced to choose between two sides (opposition and power holders) that use the same means (i.e., overpoliticization), foreign actors base their decisions on their short- and long-term interests. For them the question is: Which of the two sides of the overpoliticized state would best defend their interests?

In post-1965 Zaire, the answer to this question was a function of several factors, of which historical particularity was the most important. Authoritarian rule emerged after the protracted and acute Congo Crisis of the 1960–65 competitive rule. Foreign actors' perception of Zaire's politics in the post-1965 period was influenced by that crisis. Hence, one understands the myth of *après Mobutu, le chaos*, which accredited the idea of the ingovernability of Zaire upon President Mobutu's departure from power. To the extent that overpoliticization by the opposition was identified with crisis and, like the 1960–65 crisis, was detrimental to their interests, foreign actors preferred overpoliticization by power holders to that by the opposition. This choice was facilitated by the advantages attached to any incumbency; power holders are in a position to manipulate foreign actors by threatening to break diplomatic ties. One recalls here the various conflicts between Zaire and Belgium during which Belgium was often threatened with replacement in its privileged position by France or the United States. The choice of foreign actors was further facilitated by the ineffectiveness and real difficulties of the opposition.[54] Incapable of forcing the choice in their favor through a sustained internal struggle, the opposition allowed foreign actors to wrongly or rightly equate the protection of their interests with overpoliticization by power holders.

These factors illuminate the type of support Zaire received from Western countries in the post-1965 period; this included military assistance as witnessed by the 1977 and 1978 Shaba (Katanga) wars and economic assistance, including investments and their financing. According to USAID, loans and grants to Zaire help to 'prevent Zaire's severe short-term financial problems from causing economic disruption and undermining political stability.' They also help to maintain (US) 'access on favorable terms to Zaire's rich mineral resources.'[55] By 'political stability' USAID meant stability as provided by authoritarianism. This interpretation suggests that the behavior of foreign actors is likely to be more supportive of overpoliticization when they are beneficiaries rather than victims of it. The benefits derived from authoritarian rule by foreign actors ranged from alignment with Western allies' positions in international affairs (e. g., in the Gulf War and in the Israeli–Arab conflict) to increasing the rate of profit for foreign businesses by banning strikes.

However, the behavior of foreign actors did not always support the power holders. In those cases where overpoliticization by the latter affected them negatively, foreign actors reacted negatively. They supported the overpoliticized opposition. Recall here the alleged collusion of the American ambassador with military officers who staged a coup in 1975; Belgium's timid receptiveness to the armed opposition (FNLC) in 1977 and 1978 (even though in the end Belgium chose to maintain its support of Mobutu); and the tense relationship between the Mobutu regime and Western countries following the nationalization of their assets. In this sense, political crisis that accompanied Mobutu's authoritarian rule was also a result of the reliance on overpoliticization by foreign actors. But the conditions that led them toward reliance were not 'made abroad.'

Conclusion

I have argued in this chapter that within the context of post-1965 politics, authoritarianism and the various reactions to it expressed a reliance on overpoliticization by both the power holders and the opposition in the competition for the social product in pseudocapitalism. Such reliance took five major forms: (1) institutional authoritarianism and stringent authoritarian requirements imposed on potential beneficiaries of the social product by the power holders; (2) repression and persecution of the opposition; (3) authoritarian behavior and policies of the power holders toward foreign actors; (4) use of violence and anticonstitutional means by the opposition to respond to the power holders; and (5) embrace of authoritarianism or anticonstitutional means by foreign actors in their support of or opposition to the power holders. Reliance on overpoliticization deepened pseudocapitalism as revealed by the sectoral imalance and input–output disintegration of the economy, exacerbated socioeconomic deprivation, and fed on more overpoliticization in the form of political crisis. As under the 1960–65 competitive rule, the manifestations of overoliticiztion were consistent with the definition of overpoliticization in chapter 1; they differed from those of the liberal democratic state.

The central question of this book remains: Why was the competition for the social product under the 1960–65 competitive rule and the post-1965 authoritarian rule subordinated to overpoliticization? To attempt a theoretical answer to this question, I return now to the issues of capitalism and pseudocapitalism.

Notes

1. *Congo 1965* (Brussels: CRISP, 1966), pp. 438–444.

2. See Juan Linz, 'Totalitarian and Authoritarian Regimes,' in E. Greenstein and N. Polsby, eds., *Handbook of Political Science* (Reading: Addision-Wesley, 1975), pp. 180–273.

3. Manwana Mungongo, Le Genéral Mobutu Sese Seko parle du nationalisme Zairois authenique, quoted by Young and Turner, *op. cit.*, p. 214

4. Mpinga Kassenda and D. J. Gould, *Les reformes administratives au Zaire 1972–73* (Kinshasa: P.U.Z., 1975), p. 78.

5. D. J. Gould, 'Patrons, Clients, and the Role of the Military in Zairian Politics.' (Mimeoraph)

6. See, Th. Lukusa, 'La réforme monétaire du 24 Juin 1967,' *Etudes Congolaises*, 10, no. 4 (July–August 1967).

7. See H. Leclercq, 'Evolutions des finances publiques de 1966 à 1969,' *Cahiers Economiques et Sociaux*, 7, no. 2–3 (September 1969), pp. 147–195.

8. On the influence of these bodies, see Katwala-Ghifem, *Bureaucracy, Dependency and Underdevelopment in Zaire* (Ph.D. dissertation, Berkeley: University of California, 1979), pp. 146–158.

9. These guidelines can be found in A. Ndele, *Politique economique et financière au Congo* (Frankfurt, Germany 1969); R. Bisengimana, 'La politique gouvernementale en matière de développement,' *Zaire-Afrique*, No. 64 (1972) p. 209 ff.; Ngoy Kapaji, 'Projets d'investissements et croissance de l'economie Zairoise 1970–75,' *Zaire-Afrique*, no. 70 (December 1972), pp. 607–619; Banque du Zaire, *Bulletin Trimestriel*, No. 4 (1970).

10. The sectoral distribution given by Ngoy Kapaji, *op. cit.*, is the following: agriculture 186.55 million zaires; mining 186 million; manufacturing 42.48 million; building 40 million; energy 30.48 million; banking and services 166.14 million; transportation/communication 334.96 million; commerce 38.8 million. The percentage was calculated on the basis of these figures and the total projected capital of 1 billion zaires given in Ngoy. Example: agriculture = *186,550,000 x 100/1* billion = 18.6%. However, since the projected total capital given by Ngoy is lower than that proposed by Zaire's national bank (1.4 billion zaires), I have compared the percentage obtained in each sector above with the 1.4 billion (e.g., agriculture: 18% of 1.4 billion = about 252 million zaires) in order to obtain a more realistic sectoral distribution in value

11. See *Etudes Congolaises*, 10, no. 4 (1967).

12. See World Bank/IBRD, *Appraisal of Gecamines Expansion Project*, December 26, 1974.

13. For an appraisal of the line, see J. C. Willame, *Zaire: l'épopée d'Inga* (Paris: L'Harmattan, 1986).

14. Zaire's National Bank, Annual Reports 1971/72 and 1975; World Bank/IBRD, *The Economy of Zaire* 3 (1975): Table 5.10.

15. World Bank/IBRD, *Appraisal of GECAMINES Expansion Project*, December 26, 1974; EXIMBANK, *Inga–Shaba Transmission Line*, May 8, 1979.

16. On SODIMIZA and SMTF, see S. N. Sangmpam, 'Peripheral Capitalism, the State and Crisis,' Ph.D. dissertation, the University of Chicago, 1984, pp. 207–214.

17. Mulumba Lukoji, 'Invesir au Zaire,' *Zaire-Afrique*, no. 103 (March 1976): 148.

18. Mpinga and Gould, *Les Reformes administratives au Zaire*, p. 149.

19. Quoted by T. Callaghy, 'State Formation and Centralization of Power in Zaire: Mobutu's Pre-eminent Public Policy,' paper presented at the 1976 Annual Meeting of the African Studies Association, Boston, Massachusetts, November 3–6, 1976.

20. This view is held by Willame in *Patrimonialism and Political Change in the Congo*.
21. Koli Elombe, 'Le role de l'intellectuel, *JIWE* (1975), p. 3.
22. M. Schatzberg, 'Bureaucracy, Business, Beer: The Political Dynamics of Class Formation in Lisala, Zaire' (Ph. D. dissertation, 1977), chap. 4, p. 159. The dissertation has since been published as Politics and Class in Zaire: Bureaucracy, Business and Beer in Lisala (new York: Africana, 1979).
23. The interpretation of these events is given by Nzongola Ntalaja, 'The Authenticity of Neo-colonialism: Ideology and Class Struggles in Zaire,' *Berkeley Journal of Sociology*, 22 (1977–78): 115–129.
24. *Le Soir*, February 27, 1978.
25. D. Van Der Steen, 'Elections et réformes politiques du Zaire en 1977,' *Les Cahiers du CEDAF*, no. 2–3 (1978): 30–74.
26. See D. J. Gould, *Bureaucratic Corruption and Underdevelopment in the Third World* (New York: Pergamon Press, 1980).
27. President Mobutu, 'Discours d'ouverture du Deuxième Congrès Ordinaire du MPR' Nsele, November 25, 1977. Emphasis added.
28. Gould, *Bureaucratic Corruption and Underdevelopment in the Third World*, Appendix, pp. 123–149.
29. The case of Ghana where three former heads of state were shot in 1979 because of their involvement in corruption is well known.
30. US Department of Health, Education and Welfare, *Syncrisis: The Dynamics of Health, Zaire*. 14 (Washington, D. C., 1975), pp. 143.
31. On the debate on the class character of the state personnel, see M. Mamdani, *Politics and Class Formation in Uganda* (New York: Monthly Review, 1976), chpters 7 and 8.
32. Kamitatu-Massamba, *Zaire: Le pouvoir a la portee du peuple* (Paris: L'Harmattan, 1977), pp. 91–92.
33. 'Discours prononcé le 30 Novembre 1973 par le Président Mobutu devant le Conseil Legislatif National.'
34. Kikassa Mwanalessa, 'La stabilisation des entreprises Zairianisées et radicalisées, ' *Zaire-Afrique*, no. 102 (February 1976): 88–98.
35. Comité-Zaire, *Zaire: le dossier de la recolonisation* (Paris: L'Harmattan, 1979), p.125.
36. E. Kanyo, 'Political Power and Class Formation: The Zairianization Measures, 1973–1975' Ph. D. dissertation, Yale University, 1979), pp. 50–51.
37. Bayart, 'Clientelism, Elections and systems of Inequality and Domination in Cameroon,' in *Elections Without Choice*. Edited by G. Hermet, R. Rose and A. Rouquié (New York, 1978), p. 67.
38. *Epanza* (April 7, 1975).
39. Mobutu, *Discours, allocutions et messages* (Paris: Editions J. A., 1975), pp. 568–571.
40. World Bank/IBRD, *Appraisal of GECAMINES Expansion Project*, p. 8.
41. Bezy et al., *Accumulation et sous-développement au Zaire*, p. 164.
42. Bezy et al., *Accumulation et sous-développement au Zaire*, p. 204.
43. Nyembo, *L'industrie du cuivre dans le monde*, pp. 152–153.
44. These comparative data need to be interpreted cautiously. Data for 1966–80 are partial. For instance, data on the inputs/raw materials and intermediary goods give the situation only up to 1972. Furthermore, data for 1966–75 do not include inputs

used by the state bureaucracy and by approximately 10 percent to 20 percent of the private enterprises not included in the survey from which the data are drawn. Finally, as was seen earlier, capital spending in such sectors as agriculture had declined so dramatically from 1968 to 1975 that data on the origin of their inputs do not give the true picture. For instance, one would falsely conclude that the share of agriculture's imported inputs was very low (oscillating between 9.9 percent to 18.6 percent) by comparison with the colonial period. In reality, it reflected the very low priority given agriculture in the distribution of investment capital. Because the sector was neglected, its demand for imported inputs was also low.

45. On agricultural policies in Africa, see Robert Bates, *Markets and States in Tropical Africa* (Berkeley: University of California Press, 1981).
46. World Bank, *Zaire: Current Economic Situation and Constraints* (Washington, DC, 1979), pp. 14, 27–28.
47. IMF, *Zaire: Recent Economic Developments*, SM/77/113: 18, 51.
48. IMF, *Zaire: Review and Consultation Under Stand-by-Arrangements and Request*, EBS/80/218 (October 3, 1980), p. 17.
49. United Nations (UNDP), *Zaire: Mission d'évaluation et de formulation pour le secteur agricole et rural*, Rep. DP/ZAI/80/001, 1 (1980), p. 100.
50. 'Lettre ouverte au Commissaire d'Etat a l'enseignement supérieur,' Lubumbashi, December 6, 1977 (mimeographed).
51. 'Lettre ouverte au President–Fondateur du MPR, President de la Republique par un groupe de Parlementaires,' Kinshasa, November 1, 1980, p. 31.
52. Quoted by D. Gould, 'Patrons, Clients, and the Role of the Military in Zairian Politics,' (unpublished manuscript).
53. *Le Soir* (March 10, 1978).
54. On the role of the opposition before the 1990 democratization process, see Makidiku-Ntima, 'On the External Dimension of the Crisis of the Revolution in Zaire: Revolutionary Solidarity or National Interests,' in Nzongola-Ntalaja, ed., *The Crisis in Zaire*, pp. 289–295.
55. USAID, *FY 1976 Submission to the Congress*, Middle East Peace and Security Suporting Assistance (Washington, DC, 1975), p. 91.

8 Pseudocapitalism and the overpoliticized state: Theoretical reprise

The central question of this study is: How does one explain the invariant reliance by political actors on overpoliticization in their competition for the social product in both competitive ('democratic') and authoritarian rules? Differently put, why was the state overpoliticized in both types of regime? I have proposed, as a central thesis, that overpoliticization is an outcome of pseudocapitalism, which sets the structural limits for both competitive and authoritarian rules and explains their fundamental similarities. In conjunction with this thesis, I have maintained that the causal link between pseudocapitalism and overpoliticization cannot be properly demonstrated unless pseudocapitalism itself is explained. The definition of the problem, the central question of the study, and the proposed answer to the question demarcate this study from the dominant paradigms of the state and society in Africa. Indeed, in contrast to the prevailing view that authoritarian rule and competitive rule are qualitatively distinct categories, I have shown in chapters 6 and 7 that they are genetic twins that share the same empirical manifestations of overpoliticization. And contrary to the dominant paradigms, I have shown in chapters 3, 4, and 5 that, although the role of imperialism cannot be denied, society/pseudocapitalism is explained by the dynamism of precolonial societies and not their 'stagnation' or subjugation by imperialism. In this last chapter, I elaborate theoretically on the answer to the aforementioned central question of the study, that is, its central thesis. Therefore, the focus is the causal link between pseudocapitalism thus defined and

216

overpoliticization as described in chapters 6 and 7. This requires that, in addition to pseudocapitalism, I return to the concepts of capitalism and lineage mode.

Three levels of analysis of the state can be identified. In the first level of analysis the focus is on the 'universal' raison d'être, the status and functions of the state vis-à-vis society, irrespective of the type of society. The focus in the second level of analysis is on the specific institutions and policies shaped by a given group or class that assumes political power for a given period of time. This is generally referred to as a 'political regime.' The state in the third level of analysis is examined in relation to the prevailing mode(s) of production and society. As pointed out earlier, the state necessarily embodies the particularity of societal relationships. Consequently, the concept of the state cannot be discussed without specifying a particular form of material production and, hence, the type of society. The first and second levels of analysis of the state are useful only to the extent that they are illuminated by the third level. Hence, the crucial question about the state becomes: What type of state exists where and in what type of society?

As underscored in previous chapters, the notion of the state is unthinkable outside of politics. As an expression of competitive interests of social actors, politics aims to control or influence state power. Because state power is exercised in fulfillment of its various functions, politics concerns itself with these functions. One of these functions, the allocation of the social product, remains the central issue of politics, having become even more so with the advent of liberalism.[1] Lasswell's definition of politics as 'who gets what, when and how' is echoed by many other writers, including David Easton, who holds that the political system consists of the authoritative allocation of values.[2] In raising, then, the question about the state, two follow-up questions about politics are crucial: How is the social product distributed? And how does the prevailing type of society determine such a distribution? Answers to these questions help explain the overpoliticized state. To grasp differences, it is crucial to answer the questions first for capitalist societies of the West. In other words, to support my central thesis, I need to present first the theoretical counter-evidence to the link between pseudocapitalism and the overpoliticized state. Such counter-evidence is provided by the cause and effect relation between capitalism and the liberal democratic state.

1. The Capitalist Democratic State

The state takes shape, in a complex manner,[3] within the prevailing society, hence, within the prevailing mode of production. As a mode of production and a society, capitalism displays characteristics that distinguish its implantation from its mere expansion via commodity exchange. Its very specificity dictates the specificity of the state associated with it. A specific type of state is associated with fully established capitalism : the capitalist democratic state. As Charles Lindblom maintains, 'However poorly the market is harnessed to democratic purposes, only within market-oriented systems does political democracy arise.'[4]

Lindblom explains this relationship: 'The association between liberal constitutional polyarchy and market is clearly no historical accident. Polyarchies were established to win and protect certain liberties: private property, free enterprise, free contract and occupational choice. ... For both the specific liberties and for the exercise of self-help, markets in which the options can be exercised are required.'[5] Although not explicit, the relationship Lindblom establishes between 'market' and 'polyarchy' assumes the implantation of capitalism with its eight features as defined in chapter 1. To discover the reasons for the cause and effect relationship between capitalism and the capitalist democratic state, one needs to answer three important questions: What does capitalist democratic rule involve? What allows this type of rule? And What supports the respect and maintenance of it?

Any social class or group seeks to satisfy its interest by laying claims to a portion of the social product through influencing state power and policies that are aimed at the production and distribution of these goods and services. In this study, I define capitalist democracy as a type of rule in which claims to the social product and attempts to influence the state's policies are based on social liberty, on the equalization of opportunities for all. Such an equalization of opportunities resembles a lottery system. It stipulates that any actor, group, or social class can lay claims to the social product on an equal basis without knowing in advance the outcome of its demands. In his bid for the US presidential nomination, the African American leader Jesse Jackson expressed this idea very well. 'Democracy,' he said, 'is not a system of guarantees, but of opportunities. If you run, you may win, but if you don't run, you cannot win.' To be sure, the notion of the equalization of opportunities does not mean that all social actors in a capitalist democracy always have the opportunity whenever they wish. Nor do they, as pluralists maintain, operate from dispersed, relatively equal centers of power, competing over all kinds of resources offered by society. The argument put forward here differs fundamentally from that of the pluralists by the first rule of the game that I shall enunciate shortly.

Like a lottery, capitalist democratic rule is based on 'rules of the game.' Different social classes and groups accept, in the arena of political competition, a set of institutionalized principles and behaviors on which their demands ought to be based.[6] Three rules of the game can be identified. The first and most important is that when claims are made on the social product, capitalist core relations (relations of ownership, production, and extraction of surplus product) are not contested, let alone modified, by a class or group through state power or overpoliticization.[7] Whenever this first rule of the game is not followed, the compromise is broken and leads to the demise of democratic rule. Consider such Lockian postulates as 'personal liberty' and 'limited government.' The restriction of suffrage in the nineteenth and early twentieth centuries provides further evidence; it aimed to exclude from the political arena groups whose interests might be incompatible with the maintenance and prosperity of capitalism.[8] Locke and others, even the Utilitarians, held to this type of representation because of their fear that propertyless and 'uneducated' masses could 'use their numerical strength to take care of their interests' through political power or coercion.[9]

The second rule of the game, although allowing political debate over the claimable social product, stipulates that its distribution not take place through overpoliticization. In their attempts to influence state policies and to claim a portion of the social product, individual actors, groups, or social classes subscribe to the use of the vote based on such stipulations as the free and secret ballot and the respect of majority rule. They also elect to compete (participate) through organized institutions and procedures (democratic institutions) that allow compromise. (Hereafter, these institutions and procedures will be referred to as 'means of compromise' or 'means of democratic compromise.')

The third rule of the game ensures that the compromise reached via democratic rule endures through participants' respect for that compromise. In other words, it makes sure that rules one and two of the game are respected.

What allows the establishment of this type of rule? To answer this question, one must demonstrate why opportunities are equalized under capitalism. Of the eight features of capitalism, the separation of the worker from the means of production is the most important; it determines the modalities of the extraction of surplus labor, which, in turn, specify the fundamental relations of production in a capitalist society. Under capitalism, a 'national community' is established to the extent that all social actors become dependent on this core relationship between the capitalist and the worker. All activities (e.g., production, exchange, consumption, distribution of values, and even culture) depend on what the capitalist and the worker do.[10] As the base of liberalism's contractual freedoms (the right to accumulate wealth and capital, freedom to produce, sell, and buy), capitalist core relations generate and depend upon specific philosophical and political claims. The claims are *ipso facto* based on the ideas of liberty, right, and property. The central position of the capitalist core relations leads to a *triple convergence* in capitalist societies: (1) all social actors depend on the social product; (2) the entire social product depends on the capitalist core relations; and, (3) all social relationships also depend on the capitalist core relations.

The dependence of all social actors and relationships on capitalist core relations equalize the chances or opportunities in the competition for the social product. To return to the lottery analogy: as the dependence of lottery participants on the winning number before the drawing makes all of them and their chances equal, so the dependence of all actors on capitalist core relations equalizes their opportunities with respect to the social product. The role of social actors, individuals, classes, and groups is important. But their role is not to be understood by seeing capitalism as an hegemonic system and democratic rule as the result of that system. Given that a hegemonic system exists in every society, the association of capitalist democracy with hegemony without qualification is misleading. At the minimum, one needs to specify the type of hegemony or the conditions of hegemony. I suggest that capitalist democratic rule be viewed as the result of capitalism *qua* a specific mode of production. In any mode of production core relations specify the modalities of societal organization. Under capitalism, these core relations rely on claims such as liberty, rights, and property because the relations between capitalists and workers assume freedom and the affirmation of rights. The affirmation of these rights and freedoms presupposes and is consistent with the notion of the equalization of opportunities and vice versa. In fact, the claims of rights, freedoms, and property and the equalization of opportunities are one and the same. For by proclaiming the right and freedom of all social actors to compete for the social product, the notion of equal opportunities fits in well with the claims of rights, freedom, and property embodied in the capitalist core relations. That these claims reflect the ideology and interests of the ruling class is undeniable. But this is not because capitalism reserves for itself the exclusive attribute of a hegemonic system; it is because in every society – except, perhaps, in primitive communism, if it ever existed – the dominant position of the ruling class/group is embodied in the core relations of the mode of production.

Thus, the equalization of opportunities is a function of structural conditions, where the role of social actors is not neglected. Yet, insofar as equal opportunities aim at the competition over the distribution of the social product, it would be unrealistic to expect such a distribution to affect whatever is distributable, including the means of production and private property. Under capitalism, the selective distribution and equalization of opportunities are feasible precisely because capitalist core relations are the basis of liberalism's contractual freedoms. *It follows that the latter dictate the removal of capitalist core relations, of which private property is a major component, from political competition well before the competition occurs.* Indeed, if capitalist core relations are consistent with claims of freedom, property, and rights that, in turn, dictate equal opportunities, they (i.e., core relations) cannot be expected to be brought into the distributive process by equal opportunities. This situation is consistent with the first rule of the democratic game.

Capitalist democratic rule, that is, the equalization of opportunities, has institutional implications. Insofar as democratic rule is thus predicated upon equal opportunities, its functioning relies on a set of institutions and procedures; these are tailored toward the participation of social actors competing for the social product without knowing the outcome in advance. The electoral process, majority rule, and the representation mechanism are the major means of compromise in such participation. This situation is consistent with the second rule of the democratic game.

The test and particularity of capitalist democracy, however, reside not so much in the rules of the game as in the respect for these rules by the participants. Hence, the third major question: What helps capitalist democratic rule maintain itself? In other words, how does one explain respect for the first two rules of the game governing capitalist democracy? The common explanation is that democracy persists because of the strength of its institutions and procedures. I think not. Respect is not the result of the system of checks and balances, however elaborate, nor is it a function of 'working' regulative mechanisms. It is not even the result of the length of time the institutions have been in place. Though all of these factors do play a role in the maintenance of the rules of the game, their strength is the result of capitalist democracy itself. Respect for the rules lies in the equalization of opportunities that results from the triple convergence under capitalism. Like a lottery, the equalization of opportunities builds winning expectations; the more the outcome is unknown, the higher the expectations of each participant. This uncertainty provides participants with incentive to respect the rules of the game, for only through participation under agreed-upon conditions can their claim to the social product be possible. This process entails the acceptance of decisions reached by the majority with regard to the social product and of normal procedures and institutions of participation. Most important, however, is respect for the first rule of the game, that is, the removal of the capitalist core relations from political debate and competition. And equal opportunities, along with the winning expectations associated with them, are consistent with such removal.

Respect for the first rule of the game is at the very heart of the preservation of capitalist democratic rule. If participants (groups, classes) in competition for the social product attempt to modify capitalist core relations by overpoliticizing them, the result is the disruption of the equalization of opportunities; this introduces into the competition some predictability and guarantee for some actors. For example, the state's takeover of private assets renders the modalities of distribution predictable. There is some guarantee that everyone will have an equal share or that one group will have a bigger share. As a result, there are no longer equal opportunities, but equal outcome or predictably unequal outcome. This situation may be good news for the poor or the benefiting group/class, but in the real world of capitalist society, it is bad news. The equal or predictably unequal distribution of the social product is the opposite of the ideology of capitalist democracy, which advocates inequality through equal opportunities. If winning expectations are frustrated, the result is likely to be, at best, a lack of participation, and at worst, overpoliticization.

The triple convergence in capitalism, its attendant equalization of opportunities, and the equalization's underlying ideology spare capitalist democracy the worst possible effects. If the rules of the game of democratic rule are to be safeguarded, then it can be reasonably assumed that in the socioeconomic system itself, there are built-in mechanisms of deterrence against any disruption of these rules. Capitalism is endowed with such mechanisms because of the extensive nature of its relations of production, geographically and socially. For example, if threatened, the social classes whose positions are prevalent in the core relations can reestablish themselves because of the entrenchment of these relations within society. Consider the role of fund-raising and political contributions in gaining political office in the United States or the relationship between business and political power. The unsuccessful attempt to implement socialist policies in a country such as Mitterand's France is a further indication of this entrenchment.[11] (The same can be said of other Western European countries to the extent that the policies of social-democratic parties or the Labor party are not socialist policies.)[12]

The extensiveness of capitalist core relations is a deterrent to the modification of these relations also at the level of the 'masses.' Consider the dramatic decline and marginal position of the Socialist and Communist parties in the United States and the failure of the Communist parties to secure political power in Western Europe. The defensive position adopted by 'liberals' during US presidential elections also provides a partial illustration. So do accusations against such candidates as Jesse Jackson as being far from the 'mainstream.' Whether 'protecting a way of life' is done by ideological manipulation, coercion, or conscious effort by the masses, the latter do constitute a deterrent to the political modification of capitalist core relations that are so much a 'part of their culture.' Thus, by its very entrenchment, capitalism makes the maintenance of capitalist democratic rule possible. This is consistent with the third rule of the liberal democratic game.

The above discussion about the capitalist democratic state can be summarized in a proposition:

> Given its triple convergence (i.e., all social actors depend on the social product, and the entire social product and all social relationships are subordinated to its core relations), capitalism offers a unique possibility to equalize opportunities in the competition over the social product. Such equalization is made possible by claims inherent in capitalist core relations (i.e., rights, liberty, property). Because it is congruent with the removal of capitalist core relations themselves from political competition, the equalization of opportunities prevents overpoliticization in the competition. In so doing, it allows respect for the rules governing capitalist democracy.

2. The Overpoliticized State

As Nigeria prepared itself in 1978 for a transition to civilian democratic rule, Lieutenant General Obasanjo declared: 'From now on let the game of politics be played according to the laid-down rules. Let all players be good sportsmen. No matter the result of the competition, let all players remain friendly and without bitterness look forward to another competition.[13] The transition did take place, but the elected democratic government of President Shagari was overthrown by the military a short time after the second term had started. Not only were the rules of the game as enunciated by Obasanjo not respected during the civilian government's tenure, but they were completely repudiated by the military upon its takeover. As in Nigeria, the reliance on overpoliticization under both competitive and authoritarian rules in Zaire repudiated the democratic 'laid-down rules.' To understand the state in Nigeria and in Zaire in the context of the predicates of the capitalist democratic state, the following questions must be asked: What prevents the rules of the game for democratic rule from being maintained? Is the equalization of opportunities possible at all? To answer these questions one must first answer the two more general questions raised earlier about the capitalist democratic state: What type of society exists in Zaire? How is the social product distributed there?

The first question has already been answered in chapter 5. To briefly recapitulate: I have argued that society in Zaire is based on pseudocapitalism, which rests on two types of core relations (ideological and capitalist). An outcome of the neutralization of capitalism by the higher level of ideological routinization in precolonial societies, pseudocapitalism is characterized by specific features. The most important feature is the noncentral position of the capitalist core relations . That is, social classes and groups oscillate between capitalist and precapitalist relations, and social activities do not depend in *toto* on what the capitalist and the worker do. The ramifications of this situation are the structural traits that Zaire shares with other Third World countries as described in chapter 1 and analyzed in chapter 5. Consequently, rather than a triple convergence, pseudocapitalism displays a *triple divergence*: (1) all social actors express claims to the social product; (2) only a portion of the social product is generated by capitalist core relations; and (3) only a part of social relationships is subordinated to capitalist core relations.

This triple divergence has major implications for the state. To recall the three rules of the capitalist democratic state: (1) the removal of capitalist core relations from political competition; (2) the establishment of participatory institutions to ensure that the competition over the claimable social product results not in overpoliticization, but in compromise; and (3) respect for the democratic compromise itself, that is, respect for rules (1) and (2). These three rules are followed because of the centrality of capitalist core relations, their attendant triple convergence, and the equalization of opportunities they involve. In Zaire, by contrast, pseudocapitalism disallowed the centrality of capitalist core relations. Its attendant triple divergence removed the conditions for the equalization of opportunities by creating uneven patterns of linkage between social relationships and capitalist core relations and by stifling liberalism's contractual freedoms. Again, to use the lottery analogy: all players did not depend on the same winning number ; consequently, their chances of winning were not the same as those of participants in a lottery, as in a capitalist society. The inequality of opportunities led to the violation of the three rules of capitalist democracy and to overpoliticization.

With respect to the first rule, one must bear in mind that the removal of capitalist core relations from competition in a capitalist democratic state results from capitalist core relations and liberalism's contractual freedoms being one and the same at the center of social relations. The removal of capitalist relations from political debate deprives political competition of irreconcilable differences. In other words, it prevents the competition for the social product from being overpoliticized. In Zaire, by contrast, the claim to the social product was not predicated upon the removal of capitalist (and ideological) core relations from competition. *This stemmed from the displacement of capitalist core relations from the central position by competing core relations in pseudocapitalism.* Such a displacement removed the protective shield that is formed against overpoliticization by capitalist core relations and liberalism's claims. The result was the violation of the first rule of capitalist democracy by bringing the core productive relations into open political competition in three ways.

First, contradictory claims by competing core relations (capitalist and ideological/ 'traditional') helped rationalize the recourse to overpoliticization. The position adopted by the settlers, foreign actors, and the Katangese in the Katanga Secession illustrates this situation. As seen in chapter 6, for the settlers, Katanga's traditions were incompatible with the capitalist economy and liberal democracy. At the same time, they expressed their 'respect' for and commitment to the Katangese and their traditions. Moreover, the King of Belgium and Tshombe posited the traditional chiefs and their subjects as the prime beneficiaries of Katanga's enclave capitalist economy. Similar claims were made by other centrifugal forces during the Balkanization period of the early 1960s. The settlers' way of defending capitalist core relations against noncapitalist relations ('Katanga's traditions being incompatible with the capitalist economy') was very insidious. The defense took the form of open confrontation (secession) against the central government in the name of the Katangese and their traditions; in reality, it was designed to ensure (among other things) the victory of capitalist over noncapitalist core relations in Katanga itself. On the other hand, by positing the traditional chiefs and their subjects as the prime beneficiaries of the social product, the king and Tshombe, in effect, politically 'transfered' the ownership of Katanga's capitalist core relations to the chiefs and their subjects. In Kasai, Kalonji based his secessionist claims also on the 'traditional rights' of the Luba *Mulopwe* and his subjects over the social product. In so doing, he politically 'transfered' Kasai's core relations to the chiefs and their subjects. As a result, capitalist core relations became a claimable social product that the chiefs and their subjects sought to protect against other regions of the country; the protection took the form of a secession. In all these cases, 'tradition' (i.e., noncapitalist relations) served as a catalyst. The opposition between capitalist core relations and ideological core relations ('Katanga's traditions,' 'traditional chiefs,' 'Mulopwe') and the oscillation of social forces between these two core relations figured prominently in the political game of all the parties involved in the Katanga and Kasai Secessions; it rationalized and allowed overpoliticization – in this case, the secession – by granting it some aura of 'traditional support.'

The situation is also illustrated by authoritarian rule in a different way. Under Mobutu's rule, contradictory claims by capitalist core relations and ideological core relations expressed themselves through the notion of Zaire's 'authentic nationalism.' One of the outcomes of nationalism was the nationalization policies (e.g., the nationalization of the UMHK in 1967 and the Zairianization policies of 1973). In addition to nationalism, these policies were guided by authenticity. The latter, as seen in chapter 7, aimed to revive the distinctive social and economic values of the Zairians and repudiate contradictory foreign ideas. In other words, it revived, among other things, precolonial ideological core relations. In this sense, authentic nationalism highlighted the contradictions between capitalist core relations and ideological core relations. It matters little that authenticity simply served, in many instances, the interests of the power holders. The point is that recourse to 'authentic' values, hence to non-capitalist relations, had implications for the competition for the social product. It justified the notions of the 'traditional ethics of sharing' and 'monistic leadership,' which, in turn, justified the nationalization policies. These policies allowed the direct control of state power over capitalist core relations. The control was ensured via authoritarian means. On the other hand, ideological core relations were not always victorious in their struggle against capitalist core relations. Despite its claims of authenticity, the Mobutu regime moved to dismantle the powers of the traditional chieftainships in 1973.[14] Aimed at bringing about capitalist 'progress,' this policy revealed the competing claims of two core relations; it showed that the success of one of the competing core relations was possible only through the subordination of the other to state power. Again, authoritarianism ensured such subordination.

In short, because of pseudocapitalism, there was no agreement on the centrality of the capitalist core relations (or ideological core relations). The lack of agreement deprived them of the mechanisms of defense against over-politicization by making them claimable social product. Indeed, unlike in the capitalist democratic state, political competition under both competitive and authoritarian rules was about core productive relations themselves. Under these conditions, political power became a highly sought-after good in a zero-sum game because it was the only means through which the opposition between capitalist and noncapitalist forces could be settled in favor of one of the two sides. The choice of the protagonists for capitalist core relations or ideological core relations did not necessarily attest to their allegiance to these relations; in many cases, it simply helped to advance the prevailing interests. What is important is the fact that, because of pseudocapitalism, core relations were brought into political competition. The result was overpoliticization expressed in the form of secession, Balkanization, and authoritarianism.

The first rule of capitalist democracy was violated in a second way under pseudocapitalism. The differential rates of accumulation between noncapitalist/lineage and capitalist relations, the dissociation of many social actors from capitalist core relations, and the stagnant reproduction of socioeconomic activities directly exposed capitalist core relations to the dictates of political power. By invoking the right and the responsibility of the state to 'develop' the country, the state became an active owner of the means of production. Unlike in capitalist democratic states that limit their involvement to strategic infrastructures or in some historically chosen manufacturing industries (e.g., France's involvement in the automobile industry), the scope of state ownership in Zaire is substantial. In addition to assets inherited from the colonial state, new ones were acquired through nationalizations in the postindependence period. Direct and substantial state involvement made core relations a *claimable* social product. This was all the more so because, in addition to 'development' tasks of the state, the stagnant socioeconomic activities under pseudocapitalism made the satisfaction of material interests of the power holders and other auxiliary groups heavily dependent on state power. One recalls that in 1962 under competitive rule, 'politicians' raised their wages by 400 percent and, owing to the accumulation of wealth through their control of state power, invested in private businesses. Thus, by making productive core relations a claimable social product, pseudocapitalism exposed them to political competition. The result of this violation of the first rule of capitalist democracy was overpoliticization. This pattern continued unabated under Mobutu's rule. Authoritarianism and nationalizations (e. g., Zairianization/radicalization measures) under the Mobutu regime expressed in part the overpoliticization of the competition over core productive relations. The nationalization of the UMHK, for example, was a claim made through state power to capitalist core relations in an attempt to compete against both foreign actors and domestic political foes. Indeed, the nationalization aimed to deprive Mobutu's opponents (e.g., Tshombe) of the financial backing of the UMHK.[15] Only through authoritarianism, that is, recourse to state power, could the claim be made and protected. This situation partly explains institutional authoritarianism under the Mobutu regime.

Pseudocapitalism violated the first rule of capitalist democracy in a third way. Pseudocapitalism is characterized by the marginal position of indigenous groups or classes in capitalist ownership and production. The latter tend to be dominated by foreign actors. The prevalent position of foreign actors in core (pseudo)capitalist relations is a guarantee that one group (i.e., foreign actors) is likely to get a predetermined – larger – share of the social product. As a consequence, the competition over the social product is modified to expose core productive relations to state power or other forms of overpoliticization. The Katanga Secession and the crisis of the early years of Mobutu's rule illustrate this situation. The prevalent position of foreign-based actors and the settlers in the Katanga enclave capitalist economy was a contradiction. On the one hand, the enclave economy, and especially the UMHK, stood as the 'engine of development' of the newly independent country; on the other hand, foreign interests controlled it. Attempts to weaken foreign control over the Katanga economy, first under the Lumumba government and later under Mobutu's rule, exposed capitalist core relations to state power; the reaction of foreign actors, the settlers, and those opposed to Lumumba and Mobutu was to subordinate these core relations also to direct political competition. In so doing, they broke the first rule of the capitalist democratic game. The result was overpoliticization as exemplified by the secession (under competitive rule), the double mutiny of the former Katangese gendarmes and mercenary units, and Tshombe's armed attempts to recapture power (under authoritarian rule). The argument is further supported by the events of the later years of authoritarian rule. The overriding reason behind the 1973 Zairianization policies was to 'definitely free the Zairian economy from foreign domination.' Insofar as this task was assigned to the state, the policy meant, in effect, the subordination of core capitalist relations to state power. Its implementation took the form of authoritarian distribution of foreign assets and its end result was overpoliticization. This was confirmed by the sharpening of authoritarianism in the post-Zairianization period and the political crisis that followed, including the 1975 coup attempt.

The prevailing position of foreign actors in (pseudo)capitalist core relations has other types of outcomes. Local groups or classes do not always express antagonism toward foreign actors. In many instances, state power is used to build a coalition of interests with foreign actors. In this case, overpoliticization (e.g., authoritarianism and other forms of confrontations) serve as political means of control over core relations to protect these common interests. Mobutu's business deals with foreign actors (e.g., with Maurice Tempelsman in the diamond business) were made easier by the authoritarian control over core productive relations. Once these coalitions were threatened, as in the Shaba Wars, their protection involved the ultimate form of overpoliticization: military confrontation with the support of foreign allies.

Thus, the three ways in which capitalist (and ideological) core relations are brought into open political competition help establish the first major link between pseudocapitalism and the overpoliticized state. They show how the violation of the first rule of capitalist democracy overpoliticized the competition over the social product, leading to the manifestations of the state analyzed in chapters 6 and 7. However, the second and third rules of capitalist democracy were also violated.

One may logically assume that, where equalization of opportunities does not exist and where (capitalist) core relations are not removed from open political competition, competition for the social product is based on the inequality of chances. The inequality means that it is known in advance what group or class will get what share, or what group or class expects the outcome of the competition to be positive or negative before political competition takes place. This situation is not far from the reality in the earlier empirical discussion. Because of their 'historical' claim to the Katanga enclave economy (the result of pseudocapitalism), the Katangese knew their share of the social product in advance, or at least, expected a larger share. So did the settlers and some foreign-based actors. In addition, the nonremoval of the core relations from political power had made it possible for power holders to get a larger share of the social product or, at the very least, to expect the outcome of the competition to be positive for them. Those groups or classes that did not control state power came also to expect the competition to favor 'politicians' while expecting a negative outcome for themselves. These expectations prevailed in both the 1960–65 competitive rule and the post-1965 authoritarian rule. The distribution of the social product under authoritarian rule was discussed in chapter 7; for competitive rule, one needs only refer to the accumulation of wealth that allowed many politicians to venture into business[16] and to politics being equated with wealth. In the Hobbesian or Schmittian world,[17] where politics means 'them' against 'us,' it can be expected that those with the guarantee of obtaining a positive outcome or the larger share of the social product will attempt to protect such a system of allocation; this is possible through the overpoliticized means, both 'legal' and illegal. The protection of this mode of competition involves highly unstable coalitions based on a high level of resource manipulation. Both competitive rule and authoritarian rule offered examples of this form of protection.

Under competitive rule, the means of protection took various forms. Perhaps the most dramatic was the Katanga Secession. A secession denotes the existence of centrifugal forces. Only in rare cases, such as Burma, are some groups or regions allowed constitutionally to secede from the central government;[18] in most cases, secession occurs outside the established constitutional limits. As a corollary, it denotes a recourse to overpoliticization at variance with the existing rules of the game. In the Katanga case, the manifestations varied and included the proclamation of independence in violation of the constitutional and democratic procedures, generalized repression, political assassinations, coups, and civil war. Insofar as the existing rules of the game were consonant with democratic rule, the open challenge to it by secession revealed that these rules were repudiated. Throughout the secession the secessionists called frequently for the repudiation of universal suffrage and democracy. Traditional chiefs argued that they did not want universal suffrage extended to their subjects because they were chiefs by right, and their legitimacy emanated directly from a higher power. In his proclamation of independence, Tshombe rejected a 'carbon copy' of Western democracy and pleaded for a regime based on each region's concepts and traditions. These antidemocratic calls did not cause secession. But they do underscore the means deployed by the secessionists to protect the system of allocation in place. Indeed, failure to equalize opportunities caused those favored by the Katanga enclave economy to seek guarantees. Guarantees could be ensured and protected only through overpoliticization – in this case, the secession. The system of allocation under competitive rule was protected also by the Balkanization of the territory between 1961 and 1964, Mobutu's 1960 coup, and generalized repression against the Lumumbist and popular forces by the Adoula government.

Insofar as political competition and coalitions involved foreign actors, the latter sought also to protect a system of allocation that favored them. Thus during the Congo crisis, their competitive interference forced Belgium and the United States, despite their common interests as Western allies, to protect a system of allocation best suited to each actor's national interests. As the former colonial power, Belgium had more economic interests in Katanga than the United States did. It favored the Katanga secession because it protected a system of allocation of resources consistent with Belgian interests. The United States opposed the secession because its long-term, superpower interests required a different means of protection that only non-fragmented political power offered. American aggressive anti-secessionist stand and support for Mobutu's coups were such means of protection.

Under the Mobutu regime, strict authoritarianism constituted the best way to protect a skewed form of competition over the social product. The specific means of protection included institutional authoritarianism, authoritarian requirements imposed on would-be beneficiaries of the social product, and coalition building based on the tolerance of pervasive corruption and on the manipulation of budgetary and nationalized resources.

Five consequences follow from the inequality of opportunities and its attendant overpoliticized means of protection. (1) For social actors engaged in competition for the social product, the outcome is almost always quite predictable. Rather than compete on equal footing for unknown outcomes, participants compete for known results. (2) Winning expectations are invariably high for some actors and low or zero for others. (3) Because winning expectations for some are always predictably low or zero, their participation in the competition becomes meaningless. Coerced political participation is often the result of this situation. (4) The lack of winning expectations for some actors provides no incentive at all for them to adhere to the enunciated rules of the game. (5) Because dissatisfied actors cannot adhere to the rules of the game, they attempt to modify the modalities of the distribution of the social product. In the absence of game rule and means of compromise, modification can take place only through overpoliticization, a sure means of participation for those for whom the 'normal' channels of participation have become meaningless. These five points explain the types of opposition that took place both under competitive rule and authoritarian rule. Under competitive rule, the overpoliticized modification of the rules of the game was expressed through centrifugal forces, popular rebellions, guerilla warfare, and coups. Under authoritarian rule, overpoliticized responses took the form of peasant uprisings, coup attempts, armed invasions, rebellions, and defections.

Thus, under pseudocapitalism, lack of respect for the first rule of the democratic game and the nonequalization of opportunities lead to overpoliticization by power holders and the opposition alike. Reliance on overpoliticized means breaks the second and third rules of capitalist democracy. Because of its second rule, capitalist democracy (despite its various manipulations and outright obstructions, at times) dictates and generally functions in such a way that power holders do not block the avenues of participation for the citizens. As a result, citizens' responses are formulated in accordance with the rules of the game and through participatory institutions. In Zaire, on the other hand, recourse to overpoliticization and the institutional obstructions by the power holders dictated specific avenues of participation for the citizens; their responses to the outcome of the competition for the social product took place outside institutional limits. The second rule of capitalist democracy was thus not respected. Insofar as the third rule of capitalist democracy depends on the first and second rules, the repudiation of the first two rules rendered the third rule useless. The result was political crisis. The specificity of the political crisis in Zaire lies in its being part of overpoliticization; its explanation is contingent upon that of overpoliticization. As in the above discussion, the explanation is provided by pseudocapitalism. Even such factors as debt, unemployment, inflation and socioeconomic deprivation, which trigger the crisis, are traceable to pseudocapitalism. Moreover, as part of the social product, they are issues of political competition that are easily overpoliticized. This situation is illustrated by the crisis that occurred in the post-1973 period as the result of the exacerbation of the socioeconomic deprivation, itself the outcome of the deepening of pseudocapitalism.

Two factors under pseudocapitalism stand at the very antipodes of capitalist democratic rule. The absence of equalization of opportunities in pseudocapitalism denotes the structural limits imposed on the feasibility of capitalist democracy. More importantly, the subordination of the claimable social product and of the core relations themselves to overpoliticization attests that respect for game rules of capitalist democracy is unlikely; this severely weakens the chances of maintaining liberal democracy itself. Because of the omnipresence of overpoliticization and the lack of means of compromise, the state is not capitalist democratic but *overpoliticized*. This fact explains its particular manifestations. In the context of overpoliticization, state power, more than in Western countries, exerts extraordinarily formidable leverage over social classes and groups holding it; for this reason, state power becomes a highly sought-after good. A first corollary is the highly defensive and protectionist behavior displayed by the holders of state power, which took the form of institutional authoritarianism in the post-1965 period. During the 1960–65 competitive rule, the state still shared fundamental characteristics with the strictly authoritarian rule: 'The state having a share in many decisions; political structures being more central to social life; the chief executive constantly building and rebuilding his political support to fend off attempts to overthrow him; the indispensability of personal power for survival; the fluidity of institutions and the intense struggle over state apparatus.'[19] A second corollary is participation outside institutional limits.

I have argued that analyses of the state in the Third World would benefit a great deal by a focus on its crucial similarities rather than a description of its variations, that is, authoritarian and competitive rule. I do not intend to dismiss variations. In contrast to competitive rule, authoritarian rule more rigidly eliminates spontaneous, freely formed interest articulations and more authoritatively determines those groups that interact with the government. Competitive rule, by its attempt to resemble democratic rule, provides a more open institutional basis for participation. On this score, the 1960–65 competitive rule differed from the post-1965 authoritarian rule. The difference is explained by their respective historical particularities and forms of coalitions. Of the particularities of competitive rule, one must mention the general euphoria about and imitation of parliamentary democracy in the wake of independence; the still strong presence of European settlers; the rigid bipolarization of forces by the Cold War; and the relatively sharp ideological differences within the ruling class. Historical particularities of the post-1965 authoritarian rule include the 1960–65 protracted crisis that facilitated the advent of authoritarianism; the consolidation of power by the pro-Western Binza Group, of which Mobutu was a member; and the exclusion of the popular masses from coalition making following their defeat, especially the liquidation of the genuinely revolutionary forces led by Pierre Mulele. Any analysis ought to take these differences into account.

Yet neither these particularities nor the 'vote' nor the label of 'democratic' fundamentally distinguishes the 1960–65 competitive rule from the post-1965 authoritarian rule. After all, each of these regimes held elections and called

230

itself democratic. Dwelling on the particularities does not explain why both rules share the overpoliticized features with other Third World states. At the risk of taking the comparison a little too far, Western Europe is not more democratic than the United States because it allows important leftist and extremist parties to compete in national elections, whereas in the United States the field is much more circumscribed. These are important historical particularities, but they do not add much to the theoretical discussion. In the specific case of Zaire, these variations cannot overshadow the fact that both authoritarian and competitive rules share fundamental similarities. *In each, the overpoliticization of the competition for the social product remains an invariant.* Both are almost identical twins from the same parent, the overpoliticized state. The latter is of greater theoretical interest, as is the variable that explains it, pseudocapitalism. The discussion about the overpoliticized state can be summed up as follows:

By its triple divergence (i.e., all social actors depend on the social product, but only part of the social product and social relationships are subordinated to capitalist core relations), pseudocapitalism suppresses conditions for the equalization of opportunities. By allowing the reproduction of ideological core relations of the lineage mode, it disallows the centrality of capitalist core relations and stifles claims of right, liberty, and property inherent in capitalist core relations. Because it is antithetical to capitalist democratic rules of the game, the nonequalization of opportunities subordinates both the claimable social product and the core productive relations themselves to a system of allocation through overpoliticization. As a result, overpoliticization characterizes relationships between holders of state power and citizens at large; it also characterizes the institutional and procedural arrangements. For this reason, the state can be called an overpoliticized state.

Although competitive rule allows more participation than authoritarian rule, both types of rule are fundamentally similar in that overpoliticization remains an invariant in both. This explains similarities in their crisis patterns. Overpoliticization radically distinguishes competitive rule from capitalist democratic rule and makes it one of the two sides of the overpoliticized state.

3. The Overpoliticized State and Social Change

This study revolves around the idea that theory is the sine qua non for social prescriptions. That I have maintained that a theory of the overpoliticized state is contingent upon an explanation of pseudocapitalism underscores this principle. Having thus proposed a theory of the overpoliticized state on the basis of that of pseudocapitalism, it is essential that I turn now to the issue of social prescription ('social change') with which I started the study.

In chapter 2, I mentioned and/or took issue with three claims of the dominant paradigms: (1) that African societies could make a transition to capitalism; (2)

that the 'softness' of African states causes socioeconomic problems such as societal withdrawal from the state; and (3) that democracy is a function of institutional and sociocultural prerequisites. Each of these claims, which is the result of academic inquiry, has led to social prescriptions for Zaire, Africa, and the Third World in general. The transition-to-capitalism argument advocates – in its liberal version as opposed to the Marxist version – capitalism as the solution. The 'soft state' and 'prerequisites to democracy' arguments plead for 'efficient' and 'democratic' institutions. As I argued in chapter 2, these prescriptions have failed because of the pitfalls inherent in their underlying theories. The alternative explanation of the state–society relations I propose sheds light on these pitfalls and allows a better appreciation of the possibilities and constraints for social change.

In the foregoing analysis, the particularity of society in Zaire is not the result of the 'stagnation' of precolonial societies. Nor is it explained by what 'almighty capitalism' did or did not do. Although the exploitative role of capitalism is undeniable, its peculiar nature in Zaire must be viewed as the result of the neutralization of capitalism by the dynamism of precolonial societies. The neutralization imposed contradictory policies that led to the structural traits of the postcolonial society – pseudocapitalism. As stated earlier, the argument that the dynamism of precolonial societies played the bigger role in the making of pseudocapitalism does not 'blame the victim.' Rather, it recognizes that they followed a noncapitalist path of development with different dynamics. Recognizing this reality does two things. First, it exposes the pitfalls of an evolutionary approach that, by positing capitalism as almighty or the end point for all, vitiates the debate and perpetuates the myth of 'civilization.' Second, it better addresses the question of solutions for today's society. In this respect, one of the central issues is the role of the state and its relation to social change.

Pseudocapitalism explains the overpoliticized state. It follows that the explanation proposed for pseudocapitalism in chapter 5 has implications for the role of the state in social change. More specifically, the dynamism of the lineage mode that explains pseudocapitalism determines the overpoliticized state in a complex manner. It does so not through the empiricist notion of the 'influence of the traditional ways' (Hyden's 'economy of affection') on modern politics, but through *structural* links. That is, the overpoliticized state is the culmination of a network of social relations expressed as a triple divergence under pseudocapitalism, itself the result of the neutralization of the capitalist core relations by the ideological core relations of the lineage mode. This web of relationships provides the overpoliticized state with a life of its own (not in the neostatist sense of autonomous institutions and policy makers). Differently put, the overpoliticized state is a structural outcome of pseudocapitalism. To illustrate, consider the subordination of the capitalist core relations to political competition and the nonequalization of opportunities, the two major variables that shed light on the overpoliticized state. Both are brought in not by the 'traditional ways' but by the triple divergence that disallows agreement on the centrality of capitalist (or ideological) core relations in pseudocapitalism. That

Western actors living in Third World countries, who have nothing to do with 'traditional ways,' display the same political behavior as indigenous actors is a clear indication. 'Clan' or 'traditional politics' do take place, but as a protective device called in by the overpoliticized state; they do not make the state, which has a structural life of its own and whose understanding requires an explanation of pseudocapitalism.

This explanation of the state and society challenges the claim made by the dominant paradigms about the transition to capitalism. There is a great deal of emphasis on the phases of capitalism, that is, its transformations over time. It is generally assumed that these transformations will affect the Third World more positively, causing capitalism to replace pseudocapitalism. The analysis in this study runs counter to this view. I have argued that as dynamic as it is, capitalism is by no means almighty. Nor is it the ultimate destination for all societies, subjugated, as it were, to the 'law of transition to capitalism.' The reasons were specified in chapters 4 and 5. Given that pseudocapitalism is a structural derivative of the neutralization of capitalism by the lineage mode, its metamorphosis into capitalism is unlikely. The reproductive power of the lineage mode and colonial pseudocapitalism, coupled with today's selective capitalist expansion that generally seeks to reinforce colonial enclave economies, make such a metamorphosis difficult. The effects of this reproduction of the lineage mode do not necessarily take the form of 'traditional ways'; they are expressed in contradictory and highly exploitative policies (e.g., authenticity-inspired Zairianization policies) that reinforce pseudocapitalism (see chaps. 5 and 7).

To the reproductive power of the lineage mode one must add the role of the overpoliticized state. The relationship between pseudocapitalism and the overpoliticized state is reciprocal. Although pseudocapitalism explains the state, the state influences pseudocapitalism through a feedback mechanism. The effects of the state's influence on society in the Third World differ from those in capitalist societies because of the specificity of the overpoliticized state. The reliance on overpoliticization in the allocation of the social product goes hand in hand with the instability of political coalitions and the fragility of control over political power. Political power can be maintained only with a high level of payoffs, which, in turn, requires a higher level of resource manipulation than exists under capitalist democracy. The higher level of corruption, embezzlements, and political payoffs in Zaire and elsewhere in the Third World is a partial but clear manifestation of this situation. The hyperinflation of bureaucratic personnel also results, to a large extent, from this situation; salaries offered to practically idle bureaucrats help in many ways to maintain political coalitions. There is, therefore, a more pressing need than in capitalist democracies for power holders to accumulate resources that are used for coalition-building and 'security' needs. The subordination of the allocation of the social product to overpoliticization leads to the subordination of its accumulation to overpoliticization as well. In addition to foreign assistance, the bulk of these resources is provided by the enclave economies in pseudocapitalism. The urgent need for resources causes the state to rely on these enclave economies rather than to attempt to extend capitalist relations to other sectors. The pattern of capital investments and the policies of nationalization analyzed in chapter 7 illustate this point. In the nationalization of the UMHK, 'The decision to nationalize ... was a political act, deliberately and carefully prepared. Its objective was less, for the policy maker, the economic independence of the nation, than the consolidation of presidential power, whose budgetary support was mainly constituted by taxes on UMHK.'[20] In any case, the result is the deepening of pseudocapitalism and not a transition to capitalism.

The overpoliticized state thesis further challenges the claims of the dominant paradigms about 'soft institutions' and the need for efficient institutions to solve socioeconomic problems. Earlier in this chapter, I provided the theoretical justification for the institutional specificity of the overpoliticized state. I showed that because it is a derivative of pseudocapitalism and its triple divergence, the overpoliticized state has major socioeconomic and institutional consequences. Specifically, overpoliticization imposes a highly defensive and protectionist behavior on power holders, which takes the form of institutional authoritarianism or other forms of overpoliticization even in competitive rule as witnessed during the 1960–65 period. The institutional specificity is coupled with socioeconomic implications. The fragility of political power that results from an overpoliticized environment requires that control over political power be maintained by a high level of resource manipulation, payoffs and the deepening of pseudocapitalism. Overpoliticization and the specific institutional strategies developed by power holders is met by overpoliticization practiced by the repressed masses or the opposition. This, as seen earlier, takes the form of secession, guerilla warfare, coups and other violent reactions. The masses have other forms of response. As the higher level of resource manipulation by overpoliticized power holders diverts crucial resources and deepened pseudocapitalism leads to the deterioration of the socioeconomic infrastructure and the brutal degradation of their conditions (see chap. 7), the masses develop strategies of survival: illicit economy, parallel markets, self-enclosure, escape, and all the activities that proponents of the soft state paradigm wrongly attribute to the 'softness' of the African state. This explanation confirms the points I made elsewhere[21] against the soft state paradigm; rather than being 'soft' or 'lacking,' political institutions in Zaire/Africa reflect the prevailing type of politics and society. Moreover, 'soft institutions' do not cause strategies of survival; the latter result from the unbreakable link between pseudocapitalism and the overpoliticized state. It follows, then, that, contrary to the dominant claim, 'efficient' institutions are not the solution to Zaire's or Africa's socioeconomic problems.

The third challenge posed to the dominant paradigms by the overpoliticized state argument concerns the issue of democratization. Today's euphoria about democratization is the result of two types of pressure: external and internal. Externally, the change in the Soviet bloc has revived the debate about democracy in Zaire and elsewhere in the Third World. More importantly, perhaps, the euphoria has been maintained by Western countries, which have urged and encouraged democratic change. Internally, the deepening of pseudocapitalism, its attendant socioeconomic deprivation, and the higher level of oppression under authoritarian rule have led to calls for democracy. In either case, the debate takes place against the background of the 'prerequisites' or 'strategies' for democracy as discussed in chapter 2. But what are the chances of success for democratization? To answer this question, one must consider the ongoing democratization process in Zaire, which is a good illustration of the overpoliticized state's attempt to bring about social change.

The present democratic process began in 1990 when, faced with rising internal opposition, President Mobutu was advised by the US government to institute democratic change.[22] Through a process of 'national consultation,' the people were invited to submit their criticisms of the government. Because these criticisms overwhelmingly revealed widespread opposition to the Mobutu regime, President Mobutu was forced to announce some reforms on April 24, 1990. The press was liberated, and the MPR, the hitherto party–state, was deprived of its monopoly; two additional political parties were allowed to compete with the MPR, and Mobutu gave up the presidency of the MPR but maintained in place all MPR-established apparatuses.

The April announcement touched off a wave of demonstrations, political organizing, and popular euphoria. More than two hundred political parties were created, many of them ethnic-based. Mobutu's forces later financed a myriad of small parties to neutralize the impact of the more important political parties, such as the Union for Democracy and Social Progress (UDPS). The old coalition that sustained the Mobutu regime weakened, many of its members having joined the opposition, and a 'transition government' formed. Because the emerging opposition exceeded President Mobutu's expectations and threatened the very foundation of his power, he reacted by slowing down the democratization process. On May 3, 1990, the government announced that no political activity would be allowed until all political parties had gone through a six-step legalization process. The decision triggered a wave of demonstrations and strikes among workers and students. The government reacted with brutal violence, culminating in what came to be known as the 'Lubumbashi massacre' of May 11–12, 1990, in which an estimated one hundred university students were killed by Mobutu's elite security forces.

The May 1990 events radicalized both the opposition and the government. Emulating the trend in French-speaking Africa, Zaire's opposition parties insisted on the organization of a sovereign national conference that would lead to a transition government, a new constitution, and legislative and presidential elections. The Mobutu government responded with 'legal' maneuvering, repression, and death against students and the opposition forces. The stalemate between the government and the opposition, the withdrawal of economic assistance by France and Belgium following the Lubumbashi massacre, and the ineptness of the Mobutu-chosen transition government exacerbated the already collapsed economy. As the misery index of the masses increased, more strikes and demonstrations were met by more government repression and violence. By September 1991, the socioeconomic conditions of the country had so deteriorated that even the military was not paid. On September 23, some of the army units mutinied, leading to an orgy of looting that destroyed the basic economic infrastructure of the country. The mutiny and pressure by the opposition forced President Mobutu to name Etienne Tshisekedi, the leader of the UDPS, as prime minister of the transition government. Because of his disagreements with Mobutu, Tshisekedi was dismissed and replaced by Mungul-Diaka on October 30, 1991. Mungul-Diaka was rejected by the opposition, which named Tshisekedi as the head of government. Thus, by November 1991 three parallel governments were in place (a reminder of the 1961–63 period): President Mobutu's own inner circle government, the Mungul-Diaka government, and the Tshisekedi government. The imbroglio was ended with the appointment of Nguza Karl I Bond as prime minister of the transition government on November 22, 1991.

In the meantime, the idea of the national conference had gathered some momentum amid chaos, violence, and death. Although the Nguza government suspended the conference in January 1992 for ethnic reasons, it had become the cornerstone of the opposition's strategy for democratic change. On May 5, 1992, the conference passed the 'sovereignty act' that established the national conference as a sovereign institution whose decisions could not be interfered with by Mobutu's forces or the transitional government. On August 15, Tshisekedi was elected prime minister of the transition government by the Sovereign National Conference (SNC). However, the Tshisekedi government faced new type of violent opposition and sabotage from Mobutu-supported forces. From August 1992 throughout 1993 a new stalemate was reached, culminating in yet another parallel government appointed by Mobutu, physical violence perpetrated against Tshisekedi and his ministers, and hundreds of deaths in Kinshasa and the provinces.

Thus, the ongoing process of democratization has been characterized by six traits.

- Violent resistance by Mobutu-controlled forces marked by police and military intimidations, arrests without trial of the members of the opposition and students, and deaths. Examples of the highest level of violence include the 1990 Lubumbashi massacre of students, the April 1991 killing of forty three opposition members in Mbuji Mayi and Lubumbashi, the February 16, 1992, death of thirty two demonstrators in Kinshasa, and the post-1992 death of hundreds of people.
- Violence by the opposition: in addition to persistent guerilla warfare in Northeastern Zaire, instances of recourse to violence by the opposition include the army's mutiny, looting, attempted coup, and threats of intervention in the transitional political process; mass looting, ethnic confrontations (e.g., the Luba–Lunda conflict in Katanga Province), and the threat of secession by Nguza-led Katangese forces.
- Sharpening of ethnic conflicts and inability of the opposition to coalesce as exemplified by the proliferation of small, often ethnic, political parties. In addition to independently created parties, the list has been lengthened by Mobutu-financed splinter parties through which he sought to strengthen his

236

position and to weaken the genuine opposition. More than 250 parties have registered.

- Open political and material support for President Mobutu's antidemocratic forces by foreign actors, including the Bush administration, Israel, South Africa and, marginally, France and Belgium.
- Procedural and institutional fraud mostly perpetrated by the Mobutu forces but also commited by the opposition. The process that established political parties and the national conference and its associated institutions such as the Haut Conseil de la République (the transition parliament) have been fraught with fraud and payoffs. Not only have Mobutu's forces used tremendous stolen wealth to buy off the opposition, but many members of the opposition have also used wealth stolen during their tenure as officials under the Mobutu regime to buy their way into the transition institutions.
- Inability of the transition government and institutions to provide the needed transitional consensus for socioeconomic change on which depends long-term political change. In addition to the incompetence and corruption of the transition governments, the Tshisekedi government and the Mobutu-established parallel governments have stalemated. Policies and decisions taken by the Tshisekedi government have been ignored or sabotaged by officials still owing allegiance to the Mobutu regime. Former parliamentarians of the Mobutu regime have attempted to hold parliamentary sessions on the budget and other matters despite the illegality of the act and Mobutu parallel governments have used the army to prevent the change proposed by the Tshisekedi government.[23]

The six traits of today's process of democratization are not 'temporary difficulties of the transition period' in Zaire, which is not to dismiss the difficulties involved. They are permanent traits of 'democracy' and democratization in Zaire, Africa, and the Third World in general. The evidence for this point is abundant. First, Zaire's ongoing democratization process shares remarkable similarities with the overpoliticization of the 1960–65 competitive rule (chap. 6), thus revealing their common structural root. Second, the process in Zaire may be somewhat extreme due to local factors, but it is not unique; it reflects, as discussed in chapter 2, the democratization process in Africa and the Third World in general. In the specific case of the ongoing democratization process, Zaire shares the above six traits with other African countries. Violent resistance by authoritarian rulers to democratic change has also characterized Togo, Côte d'Ivoire, Algeria, Madagascar, Malawi, and Kenya. The opposition has also used violence in its calls for democracy in Chad, Soudan, Niger, Algeria, Uganda, and, with a caveat, Angola and Mozambique. Zaire shares the sharpening of ethnic conflicts and the inability of the opposition to coalesce with Congo, Gabon, Central African Republic, Burkina Faso, Ghana, Nigeria and so forth. As for foreign support for antidemocratic forces, Zaire is not unique either as exemplified by US and South African support for Savimbi's UNITA in Angola and France's support to Houphouet-Boigny of Côte d'Ivoire and Bongo of Gabon. Procedural fraud during the transition period augurs electoral and institutional fraud for the years to come, a feature Zaire is likely to share with, among others, Nigeria, which halted its democratic transition to democratic rule because of massive electoral fraud in 1992 and military enchroachment by the military in 1993, Ghana, and Kenya, which became competitive ('democratic') rules in 1993. Although Zaire is still in 'transition' to democratic rule, its inability to provide the needed consensus for socioeconomic change resembles that which prevails in other African countries that have already made the transition. Zambia, Benin, Mali, Cape Verde, Mauritania, and the Congo have no less shown their inability to undertake successful socioeconomic changes to demarcate the new regimes from the preceding authoritarian regimes.

These shared traits suggest that Zaire's specific conditions alone do not explain its difficulties of transition to democracy. Nor is the transition hampered by the inability to 'build democratic institutions,' a claim made by the democratizing state paradigm. Because of the focus on institutionalization in the dominant paradigms, democracy is easily equated with 'democratic institutions.' The claim is contradicted by empirical evidence (chaps. 2 and 6) that Zaire shares with other Third World countries. 'Democratic institutions' that were built in African and Asian countries in the postindependence period and between 1945–1959 in Latin America disappeared without bringing about democracy. More importantly for my purposes, the claim does not resist the theoretical argument of the overpoliticized state thesis. If what Zaire shares with other countries is the lack of 'democratic institutions,' then the real theoretical question is why they all lack democratic institutions or have difficulties in building them. Because I have shown that institutions reflect the type of prevailing politics and society and that in Zaire they are a by-product of pseudocapitalism-induced overpoliticization, democratic institutions cannot emerge from the sheer will of the elite to 'craft' them. In Zaire, and hypothetically in other Third World countries, their absence is indissociable from the overpoliticized state, which should be the real focus of theoretical inquiry.

Although I recognize the importance of the real people in the democratization process, their pressure for democracy cannot escape the structural limits imposed on it by the neutralizing power of the lineage mode, the deepening of pseudocapitalism, and, hence, the overpoliticized state. In Zaire or elsewhere in Africa, there are enough reasons to abate the democratic euphoria. In the specific case of Zaire, the 1960–65 competitive rule and the ongoing process of democratization serve as a reminder. The cases of competitive rules in Latin America, Asia, and Africa, which are confronted by overpoliticization, are also instructive. Again, I do not subscribe to predetermination or to the 'repetition of history'; rather, I stress the theoretical argument that the structural conditions within which the debate takes place impose two kinds of limits. First, they are not conducive to capitalist democracy. Second, they fix limits beyond which the two variations of the overpoliticized state cannot move. Being 'genetically,' that is, structurally, linked to the same type of state (i.e., the overpoliticized state) as authoritarian rule, competitive rule easily displays the 'genetic' behavior of its twin, authoritarian rule; or it allows the twin to take its place. Although the call for democracy is welcome, its chances of success are slim.

The claim about external support for democratic change does not resist empirical and theoretical evidence either. One considers the following facts about external support. The Lumumba government and the 1960–65 competitive rule were ended by military coups backed by the West, which supported Mobutu's authoritarian rule; the Tshisekedi government, which attempts to replace Mobutu's authoritarian rule, has been supported by Western countries some of which help Mobutu directly or indirectly to undermine the very Tshisekedi government; the 1973 coup that ended the Allende competitive rule was backed by the United States, which supported Pinochet's authoritarian rule. On the other hand, the May 1984 elections that brought about competitive rule in El Salvador were the result of US coercion, but did not end guerilla warfare until the UN-brokered peace accords of early 1990s. In 1991, the United States, which advocates democracy, tacitly withdrew its support from the deposed democratic government of President Jean-Bertrand Aristide of Haiti. Undoubtedly, these seemingly contradictory positions of foreign actors underscore that they are no friends of democracy or authoritarianism and that only their interests count. However, caution must be exercised here. Foreign actors do not act on the basis of some voluntarism to spoil or increase the chances of democracy. Their behavior is determined by pseudocapitalism and the overpoliticized state. As participants in the competition for the social product, foreign actors are bound to follow a pattern of competition based on overpoliticization. In other words, the role of foreign actors is bound to be supportive of and consistent with the overpoliticized state (see chaps. 6 and 7). It follows that foreign support for 'democracy' is not a sure helping hand for democratic change. Whatever its form, such support is not conducive to democracy, let alone liberal democracy, as evidenced by persistent overpoliticization in third world countries where the democratization process has been supported by foreign actors. At most, it can only help establish competitive rule. Such help, however, is no cause for celebration; under overpoliticized conditions, support for competitive rule by foreign actors can easily turn into support for authoritarian rule at some historical juncture as the above cases illustrate. This argument is consistent with the theoretical points raised earlier about the common roots of competitive and authoritarian rules. To put the role of foreign actors as a proposition:

> Given the conditions conducive to overpoliticization, foreign actors are structurally bound to display behavior consistent with the overpoliticized state. Insofar as internal actors have recourse to overpoliticization to express claims to the social product, the support of foreign actors for their internal counterparts is likely to reflect the counterparts' behavior. It follows that the overpoliticized state cannot be 'broken' by foreign actors. It also follows that in terms of the change of the state in question, foreign actors are unlikely to steer it beyond its two ends, that is, authoritarian and competitive rules.

Thus, contrary to claims generally made, the overpoliticized state cannot be expected to play a 'developmentalist' role in social change. The reason does not lie in the 'inefficiency of its institutions' or 'leadership.' As a structural outcome of pseudocapitalism, the overpoliticized state determines a specific type of politics and institutions. (As the structural outcome of capitalism, the capitalist democratic state determines a specific type of politics.) The effects on society are also specific in each case; in the particular case of the overpoliticized state, they are negative. Under these conditions, an individual, a group, a class, or a new ideology may make a difference through new types of coalitions ('political regime') and policies for a while. However, their chances of a sustained, long-term impact are slim. Sooner or later they will fall victim to the sapping power of pseudocapitalism and overpoliticization. In the specific case of Zaire and Africa, one needs only refer to the frustrations of Etienne Tshisekedi, Presidents Julius Nyerere of Tanzania, Abdou Diouf of Senegal, Yoweri Museveni of Uganda, and Jerry Rawlings of Ghana; to the de facto defeat of the Front for the Liberation of Mozambique (Frelimo) in Mozambique; and to the demise of President Thomas Sankara of Burkina Faso. Their probity, ideological orientations, and drive for positive change have not prevented these leaders from falling victim to overpoliticization in one way or another or expressing serious doubts about the long-term prospects for positive change.

This pessimistic assessment is not a cry of defeat. I do not suggest that the ongoing democratization process in Zaire and Africa serves no purpose. Nor do I imply that no attempt should be made to address Zaire's or Africa's socioeconomic problems because such attempt is bound to fail. I have argued that prescriptions for social change requires theory. Attempts to democratize and to bring about socioeconomic change have failed and are likely to fail in the future because they derive from 'bad theory,' which, to repeat Kitching's already used phrase, leads to simplistic prescriptions for policy and action in which constraints are wished away. My pessimistic assessment is by no means 'deterministic' and does not posit pseudocapitalism, the lineage mode, and the overpoliticized state as 'fixed causal agents,' which is a standard objection raised by Weberian scholars whose 'optimism' hardly conceals their evolutionary views; my assessment is consistent with the fact that 'good theory' identifies causes and *constraints* accurately and proposes prescriptions for policy accordingly. Far from positing the above three variables as fixed causal agents, I have shown them to be real structural constraints that must be taken into account in any meaningful discussion about social change. To act on them requires that one explains them first.

My pessimistic assessment should serve, then, as a challenge to seek new answers to the problems of Zaire and Africa. The challenge is first an intellectual one. New types of explanation must be provided by new types of theoretical efforts. Neither describing Zaire's or Africa's problems nor recycling old, already rejected explanations advances the debate about social change. Because it is totally off target and descriptive, the normative view of institutionalization in the dominant paradigms cannot be a solution; it only adds more confusion. Moreover, the emphasis on competitive rule in the now-abundant literature on 'democratization' does little to eliminate its complicity with authoritarian rule; more importantly, it leaves unassaulted the overpoliticized state, the very source of this complicity. Lost in the confusion and left unaddressed is the central issue of what strategy can best bring about democracy and socioeconomic change while inflicting maximum damage to the overpoliticized state. To devise such a strategy, the propositions advanced herein need to be tested in other African and Third World countries first. Given the crucial similarities in the explicandum shared by Zaire and these other countries, the chances of confirming these propositions are better than fair. (A disccussion of the applicability of the thesis is provided in the appendix).

Notes

1. Gionfranco Poggi, *The Development of the Modern State*, p. 125.
2. See David Easton, *A Framework for Political Analysis* (Chicago: University of Chicago Press, 1979); *A System Analysis of Political Life* (Chicago: University of Chicago Press, 1979).
3 On this, see Bob Jessop, *The Capitalist State* (New York: The University of New York Press, 1982), especially chapter 5.
4. Charles Lindblom, *Politics and Markets*, p. 116.
5. Ibid., p. 164.
6. Along these lines but with a narrower view, see Dan Usher, *The Prerequisite to Democracy* (New York: Columbia University Press, 1981).
7. This is not the same as suggesting that within limits of the rules of the game the state cannot 'correct abuses of capitalism.' In fact, in order to maintain the compromise, it is 'imperative' for the capitalist state to eliminate abuses and conditions that are likely to cause some social classes or groups to modify unilaterally the fundamental relations of production through state power/violence. Such concepts as 'welfare state' attest to this situation.
8. Poggi, *op. cit.*, p. 122.
9. In spite of their initial opposition to a form of representation which would include only the vested interests, the utilitarians also feared that the propertyless classes would use their political strength for their interests. On the issue of representation, see John Locke, *Two Treatises on Government*; John Stuart Mill, *Considerations on Representative Government* and *Utilitarianism*.
10. Poggi, *op. cit.*, p. 121; Taylor, *op. cit.*, pp. 113–115.
11. Even newspapers such as the *New York Times* (various issues of 1984 and 1985), *Christian Science Monitor* (February 4, 1985), and *Jeune Afrique* (No. 1254, January 16, 1985), conveyed the idea of incompatibility between socialist policies and capitalism in France.
12. For an understanding of the difference between 'social democratic policies and 'socialist policies,' see Casten von Otter, 'Swedish Welfare Capitalism: The Role of the State,' in Richard Scase, *The State in Western Europe* (New York: St. Martin's Press, 1980), pp. 142–163.

13. *West Africa*, October 2, 2978, p. 1935.
14. See Mpinga and Gould, *op. cit.*, pp.117–133.
15. Kamitatu Massamba, 'Problematique et rationalite dans le processus de nationalisation du cuivre en Afrique Centrale: Zaire (1967) et Zambie (1969),' Doctoral Dissertation, Institut d'Etudes Pratiques de Paris, 1976, p.181.
16. See Willame, *Patrimonialism and Political Change in the Congo*, Appendix.
17. See Hobbes, *Leviathan* and Carl Schmitt, *Der Begriff des politischen* (Berlin, 1963).
18. Note that even in the case of Burma the constitution imposed a ten-year period of the recognition of the central government by the Karens and Shans before they would be allowed to secede. The actual secession took place before the ten-year period expired.
19. Chalmers, *op. cit.*, pp. 31–32.
20. Kamitatu Massamba, 'Problematique et rationalite,' *op. cit.*, p. 181.
21. See Sangmpam, 'Neither Soft Nor Dead: The African State is Alive and Well.'
22. Testimony of Assistant Secretary of State for African Affairs, Mr. Herman J. Cohen, before the Senate Foreign Relations Subcommittee on Africa, November 6, 1991, p. 2.
23. *Jeune Afrique*, no.1659, October 1992, pp. 20–22.

Appendix:
Notes on class, ethnicity and the appplicability of the lineage mode of production

The propositions presented in this book in support of its major thesis are working hypotheses to be tested in other countries of Africa, Asia, and Latin America. Only such testing can lead to the refinement of the propositions. One can easily imagine the types of objections the claim is likely to generate about one of the leading explanatory variables: the lineage mode of production. First, is lineage, hence the lineage mode, to be found everywhere in the Third World? Second, does the notion of lineage mode reinforce the existing platitudes about the Third World?

The form lineage took in various precolonial societies varied, as did lineage practices. For several reasons, one of which is the dual structure (state and lineage) in which the state had an impact on lineage, lineage was structured in different ways. Thus, for instance, the lineage structure and its relation to the state in northern Nigeria, Ethiopia, and Rwanda differed somewhat from that which prevailed in Zaire. For this reason, the misleading label of 'feudal' has been applied to these societies. What is true of African societies is even more true of Asia and South America. That the Inca *ayllu* and the Aztec *calpulli* were not structured the way the Kongo *kanda* was and that the Chinese or the Southeast Asian clan was not organized exactly the same way that the Luba's was does not detract from the fundamental issue: there was a lineage structure in all these societies. In addition to Marc Bloch's previously quoted suggestion that lineage ties were weakened only in those societies characterized by feudalism, numerous anthropological and historical studies confirm the claim. My own preliminary research on Asian and South American societies also strongly supports this view.

In any case, lineage is not *the* explanation. The empirical investigation into lineage has been undertaken not so much for its descriptive value as for its theoretical implications. From it one can deduce the concept of the lineage mode of production. The latter allows theoretical comparisons between Third World societies and other societies (e.g., Western societies) by allowing comparisons of their modes of production. Lineage, an empirical category, is not the same as the lineage mode of production, a theoretical category. It follows that the lineage structure itself is not of major theoretical significance. This further illustrates that differences in the form of lineage structure in different historical settings should not be a major reason to deny the applicability of the propositions advanced in this work.

What is crucial is the deduction of the concept of the lineage mode from the lineage structure, regardless of its form. Central to the concept of the lineage mode is the notion of ideological core relations. The important question is: Did ideological routinization characterize even those lineage-based societies that did not practice such rituals as the ancestral cult or did not organize them as explicitly as Central African societies did? In chapter 4, I referred to Bwakassa's plausible hypothesis about the collective cult of the spirits in some villages aimed at calming the spirits of those who were vanquished by the new occupants of the village. Because villages were generally organized around a core lineage, such cults had an indirect link to the core lineage. In this case, even though the organization of the lineage may not have had all the usual trappings and may not suggest a direct link between the lineage and the collective cult of the spirits, a closer look may reveal the presence of the lineage mode. In fact, the effects of the lineage mode can be felt without the localized lineage organization itself being present. To understand this, one needs to bear in mind the theoretical points made in Chapter 4 about ideological routinization. Insofar as the lineage mode rests on ideological core relations, it maintains, in times of change, the inner characteristics of ideology. As part of highly routinized ideological core relations, individual actors are likely to carry on the rituals/ practices of the lineage mode wherever they may be, even outside the lineage structure. Routinization results from imaginary relationships, which differ from the actual, concrete social order. Once ideology has created these relationships, they can survive and be reproduced in the absence of the concrete lineage structure. The effects of the lineage mode are all the more pervasive given their basis in ideological *core* relations and the double dependence of social life on ideology and its imaginary relationships.

In any case, to accept or reject the applicability of the propositions advanced here, one needs to investigate the different forms of lineage organization in precolonial non-European societies. Only such an investigation can help determine whether the concept of the lineage mode can be derived from these different forms. Unfortunately, such an investigation is lacking. I do not suggest that the concept of the lineage mode has not been used or discussed; rather, existing analyses have not provided a convincing definition of the concept. One of the reasons for this lack is the focus on the misleading notion of the 'Asiatic' or 'tributary' mode, elaborated from a typology of modes of production in which the tributary mode is differentiated from the lineage mode, the slave mode, and so forth. It comes as no surprise, then, that in many studies the lineage mode would exist only in Africa where kinship ties 'hold strong,' but not in Asia and South America. Moreover, the evolutionary view in the studies of mode of production has vitiated the debate. The lineage mode is supposed to precede the others, and the final destination is capitalism. Consequently, capitalism's failure to destroy precapitalist relations in all non-European societies is ascribed to what almighty capitalism did or did not do rather than to what these societies may have done and may have had in common.

An investigation into the various forms of lineage organization in Africa, Asia, and South America would not reveal uniformity in their morphological makeup but would likely show that their mode of production rested on ideological core relations. By taking the core relations as the fundamental definitional element, one avoids the pitfalls mentioned; it becomes clear that what makes the lineage mode is not the specific form of lineage organization but these core relations. The applicability of the propositions I have advanced in this work to Asia, South America, and other parts of Africa rests on whether these different forms of lineage organization were based on ideological core relations. This means, in the end, that the term 'lineage' attached to 'mode of production' is dispensable. Inasmuch as ideological core relations are the real issue, a substitute can be found for 'lineage.' Before settling on such a substitute, I have used the term 'lineage' mode. This usage is preferred to that of 'communal mode' to avoid the false debate over the form of ownership that prevailed in precolonial times (communal property vs. private property).

It is quite possible that specific historical cases may reveal the absence of the link between the lineage structure and ideological core relations. But such a claim can be made only on the basis of macrocomparative analyses, which are lacking. Whenever an analysis of modes of production is attempted, the focus is on their 'articulation,' that is, the colonial period. The theory of articulation being what it is, one understands why the dynamics of precolonial societies cannot be adequately seized. Furthermore, in some studies on the modes of production in Latin America, what is referred to as 'precapitalist modes' is the so-called feudalism introduced by Spanish and Portuguese colonialism.[1] No mention is made of precolonial Indian modes of production. Even more surprisingly, works by Latin Americans themselves on modes of production hardly concern themselves with in-depth analysis of pre-Hispanic modes and their effect on colonialism and capitalism. The focus is on the effects of 'feudal' or capitalist domination. One wonders how an articulation can take place without one of the parties influencing the other party. Even though the patterns of Indian settlements were uneven throughout Latin America, one still needs to inquire about their modes of production. Such an inquiry necessarily leads to the question of their effects on colonial and capitalist penetrations, at least where Indian societies did exist. This, in turn, raises the question of by what means the prevailing precolonial mode exerted such an influence. It is in light of these issues that the propositions put forward here, especially that related to the routinizing ability of the lineage mode, constitute working hypotheses for Latin America as well.

In South America two situations present themselves. The first concerns those societies, as in Central America, where Indian settlements remained strong even after colonialism. The second situation is identified with such cases as Argentina or Chile, where the Indian settlements were scattered and completely marginalized after colonial rule. In the first situation, there is no a priori reason why the propositions cannot be tested. Indeed, these societies defy the conventional wisdom of incomparability between Africa (Asia) and Latin America. More problematic is the second situation, where there is a prima facie reason to deny the applicability of the propositions. But prima facie evidence is not tested evidence. The real test for the propositions comes when the following questions are addressed. First, have there been pseudocapitalism and overpoliticization in countries such as Argentina and Chile? Second, if so, are the two variables explained by the explanatory variables I propose in this study? Given that pseudocapitalism involves a triple divergence in which social relationships are not entirely dependent on capitalist core relations, what prevents such total dependence in these countries? Can this situation be ascribed to the prevalence of ideological core relations and their attendant routinization?

If the answer is positive, how does one explain these ideological core relations? One needs to inquire about the possible role of the lineage mode. If this possibility is denied, then one has to inquire into the so-called feudalism that accompanied Spanish and Portuguese rule in South America. Given that this feudalism did not allow transformations to take place along Western European lines in Latin America, is there something in it that resembles the lineage mode, hence its ideological routinization? Or, for that matter, was it feudalism? The answer to the question of whether the triple divergence in pseudocapitalism that prevails in such countries as Argentina and Chile is ascribable to ideological core relations may be negative. In this case, one must be prepared to think of these countries as the exceptions that confirm the rule, that is, the propositions. After all, Latin America is not reducible to 'white South America.'

The second objection about the concept of the lineage mode is that it may lend ammunition to erroneous interpretations such as those that reduce all historical trends in the Third World today to clanism and tribalism. Undoubtedly, the danger of such interpretation is real, but the concept of the lineage mode does not contribute to it. On the contrary, it and the whole foregoing analysis help avoid the danger by shedding light on the issue. To better answer the objection, it is worth turning to the twin issues of ethnicity and class.

Third World observers have addressed the issues of ethnicity and class in different ways; two extremely antipodal views have dominated the debate. On the one hand are those who see ethnicity everywhere and, on the other hand, those who see it nowhere. The same holds true with the concept of social class. Between the two extremes have been attempts to treat the two concepts as not mutually exclusive. The two extremist positions result from pitfalls in the inquiry into Third World societies. Even the 'middle ground' position, which mixes ethnicity and class, does not succeed in explaining why the two coexist. The impact of both ethnicity and social class in Africa and the Third World in general is undeniable. This in itself is not a big discovery because the Third World does not deserve pride of place for the existence of both categories. Hence, to be able to explain their status and role, one needs to relate them to the type of society that makes them specific.

It is true that the colonial administration played a major role in shaping 'tribal identities,' sometimes imposing such identities where they were not acutely felt. It is also true that ethnicity has played a much more instrumentalist role in postcolonial politics than its real primordial ties would allow. Nevertheless, such an instrumentality of ethnicity, under colonial rule or in the postcolonial era, still raises a question. How is it that colonial officials and postcolonial politicians succeeded in persuading their targeted population to subscribe to ethnic or tribal rivalries? After all, they could have done the same with class affiliations, persuading the populations to fight a class war. The attempts by the colonial officials or politicians would have been unsuccessful had it not been for the reliance of the population on routinized ideological social ties that could be extended, stretched, and manipulated. These ties are the real or 'created' outcomes of the lineage mode. It is this reliance on ideological core relations in the lineage mode that explains their persistence. Again, that ethnic ties are tributary to the lineage mode by no means implies that the actual localized lineage or clan structure today provides ethnicity with its dynamism. The link between the two is theoretical and structural. Only by considering the concept of ideological routinization does the link become clear. What are referred to today as tribes or ethnic groups were in many cases precolonial centralized and noncentralized societies. The analysis in chapters 3 and 4 showed their dependence on the lineage mode, hence on ideological core relations. Pseudocapitalism and overpoliticization exacerbate these ties, making them specific in the Third World. They are, indeed, prominent in the social configuration and in the dominant discourse. Rivalries that they generate often take on the form of open confrontations. Therefore, recourse to the concept of lineage mode does not encourage 'tribalist' interpretations of contemporary societies. On the contrary, it deprives such interpretations of their academic aura by showing the following: (1) ethnic conflict is specific and expresses itself differently in the Third World; and (2) this specificity cannot be explained unless one explains first pseudocapitalism and the over-politicized state.

The specification of class under pseudocapitalism is a risky exercise at best. Not all social groups that emerged from colonial differentiation are classes. Unfortunately, this reasoning has been taken to the extreme by some writers. The prominence of ethnic ties has been used as evidence for the absence of class ties. Such an extreme position is, however, baseless. There is no reason why class and ethnicity cannot cross-cut each other. I have maintained that precolonial African and Third World societies were not based on class because of what I consider the minimum prerequisite for class relations. I take it for granted that neither inequality nor conflicts are sufficient conditions for the existence of a class. Moreover, political power and its attendant domination are not, in themselves, criteria for class relations. This is not to deny their role in a class situation or to suggest that the political superstructure is not impor-tant in class relationships. The point is that these factors are necessary but not sufficient conditions for the existence of classes. They need to be analyzed in conjunction with the existing relations of production.

There is, of course, the evident danger that for those subscribing to depend-ency theory, reliance on the relations of production may lead to the question-able conclusion that ruling classes in the Third World are mere puppets of foreign economic classes. For those avoiding this kind of conclusion, the temptation is to develop a theory of class based on 'relations of power and not production.'[2] The temptation is even greater when one is reminded of one writer's cogent observation that if one restricts oneself to relations of produc-tion in Africa, there is no way to find the type of class exploitation Marx had in mind. Maybe so, but political power cannot develop in a vacuum. It is possible to avoid dependency theory and still be able to analyze class relations in light of the relations of production. For this one needs to look no further than pseudocapitalism; its productive relations, however truncated, do allow appropriation of surplus production on the basis of which class exploitation can be determined. Indeed, given the overpoliticized state, political power in pseudocapitalism, unlike capitalism, directly determines the production and circulation of the surplus product. The class nomenclature, therefore, ought to be proposed from the top down, taking into account political power. Although I have argued that the relationship between state officials and subjects is not a class relation, the relationship between power holders in the overpoliticized state and society is *susceptible* to developing into a class relation. By directly controlling productive relations with an exploitative (capitalist) content, the holders of state power control potential class relations. In fact, by virtue of this specific control and its attendant accumulation they often engage in many productive activities using wage labor.

Class relations , then, are to be examined at two different levels. The first one involves foreign or national owners of the means of production engaged in productive relations with workers to whom a wage is paid. And the other involves those in control of state power with direct control over productive relations or able to establish such relations because of their private accumulation through the exercise of state power. Various names have been given to this class closely associated with state power; it can be referred to simply as the 'ruling class.'

Given the presence of ethnicity, these class relations obviously coexist with ethnic ties. One can belong to one ethnic group and at the same time be a member of a given social class. It also means that one can be involved in both ethnic and class practices at the same time. Intraclass ethnic conflicts are an example. Moreover, ethnic politics may dominate class politics and vice versa, or both may equally be present. However, it is highly improbable that one ethnic group can be a social class, dominating another 'ethnic group-class.' I am also skeptical about the notion of contextual class relations developed by some authors, such as Michael Schatzberg, who argues that 'Africans, like others, can and do maintain more than one ethnic identity.' He concludes that the same holds true for social class: 'As the context changes, the same individual may well display more than one class identity.'[3] Because this study does not concern itself particularly with the issue of social class, there is no way to address fully the problem here. Nevertheless, it is true that ethnic consciousness can shift depending on the context, because ethnicity, as pointed out earlier, is essentially an ideologically maintained relationship that can be expanded and manipulated according to context. This is not the case with social class. One does not need to rely on 'Marxian trappings' or 'objective conditions' to make this point.

Schatzberg is quite right when pointing to the class nature of the state, which is perhaps even more pronounced in the Third World because of overpoliticization. But this by no means indicates that even the police can be seen as a class because they have a 'consciousness' that extorts peasants within the state hierarchy. If political power by itself is to be a point of reference for class analysis, a view to which I do not subscribe, then one still needs to know who controls state power and how. If a class is a relation of exploitation, those involved in it have a common bond – a bond determining the modality of exploitation. In those cases where relations of production are not taken into account, state power should be such a bond. But even in this case, where Marxian trappings are repudiated, it cannot be said that social class is contextual. Neither the peasants who find ways to extort other peasants after moving to town nor the police hold state power. That bureaucrats and local officials have the 'consciousness' of being different does not make them a class. I do not a priori deny their potential class status, but not because of their 'consciousness.' One needs to link them to the whole state apparatus in the Third World context to understand their actual class status.

249

Thus, here also, it becomes quite clear that the lineage mode cannot provide ammunition to those interpretations of the Third World that attribute everything to 'tribalism.' Not only is the lineage mode different from lineage organization, but focus on the lineage mode does not deny the existence of social classes in the postcolonial period. Yet, as I hinted in chapter 2, as a category, social class is no substitute for explanation. Its mere presence does not explain why political competition among classes in the Third World is overpoliticized. The overpoliticized state thesis developed in this book has attempted to answer this question.

Notes

1. See Gustavo Rodriguez, 'Original Accumulation, Capitalism, and Precapitalistic Agriculture in Bolivia,' *Latin American Perspectives*, Issue 27, Fall 1980, Vol VII, no. 4: 50–65; Rodrigo Mantoya, 'Class Relations in the Andean Countryside,' *Latin American Perspectives*, Issue 34, Summer 1982, Vol. IX, No. 3: 62–77.
2. Richard Sklar, 'The Nature of Class Domination in Africa,' *Journal of Modern African Studies*, 17, 4 (1979): 17, p. 537.
3. Michael Schatzberg, *Politics and Class in Zaire*, p. 173.

Supplementary references

Abner, Cohen. *Customs and Politics in Urban Africa: A Study of Hausa Migrants in Yoruba Towns*. Chicago: University of Chicago Press, 1969.

Academie Royale des sciences d'outre-mer. *Bulletin des seances*. 1ère ser. 1930–54; vol.1, 1955.

Afanasyev, L. et al. *The Political Economy of Capitalism*. Moscow: Progress Publishers, 1974.

Agarwal, N. *The Development of a Dual Economy*. Calcutta, India: K.P. Bagchi & Company, 1983.

Alavi, Hamza. 'The State in Post-Colonial Societies: Pakistan and Bangladesh.' *New Left Review*. (July–August, 1972): 59–81

Alford, Robert and Roger Friedland. *Powers of Theory*. Cambridge: Cambridge University Press, 1986.

Althusser, Louis. *Lenin and Philosophy and Other Essays*. New York: Monthly Review Press, 1972.

—— and Etienne Balibar. *Reading Capital*. London: NLB, 1970.

Ameringer, Charles. *Don Pepe: A Political Biography of Jose Figueres of Costa Rica*. Alburquerque, NM: University of New Mexico Press, 1978.

Amin, Samir. *Eurocentrism*. New York: Monthly Review Press, 1989.

—— *Unequal Development*. New York: Monthly Review Press, 1976.

—— *Le développement du capitalisme en Côte d'Ivoire*. Paris: Edition de Minuit, 1967.

—— *Accumulation on a World Scale*. New York: Monthly Review Press, 1974.

Anderson, Perry. *Lineages of the Absolutist States*. London: Verso, 1979.

—— *Passages from Antiquity to Feudalism*. London: Verso, 1980.

Anglade, C. and C. Fortin, eds. *The State and Capital Accumulation in Latin America*. Pittsburgh: University of Pittsburgh Press, 1985.

251

Anstey, Roger. *King Leopold's Legacy*. London: Oxford university Press, 1966.

Apter, David. *The Politics of Modernization*. Chicago: The University of Chicago Press, 1965.

Arrighi, G. and J. Saul. *Essays in the Political Economy of Africa*. New York: Monthly Review Press, 1973.

Azarya, V. and Noami Chazan 'Disengagement from the State in Africa: Reflections on the Experience of Ghana and Guinea. *Comparative Studies in Society and History*. Vol. 29, No. 1 (1987): 106–131.

Baeck, L. 'Une société rurale en transition: Etude socio-économique de la région de Thysville, *Zaire*. Vol. XI, 2 (February 1957): 115–186.

Bagchi, Amiya Kumar. *The Political Economy of Underdevelopment*. Cambridge: Cambridge University Press, 1982.

Balandier, Georges. *Daily Life in the Kingdom of the Kongo*. New York: Pantheon Books, 1968.

Baker, Hugh D.R. *Chinese Family and Kinship*. New York: Columbia University Press, 1979.

Bascom, William and Melville Herskovits, eds. *Continuity and Change in African Cultures*. Chicago: University of Chicago Press, 1959.

Bates, Robert. *Markets and States in Tropical Africa*. Berkeley: University of California Press, 1981.

Baudin, Louis. *A Socialist Empire: The Incas of Peru*. Princeton, NJ: D. Van Nostrand Co., 1961.

Bauer, P. *Dissent on Development*. Cambridge: Harvard University Press, 1983.

—— *Equality, the Third World and Economic Delusion*. Cambridge: Harvard University Press, 1972.

—— and B. Yamey. 'The Third World and the West: An Economic Perspective' in *The Third World: Premises of US Policy*. Ed. W. S. Thompson. San Francisco: Institute for Contemporary Studies, 1978.

Bayart, J. F. 'Clientelism, Elections and Systems of Inequality and Domination in Cameroon.' in *Elections Without Choice*. Ed. G. Hermet, R. Rose and A. Rouquie. New York, 1978.

—— *L'Etat en Afrique: la Politique du Ventre*. Paris: Fayard, 1989.

Beattie, J. H. N. and R. G. Lienhardt. *Studying Social Anthropology*. Oxford: Oxford University Press, 1975.

De Beaucorps, R. *Les Basongo de la Luniungu et de la Gobari*. Brussels: Librairie Falk Fils, 1941.

—— *L'evolution economique chez les Basongo de la Luniungu et de la Gobari*. Brussels, 1951.

Belgian Government (Ministere des Colonies). *Annuaire officiel 1910*. Brussels, 1910.

—— *Le Plan Decennal pour de le Developpement Economique et Social du Congo Belge*. Brussels, 1959.

—— *La situation economique du Congo Belge et du Rwanda–Burundi*. (Yearly Publication from 1951 to 1959). Brussels, 1951–1960.

Bell, Daniel and Irving Kristol, eds. *Capitalism Today*. New York: New American Library, 1971

Bendix, Reinhard. *Kings or People: Power and Mandate to Rule*. Berkely: University of California Press, 1978.

—— et al. *State and Society*. Berkeley: University of California Press, 1968.

Berg-Schlosser, Dirk. *Tradition and Change in Kenya*. Munich, Germany: Ferdinand Schoningh, 1989.

Berger, Peter. 'Underdevelopment Revisted.' *Commentary*. (Jul. 1984): 41–45.

Bezy, F., J.P. Peemans, and J.M. Wautelet. *Accumulation et sous-developpement au Zaire 1960–1980*. Louvain-la-Neuve: Presses universitaires de Louvain, 1981.

—— and J.L. Lacroix. *L'industrie manufacturiere a Leopoldville et dans le Bas Congo et ses problemes d'approvisionnement 1960–1961*. Leopoldville: IRES, 1962.

Biebuyck, Daniel. *Lega Culture*. Berkeley: University of California Press, 1973

Biletsi, Eugene. 'La Solidarite chez les Ambuun.' *Etudes Congolaises*. Vol. XI, No. 1 (1968): 4–24.

Block, Marc. *Feudal Society*. Vol. 1. Chicago: University of Chicago Press, 1974.

Bloch, Maurice. *Marxist Analyses and Social Anthropology*. London: Mohaby Press, 1975.

Boelaert, E. 'Les trois fictions du droit foncier Congolais'. *Zaire*. Vol. XI–4 (April 1957): 399–427.

Boelaert, R. P. E. 'L'etat independant et les terres indigenes.' *Academie Royale de sciences Coloniales*. T.V. Fasc. 4, 1956.

Bratton, Michael. 'Patterns of Development and Underdevelopment: Toward a Comparison.' *International Studies Quarterly*. No. 26 (Sept. 3, 1982): 333–372.

Brausch, George. *Belgian Administration in the Congo*. London: Oxford University Press, 1961.

Buelens, K. 'Analyse economique du probleme de la propriete fonciere au Congo Belge.' *Zaire*. Vol. XII–3 (1958): 227–249.

Burns, E.B. *Latin America: A Concise Interpretive History*. Englewood Cliff, NJ: Prentice Hall, 1986.

Burton, W.F.P. *Luba Religion and Magic in Custom and Belief*. Tervuren, Belgium: Musee Royal de l'Afrique Centrale, 1961

Bustin, E. *Lunda Under Belgian Rule: The Politics of Ethnicity*. Cambridge: Harvard University Press, 1975.

Bwakasa, Tulu. *L'impense du discours: Kindoki et nkisi en pays Kongo du Zaire*. Kinshasa, 1980

Callaghy, Thomas. *The State–Society Struggle: Zaire in Comparative Perspective*. New York: Columbia Univeristy Press, 1984.

Cardoso, F. and E. Faletto. *Dependency and Development in Latin America*. Berkeley: University of California Press, 1979.

Chazan, N. *An Anatomy of Ghanaian Politics: Managing Political Recession*. Boulder, CO:Westview Press, 1982.

—— and E. Rothchild, eds. *The Precarious Balance: State and Society in Africa*. Boulder, CO: Westview Press, 1988.

Chilcote, R. and Dale Johnson, eds. *Theories of Development*. Beverly Hills: Sage, 1983.

Chome, Jules. *Moise Tshombe et l'escroquerie Katangaise*. Brussels, 1966.

Clapham, C. *Third World Politics*. Madison: University of Wisconsin Press, 1986.

Clough, E. *Africa*. Detroit: n.p., 1911.

Collier, David. *The New Authoritanianism in Latin America*. Princeton: Princeton University Press, 1979.

Congres Colonial Belge. *Comptes Rendus et Rapports*. Brussels, February 6 & 7, 1926.

Cornevin, R. *Histoire du Congo*. Paris: Berger-Levraut, 1970.

CRISP. Congo. (1959, 1960, 1961, 1962, 1963, 1964, 1965). Brussels: 1960–1966.

Crouch, Colin, ed. *State and Economy in Contemporary Captialism*. New York: St. Martin's Press, 1979.

Crummey, D. and C.C. Steward, eds. *Modes of Production in Africa*. Beverly Hill: Sage, 1981

Dahl, R. *Polyarchy*. New Haven: Yale University Press, 1971.

—— *A Preface to Democratic Theory*. Chicago: University of Chicago Press, 1956.

De Decker, J. M. *Les clans Ambuun (Bambunda) d'apres leur litterature orale*. Brussels,1950.

Delcommune, A. *L'avenir du Congo Belge menace*. Brussels: Lebegue, 1919.

—— *Vingt annees de vie Africaine: Recits de voyages d'aventures et d'exploration au Congo Belge 1874–1893*. Vol. 2, Brussels, 1922.

Dhanis, E. 'Recrutements de main d'oeuvre chez les Bayaka.' *Zaire* Vol. VII, No. 5 (1953): 489–496

Diamond, Larry, Juan Linz, and S.M. Lipset, eds. *Democracy in Developing Countries: Africa*. Boulder, CO: Lynne Rienner, 1988.

Doornbos, M. 'The African State in Academic Debate: Restrospect and Prospect.' *The Journal of Modern African Studies*. Vol. 28, No. 2 (1990): 179–198.

Dumont, Fernand. *Les Ideologies*. Paris: PUF, 1969.

Essor du Congo. (Several Issues).

Evans, Peter. *Dependent Development: The Alliance of Multinational, State, and Local Capital in Brazil*. Princeton: Princeton University Press, 1979.

Fallers, L. *Bantu Bureaucracy*. Chicago: The University of Chicago Press, 1965.

Fatton, Robert. 'The State of African Studies and Studies of the African State: The Theoretical Softness of the "Soft State."' *Journal of Asian and African* Studies, Vol. 24, Nos. 3–4 (1989): 170–185.

Fischlow, et al. *Rich and Poor Nations in the World's Economy*. New Haven: Yale University Press, 1976.

Fooz, Hauzeur de. *CSK: Comite Special du Katanga 1900–1950*. Brussels: Editions Cuypers, 1950.

—— *Un demi-siecle avec l'economie du Congo Belge*. Brussels: Imprimerie Mondiale, 1957.

—— *Du Congo de Leopold II au Congo Kinshasa*. Brussels: Imprimerie Mondiale, n.d.

Fortes, Meyer. *Kinship and the Social Order*. Chicago: Aldine Publishing Co., 1963.

—— and E. Evans-Pritchard, eds. *African Political Systems*. London: Oxford University Press, 1958.

Frank, Andre G. *Crisis in the Third World*. New York: Holmes and Meier, 1981.

—— *Dependent Accumulation and Underdevelopment*. New York: Monthly Review Press, 1979.

—— *Latin America: Underdevelopment or Revolution*. New York: Monthly Review Press,1969.

—— *Mexican Agriculture 1521–1630*. Cambridge: Cambridge University Press, 1979.

Gann, L.H. and P. Duignan. *The Burden of Empire*. New York: Praeger, 1967.

—— *Colonialism in Africa 1870–1960*. Cambridge: Cambridge University Press, 1975.

—— *The Rulers of Belgian Africa 1884–1914*. Princeton: Princeton university Press, 1979.

Gelders, V. *Le Clan dans la societe indigene*. Brussels: Institut Royal Colonial Belge, 1943.

Gerard-Libois, J. *Katanga Secession*. Madison : University of Wisconsin Press, 1966.

Giddens, Anthony. *Capitalism and Modern Social Theory*. Cambridge: Cambridge University Press, 1971.

—— *The Class Structure of the Advanced Societies*. New York: Harper and Row, 1973.

Godelier, Maurice. *Horizons, Trajets Marxistes en anthropologie*. Paris: Maspero, 1973.

Goody, Jack. *Comparative Studies in Kinship*. Stanford: Stanford University Press, 1969.

Galtung, Johan. 'A Structural Theory of Imperialism.' *Journal of Peace Research*. Vol. VIII, No. 2 (1971): 81–117.

Gould, D. J. *Bureaucratic Corruption and Underdevelopment in the Third World: The Case of Zaire*. New York: Pergamon Press, 1980.

Gramsci, Antonio. *Prison Notebooks*. New York: International Publishers, 1971.

Gran, G. ed., *Zaire: The Political Economy of Underdevelopment*. New York: Praeger, 1979.

Griffin, Keith. *Underdevelopment in Spanish America*. London: George Allen and Unwin, 1969.

Gutkind, P.C.W. and I. Wallerstein, eds. *The Political Economy of Contemporary Africa*. Beverly Hill: Sage, 1976

Hamilton, Nora. *The Limits of State Autonomy: Post-Revolutionary Mexico*. Princeton: Princeton University Press, 1982.

Hanke, Lewis, ed. *History of Latin American Civilization*. 2 Vols. Boston: Little, Brown and Co., 1973.

Harms, Robert. *River of Wealth, River of Sorrow: The Central Zaire Basin in the Era of the Slave and Ivory Trade, 1500–1890*. New Haven: Yale University Press, 1981.

Harrison, Laurence. *Underdevelopment is a State of Mind: The Latin American Case*. Cambridge, MA: Center for International Affairs, Harvard University, 1985.

Heilbroner, Robert. *The Nature and Logic of Capitalism*. New York: Norton, 1985.

Held, David, et al. *States and Societies*. New York: University Press, 1983.

Hemptine, J. de. 'La politique indigene du Congo Belge.' *Congo*. T2, No. 2. (Oct. 1928): 359–374.

Higgins, B. 'The Dualistic Theory of Underdeveloped Areas: Economic Development and Cultural Change.' *Leading issues in Development Economics*. Ed., G. M. Meier. New York: Oxford University Press, 1984.

Hilton, Anne. *The Kingdom of Kongo*. New York: Oxford University Press, 1985.

Hilton, Rodney et al. *The Transition from Feudalism to Capitalism*. London: Verso, 1978.

Hindess, Barry and Paul Hirst. *Pre-Capitalist Modes of Production*. London: Routledge and Kegan Paul, 1977.

Hobson, J.A. *Imperialism: A Study*. Ann Arbor: University of Michigan Press, 1965.

Hoskyns, Catherine. *The Congo Since Independence*. London: Oxford University Press, 1967.

Hulstaert, G. *Elements pour l'histoire Mongo ancienne*. Brussels: Academie Royale, 1984.

Hunter, Guy. *Modernizing Peasant Societies: A Comparative Study in Asia and Africa*. Oxford: Oxford University Press, 1969.

Hyden, Goran. *Beyond Ujamaa in Tanzania: Underdevelopment and Uncaptured Peasantry*. Berkeley: University of California Press, 1980.

—— *No Shortcuts to Progess: African Management in perspective.* Berkeley: University of California Press, 1983.

IRES. *Independance, inflation, developpement: l'economie Congolaise de 1960 a 1965.* Paris: Mouton, 1968.

Jackson, R. and C. Rosberg. *Personal Rule in Black Africa.* Berkeley: University of California Press, 1982.

—— and Rosberg, C. 'Sovereignty and Underdevelopment: Juridical Statehood in the African Crisis.' *Journal of Modern African Studies.* Vol 24, No. 1 (1986): 1–31.

Jewsiewicki, Bogumil. 'Lineage Mode of Production: Social Inequalities in Equatorial Central Africa.' *Modes of Production in Africa: The Precolonial Era.* Ed. Donald Crummey and C.C. Stewart. Beverly Hills: Sage Publications, 1981.

—— and Letourneau, J., eds. *Mode of Production: The Challenge of Africa.* Ste-Foy, Canada: Safi Press, 1985.

Kanza, Thomas. *Conflict in the Congo.* Baltimore: Penguin Books, 1961.

—— *The Rise and Fall of Patrice Lumumba (Conflict in the Congo).* Boston: G.K. Hall Co, 1979.

Kapaji, Ngoy. 'Projects d'investissements et croissance de l'economie Zairoise 1970–75.' *Zaire-Afrique.* No. 70 (Dec. 1972): 607–619.

Kitching, Gavin. *Class and Economic Change in Kenya.* New Haven: Yale University Press, 1980.

Lamal, F. *Basuku et Bayaka des Districts Kwango et Kwilu au Congo.* Tervuren, Belgium: Musee Royal de L'Afrique Centrale, 1965.

Lasswell, H. *Politics: Who Gets What, When, and How?* New York: McGraw-Hill, 1936.

Legun, Colin. *Congo Disaster.* Baltimore: Penguin Books, 1961.

Lemarchand, Rene. *Political Awakening in the Belgian Congo.* Berkeley: University of California Press, 1969.

Lenin, V.I. *Imperialism: The Highest Stage of Capitalism.* New York: International Publishers, 1977.

Leplae, Edm. 'Resultats obtenus au Congo Belge par les cultures obligatoires alimentaires et industrielles.' *Zaire.* Vol. 1, no.2 (Feb. 1947): 115–140.

Levi-Strauss, Claude. *Structural Anthropology.* New York: Basic Books, 1963.

—— *Tristes Tropiques.* Paris: Plon, 1955.

Leys, Colin. *Underdevelopment in Kenya.* Berkely: University of California Press, 1975.

Lindblom, Charles. *Politics and Markets.* New York: Basic Books, 1977.

Lipset, Seymour M. *Political Man.* New York: Doubleday & Co., 1960.

Locke, John. *Two Treatises on Government.* New York: New Library 1965.

Lucas, Stephen. 'L'Etat traditionnel Luba.' *CEPSI*, no. 74 (1966): 83–93 and no.79 (1967): 93–115

Luckas, G. *History and Class Consciousness.* London, 1971.

Lusanga, T. Kanyinda. 'Pouvoir traditionnel et institutions politiques modernes chez les Baluba du Sud-Kasai.' MA Thesis, Lovanium University, Kinshasa, 1968.

Macridis, Roy. *Contemporary Political Ideologies.* Boston: Little, Brown, 1982

Maes, J. *Notes sur les populations des bassins du Kasai, de la Lukenie et du Lac Leopold II.* Brussels: Annales du Musee du Congo Belge, 1924.

Mandel, Ernest. *Late Capitalism.* London: Verso, 1978.

Manley, M. 'We Are Told . . . We Must Have More of the Same Disease. *Third World 88/89.* Guilford, CT: Dushkin Publishing Group, 1989.

Markovitz, Irving Leonard. *Power and Class in Africa*. Englewood Cliffs, NJ: Prentice Hall, 1977.

Martelli, G. *Leopold to Lumumba: A History of the Belgian Congo 1877–1960*. London: Western Printing, 1962.

Mason, J. Alden. *The Ancient Civilization of Peru*. Baltimore, MD: Penguin Books, 1957.

Meillassoux, Claude. *Anthropologie economique des Gouro de Cote d'Ivoire*. Paris: Mouton, 1964

—— *Maidens, Meal and Money*. Cambridge: Cambridge University Press, 1981.

Merriam, Alan. *An African World: The Basongye Village of Lupuya Ngye*. Bloomington: Indiana University Press, 1981.

—— *Congo: Background of Conflict*. Evanston, IL: Northwestern University Press, 1961.

—— *Culture History of the Basongye*. Bloomington: Indiana University Press, 1975.

Mertens, Joseph. *Les Badzing de la Kamtsha*. Brussels: Librairie Falk Fils, 1935.

Mill, John S. *Considerations on Representative Government*. Library of Liberal Arts, 1958.

Mittelman, James. *Out From Underdevelopment*. New York: St. Martin's Press, 1989.

Morel, E.D. *Red Rubber*. London: Fischer, 1906.

Mugubane, B. and Nzongola-Ntalaja, eds. *Proletarianization and Class Struggle in Africa*. San Francisco: Synthesis Publications, 1983.

Munoz, Heraldo, ed. *From Dependency to Development: Strategies to Overcome Underdevelopment and Inequality*. Boulder, CO: Westview Press, 1981.

Mwabila, Malela. 'Proletariat et conscience de classe au Zaire.' *Annales*. No. 2 (Mar. 1974). Lubumbashi. (Special issue.)

Myint, H. *The Economics of the Developing Countries*. London: Hutchinson, 1964.

Nseka Ngimbi, ed. *Actualite et inactualite des 'Etudes Bakongo' du P. Van Wing*. Mayidi, Zaire, 1983.

Nguyen, Khac Kham. *An Introduction to Vietnamese Culture*. Tokyo: Tokyo Press Co, 1967.

—— *Traditional Vietnam: Some Historical Stages*. Hanoi: Hanoi Institute of Historical Studies, n.d.

N'Krumah, Kwame. *Challenge of the Congo*. New York: International Publishers, 1966

Nordlinger, Eric. *Soldiers in Politics*. Englewood Cliffs: Prentice Hall, 1977.

Nyang'oro, J. and T. Shaw, eds., *Beyond Structural Adjustment in Africa*. New York: Praeger, 1992

Nyembo Shabani. *L'industrie du cuivre dans le monde et le progres economique du Copperbelt Africain*. Brussels: La Renaissance du Livre, 1975

Nzongola-Ntalaja, G. 'The Authenticity of Neo-colonialism: Ideology and Class Struggles in Zaire.' *Berkeley Journal of Sociology*. Vol. 22 (1977–1978): 115–129.

—— 'The Bourgeoisie and Revolution in the Congo.' *Journal of Modern African Studies* Vol. 8, No. 4 (Dec. 1970): 511–530

—— *Class Struggle and National Liberation in Africa*. Roxbury, MA: Omenana,1982

—— ed. *The Crisis in Zaire: Myths and Realities*. Trenton, NJ: Africa World Press, 1986.

—— *Revolution and Counter-Revolution in Africa*. London: Zed, 1987

Offiong, D. *Imperialism and Dependency*. Washington, DC: Howard University Press, 1982

Oliver, R. and Atmore, A. *The African Middle Ages 1400–1800*. New York: Cambridge University Press, 1981.

Oropeza, Louis. *Tutelary Pluralism: A Critical Approach to Venezuelan Democracy*. Cambridge, MA: Center for International Affairs, Harvard University, 1983.

Osaghae, E.E. 'The Character of the State, Legitimacy Crisis and Social Mobilization in Africa: An Explanation of form and Character. *Africa Development*. Vol. 14, No. 2 (1989): 27–46.

Packard, Randal. *Chiefship and Cosmology*. Bloomington: Indiana University Press, 1981.

Pagden, A.R., ed. *The Maya*. Chicago: J. Philip O'Hara Inc., 1975.

Palmer, R. and N. Parsons. *The Roots of Rural Poverty in Central and Southern Africa*. Berkeley: University of California Press, 1977.

Peeler, John. *Latin American Democracies: Colombia, Costa Rica, Venezuela* Chapel Hill: The University of North Carolina Press, 1985.

Peters, G. 'L'agriculture Congolaise et ses problemes.' *Zaire*. Vol XII, No. 5 (1958): 451–478.

Pirenne, Henri. *Economic and Social History of Medieval Europe*. New York: Harcourt, Brace and World Inc., 1937.

Poulantzas, Nicos. *Political Power and Social Classes*. London: Verso, 1978.

—— *State, Power, socialism*. London: Verso, 1980.

Przeworski, A. 'Class Compromise and the State: Westen Europe and Latin America.' 1980. (Mimeographed.)

—— and Henry Teune. *The Logic of Comparative Social Inquiry*. New York: Willey Interscience, 1970.

—— 'Material Bases of Consent: Economics and politics in a hegemonic System.' *Political Power and Social Theory*, Vol. 1 (1980): 21–66.

Randles, W.G.L. *L'ancien royaume du Congo des origines a la fin du XIX siecle*. Paris: Mouton, 1968.

Reefe, T. *The Rainbow and the Kings: A History of the Luba Empire to 1891*. Berkeley: University of California press, 1981.

Rejai, M. *Comparative Political Ideologies*. New York: St Martin's Press, 1984

Rey, P.P. *Colonialisme, neocolonialisme et transition au capitalisme*. Paris: Maspero, 1971

Rodney, Walter. *How Europe Underdeveloped Africa*. Washington, DC.: Howard University Press, 1981.

Sandbrook, R. *The politics of Africa's Economic Stagnation*. Cambridge: Cambridge University Press, 1985.

Sangmpam, S. N. 'Neither Soft Nor Dead: The African State is Alive and Well.' *African Studies Review*, Vol. 36, no. 2 (September 1993): 73–94.

—— 'The Overpolitized State and Democratization: A Theoretical Model.' *Comparative Politcs*, Vol. 24, no.4 (July 1992): 401–417.

—— 'The State–Society Relationship in Peripheral countries: Critical Notes on the Dominant Paradgms.' *The Review of Politics*. Vol. 48, No. 4 (Fall 1986): 596–619.

—— 'Peripheral Capitalism, the State and Crisis.' Ph.D dissertation, the University of Chicago, 1984.

Sartori, Giovanni. *The Theory of Democracy Revisited*. T2 (Chatham House, 1987).

Scase, Richard. *The State in Western Europe*. New York: St. Matin's Press, 1980.

Schapera, I *Government and Politics in Tribal Societies*. London: C.A Watts, 1963.

Seddon, David. *Relations of Production: Marxist Aproaches to Economic Anthropology.* London: Frank Cass, 1978.

Seidman, Ann. and Neva Seidman Makgetla. *Outposts of Monopoly Capitalism.* London: Zed Press, 1980.

Seliger, Martin. *The Marxist Conception of Ideology.* Cambridge: Cambridge University Press, 1977.

Sendwe, J. 'Traditions et coutumes ancestrales des Baluba Shankadji.' *CEPSI*, no. 24 (1954): 88–120.

Shatzberg, M. *The Dialectics of Oppression in Zaire.* Bloomington: Indiana University Press, 1988.

Shenton, Robert. *The Development of Capitalism in Northern Nigeria.* Toronto: University of Toronto Press, 1986.

Shills, Edward. *Center and Periphery.* Chicago: The university of Chicago Press, 1975.

Shonfield, Andrew. *Modern Capitalism.* London: Oxford University Press, 1969.

Smith, Anthony. *State and Nation in the Third World.* New York: St. Martin's Press, 1983.

Stavrianos, L. S. *Global Rift: The Third World Comes of Age.* New York: William Morrow & Co., 1981.

Stepan, Alfred. *The State and Society: Peru in Comparative Perspective.* Princeton: Princeton University Press, 1978.

Stern, R. W. *The Process of Opposition in India.* Chicago: University of Chicago Press, 1970.

Szentes, T. *The Political Economy of Underdevelopment.* Budapest: Academia Kiado, 1975.

Taylor, John. *From Modernization to Modes of Production.* The Macmillan Press, 1979.

Terray, Emmanuel. *Le Marxisme devant les Societes primitives.* Paris: Mapero, 1972. (Translated as *Marxism and Primitive Societies.*)

Theuws, P.T. 'Outline of Luba Culture.' *Cahiers Economiques et Sociaux*, Vol. 2, no. 1 (1964)

Thornton, John. *The Kingdom of Kongo: Civil War and Transition 1641–1718.* Madison: University of Wisconsin Press, 1983.

Torday, E. *On the Trail of the Bushongo.* New York: Negro University Press, 1969.

Tshimbombo, Mudiba P. 'La Famille Bantu–Luluwa et le Developpement.' (Doctoral. dissertation, St Thomas Aquinas, Rome, 1975.

Van Der Kerken, G. *L'Ethnie Mongo.* Brussels: Institut Royal Colonial Belge, 1944.

Van Der Streten. *L'agriculture et les industries agricoles au Congo Belge.* Brussels, 1945.

Van Wing, J. *Etudes Bakongo: Sociologie, Religion et magie.* Museum Lessianum section Missiologique. No. 39, 2nd ed. Louvain: Desclee DeBrouwer, 1959.

Vansina, Jan. *The Children of Woot: A History of the Kuba People.* Madison: University of Wisconsin Press, 1978.

—— *Introduction a l'ethnographie du Congo.* Kinshasa, 1966.

—— *Kingdoms of the Savanna.* Madison: University of Wisconsin Press, 1966.

—— *Oral Tradition as History.* Madison: University of Wisconsin Press, 1985.

—— 'Le Regime foncier dans la societe Kuba.' *Zaire.* Vol. X–9 (Nov. 1956): 900–926

—— *The Tio Kingdom of the Middle Congo 1880–1892.* Madison: University of Wisconsin Press, 1973.

—— *Les tribus Ba-Kuba et les peuplades apparentes*. Tervuren, Belgium: Musee Royal du Congo Belge, 1954.

Verhaegen, B. *Rebellions au Congo*. 2 Vols. Brussels: CRISP, 1966; 1968.

Wallerstein, I. *The Modern World-System*. Vol. 1. New York: Academic Press, 1976.

—— *The Modern World-System*. Vol. 2. New York: Academic Press, 1980.

—— *The Politics of the World Economy: The States, the Movements and the Civilizations*. Cambridge: Cambridge university Press, 1984.

Wiarda, Howard, ed. *New Directions in Comparative Politics*. Boulder, CO: Westview Press, 1985.

—— and Harvey Kline, eds. *Latin American Politics and Development*. Boulder, CO: Westview Press, 1985.

Willame, J.C. *Patrimonialism and Political Change in the Congo*. Stanford: Stanford University Press, 1972

Worsley, Peter. *The Three Worlds: Culture and World Development*. Chicago: Chicago University Press, 1984.

Young, C. *Politics in the Congo*. Princeton: Princeton University Press, 1965.

—— and T. Turner. *The Rise and Decline of the Zairian State*. Madison: University of Wisconsin Press, 1985.

Zolberg. A. *One-Party Government in the Ivory Coast*. Princeton: Princeton University Press, 1964.